Marko Milivojevic.

BC 1544/96   E16

D1420482

THE EAST GERMAN ARMY

THE EAST GERMAN ARMY

The Second Power in the Warsaw Pact

Thomas M. Forster

With an introduction
by
General Sir Harry Tuzo, G.C.B., O.B.E., M.C., M.A.

Translated by
Deryck Viney

London
GEORGE ALLEN & UNWIN LTD
Boston   Sydney

Published in Germany under the title
DIE NVA - KERNSTÜCK DER LANDESVERTEIDIGUNG DER DDR
by the Markus-Verlagsgesellschaft mbH., Köln

Copyright in the German original and this translation
Markus-Verlag Köln 1980 ©

Published in Great Britain 1980
by George Allen & Unwin, Ltd.

GEORGE ALLEN & UNWIN LTD
40 Museum Street, London WCIA ILU
ISBN 0 04 355012 6

Printed in Germany by
Rock & Co., Wolfenbüttel

Introduction

by

General Sir Harry Tuzo, G.C.B., O.B.E., M.C., M.A.

If we are right in assuming that military factors will play a greater rather than diminishing role on the international scene in the new decade, we need to take a closer look at those instruments of military power which may take the stage in the years to come. Before the invasion of Afghanistan few people in Western Europe saw the threat of World War Three as anything but an improbable nightmare. For many reasons – and this is not the place to go into them – I believe that this war will only happen if we bury our heads in the sand and ignore realities. Peace can only be preserved if we look to the defences of NATO as a whole and to our national contribution in particular. It follows that a clear understanding of the various Warsaw Pact forces is in every way necessary.

As I write the Soviet Army, despite Brezhnev's protestations that "détente" must continue, is in action. In areas from which Soviet "military advisors" were forced to withdraw, other "socialist" personnel have replaced them, such as Fidel Castro's "volunteers" – and the East Germans. If we compare Cuba's economic potential with that of East Germany it is not difficult to see the latter, with an army which has belonged for years to the First Strategic Echelon of the Warsaw Pact, fighting a proxy war on Soviet behalf in any part of the world where Big Brother might find it convenient and where a plausible "cause" could be contrived.

Over the last ten years East Germany has won diplomatic recognition as the "German Democratic Republic". She is also one of the 35 states to sign the Final Act of the Helsinki Conference on European Security and Cooperation in 1975. If "détente" is revived the Helsinki agreements may permit closer scrutiny by outsiders of East Germany's army, the Nationale Volksarmee (NVA). While possessing all the typical characteristics of a Communist Military establishment it also derives a character of its own from martial traditions strongly embedded in history.

Mr. Forster's excellent book provides a total picture of the armed forces of that "other" Germany. I recommend it not only to those professionally concerned but to all who are interested in world affairs and the military balance.

In expanding the material used in the first English edition of 1967 (also published by George Allen & Unwin) the German author has made it clearer than ever that the capability of the NVA depends on more things than purely military factors and national policies. He shows us the NVA as part of a society that has become, thanks to "socialist military education", militarized through and through. It is important to realize – and our representatives at the Mutual and Balanced Force Reductions talks in Vienna might make use of the fact – that East Germany possesses, in addition to a regular army of some 200,000, paramilitary forces numbering about half a million. These Working Class Combat Groups constitute an army on their own which figures prominently in Warsaw Pact calculations, even though disregarded by international arms control experts.

As a purely Soviet product the East German Army does not formulate its own broad military doctrines. It is useful therefore to have from Mr. Forster an outline of the Soviet theory of war. This will help the reader to understand many contemporary developments even where the East German military are not directly involved.

For all these reasons – the growing importance of military factors in the eighties, the increased part played on the world stage by the GDR itself during the last ten years, and the pace of that country's internal militarization – I welcome this new edition of Forster's standard work. Central Europe may appear calm at the moment. But new crises in that area could come upon us with great suddenness. The single word "Berlin" is sufficient to support this possibility.

Mr. Forster's book will make a great contribution to our understanding of the forces which could be closely involved. His work will be widely welcomed and highly respected.

Contents

Foreword

The general reader's interest in military affairs has changed considerably over the last generation or two, not so much in intensity as in motivation. The older generation, all of whom had experienced the Second World War and many the First World War as well, would have expected any account of a country's army to pay attention to the ethical dimension of its fighting power – the "soldierly virtues". Later descriptions were satisfied with outward appearances and technology, establishment figures and weapon statistics. Only when the "old soldiers" had left the stage did writers appear who saw armies rather as an integral part of the state, and the military as members of society. They were largely concerned to prove that army regulations and precepts of behaviour either were, or were not, in line with the general principles of the society in question. Where their elders, having readers in mind who were either soldiers too, or civilians with military connections, often wrote from an emotional standpoint in terms of "our" side and "theirs", the new authors were products of scientific disciplines – political science, sociology, educational theory or economics.

There are several reasons for the public at large, both in West Germany and in the West generally, to be increasingly interested in publications about armies such as that of the other, communist, German state. There is in the first place general support in the West for a defence effort which is only justified by the military potential of the other side; support, therefore, both for the outlay on its own forces and for membership of the Western alliance. This consensus is tacit rather than vocal, and certainly not jubilant. But the willingness of the taxpayer to reach so deeply into his pocket, and of hundreds of thousands of young men in Western Europe to undergo the inconvenience of national service, is no trivial sign in the long run, considering the growth of political awareness. And this is all the more significant in view of the decisive importance now attached to security, and hence to the armed forces, in every country – in the Third World as much as in the regions overshadowed by the Superpowers.

In offering this new, fifth, edition of Forster's standard work on the East German armed forces both author and publisher are as aware of this change in readers' attitudes to military literature as they are of the military factors and dangers themselves. Much of the picture, perhaps the greater part of it, has been transformed since the first edition appeared in 1964. There have been changes of detail; this is not surprising in view of the lapse of time, but the National People's Army (NVA) of the German Democratic Republic (GDR) has made more progress than that alone would account for. Secondly, the range of topics has been extended. In the first years after its emergence from the "Garrisoned People's Police" of the Soviet-occupied Zone of Germany, the NVA's men and officers were grateful even to be saluted by their opposite numbers in the other Warsaw Pact armies. Yet nowadays we find NVA personnel "in the service of proletarian internationalism" helping to train and supply several armies and guerrilla groups in Black Africa and even playing operational roles that at one time were initiated and fulfilled by the "invincible" troops of the Soviet Big Brother alone. The NVA has indeed acquired the status of No. Two.

The general political section of the book has also been considerably expanded. It was necessary to show how the "coordination of economic policy" in Comecon, and East Germany's specially close cooperation with the Soviet Union, had brought her with her sophisticated chemical, electronic, optical and other key industries into the second leading position in the East Bloc in terms of technical, and hence also of military, progress. For East Germany, saddled as she is with recurrent economic crises in an East Bloc which nowadays has to cope with the challenges of the world market as well, this all means extra effort. And for the NVA itself, it means greater compulsion to "think economically" in the sense of using more labour and less material.

Our fifth edition, then, provides more insight into the overall system of "socialist national defence" and the worldwide endeavour to "guarantee the onward march of socialism" than its predecessors did. It is therefore longer, despite the abridgement of some other sections: this applies particular to some of the technical material on weapons, whose growing complexity everywhere makes description harder. However, the military specialist can obtain this information elsewhere[1].

Addressing as it does an international readership – English, French and Italian translations[2] appeared as early as 1967–69 – this standard work remains unchanged in one respect noted by the Vienna *Truppendienst* back in 1965[3]: "The author has at every point striven to render an objective account, as far as this is possible in such a case". And the *Neue Zürcher Zeitung* at that time made a comment which still applies: "Forster emphasizes strongly the dependence of the NVA's reliability as an instrument of communist government on factors other than military ones. One of the most interesting sections of the book deals with political schooling in the army, an area which remains one of continuous concern for the GDR authorities."[4]

In the fourth edition, in early 1972, three points were particularly stressed which remain true today[5]:

1. The NVA is more closely tied to the Soviet Army than ever.

2. It has no military doctrine of its own, but relies for its thinking on Soviet policies that give more than theoretical place to the modalities of a modern nuclear missile war.

3. As the main pillar of "socialist national defence", the NVA has extended its influence throughout East German society and government and thereby increased its leverage in the domestic political scene.

All three tendencies are now more apparent than ever.

1. The still closer ties between the NVA and Soviet Army follow logically from a series of amendments to basic documents. The new Constitution of October 7, 1974, states that the GDR is "permanently and irrevocably allied to the U.S.S.R." and forms an "inseparable

part of the commonwealth of socialist states"[6]. Again, the October 1975 treaty with the Soviet Union is said to have "given our state a new dimension"[7].

2. It is not only a native military doctrine that the NVA lacks. Like the whole country, it is preparing the way through promotion of Russian language teaching for a complete adoption of Soviet behaviour and ways of thought. The growing assumption of the need to face nuclear war is evident among other things from recent arms procurement: tanks, personnel carriers, transport vehicles and self-propelled artillery are all being designed to protect crews against radiation.

3. A further example of the enhanced influence of the NVA is the transfer of control in 1978 over the entire civil defence system from the Ministry of the Interior to the Defence Ministry. And the militarization of East German life was reflected by the introduction, in September 1978, of "defence instruction" as a compulsory subject in the 9th and 10th grades of *Polytechnische Oberschulen* despite the opposition of the churches in particular to the "hate training" that formed part of it.

One expectation, expressed in 1972 in connection with these three theses, has not been fulfilled in all cases, probable though it seemed in the nature of things. This was the prognosis that "the era of the old-time veteran communists will soon come to a close"[8]. The top man in the NVA is still General Heinz Hoffmann – born 1910, member of the Communist Youth League since 1926 and of the Party since 1930; International Brigade fighter in Spain 1936–39 and from 1950, after lengthy training in the Soviet Union, Inspector General of the Garrisoned People's Police. The Ministry for Security with its own armed agencies is still controlled by Erich Mielke – born 1907, member of the Spartacus Youth League from 1921 and of the Party from 1925; involved in the murder of two police captains in Berlin in 1931; International Brigade member 1936–39; Vice-president of the Central Administration for Internal Affairs in the Soviet Zone, 1946, and connected with the State Security Service without interruption since 1950. At the head of the Ministry of the Interior and that body's armed agencies we still find Colonel General Friedrich Dickel, military science graduate, born in 1913, member of the Communist Youth League since 1928 and of the Party since 1931; member of the International Brigade in Spain and connected with the People's Police since 1946.

In its personnel policy East Germany evidently follows the Moscow line of having a very high average age among the top leadership, in the forces and elsewhere. This is not the place to pursue the pros and cons of preserving men in their seventies in commanding positions. But against their experience and esprit de corps one must obviously set the lose of flexibility the policy entails, preventing new blood from coming into posts of supreme responsibility.

There is no reason to assume that the up-and-coming generation of leaders will be more "humane". The veterans, after all, have had their bitter experiences with their own Party as well as with Moscow. The Soviet old guard themselves agreed after Stalin died to stop killing each other and to settle their differences in less bloody fashion. Apart from the unexplained "fatal fall from a window" on May 12, 1961, of Vincenz Müller, the former "Hitler General" who was dropped in 1957 from the posts of NVA Chief of Staff and Deputy Defence Minister, there is no known case of an East German general having been dramatically liquidated. There seems to be a certain solidarity here which, if genuine, can certainly benefit the army as a whole.

It may be questioned whether the NVA's new generation of military and scientific technocrats really understands and practices "comradeliness" as an important ingredient of combat-readiness. The frequent stress laid on this quality in pronouncements from above suggests that there is cause for worry here.

There is evidence that the NVA and its top leaders have been touched by a general trend reflected most clearly in the Final Act of the Helsinki Conference. Communication across state frontiers, facilitated by modern technology and made necessary by the higher intellectual demands imposed – for the mastery of that same technology – on soldiers as on other citizens, means that a new style of leadership is required. Ten years ago it would have been unthinkable for Defence Minister Hoffmann to make the kind of remark he included in his comments on command and training tasks for 1978/79: ". . . These young men on whose brains and hands the effectiveness of our very costly, and very powerful, weapon systems depends are not going to respond to a commander quite in the fashion of left-turn and right-turn on the parade ground."[9] Hoffmann went on to demand a "new quality in our political work". And no doubt in allusion to the concept of "citizens in uniform" in the West German army, he said that what the NVA needed was "communists in uniform".

The author of this book takes it for granted that the NVA has long since reached the same standards as any other operationally capable army with a long tradition behind it. Western observers concede that the NVA is well trained. And if one is to accept the plentiful testimony from the communist side, this applies not only to the GDR's active Land, Air and Sea forces but its paramilitary organizations as well. As for the NVA's present arsenal of weapons, some at least will be obsolete in a few years and have to be replaced by new systems. Not that the fighting power of an army is purely a function of its training and equipment, but both can be decisive factors. If the NVA is not to accept a loss of efficiency, rearmament in some fields will be needed, and this will present a propaganda problem as well as an economic burden for the East German leaders.

The high command of the NVA is always anxious to represent its current sophistication as something planned from the beginning in consistent fulfilment of Lenin's doctrine of the "working class under arms". This claim has increasingly coloured the NVA's publicity about itself and encouraged a standard view among foreign observers such as was indeed reflected in the first edition of the present work[10]. However, it was a simplification that presents a difficulty for NVA historians themselves in regard to the exact moment of origin of the East German armed forces.

In Forster's first edition it was argued, with evidence, that "the Soviets proceeded deliberately, as soon as the war was over, to build up communist German military formations in their zone of occupation under the guise of creating a police force"[11]. Defence Minister Hoffmann rejected this account, insisting that all the measures then taken were "part of the answer of Europe's socialist states to the remilitarization of West Germany"[12]. In his counter-version, however, he admits that "our government was not so naive ... as to react to the 1948/49 plans for setting up a West German mercenary army with protests alone". It was necessary at the same time to turn "the Garrisoned People's Police ... into a cadre school for the possible creation of national armed forces". Hoffmann went on to claim that "all these assumptions" could have been "fairly quickly reversed". But to suggest that "reversal" was seriously built into a communist planning strategy would mean that communists in this case were not merely following Lenin's "One step back, two steps forward!" axiom, but were prepared to renounce the creation of a communist state, since that is "unthinkable", according to recent NVA pronouncements, without the presence of armed forces.

In regard to certain problems of research and description one can confidently repeat now what was said in the introduction to all previous editions. The habit of communist regimes of cloaking all their activities in a veil of secrecy makes it difficult to form a clear picture of military structures. There is first of all the tendency of every dictatorship to reverse the democratic theory and practice by which the public, as the constitutional source of government, has the right to maximum information. In addition, the inclination to secretiveness in Moscow-line communist countries has been reinforced by Bolshevik, and by traditional Russian, influence. Another important factor contributing to communist aversion for publicity is the gap, of which they are only too aware, between reality and the targets set by their own propaganda, a gap which can only be treated with the utmost discretion in official writings. As these present it, the communist world is sacrosanct.

All the same, it is not impossible for an outside observer to form some picture of a communist institution, including ones like the army which even in democratic states enjoy a certain security protection. Indeed the communists are anything but reticent. Their endless stream of agitprop writings make pronouncements on every conceivable subject in order to "reach the masses". They are not merely concerned to manipulate those masses. In this age of advanced technology with its increased demands on every citizen a communist government, like any other, must use every means, including the information media, to rally the public's support. It has to explain to its own people – in this case the officers and men of the NVA – exactly what it wants from them. And all the more so since communists subscribe a priori to a rationalist dogma which gives pride of place to universal "awareness".

If then one takes the trouble carefully to sift through and compare the mass of material produced by the NVA about itself, the objective accounts and directives as well as the propaganda, one can reach quite sound conclusions. The most fruitful source is the output, periodical and otherwise, of the GDR Military Publishing House (*Militärverlag der DDR*), which as an agency of the

Defence Ministry enjoys a certain monopoly of publication in the military field, both popular and specialized. The problem here lies rather in an excess than a shortage of material, but a few textbooks have appeared in recent years which make the gleaning of information – and misinformation, of course – more easy. Any Western writer interested in the NVA will also do well to take note of the many accounts given by refugees, including those formerly in GDR uniform. No piece of evidence can be accepted without checking, and despite all efforts errors can get through. Among the many thousands of details in this book some mistakes have doubtless crept in: author and publisher would be grateful for corrections.

As we have said, there is considerable interest in the NVA among the Western public, above all of course in the Federal Republic of Germany. An ample literature from pens of all colours bears witness to this, and it is a gratifying fact that the tone of comment is on the whole sober. In the field of West German writing on communist military affairs the Cold War is over. Now, by contrast, we find analyses proliferating which claim to draw exclusively on "authentic sources" and yet completely ignore the real factual and human background. But if anyone fifty years from now were to try and form a picture of conditions in West and East Germany respectively from these authentic sources, including the daily press, they would conclude that the former was hell on earth and the latter a veritable paradise. Which is not quite the case.

A certain amount of repetition and overlapping in the present work is intended to make the material easier for the non-specialist to follow. Quotations have often been given at some length, partly for authenticity, partly to provide usable references in points of detail. A list is provided for the reader's convenience.

It may disappoint some readers that, except in a few cases where they were particularly illuminating, no detailed comparisons have been made with Western armies. But to do so would have meant expanding the book unreasonably.

The German publisher would like to thank the author, his assistants and all those who have given advice and help in preparing this new edition. Readers' comments have been particularly taken to heart.

Cologne, November 1979

Markus Verlag

Notes

[1] Particularly from such specialist periodicals and series as: Adelphi Papers, London; Aerospace International, Washington D. C.; Air Force Magazine, Washington D. C.; Allgemeine Schweizerische Militärzeitschrift, Frauenfeld; Armee-Motor; Zürich; Armee-Rundschau, East Berlin; Armed Forces International, New York; Armor, Washington D. C.; Army, Washington D. C.; The Army Quarterly and Defence Journal, London; Army Research and Development, Washington D. C.; Aviation Week and Space Technology, New York; Défence Nationale, Paris; Elektronische Informationsverarbeitung und Kybernetik, München; Forces Aérien-

nes Françaises, Paris; Forces Armées Françaises, Paris; Informatik, East Berlin; Interavia, Genf; Military Review, Fort Leavenworth, Kansas; Militärtechnik, East Berlin; National Defense, Washington D. C.; Österreichische Militärische Zeitschrift, Wien; Royal Air Forces Quarterly, London; Soldat und Technik, Frankfurt am Main; Survival, London; Voenniy Vestnik, Moscow; Wehrkunde, München.

2 Thomas M. *Forster*, The East German Army. A pattern of a Communist Military Establishment, with an introduction by Brigadier W. F. K. *Thompson*, George Allen & Unwin Ltd, London 1967, 255 pp.: Do., L'Armée Est-Allemande, with a foreword by General Paul *Stehlin*, Nouvelle Edition Latine, Paris 1968, 274 pp.: Do., Le Forze della Germania Orientale, with an introduction by General Giorgio *Liuzzi*, Edizioni Mundus, Roma and Milano 1969, 274 pp.

3 *Truppendienst*, Wien, 2/1965.

4 *Neue Zürcher Zeitung*, November 26, 1965.

5 T. M. *Forster*, Die NVA. Kernstück der Landesverteidigung der DDR, 4th revised edition, Köln 1972, p. 7 f.

6 GDR Constitution of April 6, 1968, in the version of the Gesetz zur Ergänzung und Änderung der Verfassung der DDR vom 7. Oktober 1974, quoted from: *Neues Deutschland*, East Berlin, September 28, 1974.

7 Die Sowjetunion ist die Hauptkraft des Friedens. Address by Colonel General *Kessler*, Central Committee member of the SED, in: *Neues Deutschland*, May 8, 1978.

8 T. M. *Forster*, op. cit. note 5, p. 7.

9 General *Hoffmann*, Zu einigen Führungs- und Erziehungsaufgaben im neuen Ausbildungsjahr, in: *Militärwesen*, East Berlin, 1/1979, p. 8.

10 T. M. *Forster*, NVA. Die Armee der Sowjetzone, Köln, 1964, p. 33 ff.

11 Ibid., p. 35.

12 General Heinz *Hoffmann*, Die NVA auf Friedenswacht, in: *Deutsche Außenpolitik*, East Berlin, May 1965, Sonderheft, quoted in: Heinz *Hoffmann*, Sozialistische Landesverteidigung. Aus Reden und Aufsätzen 1963–1970, East Berlin 1971, pp. 252–258.

CHAPTER ONE

Ensuring the Onward March of Socialism

An enquiry into the origins of the armed forces of what is now the *German Democratic Republic (GDR)* can either dwell on the contemporary political situation at the close of World War II on the territory of the German *Reich* or, equally well, on the ideology then prevailing in the area of East Germany.

For many years attention was focussed on the historical view that the creation of armed forces in the *Soviet-occupied Zone,* which became the German Democratic Republic in 1949, must be related par excellence to the division of the country in consequence of the East-West conflict in power politics. The question was posed, who started it all, whether rearmament was instigated by the West first, or by the East, to ward off the acute dangers that loomed. Each side sought publicly to cast the blame on the other. It was taken for granted that there was something objectionable about such rearmament, for one side an "unavoidable evil"[1], for the other a "response"[2], in any case the result of tensions that were waxing but might also wane again. The Germans, who only a few years before had emerged from a catastrophic world war either "defeated" or "liberated", but above all "guilty", could only reluctantly be persuaded to "take a gun in their hands"[3]. For the victors, too, the notion of rearming the Germans was for a long time an odious one.

Today, thirty-five years after the war and with world politics no longer exclusively determined by the East-West conflict, the rearming of both German states that completed its course in the 1950s strikes world opinion only as an example of the general phenomenon that arsenals everywhere have grown larger, not smaller, since that war ended. International acceptance of the fact of two German armies – the *Bundeswehr* and the *Nationale Volksarmee (NVA)* – was eased by the discovery that Central Europe, though still a region of paramount political and economic importance, was no longer a hotbed of crises. Central Europe has been spared from warfare ever since 1945.

The GDR has become a most important, and apparently irremovable, component in the group of states fashioned by Moscow. The existence of its National People's Army *(Nationale Volksarmee)* is founded in this association and in the Great Power policies of the Soviet Union. It is founded equally in the ideological fixation that the GDR's own forces are there not only to protect the "socialist fatherland", the "socialist community of states" and "peace" itself, but moreover to ensure the "victory of socialism round the globe". If we ask, then, how the NVA came to be born, mention of particular dates in history is far less revealing than the manifestation of the relevant ideological doctrine.

In this introductory chapter, designed to sketch out the character and the aims of the National People's Army, we must recognize and elucidate both

"Day of Liberation" on May 8 – SED Combat Groups at the Soviet War Memorial in Berlin-Treptow.

these roots – the almost forgotten historical one as well as the ideological. The ever tighter involvement of the NVA in the Soviet-led military bloc requires attention to the theory of war taught in the Soviet Army and to the main forms of struggle advocated – not least in an era of "détente".

The historic background

On June 5, 1945, one month after the unconditional surrender of the *Deutsche Wehrmacht,* the U.S.A., Great Britain, France, and the Soviet Union assumed the powers of government. Their army commanders in the occupied country signed that day a statement on the control machinery in occupied Germany. An *Allied Control Council,* which could only take unanimous decisions, was set up in Berlin with representatives of all four Powers on it.

Germany was divided into *Occupation Zones.* The *Potsdam Agreement*[4] of August 2, 1945, assigned about 25 per cent of the country's territory within the 1937 frontiers to Polish or Soviet administration, viz. the provinces east of the Oder-Neisse Line, Silesia, East Brandenburg, Pomerania and most of East Prussia to Poland and the northern part of East Prussia to the Soviets. The agreement prescribed that the final settlement of Germany's eastern frontier should await a Peace Conference – one that has still not taken place, 35 years after Potsdam. It was laid down at the same time that the German people should be disarmed, as well as de-nazified and democratized.

As well as providing for central control of finance, transport, communications, foreign trade and industry throughout the country, the Potsdam Agreement foresaw the creation of administrative bodies in each of the occupation zones, committed to the "free and democratic rule of law". The U. S. S. R., however, interpreted this concept quite differently from the Western Powers. For the Soviets, democratization meant simply the establishment of a formal façade of democracy behind which they could pursue, step by step, the resolute sovietization of their own zone. The *Sowjetische Militäradministration in Deutschland (SMAD),* set up on June 9, 1945, with its headquarters in the Berlin suburb of Karlshorst, began to issue binding orders for the Soviet Zone on its own authority, regardless of the Allied Control Council's responsibility for the whole of Germany. This was a violation of the Potsdam Agreement. As Erich Honecker, First Secretary of the SED (Socialist Unity Party), was to put it in 1971, "a process of delimitation" *(Abgrenzung)* had begun between the western and eastern parts of Germany that was to cut deeper and deeper "in all spheres of society"[5].

The Soviet Union had at an early stage envisaged approval for German armed forces, provided political development went their way. On November 6, 1942, in the middle of the war, Stalin declared:

> It is not our task to destroy all organized military power in Germany. Anyone with the slightest education will appreciate that for Germany, as for Russia, this is not only impossible, but also from the victor's

standpoint undesirable. To destroy the Hitlerite army, however, is something one can do and must do[6].

The idea of having German military potential available for Soviet use had been tried out earlier when, with the help of German communist emigrés, a "Free Germany" National Committee *(Nationalkomitee „Freies Deutschland")* was set up among German prisoners of war in the Soviet Union on July 12/13, 1943, and then a German Officers' League *(Bund Deutscher Offiziere)* on September 11/12 of the same year. The Committee did not give rise to any military units, but individual members were used by the Red Army in combat against the German forces. These organizations also enabled the U.S.S.R. not only to exploit the knowledge of German military specialists for its own army but to find assistance for the subsequent establishment of a communist-oriented German army in its occupation zone. Such assistance came, for example, from former *Wehrmacht* generals like Vincenz Müller, Arno von Lenski, Dr. Otto Korfes, Hans Wulz and many others who were to help set up the Soviet Zone's armed formations. In the autumn of 1945 Moscow dissolved, it is true, both the National Committee and the Officers' League, but it intensified political re-education of German POWs along Marxist-Leninist lines, to which military training was later often added.

Immediately after the war the U.S.S.R. took deliberate steps in its own zone of occupation to build up German communist military units through the device of creating a police force. Max Opitz, who was police chief in Dresden from June 12, 1945, until 1949, lord mayor of Leipzig from then till 1951, and head of the Presidential Chancellery and State Secretary under GDR-President Pieck from 1951 to 1960, stated in 1959 that "the birth of the armed forces in the first German Workers' and Peasants' State" had occurred as far back as October, 1945.

> Arming of the People's Police was approved by SMAD on October 31, 1945. This was the moment of birth for the armed forces of the German working class, the armed forces of the first Workers' and Peasants' State in Germany ...[7]

The Soviets had often held it against the British, in particular, that they were planning, in violation of the Yalta and Potsdam agreements, to create military units out of the disarmed ex-members of the German forces gathered in British camps. This complaint was used to put the Western allies under pressure. Yet in their own zone of occupation they had created the basis of a central police apparatus. And while, in May and June, 1945, the non-military police in the

Right, top to bottom: German prisoners of war in the Soviet Union in 1944. – Foundation of the "Free Germany" National Committee in 1943 near Moscow. – Many went directly from POW camps into the People's Police: officers at a parade in 1952.

Länder (States) of the three Western zones was decentralized and could only be established at community level, the Soviet Military Administration of Germany (SMAD) rapidly centralized the police, beginning at *Länder* level. Clear evidence of this is provided by the instructions issued by the various Soviet Military Administrations, in October, 1945, to the *Länder* authorities of Brandenburg, Saxony, Sachsen-Anhalt, Thuringia and Mecklenburg-Pomerania, authorizing their administrations to amalgamate community-level police forces and centralize them in the *Länder*.

Only two months later, in December 1945, the various police forces in the *Länder* were subordinated to the Ministers of the Interior, all members of the Communist Party. Thus, within six months of the war ending, each of the five *Länder* of the Soviet Zone had a central police body, the *Landespolizeibehörde (LPB)*. This was a clear breach of inter-allied understandings.

The Soviet authorities made a major step in the spring of 1946 toward permanent incorporation of their zone into the communist bloc by forcibly fusing the Social Democratic Party of Germany *(SPD)* in the zone with the Communist Party of Germany *(KPD)* into a Socialist Unity Party – *Sozialistische Einheitspartei Deutschlands (SED)*. As Ulbricht was to say at this party's 25th anniversary, its policy was "from the beginning characterized by the struggle to preserve peace and to fasten the alliance with the Soviet Union"[8]. Or as Colonel Professor Dr. Brühl put it in 1971, reviewing the initial period of the SED's military policy:

> The Party's antifascist-democratic and anti-imperialist programme from the start included the task of employing revolutionary force to frustrate any counter-revolutionary use of force by the propertied classes. This showed a clear marxist position on the role of force in revolutionary historical change, patently distinct from bourgeois ideology and hence from social-democratic doctrine[9].

A new chapter began in August, 1946, when on instructions from SMAD a centralized German Administration of the Interior *(Deutsche Verwaltung des Innern – DVdI)*, was set up in East Berlin under a veteran communist, Erich Reschke. It was given discretionary powers vis-à-vis the *Länder* ministries of the interior and so enjoyed supreme authority over all levels of the People's Police *(Volkspolizei)* in the Soviet occupation zone. Key positions in the DVdI were entrusted to reliable communists, who in many cases took their orders straight from SMAD in Karlshorst.

By the end of November 1946, this centrally-directed People's Police force already numbered 45,000.

On November 28 the SMAD gave the DVdI the further task of instructing the *Länder* police authorities to set up a German Frontier Police *(Deutsche Grenzpolizei – DGP)*. By December 3,000 Frontier Police were installed in their barracks; they received training in the first half of 1947 and were then despatched in equal proportion to the five *Länder*. By September 1947, 4,000 men were in readiness, armed with the pistols and the 98 k carbine of the old *Wehrmacht*.

Both the creation and functions of the DGP were a clear breach of Allied Control Council directives entrusting control of frontiers and demarcation lines exclusively to Allied soldiers until the conclusion of a German Peace Treaty. The U. S. S. R., while giving its approval to such directives as a Council member, had no intention of respecting them in its own occupation zone.

In the summer of 1948, as international relations were exacerbated by the communist coup in Prague, faster rearmament in the U. S. S. R. itself and the Berlin blockade, the Soviets took a further step[10]. An order issued by SMAD on June 3, 1948, ushered in the final phase of the creation of regular military units. The DVdI was instructed to set up training facilities and units for the creation of military cadres.

Due preparations had already been started to provide the personnel. Some 1,000 former Wehrmacht officers, still in Soviet POW camps, were to be persuaded to serve in the new Soviet Zone units.

By the summer of 1948, then, three types of armed forces existed:

- the regular People's Police,
- the German Frontier Police, and
- the Garrisoned Alert Squads.

These last were soon to be renamed Garrisoned People's Police *(Kasernierte Volkspolizei – KVP)*, though the name was only made official in 1952. They were to provide the cadres for the future land, air and naval forces.

A new era in the evolution of East German armed forces opened with the self-styling, in October 1949, of the German Democratic Republic. The Soviet Military Administration in Germany was now wound up. In its place came the Soviet Control Commission *(Sowjetische Kontrollkommission – SKK)*, which henceforth exercised overall supervision of all military and police units. The DVdI was turned into a Ministry of the Interior, including the Main Administration of German People's Police *(Hauptverwaltung der Deutschen Volkspolizei)* in charge of both the regular German People's Police *(DVP)* and German Frontier Police *(DGP)*. The Garrisoned Alert Squads of the KVP remained under the control of a Main Administration for Training *(Hauptverwaltung für Schulung – HVS)* which became an increasingly independent authority. A few weeks later the Alert Squads were reorganized into units of the various arms of service.

Meanwhile the Federal Republic of Germany *(Bundesrepublik Deutschland)* had been created out of the three western-occupied zones, with the approval of the Western Allies and the democratic support of the public. Here there were no garrisoned police units, let alone military ones. The police were indeed not even centralized at *Länder* level.

In face of the situation that had arisen in the Soviet Zone the Allied High Commission representing the Western powers now issued orders[11] authorizing the Federal *Länder* to organize separate police corps subject to the provisions of the Occupation Statute. The towns were accordingly permitted to merge their police units with those of other communes, "provided that no resultant police unit has more than 2,000 members, and ... that no area thus covered exceeds that of a District" *(Regierungsbezirk)*.

Still more revealing of the situation then prevailing in West Germany was the Allied High Commission's Law No. 16, of December, 1949, forbidding, under threat of severe penalties, any activity "directly or indirectly concerned with imparting the theory, principles or techniques of warfare, or designed to prepare for any warlike activity or to promote the revival of militarism"[12].

By the end of 1950, the rearmament of East Germany had reached the following point.

1. The KVP comprised
    - 39 Alert Squads,
    - 12 Weapon Schools,
    - 12 Cadet Schools, and
    - 5 Special Schools,

with a total personnel of 70,000.

2. The DGP had an establishment of 18,000 frontier police.

3. The Transport Police numbered 11,500.

4. There was a 5,000 strong Guard Corps *(Wachverband)* under the Ministry for State Security.

In addition there was the 80,000 strong non-military part of the DVP, consisting of the criminal, traffic, general and administrative police branches.

Only at this point did Western thoughts on whether the Federal Republic of Germany should be armed again produce a definite decision. After the communist attack on Korea, on June 25, 1950, and in view of continued East German rearmament the Conference of Foreign Ministers in New York agreed, in September 1950, to the establishment of garrisoned police forces to a total strength of 30,000 men. On March 16, 1951, the West German President announced a bill for the foundation of a Federal Frontier Guard *(Bundes-grenzschutz)* with its controlling bodies; a force of 10,000 men was envisaged. Only reluctantly did the *Länder* of West Germany agree to recruit their own alert squads, totalling another 10,000.

The possibility of halting the trend toward two mutually hostile German military camps seemed to be raised once more by the *Soviet Note of March 10, 1952*, offering the Western powers a united, democratic Germany "with its own national armed forces". A draft German Peace Treaty was appended[13].

This note had been preceded by a message from the GDR government to those of the four occupation powers, on February 13 of the same year, demanding a peace treaty "in the name of the German people". This message was referred to in the Soviet note as a way of involving the GDR *ab initio* as a German state. In the Federal Republic, the note started a public argument that dragged on for years. Taking into account previous Soviet documents, it offered no guarantee that once Federal Germany had been prevented from integrating itself with the West, the whole of Germany would not then be swallowed up into the Soviet bloc. Indeed, there were plenty of East German commentaries that justified the suspicion. On May 3, 1952, the SED's Secretary General, Walter Ulbricht, gave a lecture in East Berlin's Humboldt University on "the scientific significance of the Soviet government's note". He said it was of cardinal importance which group of states a future "peaceloving and democratic" Germany allied itself with. "Does Germany belong to the great camp of world peace, or to the Atlantic war-pact coalition?" Germans, he declared, could live in peace "provided the aggressive Powers knew that this Germany was protected by national armed forces, and was firmly tied to the world peace camp"[14].

In the protracted exchange of notes that followed between the Soviets and the West, the ever-recurring question was that of free German elections. In their fourth note on September 23, 1952, the Western Powers suggested a four-power meeting in October to discuss, for a start, the setting up of an "impartial commission of enquiry"[15].

Meanwhile, however, a Convention on Germany was signed in Bonn on May 26, 1952, and an agreement on a European Defence Community in Paris the next day. The Soviet note of March 10 turned out, then, neither to have prevented nor even delayed West Germany's integration with the West. To the Western Powers, and to most people in West Germany, it had seemed only too clearly to be an attempt to neutralize the whole country, with a view to sovietizing it later.

Parade for the GDR's 15th anniversary, October 7, 1964, in East Berlin.

At the 2nd SED Party Conference of June 1952, a further development occurred, certainly with Soviet approval, in which ideological factors were quite apparent. Reviewing the events in 1970, the East German periodical *Militärgeschichte* (Military History) wrote:

> The importance of military policy as an inseparable component of overall policy in the Workers' and Peasants' State grew larger as conditions ripened in the GDR for the transition to the phase of constructing the foundations of socialism, and this in turn became an objective require-ment in the struggle to resolve the vital issues of the German people. At the 2nd SED Party Conference of July 1952, Wilhelm Pieck quoted Lenin's conclusion in 1919 that the Soviet Republic could not survive without an armed defence capability, and applied it to the historical context of the GDR ...

> The military policy concept evolved at the 2nd Party Conference was of programmatic significance for the solution of the military question in the GDR, for:

> the Conference established the objective historical need to ensure the military defence of the GDR in the conditions of intensifying class conflicts; and

> the Conference answered the question of the class character and function of the first socialist army in the history of the German people. It point-ed out that the creation of armed forces in the GDR was the expression of a progressive military policy in harmony with the interests of the entire German nation, whereas the militaristic policy of setting up a West German army of revenge was reactionary and anti-national in character[16].

The establishment of East German forces proceeded openly in accordance with military requirements from 1952 on, albeit under the label of the Garri-soned People's Police. Following the popular uprising of June 17, 1953, in which the People's Police failed to fulfil expectations as Party troops, there was a major purge resulting in the dismissal of 12,000 members of all ranks as "unreliable elements". Supervision by Soviet "advisors" was for a period intensified.

The next organizational step was taken in September 1953. Various bodies were merged into a central command within the framework of the Ministry of the Interior, entitled Ministry of the Interior Garrisoned People's Police *(MdI/KVP)*.

On January 18, 1956, the East German parliament passed a bill for the creation of a National People's Army and a Ministry for National Defence *(Ministerium für Nationale Verteidigung)*[17]. In propaganda terms, this "sponta-neous" act was supposed to influence the debate in the Federal Republic on the need for a German contribution to a western defence organization. In reality, however, the first major phase in the establishment of East German armed forces was already over, and they totalled at this time 120,000 men. (West

Veteran communist Major General Ewald Munschke (left), Chief of Cadre during the years of establishing the NVA, and Lieutenant General Vincenz Müller, during World War II Deputy Commanding General of the Twelfth Army Corps of the German Wehrmacht, during the years of establishing the NVA Chief of Staff and First Deputy of the Minister for National Defence.

Army General Willi Stoph, the GDR's first Minister for National Defence, while concluding the stationing-agreement of Soviet Troops in May 1957, with the Soviet Minister of Defence, Marshal of the Soviet Union G. Zhuhov.

Germany was then only just beginning to muster its first 1,000 volunteers for the Bundeswehr.)

The Supreme Command of the KVP was now renamed the Ministry for National Defence. It was headed by the Vice-Premier, Colonel General Willi Stoph, who took with him from the KVP as Chief of Staff Lieutenant General Vincenz Müller, a former *Wehrmacht* general and member of the "Free Germany" National Committee in his POW days in Russia. As Deputy Chief of Staff he had Major General Bernhard Bechler, former *Wehrmacht* major and another "Free Germany" committee member.

The old *Wehrmacht* uniform was reintroduced, except for a new steel helmet. This was meant to give moral and visible emphasis to the "national" character of the NVA in accordance with the current efforts to gain recognition and sovereignty. At home, the SED leaders evidently hoped that this ostentatious maintenance of German military tradition would win approval for the still unpopular NVA.

The *Defence Law*[18] of September 20, 1961, set a further seal on the militarization process. A further Defence Law, passed 17 years later, added nothing fundamentally new, but reinforced the trend toward militarization already apparent in the earlier one. It had laid down the basic civil obligation to undergo service in the NVA, in one of the other arms or in the air defence organization. This prepared the way for the introduction of compulsory military service, which was enacted in the conscription bill of January 24, 1962[19].

From then on the organization, equipment and training of the NVA followed increasingly the lines of a modern army. As Defence Minister Hoffmann was to boast on its 15th anniversary in March 1971, the NVA is "ready and able to do combat under any conditions of conventional or nuclear warfare"[20].

The ideological roots

The idea that the NVA should have arisen, and remained, as a mere reaction to the arming of "West German imperialism" was not one to satisfy the *aggressively-minded communist*. Clear support for an "offensive" attitude appears in the reply given by a delegate to the 8th Party Congress when a soldier, Claus Pöschel, enquired:

> Is it only because West German imperialism has become more aggressive that we now speak of greater tasks, of deeper responsibility for the protection of socialism?

To which the delegate, Colonel Beckmann, replied:

> Of course not. Such an attitude would be both onesided and defensive ... What is true – and this perception is no doubt at the back of the questioner's mind – is that the need to reinforce the defensive power of

the socialist community results from the external conditions and aggressive efforts of international, and not merely West German, imperialism ... But as has already been indicated, that is not the whole truth. In his address to the 24th Congress of the CPSU Marshal of the Soviet Union Grechko stressed: "Constant strengthening of the armed forces ... follows from the laws of social development and from the special circumstances of the class war between capitalism and socialism." One special circumstance is that socialism is today on the offensive, and this offensive has to be secured militarily. The military might of the countries of the socialist community, the military superiority of the socialist armed forces, have a powerful influence on all revolutionary processes throughout the world ...[21]

The argument runs like a thread through all the NVA's self-portraits that though socialist forces were only set up after West Germany rearmed, they are nevertheless an integral component of a socialist state. In 1976 Colonel General Heinz Kessler declared that "after the smashing of fascism" the stationing of Soviet forces on the territory of what was be the GDR had meant the presence at hand of "reliable protectors of the revolutionary processes awaiting completion here". He went on: "This however did not relieve the GDR's working class ... of the need to respect and fulfil the objective law of providing a military guarantee of revolutionary progress through their own measures and endeavours."[22]

In 1978 we find SED leader Honecker mentioning the defence of "social progress" as one of the duties of the armed forces[23].

The NVA is not seen as a non-party instrument of the state, but as the tool of the SED, since it is "the product of the SED's ongoing military policy"[24].

Like the Soviet Union's Communist Party, so also the Socialist Unity Party of Germany follows the Leninist principle that the undivided leadership of the army by the party of the working class and its Central Committee is an objective law governing the construction of socialist armed forces[25].

In a basic lecture on "The Armed Forces in Our Time", Army General Hoffmann stressed in 1975 the importance for the armed forces of the supreme ideological aim of "spreading socialism/communism throughout the world".

What is the role ... of military force in determining the victory or defeat of a revolution in the period of transition from capitalism to socialism? Does such a revolution come about without a shot being fired, can it achieve bloodless victory? So far, in truth, history has witnessed no case in which a socialist revolution was led to victory without the guns speaking their message of power – or at least being aimed and loaded[26].

Hoffmann, too, admits that the NVA is an instrument of ideology, designed to secure the victory of "socialism/communism" on a world scale.

The duties of socialist armed forces nowadays extend far beyond the frontiers of the individual socialist country ... They demand that in case of war we should fight alongside our brothers-in-arms for socialism and communism, risking our own lives for victory.

Lenin, according to Hoffmann, was profoundly convinced that the interests of the working class "will be immeasurably better promoted by peace than by war", but he was equally opposed to "any absurd fantasies about growing peacefully and without conflict into socialism via the path of reform".

As the most fundamental social upheaval in history, the socialist revolution can only bring about a new, human order if it has first rased the old class tyranny to the ground ...

Theory of war

Whereas armies are largely seen in the West as serving to deter an attack- and hence as mere tools for the prevention of war[27], communist doctrine regards war, even in the atomic age, as an *instrument of politics*. Clausewitz' thesis that war is the continuation of politics by other means, a view looked askance at by Western students because of the nature of modern warfare, is endorsed without qualification in communist teaching. And this is not merely a reflection of the high opinion Lenin had of the Prussian general. To quote Hoffmann again:

We do not share ... the view, expressed even by progressive people in the peace movement, that a just war is no longer possible in the atomic age, or that a war waged with nuclear missiles would be a mere atomic inferno and the end of the world rather than a continuation of the policies of the struggling classes[28].

Indeed, the doctrine of a *"just war in our epoch of history"*[29], as repeatedly expounded by Soviet specialists, is basic to the prevailing theory in the NVA. Thus the East German periodical *Militärwesen* (Military Affairs) quotes from an article by the Soviet expert Colonel Professor Khalipov:

Marxist-Leninists have condemned imperialist wars of conquest, but they justify and support wars to protect the achievements of the nations from imperialist aggression, wars of national liberation and wars waged by the revolutionary classes to fend off attempts by reactionary forces at maintaining or restoring their hegemony by force of arms[30].

These ideas incorporate what the Soviet theory of war has always averred: that there can be no such thing as an unjust war waged by a socialist state, since "a socialist state does not aim at conquest or enter into any relationship with the imperialists at the cost of other nations"[31].

According to this view, wars in defence of the socialist fatherland are a continuation of the "politics of socialist revolution"[32].

> The Leninist concept of the defence of the socialist fatherland rests on the firm theoretical and methodological basis of the theory of imperialism, the theory of socialist revolution, the theory of the socialist fatherland and the manifold and wealthy experience of the struggle of our working people to defend the fruits of the October Revolution. Marxist-Leninists consistently defend and implement the civic ideal that the proletariat would prefer to take over power peacefully. It is not the working class, but their enemies within and without who are the instigators of armed force[33].

A *just war*, again, is

> a war that conforms to the basic interests of the majority of the population, to the basic interests of all the working people of the country in question. It is waged by the people for the purpose of paramount social justice, for freedom and for the independence of their country[34].

It is, of course, to be borne in mind that the "basic interests of the majority of the population" means, not the desires expressed by that majority, but those endorsed by the communists as their "avantgarde". Again, the "independence of their country" cannot mean, in the case of a socialist country, its independence from Soviet domination.

The distinction between just and unjust wars is a familiar theme in communist theory which turns up in various guises but remains constant in its main features, and recurs continually in specialist literature designed for the East German forces. The standard work on the History of the CPSU (B), ascribed to Stalin and enjoying official status up to 1956[35], offered these definitions:

Just wars are:
1. Wars waged by the proletariat to liberate the working people of their country from the yoke of capitalist exploitation . . .
2. Wars of national liberation waged by oppressed peoples and dependent countries against imperialism . . .
3. National wars of liberation from imperialist occupiers . . .
4. Wars of socialist states against the capitalist world to safeguard socialist achievements . . .

Unjust wars are:
1. Wars of the exploiting class against the working people inside their own country . . .
2. Wars of imperialist states against the national liberation movement of the people . . .
3. Wars between imperialist states to re-divide the world, conquer colonies and enslave their peoples . . .
4. Wars of imperialist states against the Soviet Union and the other people's democratic countries . . .

31

Amongst the just wars are also to be counted wars of revolution.

> Revolutionary wars in the narrower sense are wars waged by the revolutionary working class and other popular strata of a capitalist country to consolidate democracy and particular revolutionary achievements. These wars can either arise in the course of a revolution that has started, or take the form of civil war, or merge with a war against imperialist aggression[36].

Though war and *revolution* may be linked together, there can be no "equation or rigid connection" between them[37]. Especially complex is the "relation in our own epoch between world war and socialist revolution"[38].

> History is familiar enough with victories of revolution under the conditions of two world wars. If the reactionary forces of imperialism were to unleash another world war, there is no doubt that the nations would of course refuse to tolerate a system that condemned millions to suffering and death[39].

For those curious about the differences between the "*marxist-leninist theory of war*" and the "*views and doctrines of the bourgeoisie*" we have another Soviet authority, Colonel General Sredin:

> Firstly, the marxist-leninist theory of war and the armed forces is profoundly partisan in its origin and essence ... The superiority of a class political approach to the analysis of military questions is an essential condition for the correct solution of contemporary problems concerning war and armed forces, and for the further creative development of that analysis.
>
> Secondly, the marxist-leninist theory is in its content deeply scientific ... This is ensured by all-round study of warfare from a marxist-leninist standpoint in the unity of all its parts, and is achieved by applying the ideas and methods of dialectical materialism, economics and scientific communism, and using the achievements of the other social sciences, especially history.
>
> Thirdly, the marxist-leninist theory of war and the armed forces has a creative character, evolving continuously through generalization and the analysis of new phenomena in the life of society[40].

According to Colonel General Sredin we find in contrast to marxism-leninism "various views held by its political and ideological opponents, from war-mongering militarists and ultra-right fascist groups to leftist adventurists and reactionary bourgeois pacifists"[41]. No further details are provided about their "views", but of the "imperialist" camp it is stated in general that

> the arms race and preparations for war ensure huge profits for the monopolies. They have a direct and indirect interest in an acceleration of the arms race, in the modernization of armed forces and in the maintenance of international tensions. The military-industrial complexes

possess enormous potential for decisively influencing the policies of the ruling circles and for using this potential in their own interest . . .

The role of the armed forces in the societies of the imperialist states is a growing one. It conditions the ideological and psychological preparation of the soldiers and officers of the bourgeois armies. Personnel instruction amounts increasingly to training zealous servants of the ruling class who are ready for murder and shrink at no crime[42].

In view of the origins of the Soviet Union it is understandable that *civil war* should be given special priority. According to Marshal Sokolovsky the Russian Civil War was "a just war par excellence, the most intense form of the class struggle, the continuation of proletarian policy in the socialist revolution – the policy of overthrowing the bourgeoisie and landowners"[43].

That war should also, and primarily, be seen as a class struggle follows from the definition of war in the East German *Militärlexikon* (Military Lexicon):

War. A continuation of the policies of classes, peoples, nations, states or coalitions by means of organized armed force for the promotion of economic interests and political aims[44].

Just wars are those which accord in their objective political content with the interests of the revolutionary working class. In our own epoch this includes above all wars for the defence of socialism, revolutionary civil wars, national liberation wars of the peoples of colonial and dependent countries, wars to defend the independence of young nation-states and liberation wars of the peoples of capitalist countries who have been victims of imperialist aggression[45].

Unjust wars are those which by their objective political content conflict with the interests of the revolutionary working class[46].

Although "organized armed struggle" represents "the main form in which political conflict between the classes or states in question is worked out", it remains a combination of "military, political, economic, ideological and psychological forms of struggle"[47].

Wars between socialist states are not envisaged in communist theory. This is inevitable, since war is

a historical phenomenon, which arose with the appearance of private ownership of the means of production, the division of society into antagonistic classes and the growth of the exploitative state, and will likewise disappear when these do[48].

In 1956 and 1968, when the armies of the socialist Soviet Union were pitted against those of socialist Hungary and socialist Czechoslovakia, Moscow resorted to explaining these actions as *assistance to the two nations and their ruling communist parties in suppressing "counter-revolutions"*.

33

In 1957 an NVA military delegation, led by Minister for National Defence Willi Stoph visited the Chinese People's Republic, with the People's Liberation Army of which the NVA declared itself to be united in "unassailable brotherhood-in-arms".

In February 1979 Stoph in his function as Chairman of the Council of Ministers signed a declaration condemning the "criminal Chinese aggression against the SRV". – Text quoted in "Neues Deutschland": "Hands off Vietnam!"

Hände weg von Vietnam!

Protesterklärung der DDR gegen den ungeheuerlichen Überfall Chinas auf die SRV

Mit tiefster Empörung hat das Volk der Deutschen Demokratischen Republik die Nachricht von dem ungeheuerlichen militärischen Überfall Chinas auf die Sozialistische Republik Vietnam vernommen. Am 17. Februar 1979 sind chinesische Streitkräfte — Infanterie, Artillerie, Panzer sowie Einheiten der Luftstreitkräfte — unter Verletzung der Grenze in vietnamesisches Territorium eingedrungen und haben damit die Souveränität und Unabhängigkeit Vietnams angegriffen.

Das ist ein Verbrechen gegen den Frieden und die internationale Sicherheit! Das ist eine Herausforderung aller friedliebenden Völker!

Im Namen des Volkes der Deutschen Demokratischen Republik erheben wir entschieden Protest gegen diese Aggression Pekings auf Vietnams Heldenvolk. Wir fordern die sofortige bedingungslose Einstellung aller kriegerischen Handlungen und den unverzüglichen Rückzug der chinesischen Truppen.

Dem Brudervolk Vietnam versichern wir erneut die tatkräftige Solidarität der Deutschen Demokratischen Republik.

Zentralkomitee der Sozialistischen Einheitspartei Deutschlands
Staatsrat der Deutschen Demokratischen Republik

E. HONECKER
Generalsekretär und Vorsitzender

Ministerrat der Deutschen Demokratischen Republik

W. STOPH
Vorsitzender

Berlin, 17. Februar 1979

A delicate question arose, of course, with the Soviet-Chinese border conflicts in 1969. But when on February 17, 1979, Peking "attacked Vietnam with more than 20 divisions"[49], this constituted war. Peter Florin, East Germany's Deputy Foreign Minister and permanent UN representative, made no bones about it.

> China's aggression against the Socialist Republic of Vietnam is a crime against peace and international security, a challenge to all peaceloving peoples. The Security Council should resolutely condemn this aggression and its authors, and demand the immediate and unconditional cessation of the aggression and the withdrawal of Chinese troops from the territory of the SRV forthwith[50].

Soviet Foreign Minister Gromyko also failed to mention that China was a *socialist* state when he declared that "this crime was committed by Chinese leaders obsessed with notions of hegemony and expansion"[51].

In East Germany a massive "Hands off Vietnam!" campaign was launched. Volunteers were sought in the factories to fight alongside their Vietnamese "brothers-in-arms". Meanwhile the Politburo debated in private whether the Chinese People's Republic should be deprived of its status as a "socialist state". It would be surprising under these circumstances if the communist axiom, that there can be no wars under socialism, was not also discussed by the East German public and particularly by soldiers of the NVA, and seen to be highly questionable.

Under conditions of "détente"

Socialist revolution need not necessarily be associated with war[52], even if, as Army General Hoffmann said, history in fact "has witnessed no case in which a socialist revolution was led to victory without the guns", indirectly at least, "speaking their message of power"[53]. Nowadays, "when the world of socialism exists and is consolidating itself", the defence of its achievements, including that of international progress, depends on "scientifically-based activity at many levels, political, economic, ideological and military"[54].

> The political part of this activity consists of creating and perfecting favourable external conditions for the construction of socialism and communism; of actively cooperating with other contemporary revolutionary forces; of struggling for peace and international security, for the victory of the Leninist principles of peaceful coexistence and the intensification of the process of international détente[55].

Now the policy of "*peaceful coexistence*" between the two systems did not first enter the picture with the development of nuclear weapons in the mid-fifties. The American scholar Gerald Steibel, in a study of six decades of American-Soviet relations, finds that they covered at least six distinct cycles of tension and relaxation. Six decades of "détente politics" have taught the American people what it is all about. On whether this lesson is taken to heart or forgotten will depend "whether détente turns out to be an American art or an American tragedy"[57].

Communists make no secret of the fact that détente, and the "peaceful coexistence" theory which for them underlies détente, in no way imply abandonment of that *international class struggle* whose aims include Soviet hegemony. In 1973 the SED daily *Neues Deutschland* (New Germany) published an article by two Soviet authors pointing out that

> if the Soviet Communist Party and government are now pressing for cooperation with the capitalist countries, including the USA, the Federal Republic of Germany, France and Japan on the basis of peaceful coexistence, we are naturally quite aware of the permissible limits which the class struggle imposes on this policy. Peaceful coexistence is one form of the class struggle. Through their very nature and ultimate aims, the imperialist states remain irreconcilably hostile to socialism and social progress[58].

In answer to those who "falsify the concept of peaceful coexistence" the point is made that the use of this policy helps to create a situation "in which the worldwide revolutionary process can seize new opportunities for development"[59]. For it "facilitates solving the tasks of the national liberation movement, by hindering interference from the imperialist states in the domestic affairs of peoples who are struggling for their freedom, and by helping to expand the working-class and democratic movement in the capitalist countries".

And in 1978 we find the East German periodical *Militärwesen* stressing once more that

> under current conditions we often hear the question raised, both in the international workers' movement and among its opponents, as to how détente affects the class struggle. Certain bourgeois politicians express amazement and alarm at the solidarity shown by Soviet communists and the Soviet people with the struggles of other nations for freedom and progress. This is either naiveté or, more likely, a deliberate effort to confuse people's minds.

> ... Détente, however, in no way eliminates or changes the laws of class struggle ... We make no secret of our opinions.

> ... In the Party's view détente does not, and cannot, mean a freezing of the objective processes of historical evolution[60].

It is important to grasp that such interpretations of "peaceful coexistence" and "détente" are not designed for a restricted audience, but are spread around quite publicly. The *Militärlexikon*, for example, writes of peaceful coexistence as a "particular form of the class struggle between socialism and capitalism", calculated to create favourable conditions "for the international proletariat's fight to destroy imperialism and for the revolutionary transformation of society"[61].

There is another form of struggle, namely *economic activity* in the "world-wide conflict between classes and states", which is less strongly emphasized in periods of détente, at least as regards *economic warfare*. The "role of the economic factor" in war is greatly stressed. According to Sokolovsky the capitalist economies, albeit "in general keyed to preparation for war", are at a disadvantage in that they "have no central planning to rely on". In contrast to those of the socialist states they have "no clear prospect of expansion, since they are basically at the mercy of the random forces of competition"[62].

Honecker also claims that the GDR army is "equipped to meet the requirements of the class struggle, in accordance with scientific-technical advances". But he qualifies this with a reference to "economic possibilities"[63], i.e. economic limitations. The question of arms supplies to the GDR forces is one we shall deal with in a later chapter; at this point we are concerned with economic warfare as "one of the forms of the class struggle". In contrast to Khrushchev's utopian idea[64] that the "main economic task" was to match and overtake the United States, the latest targets present a more modest picture. The main tasks, we are now told, include

> intensification of socialist economic integration; the struggle to extend international economic cooperation and achieve equitable and mutually advantageous economic relations; the purposeful expansion of the economy of each fraternal country and of our whole community, which must objectively lead to enhancement of the defence capability of the socialist states[65].

On the economic battlefield the communists rest their hopes less on the superiority of their own system than on the *difficulties experienced by capitalism*. Industrial quarrels and strikes in the capitalist world are regarded by the communists as victories for their own side in the international class struggle.

Another form of the struggle, the *ideological* one, becomes more and more fierce "in the conditions of visible reduction of tension"[66]. "As the marxist classics repeatedly stress", ideological warfare is "one of the chief forms of the proletariat's class struggle". It is also assisted by the "*increasing scope of the mass media*". While these may "bring the two opposed systems face to face", as a West German specialist, Günther Wagenlehner[67], puts it, it appears that the "war of ideology" only goes well for the communists to the extent that "they can hermetically seal off their own territory from the non-communist world". To quote a Soviet view:

> Despite the undeniable fact that the crisis of bourgeois ideology is becoming more acute and that the ideological resources of anti-communism are running out, it would be wrong on that account to ignore the scope which contemporary capitalism still possesses for waging a struggle to control the minds of men ... Our adversaries are seeking ... to carry the ideological war into our territory[68].

The Helsinki *Conference on European Security and Cooperation* demonstrated that the communist camp fears any East-West contacts other than those conducted through State or Party organizations as potential infiltration and "interference in domestic affairs". Its Final Act gave the West a lever, for the first time, for speaking directly to the Soviet and East European public. "What the Soviet Union has always practised, and clearly regarded as its ideologically presupposed right – namely addressing Western societies directly over the heads of their governments – could now be practised against them"[69].

The GDR, because of its immediate proximity to West Germany, had lived with this problem for a long time. Back in November 1974, Honecker had complained:

> Every day, every hour, the GDR has had bourgeois ideology delivered to it from West Germany and West Berlin – free on the house, so to speak[70].

He accordingly challenged the mass media in particular to pay ever closer attention to their "great political-ideological tasks in propagating our ideas".

Human contacts in the form of meetings and exchanges of information having increased in the wake of East-West German agreements and of Helsinki, the ideological struggle has bulked even larger in Soviet doctrine. As Honecker pointed out in September 1977:

> It may sound odd, but the fact remains: at a time when people are talking – quite rightly, I believe – of détente making great progress, and of the need to make détente irreversible, international tension has increased in quite a few areas[71].

In 1975, a few days after the signature of the Final Act, Honecker termed it "the result of the greatest international collective action since the anti-Hitler coalition to reinforce security and make a reality ... of peaceful co-existence." It was the greatest flowering of European détente to date, he said. Yet class differences in the social system continued, and could not "disappear as a result of negotiations or agreements"[72].

To appreciate the place which war, and armed forces for securing the advance of socialism/communism, occupy in the minds of the ruling SED Party, one has to look at the system of "socialist defence education" by which the GDR seeks with growing intensity to indoctrinate the entire populace and, within the bounds of possibility, to educate it in the martial arts.

Notes

[1] Erich *Dethleffsen* und Karl Heinrich *Helfer*, Soldatische Existenz morgen, Bonn 1953, p. 23; Werner *Picht*, Wiederbewaffnung, Pfullingen 1954, p. 15.
[2] Cf. Heinz *Hoffmann*, Die Nationale Volksarmee auf Friedenswacht, in: *Deutsche Außenpolitik*, East Berlin, May 1965, Sonderheft, excerpted in: Heinz *Hoffmann*, Sozialistische Landesverteidigung. Aus Reden und Aufsätzen 1963–1970, East

Berlin 1971, pp. 252–258; Willi *Stoph,* GDR Vice-premier, addressing the People's Chamber in the debate on the bill for the creation of the NVA and Defence Ministry, in: *Neues Deutschland* (Organ of the SED Central Committee), East Berlin, January 19, 1956.

[3] Cf. on West German rearmament Gerhard *Wettig,* Entmilitarisierung und Wiederbewaffnung in Deutschland 1943–1955, vol. 25 in the documents published by the Forschungsinstitut der Deutschen Gesellschaft für Auswärtige Politik, München 1967.

[4] Ernst *Deuerlein,* Die Einheit Deutschlands, vol. 1, Die Erörterungen und Entscheidungen der Kriegs- und Nachkriegskonferenzen 1941–1949, Frankfurt am Main 1961, p. 347 ff.

[5] SED Central Committee report to the 8th Party Congress of the SED, in: *Volksarmee,* Militärverlag der DDR, East Berlin, June 1971 documents.

[6] J. V. *Stalin,* Über den Großen Vaterländischen Krieg der Sowjetunion, East Berlin 1945, p. 59.

[7] Max *Opitz,* October 1959, in a report of the SED Central Committee's Institute of Marxism-Leninism for the SED Party schools.

[8] Walter *Ulbricht,* 25 Jahre nach der Einigung der Arbeiterklasse, in: *Neues Deutschland,* January 14, 1971.

[9] Reinhard *Brühl,* Militärpolitik für Frieden und Sozialismus. Zum 25. Jahrestag der SED, in: *Militärgeschichte,* East Berlin, 3/1971, p. 262.

[10] Theo *Sommer,* Wiederbewaffnung und Verteidigungspolitik, in: Die zweite Republik. 25 Jahre Bundesrepublik Deutschland – Eine Bilanz, ed. Richard *Löwenthal* and Hans-Peter *Schwarz,* Stuttgart-Degerloch 1974, p. 580 f.

[11] Handbuch der NATO, Frankfurt 1957, p. 393; Lord Ismay, Secretary General of NATO, NATO – The First Five Years 1949–1954, Paris 1954, p. 32 f.

[12] Norbert *Tönnies,* Der Weg zu den Waffen. Die Geschichte der deutschen Wiederbewaffnung 1949–1957, Köln 1952, p. 59 f.

[13] Die Bemühungen der Bundesregierung um Wiederherstellung der Einheit Deutschlands durch Gesamtdeutsche Wahlen. Dokumente und Akten, pt. I., Oct. 1949 – Oct. 1953, 4th enlarged edition, Bonn 1958, p. 290.

[14] *Tägliche Rundschau,* Blatt der Sowjetischen Militärverwaltung für die deutsche Bevölkerung, East Berlin, May 4, 1952.

[15] Die Bemühungen … (cf. note 13), pp. 109–112.

[16] Toni *Nelles,* Der Aufbau und die Entwicklung der NVA – schöpferische Anwendung des Leninschen Militärprogramms durch die SED (I), in: *Militärgeschichte,* 1/1970, p. 23 f. (Source given: Protokoll der Verhandlungen der II. Parteikonferenz der SED, East Berlin 1952, p. 216.)

[17] *Neues Deutschland,* January 19, 1956.

[18] *Gesetzblatt der DDR,* pt. I, No. 18, September 20, 1961.

[19] Conscription Law of January 24, 1962, in: *Volksarmee,* 2/1962.

[20] Armeegeneral Heinz *Hoffmann,* Wir sind und bleiben an der Seite der stärkeren Bataillone. Speech at commemoration of NVA's 15th anniversary, in: *Volksarmee* 10/1971.

[21] Forum des Soldaten, in: *Volksarmee* 25/1971.

[22] Heinz *Kessler,* Die historische Leistung der SED bei der Entwicklung der NVA zu einer modernen sozialistischen Armee, in: *Militärgeschichte,* 1/1976, p. 6.

[23] Address given to troops by Erich *Honecker,* in: *Neues Deutschland,* June 9, 1978.

[24] Heinz *Kessler,* (cf. note 22, p. 6.)

[25] Ibid. p. 10.

[26] Armeegeneral Heinz *Hoffmann,* Streitkräfte in unserer Zeit, in: *Einheit,* Zeitschrift für Theorie und Praxis des wissenschaftlichen Sozialismus, pub. SED Central Committee, East Berlin, 3/1976.

[27] Raymond *Aron,* Frieden und Krieg, Frankfurt am Main 1963; Bernard *Brodie,* Strategy in the Missile Age, Princeton 1959; Stanley *Hoffmann,* The State of War, New York 1965; Henry *Kissinger,* Kernwaffen und auswärtige Politik, Frankfurt

am Main und München 1959; Robert *McNamara,* The Essence of Security, New York 1968; Thomas *Schelling,* Arms and Influence, New Haven and London 1966.

28 *Hoffmann,* Streitkräfte in unserer Zeit, loc. cit.

29 Col. Prof. *Chalipow (Khalipov),* Gerechte Kriege in unserer Epoche, in: *Militärwesen,* East Berlin, 9/1978, pp. 17–23. Abridged and edited translation from the Soviet military press.

30 Ibid. p. 17.

31 Ibid. p. 18 f.

32 Ibid. p. 18.

33 Ibid.

34 Ibid.

35 Geschichte der Kommunistischen Partei der Sowjetunion (Bolschewiki), Kurzer Lehrgang, East Berlin 1952, p. 210.

36 Chalipow, loc. cit., p. 20.

37 Ibid. p. 21.

38 Ibid.

39 Ibid. p. 22.

40 Generaloberst G. *Sredin,* Die marxistisch-leninistische Lehre vom Krieg und von den Streitkräften in der Gegenwart, in: *Militärwesen* 7/1978, p. 81 f. Abridged and edited translation from the Soviet military press.

41 Ibid. p. 79.

42 Ibid. p. 84.

43 Militär-Strategie, ed. Marshal *Sokolovsky,* German translation of the 3rd revised and enlarged Russian edition, Köln 1969, p. 358.

44 Militärlexikon, Militärverlag der DDR, East Berlin, 2nd ed. 1973, p. 183.

45 Ibid. p. 184

46 Ibid.

47 Ibid. p. 183.

48 Ibid.

49 Der Krieg Chinas gegen Vietnam, in: *Neues Deutschland,* February 28, 1979.

50 *Neues Deutschland,* February 27, 1979.

51 Ibid.

52 Chalipow, loc. cit., p. 22.

53 *Hoffmann,* Streitkräfte in unserer Zeit, loc. cit., p. 359.

54 *Chalipow,* loc. cit., p. 17.

55 Ibid.

56 Dr. Gerald *Steibel,* Director, Research Dept. for Foreign Affairs of the Research Institute of America, Detente. Promises and Pitfalls, in: Strategy Paper No. 25, National Strategy Information Center, New York 1975.

57 Ibid. p. 15.

58 W. *Kudinow* und W. *Pletnikow,* Der ideologische Kampf zwischen den beiden Systemen, from Mezhdunarodnaya Zhizn, in: *Neues Deutschland,* February 3, 1973.

59 Ibid.

60 *Chalipow,* loc. cit., p. 22.

61 Militärlexikon, 1973, p. 110 f.

62 *Sokolovsky,* loc. cit., p. 91.

63 Speech by Erich *Honecker,* Schutz des Vaterlandes in guten Händen, in: *Neues Deutschland,* June 9, 1978.

64 Cf. Boris *Meissner,* Politische Entwicklung und sozialer Wandel in der Sowjetunion, in: Elemente des Wandels in der östlichen Welt, Köln 1976, p. 90.

65 *Chalipow,* loc. cit., p. 17 f.

66 *Kudinow* und *Pletnikow,* loc. cit.

67 Günther *Wagenlehner,* Die gegensätzlichen Systeme im Kontakt. Zur Frage der Freiheit des internationalen Personenverkehrs, des Informationsaustausches und der Medien in Europa, in: *Beiträge zur Konfliktforschung,* Köln 1/1975, pp. 5–27.

68 *Kudinow,* loc. cit.

69 Curt *Gasteyger,* Die Aussichten der Entspannung. Europa nach dem KSZE-Folgetreffen in Belgrad, in: *Europa-Archiv,* Bonn, August 10, 1978, p. 472.

[70] Cf. *Die Welt*, Hamburg, December 14/15, 1974.
[71] *Honecker*, Die sozialistische Revolution in der DDR und ihre Perspektiven, East Berlin 1977, p. 6.
[72] Helsinki und wir. Interview with Erich *Honecker, Neues Deutschland*, August 6, 1975.

CHAPTER TWO

Socialist Military Education

Article 23 of the GDR *Constitution* says that every citizen is obliged to render "service and other contributions to the defence of the German Democratic Republik"[1]. The *Party Programme* of 1976, which calls the SED "a section of the international communist movement", terms it "a right and debt of honour of every citizen" to defend "the achievements of socialism and of the socialist fatherland", and adds that "the constant and alert attention of the Party, the State and all social organizations" is required to further "the readiness and competence of all citizens to afford military protection to socialism"[2]. The increasing tendency to put "*the fatherland*" in second place after "*internationalism*" is noticeable if one compares, for example, the 1971 and 1973 editions of the *Militärlexikon*. In the former, the "socialist fatherland" is mentioned before the "socialist community of states"[3]. But in the later edition we read:

> The basis of socialist military education is to educate citizens toward socialist internationalism and socialist brotherhood-in-arms, toward socialist patriotism, love of the socialist fatherland, self-sacrifice on behalf of the achievements of socialism[4].

The GDR's close ties with the Soviet Union meant that its military training was from an early stage modelled on the Soviet pattern. Though in Khrushchev's Russia all education was slanted towards work-worship as a means of increasing civilian production, great attention was also paid to preparing the public for war, especially in an ethical-political sense. Marshal Sokolovsky wrote in 1963 in his *Military Strategy:*

> Preparing the public in moral-political terms is critically important at the present time, since the introduction of weapons of mass destruction places greater demands than ever on the political and moral stance of the population.
>
> The moral-political preparation of the Soviet people for war consists in the first place of educating it in the spirit of Soviet patriotism, in the spirit of love for one's homeland and for the Communist Party, and in inculcating willingness to bear any burden that war brings in order to achieve victory.
>
> The Soviet people is brought up to defend its fatherland and the achievements of the socialist revolution, to realize the superiority of the socialist over the capitalist system, and to believe firmly in the creation of a communist society . . .
>
> The moral-political preparation of the people for war is conducted by

all the country's state and social organizations, and by the entire educational and training system, under the guidance of the Communist Party and the Soviet government. All the media of propaganda and agitation are mobilized to this end – press and periodicals, science, literature, the cinema, theatre and so on[5].

After the fall of Khrushchev in 1964 a fresh impulse was given to the inculcation of patriotism and to the closely associated pre-military training of the young, both of which had featured in Soviet educational policy since Lenin's days. Military-patriotic education received more stress than ever. Borys Lewytzkyj, a specialist living in the West, commented in 1971:

> Military-patriotic schooling is an integrated concept in which two streams of interest converge. The military insist that the young should be trained to cope with the demands of a modern atomic war; the politicians have become increasingly aware that the standard ideology has worn thin and is more and more detached from reality, so they seek an effective substitute in military-patriotic training. At the same time there was an intention to counter the much-lamented softening of the fibre in a generation continually reminded that it had not gone through the discipline and privations of the October Revolution or the Second World War[6].

When the U.S.S.R.'s *new conscription law* came into effect on January 1, 1968, "military-patriotic education" acquired fresh definition and stronger commitments. Basic pre-military training became mandatory for all schools. The *DOSAAF* (Voluntary Association for Cooperation with the Army, Air Force and Fleet – cf. the East German GST, Ch. 6 below) was reorganized and given massive support.

In East Germany, whose leaders could boast of having maintained their hard line even during the Khrushchev era, the SED's Central Committee hastened with its resolution of June 11, 1968, to proclaim the "enhanced tasks and main lines of military education work"[7] and to lay down the responsibilities in this field of the various sectors of society. In the East German case it was not of course possible to speak primarily of military-patriotic education, nor to lay the sole emphasis on "unity of people and army".

> The new element is that the unity of people and army is today no longer confined within a national framework. The GDR public increasingly sees all the armies of the Joint Armed Forces as its protectors, and is guided by this principle in its practical attitude and dealings with them. Its love and commitment to all the armies of the coalition, especially the various forms of active public participation in fulfilling the tasks required of the troops, were particularly apparent during Exercise "Brotherhood-in-arms", the high point so far in the socialist states' successful development of collective defence.
>
> With a view to further consolidating the unity of people and army, the SED Central Committee and the state leaders of the GDR have elevated

socialist military education for the public during the 1960s to a higher level as an inseparable part of their overall effort in political-ideological education.

Socialist military education, we learn, "is aimed, like any educational process, at the feelings as well as the mind. It is conducted systematically and with differential regard to political and military needs, to the age and activities of the pupils"[8]. It constitutes "class education and training for every GDR citizen"[9]. "It implements educational aims, and applies tools and methods, calculated to promote defence awareness, defence morale, defence motivation, defence preparedness and defence competence."[10] It encourages the overall development of a socialist personality and the growth of qualities such as

> loyalty to socialist ideals, proletarian internationalism, socialist patriotism, solidarity, firmness, courage, discipline, confidence in victory, loyalty to the Party of the working class, self-sacrifice, and hatred for the enemies of the people and the enemies of socialism[11].

Overcoming pacifism

Back in the late 1940s, when the SED was still keeping secret its support for rearmament in the territory it controlled, it was already planning to involve the whole population in its military policies. In 1948 "a start was made with the creation of Alert Squads of the People's Police and the process of educating working people toward active defence-preparedness was embarked on"[12]. It was imperative "quickly to step up the defence-preparedness of the working people"[13].

The first need was to exorcize pacifism. "Large sectors of the public nurtured pacifist views stemming from their bitter experience in the Second World War."[14] At the 4th Parliament of the Free German Youth organization in Leipzig, its then chairman Erich Honecker declared that it would be quite logical for "peaceloving German youth" to regard it as an honour and a duty to undertake "the organization of armed defence for our homeland". And he added that "service in the German People's Police is for every member of the Free German Youth a debt of honour to the German people"[15]. The recruitment campaign for the People's Police did not go as well as had been hoped. At the 2nd Session of the Central Council of the Free German Youth in Halle, Honecker had to admit that "strengthening the ranks of the armed forces, the basis of our future People's Army", was an honourable task, but had proved a "difficult" one[16].

As early as July, 1952, at the 2nd SED Party Conference, the then Party Chairman Wilhelm Pieck demanded

> the complete elimination of any unclear thinking and vacillation in the Party ranks . . .

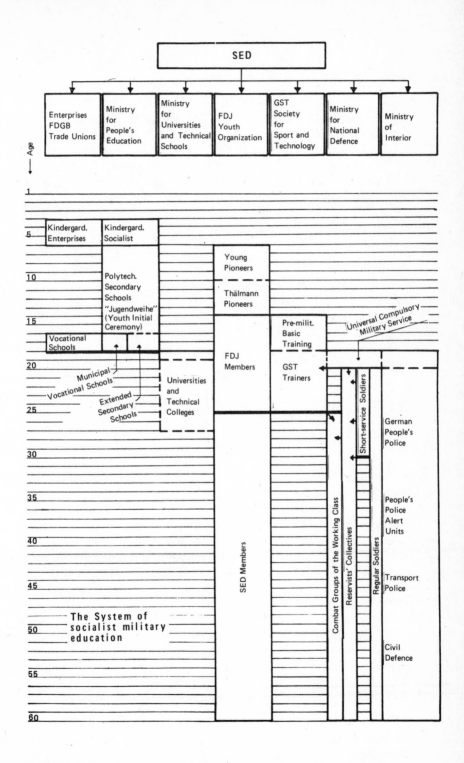

The two great founders of scientific marxism sharply denounced the mischievous cliché that "war in any form" was to be deplored[17].

What was particularly denounced, in the autumn of 1955, was "the view being increasingly put about by today's enemies that there is no difference in principle between the armies of the imperialist and of the socialist states"[18].

By propagating this theory the West German imperialists hoped to counter the growth of socialist defence-motivation in large sections of the GDR public, to set working people at odds with the military policies of the Party and the state leaders, and at the same time to distract attention from the reactionary and aggressive nature of the West German army, whose build-up has progressed apace since 1955[19].

In current conditions "the effect of pacifism in the workers' movement is objectively anti-progressive".

Pacifism paralyses the fighting power of the masses and restrains them from actively struggling against unjust wars or supporting just ones[20].

But "as an ideological current alien to the working class's scientific outlook" pacifism, we learn, has nevertheless "points in common with the peace policy of the socialist states and the international workers' movement" in cases where it opposes "imperialist" military measures.

Refusal of service

There is no such concept as refusal of military service in the official usage of the GDR. There is, however, alongside service in the NVA and Frontier Troops, the institution of substitute service *(Wehrersatzdienst)*. Unlike civilian service in lieu of conscription, as the West knows it, *Wehrersatzdienst* is seen simply as conscript service rendered *outside the armed forces*. A resolution of the National Defence Council[21] has defined service in the *Ministry for State Security,* in the *People's Police* and *Transport Police,* and in the *Construction Units (Baueinheiten)* as forms of substitute service in the sense of paragraph 25 of the Conscription Law.

While service in the Security Ministry and the police is comparable with basic military service in the NVA, that performed in the Construction Units differs in some respects. "Construction troops" are conscripts who "for religious or similar reasons refuse to carry arms".

The status and function of construction troops are clear from the principal regulations governing Construction Units, viz.

– Construction Units are used for the construction of military facilities, for the repair of damage caused by military exercises and for coping with natural disasters.

– Members do not carry arms.

– Members carry the rank of Construction Private; they do not swear allegiance to the colours, but make a promise of loyalty.

– They take orders from "reliable officers, NCOs and other ranks of the National People's Army".

– They wear uniform, "branch colour olive", with special insignia.

– In addition to work they receive the following types of training: Political schooling, instruction in legal and military regulations, parade-ground drill without weapons, army-style physical exercise, pioneer service and specialist training, civil defence and first-aid instruction.

– Construction troops are subject to the same legal and military ordinances as regular conscripts unless expressly stated otherwise in these Regulations.

School of hatred

Those in charge of socialist military education are not content with overcoming pacifism as an obstacle to defence-preparedness. What they find indispensable is an *image of the enemy* – not merely of a particular system, state, coalition or class, but of an enemy personified and even named. If the enemy is to be fought, he has to be hated, and hatred is something for which men must be trained.

In socialist military training hate is represented in the first place as a necessary complement to "respect and love for the working class and the Party, for the people of the GDR, and particularly for the peoples of the Soviet Union, of the whole socialist community and of other countries"[22]:

> As we deeply love all that is progessive, noble and conducive to human dignity, so we deeply hate forces that obstruct or even jeopardize these things. Our hatred rests accordingly on other moral foundations than that of the imperialists and their minions. We neither want nor need the kind of hatred that is typical of the imperialist states, especially of their armies. There is no place in our country for the brutal killer with no conscience, who slaughters with pleasure, unhesitatingly, because that is his "job" and he is paid for it.

This is not the place to point out that in *Western society, based on Christian values, a formal doctrine of education in hatred would be out of the question.* Such training also conflicts with the knowledge that in a technologically sophisticated army, especially, emotional and negatively argued exhortations would be militarily counter-productive, even as a short-term device, for soldiers who are rationally and ethically motivated. That is the position on the Western side. But in the East, we read[23], inculcation of hatred "does not conflict with the noble aims of socialism". "The status of friend or enemy" is determined "not by subjective attitudes and notions, but by particular social conditions. The dividing line between friend and enemy is first and foremost a class line"[24]. As Defence Minister Hoffmann has explained, it is not sufficient "simply to reject and hate imperialism as a system; one must above all direct this hatred against everyone who acts under the orders of imperialist generals and officers"[25].

The Working Class Combat Groups' monthly periodical *Der Kämpfer* (The Fighter), published by the SED Central Committee, takes hate-training a step further in identifying individual enemies by name. Every issue features a column called "Deadly Enemies of the People at the Levers of Power in the Federal Republic", in which the finger is pointed at some West German public personality, usually a politician or businessman – say Helmut Schmidt or Peter von Siemens. The column ends each time with such advice as "to be removed", "to be eliminated" or "to get out of the way", as if members of the Working Class Combat Groups were expected to take the article around with them when engaged in "ensuring the onward march of socialism". A photograph of the relevant "enemy of the people" is provided. Certainly, the fact that it is "progressive forces" in West Germany which are being appealed to for the removal of "deadly enemies of the people" from positions of power cannot disguise the aim of the campaign – to identify proscribed persons and publish details in the form of instructions to the Combat Groups.

Hate-training begins in *school* at full pitch. An official textbook on the "Benefits of Socialist Military Education for Schoolchildren in the GDR" repeatedly emphasizes the need to instill hatred. Its general advice runs:

> Training pupils to love the working class and its Party, to respect the creative efforts of the working class and all working people, and to trust their leadership, must be accompanied by training in hatred toward every form of exploitation and oppression[26].

Attention is drawn to particular opportunities for inculcating hatred in various age and subject groups. Thus in 5th grade *history lessons* dealing with "the decline of primitive society and the rise of the earliest class societies in the East in ancient times ... the realization that armies were used for pillage and conquest as well as to subject the masses ... should induce hatred and disgust in the pupils towards the social forces responsible"[27]. In *music teaching*, again, "the artistic experience of music, the emotional impact of singing and listening to music, and appreciation of the intellectual content of works of music and their social and historic background" should help pupils in all grades "to take issue with the enemy's ideology and intensify their hatred for the imperialist system"[28]. *German lessons* are to be used to create "a quite rationally directed, yet emotionally rooted, image of the enemy"[29]. Discussion out-of-hours of *Soviet war books* and memoires is recommended, with the appreciative remark that "such literature helps to intensify hatred for the enemy"[30].

Hatred being regarded as of such cardinal importance in defence-preparedness, it is inevitable that hate-training should be prescribed in the statutes of the *Free German Youth* movement.

The Free German Youth movement will steel the young people of the GDR in their irreconcilable hatred for imperialism and its reactionary policies[31].

But no section of the public is so exposed to the hate-campaign as the *members of the NVA*. This is clear from every military newspaper and periodical, where inculcation of "bottomless hate toward the inhuman tyranny of imperialism and militarism" is demanded as an "inseparable element in the creation of socialist awareness"[32]. The NVA's service regulations also specify hate-training[33].

It is noticeable that neither the signing of the various agreements between East and West Germany, nor the recommendations of the Helsinki Conference, have led to any diminution in hate-education in the GDR.

No individual, no subject escapes the net

Socialist military education "aims to ensure that every citizen of our Republic is brought up to be a conscious pioneer for the nation and a passionate defender of the socialist fatherland"[34]. This follows logically, we are told, "from the conditions of modern warfare", where "all spheres of social life are in some way related to national defence"[35]. A further argument is ad-

Under the slogan "Strengthen our people's power! Defeat militarism!" Combat Groups parade in East Berlin.

duced, for example, in the Manifesto of the SED's 7th Party Congress of April 1967:

> An advanced socialist society requires everyone's readiness to defend jointly what was jointly created[36].

Not only must socialist military education involve every member of the public, but it has to be seen as an integral part of "educating an all-round personality". In the previously quoted textbook of socialist military training put out by the Ministry for People's Education in 1974 there is a special warning against the mere "grafting on" of military lessons to the various school subjects[37].

> Training in defence preparedness and efficiency must be seen as a duty required of socialist schools by the working class. It is no mere appendage to socialist education, but in our particular historic conditions is clearly part of the education of an all-round socialist personality[38].

To put it bluntly, then, the purpose of socialist military education is to create not just a militarized society but at the same time, "in our particular historic conditions", militarized individuals.

In 1976 at the SED's 9th Party Congress Colonel General Horst Stechbarth presents to Secretary General Honecker a formation of honour comprising the 500 best of the NVA and the GDR Frontier Troops.

Socialist military education is of course directed foremost at the younger generation in the *schools, universities* and *factories,* with the 16 to 18 age bracket as the target for one part of it – pre-military training. The scope of the exercise can be judged from the announcement that "in recent years eight out of every ten men called up to the NVA" have undergone pre-military training already[39]. General Lieutenant Günther Teller, chairman of the pre-military Society for Sport and Technology, was able to boast in 1976:

> We have reached a stage where nearly 95 per cent of all young men between 16 and 18 each year take part in the Society's pre-military courses[40].

Socialist military education starts with the three to six-year olds, more than half of whom attend one of the socialist kindergartens under the direct control of district or regional councils. (East Germany also has factory kindergartens, again run on strict Party lines, and others run by the churches.)

After that the Ernst Thälmann Pioneer Organization *(Pionierorganisation "Ernst Thälmann")* takes over the job, preparing about 85 per cent of all children between 6 and 14 for the Free German Youth. Young children engage in manoeuvres to show how far their military training has progressed. They receive specialist advice from class instructors, NVA officers, and officials of the Free German Youth and the Society for Sport and Technology.

The Pioneer Organization, then, is a stepping stone to the Free German Youth *(Freie Deutsche Jugend – FDJ)* and the Society for Sport and Technology *(Gesellschaft für Sport und Technik – GST),* the latter of which is officially dubbed a "school for the soldier of tomorrow"[41]. And this form of education culminates in the NVA itself.

Since the 4th Congress of the SED in January 1963 pre-military courses have been absorbed into an overall system of Complex Military Education *(Komplexe Wehrerziehung)*, in which political and ideological indoctrination ranks equally with purely military instruction.

Inside the framework of Complex Military Education, which covers all aspects of life, there is a division of labour as between the GST and the FDJ. While the former prepares young people physically and technically for *basic military training* or a *military career,* the latter seeks by intensive ideological education to arouse defence-willingness and alertness. Accordingly the FDJ holds discussion nights on military policy, organizes trips to "national monuments", and runs exhibitions and competitions to do with morale and defence issues. It has set up working groups of "Young Military Theorists" in which 10th to 12th grade secondary school-boys receive cadet training from NVA reserve officers. The FDJ also seeks to enliven military instruction with farewell parties and ceremonies for those who are called up. Not the least of the FDJ's tasks is to assist the GST in conducting and checking pre-military training in the schools and universities and in factories. The GST's purely pre-military role will be discussed in a later chapter along with that of other non-NVA elements of the defence apparatus.

Details of the "right and duty of the young to defend socialism" are to be found in the text of the 1974 GDR Youth Law[42]. The defence of socialism is there shown to embrace both "the defence of the socialist fatherland" and that of the "socialist community of states".

> It is the duty of the young to acquire instruction in defence policy and pre-military knowledge and skill, as well as to serve in the NVA and other national defence bodies.

The same law makes state and economic officials as well as schoolteachers and other educators "responsible for preparing the young to defend socialism".

> It is their duty to promote defence training and education, pre-military, civil defence and army sports training in the schools, in the vocational training institutes, FDJ and GST, and ambulance instruction in the GDR Red Cross. Particular attention is to be given to recruiting and training new aspirants for military careers.

A joint statement by the Ministry for People's Education and the Central Board of the GST, in March 1963, made the establishment and conduct of "active and purposeful pre-military training by GST branches" mandatory in all secondary and vocational schools. Military combat and marksmanship were to be included in competition programmes and school sports events.

Documents put out by the Ministry for People's Education, in 1965, likewise required that teachers should "inculcate socialist defence motives as part and parcel of the curriculum"[43]. And in 1974 we find it said that "neither pre-military training nor out-of-school activities, nor a single subject such as Civics, suffice to implement the comprehensive tasks of socialist military education"[44]. As good examples of the mutual reinforcement of formal schooling and extramural activity in socialist military training the Ministry for People's

Young riflemen of the Goethe secondary school in Neustadt-Glewe being trained by the deputy director Jürgen Sternhagen.

Education instances the strengthening of discipline, and familiarization with military tasks through mathematics and the natural sciences.

> A consciously exercised discipline is of crucial importance for the structuring of school life, for the fulfilment of production plans and, not least of course, for coping with military problems.
>
> In the NVA an approximation formula is used to determine the distance of an object in the open whose horizontal and vertical dimensions are known. Inclusion in mathematics lessons on algebraic manipulation of this so-called one-to-a-thousand formula will not only equip pupils for describing military situations in mathematical terms and handling variables confidently, but also for estimating distances, describing terrain and sighting targets[45].

The same textbook finds connections between schoolwork and the military art where none are immediately apparent. A wallpaper frieze with flowers and houses done in the art class to illustrate the subject "Erfurt, city of flowers" is "not immediately relevant", it admits, "to military education since other educational purposes are primarily involved", but it could still be donated to some NVA unit to decorate its barracks[46].

Even before the 1974 Youth Law teachers had been duty bound to promote socialist military education through *out-of-school activities*.

In grades 8 to 10 of the secondary schools so-called Hans Beimler Contests *(Hans-Beimler-Wettkämpfe)*[47] have become the main element in the system of socialist military education organized by the FDJ with different programmes for different groups and ages. These contests include ones with a military angle, such as cross-country and obstacle racing, grenade throwing, air-rifle shooting, forced marches, trecking and so on. The contests themselves are supplemented by a variety of organized events with a military interest.

As an extension to the work brigade activity of the 9th and 10th grades a syllabus for "Defence Training Brigades" *(Arbeitsgemeinschaften „Wehrausbildung")* was introduced in September 1973, concentrating on rifle practice, field exercises, self-defence and ambulance training, for which 100 hours were earmarked, 60 in the 9th grade and 40 in the 10th. A period of four consecutive hours on one afternoon every other week was recommended for this brigade activity.

An optional course in "Foundations of Military Policy and Armed Defence of the GDR" is a particularly important part of socialist military education in the last year of school. It is calculated to "help pupils in opting for a military vocation, reinforcing the decision and stabilizing career motivation"[48].

A big leap forward occurred with the introduction, on September 1, 1978, of Defence Instruction as a compulsory subject in the 9th and 10th grades of the Polytechnic Schools *(Polytechnische Oberschulen)*. Until then, young people had consistently managed to evade military training in spite of the considerable moral compulsion exercised. Despite a broad front of resistance, particularly that directed by the churches against the hate propaganda associated with weapon training, the government forced the new measure through.

The first, 1978, edition of the textbook on Civil Defence for Nine Grades *(Zivilverteidigung 9 – Lehrbuch für Klasse 9)* shows just what the new course involved[49]. It does indeed partly deal with civil defence, but it also covers pre-military training, field exercises, drill "life in war conditions" and "maintenance and care of weapons and uniform".

The section of the textbook devoted to theory – "Civil defence – a component of socialist national defence" – contains the usual polemics. What is striking, however, is the justification offered for the erection of an East-West German frontier barrier and the sealing off of West Berlin by the Berlin Wall on August 13, 1961. Where previously the main reasons given were the alleged luring away of manpower by West Germany, desertion of the GDR and consequent "billions of marks' worth of damage to the economy", the new book says nothing of a mass exodus from East Germany and speaks instead of a direct threat of war from the imperialist side.

The arguments for taking part in Civil Defence studies are summarized as follows[50]:

– As long as imperialism exists, there is a danger of it embarking on war. Imperialism as ever remains aggressive and piratical . . .

– War in the modern era would be basically different from earlier wars. A modern war would mean heavy burdens, sacrifice and efforts for the civilian population of socialist countries.

– Since the possibility of a modern-style war must be assumed, expansion of civil defence is needed to enhance the socialist state's ability to protect itself . . .

Older school children and teenagers are urged to help teachers, and especially to assist in protecting and supervising their juniors. To do this effectively they should acquire appropriate knowledge and skill through civil defence training.

Industrial apprentices are drawn into socialist defence education equally thoroughly. The Vocational Training Institute *(Institut für Berufsausbildung)* lays down the following requirements among others:

All apprentices are to be trained

– to understand relationships within society;

– to give conscious support to the all-round strengthening and defence of the socialist fatherland;

– to draw appropriate lessons for their class role by showing willingness to put their vocational knowledge and skill, their general education and their best physical abilities at the service of national defence, and to prepare themselves during their apprenticeship for the discharge of duties in national defence generally[51].

In December 1976, the SED, government and trade unions launched a joint demand with the FDJ for the socialist military education of apprentices to be intensified:

. . . pre-military training and civil defence are to continue as an integral part of their instruction and extramural activity. Good showing in pre-military training and defence sport will prepare apprentices for service in the NVA and other arms. Stress will be placed on strengthening defence motivation and instilling the same knowledge and skills as basic military training and military technology. Greater attention is to be paid to career formation and winning new recruits for the military profession . . .[52]

At the same time "everything must be done to enhance the physical stamina of apprentices"[53]. In addition to vocational expertise they will be required to display knowledge of

– Marxism-Leninism, in particular its theory of war and armed forces;

– the causes and nature of possible wars;

– Lenin's teaching on the defence of the socialist fatherland; and

– the military policy of the SED[54].

The following example shows how the organization of pre-military training in *vocational schools* is supposed to function, as well as the role of NVA *reservist "collectives"* as training cadres and the interplay of the various bodies.

> The Vocational School of the *Landbaukombinat* (Rural Building Combine) People's Enterprise has already set an example and shown in practice how the new pre-military training measures can be carried out.
>
> Party organization leaders, management, leaders of the army reserve collective, GST and FDJ join in working out a programme of socialist military training.
>
> Its aim is steadily to prepare future soldiers, ideologically, technically, physically and psychologically, for NVA service . . .
>
> In Civics lessons, for example, problems of military policy will be given their due place.
>
> Sports instruction will be largely structured to meet NVA needs, e.g. club and dart throwing, obstacle tracks, running under handicaps, and gunfire . . .
>
> On the initiative of reservists, youth brigades were set up so that they could be given pre-military training on construction sites at squad strength . . .
>
> Exemplary discipline and order is inculcated in the hostel, where wall-newspapers are posted dealing with current military political events and a "Military Political Cabinet" has been organized.
>
> Pre-military training proper is given at weekends by the GST to platoons and squads, only ex-service reservists acting as instructors.
>
> The Güstrow District Defence Command is endeavouring, in cooperation with the SED District Leadership, the District Council, mass organizations, Commission for Socialist Military Education, headmasters and enterprises to convert the experience of the *Landbaukombinat* Enterprise into general practice for the whole district[55].

Military training is equally obligatory for *university* and *technical college* personnel – teachers and other staff as well as students. Since the large majority of male students have already undergone military service before entering college, a great deal is expected of them. These requirements are intended to convince all students that vocational and defence-oriented interests form a single whole. As reservists of the NVA and other arms they are supposed to keep themselves up to the mark in military theory and practice while at the same time helping to give pre-military training to students who have not done their conscript service and to young men outside the university as well.

As early as 1960 the GST had already drawn up a comprehensive pre-military syllabus for students. It runs for two college years and takes up 100 hours in all. From 10 to 15 per cent of the training is done at night. Thirty-eight hours are set aside for Tactics, twenty-four for Marksmanship, fourteen hours each for Topography and Physical Fitness and ten for Drill. The leaders of Hundreds or faculty heads in the GST are empowered either to decrease or increase the numbers of hours according to the student's progress. "The essential consideration is that every student should have mastered the subjects before the end of his training."[56] After the two years of instruction the student has to qualify for the GST badge. From his third academic year on he is in principle obliged to take part in group contests, rifle competitions, combat practice and motorized trecking.

Students who earn bad marks for discipline during pre-military training can be given a warning by the rector in accordance with regulations, or expelled.

Female students do not escape socialist military education either. Like those of their male colleagues who are found unfit for active service, they are trained for work in Civil Defence or in the German Red Cross.

The obligation for students to do pre-military training follows in principle from the 1974 Youth Law. This states that "study at a university, senior college or technical school is a high social honour and represents a personal obligation for every student vis-à-vis the working class and the socialist state"[57]. Participation in socialist military education is therefore a very serious duty for the student, especially since admission to higher education is granted not only on academic ability but also for "social performance in accord with the needs of a socialist society", and the FDJ leaders "have the right of codecision over admission to study". Moreover the rectors of universities, technical school heads, and teaching staff in both, carry "responsibility for the class-oriented education" of students. Socialist military education had been declared obligatory for all students in directives of the Ministry for Higher Education as early as 1970.

In 1968, when Soviet pre-military training received a considerable fillip along with military education generally, East Germany created closer ties between *sport* and defence. A resolution of the State Council of September 20, 1968, for example deals with the tasks of physical culture and sport in the development of a system of "advanced socialism" in the country. Under the heading "Outstanding physical and sports efficiency promotes citizens' defence readiness and capability", we read in Section II, Point 4, the following:

> Healthy and efficient human beings, steeled by sports training, are better able to meet the requirements of the GDR's national defence.
> Physical education that meets the enhanced demands of service in the armed forces is also in line with the progressive and revolutionary traditions of the national people's struggle ... and the military traditions of the German and international working class[58].

Subsequently the close connection between sport and defence training was cast in a more binding form by the Youth Law of 1974. This states that the East German sports badge campaign entitled "Ready for Work and Homeland Defence" is an "integral part of the education of young working people, of school children, apprentices and students"[59].

The Olympic Games, too, are seen as a "political sporting event" and an example of "ideological class conflict". In April 1971 Major Wittek, head of the Youth Department in the Main Political Administration of the NVA, explained that

> an ideological class conflict awaits us in connection with the coming 1972 Olympics in Munich. In line with the socialist content of physical culture and sports in the GDR, all FDJ branches must conduct, in close cooperation with army sports clubs and groups, offensive discussions on the politics of sport, so as to help our younger comrades to adopt the right class standpoint[60].

The *Volksarmee* coverage of the Munich events certainly gave priority to the political angle. "For the first time in the Olympic summer games we saw an independent, fully sovereign Olympic team entering the arena on behalf of the socialist German state." The time had passed when GDR athletes could be subjected to "Bonn's cold-war highhandedness over so-called all-German teams"[61]. Some of the reportage, however, especially conversations with returning sportsmen, was quite human and non-political[62]. And the propaganda of "triumphal jubilation" was then scaled down to such wistful remarks as: "Who could resist hoping that his country's flag should fly as often as possible from the victory mast and its anthem ring out for another Olympic win?"[63]

After the Montreal Olympics in 1976 *Volksarmee* had a new thought. Under the headline "Final Totals" it presented the "share of all medals going to the socialist countries", viz. 56 per cent, as an "historic event" – 121 gold medals, 107 silver and 116 bronze. There followed a list of GDR victories, with special note of those (in parentheses) won by NVA members. While at the 1972 games there had been 20 (3) gold, 23 (4) silver and 23 (4) bronze medals, the corresponding results for 1976 were 40 (5) gold, 25 (1) silver and 25 (7) bronze ones.

NVA reporter Karl-Heinz Wehr, army colonel and Vice-president of the International Boxing Federation, swore on his return from Montreal that "each of us left the stadium after the closing ceremony firmly resolved to continue the struggle to uphold the Olympic ideal of bringing nations together, against all those forces who would destroy that ideal and simultaneously seek to frustrate peace and progress"[64].

The implication that support for the Olympic idea is a speciality of the "socialist countries" in opposition to the "imperialist" ones – where the idea nevertheless originated – is another feature of socialist military teaching. Insistence that the socialist countries support the Games purely to promote détente was, of course, further stressed in January, 1980, when the Soviet invasion of Afghanistan led to calls in the West for a boycott of the impending Moscow Olympics.

Recruitment for the NVA

Even before socialist military training had taken its place as an "inseparable part of the whole educational process in the GDR"[65], large sections of the population had already been obliged to demonstrate their willingness to play a "voluntary" part in East German rearmament. There was ample scope for this between mid-1955 and January 1962, i.e. before the formal creation of the NVA up to the introduction of *universal conscription*.

There were several reasons why the voluntary principle was not abandoned in favour of conscription until six years after the birth of the NVA and indeed 14 years after the Garrisoned People's Police had been set up.

For foreign policy reasons alone it was impracticable in the early post-war years for the Soviet Union openly to endorse conscription for a populace that was supposed under the Potsdam Agreement to remain disarmed for all time. The Soviets were also aware of the unpopularity of the communist regime they had forced on the Germans, so that politically reliable cadres had first to be reared for the new army they had long since decided on creating. In 1945 and for a few years thereafter, again, East Germany's economic potential meant more to the Russians than her military potential.

An account written in 1970 offers the following explanation, in addition to the need to support the "struggle against Bonn's headlong rearmament" and a desire to "contribute to the worldwide disarmament initiative of the peace-loving peoples":

> On the other hand, the delay complied with the requirement of the Leninist military programme – often proved right subsequently – that in setting up an army of the new type the class principle must be consistently followed in making personnel appointments[66].

Thus the "people's army" was destined from the first to be a "class army".

The "voluntary" principle of recruitment could not be allowed to function "in a random way". On the contrary, it was essential that the Party and mass organizations should be committed to "participate in defence efforts".

The 1946 Statutes of the SED[67] with their insistence on strict Party discipline themselves imposed an indirect obligation on members in this direction. The 1950 Statutes made the requirement to "accept Party decisions" still more explicit, and the version passed at the 4th Party Congress, four years later, formulated it as an express duty of members to win recruits for military service.

> The Party educates and organizes working people for all-round active defence of the homeland, the workers'-and-peasants' state, against all its enemies' deeds of aggression[68].

Similarly decisions, binding members to join the armed forces themselves where possible as well as to encourage others to, are equally mandatory for the SED's daughter organizations.

The military duties of FDJ members were laid down as early as the Statutes of May, 1955.

FDJ members regard it as their honour and duty to acquire pre-military knowledge and abilities. Service in the armed forces of the GDR is a matter of honour for everyone in the FDJ[69].

In the 1976 FDJ Statutes it is stated in more detail that each member is obliged

to exert all his efforts self-sacrificingly for the defence of the workers'-and-peasants' power, to be on the alert for assaults by the enemies of peace and socialism, and to be active in support of the GDR's armed forces;
steadily to acquire knowledge and skill for the sure defence of socialism, especially by way of army training; by service in the NVA, Frontier Troops or other defence and security forces to aspire to the highest military competence and to display paramount discipline and combat-readiness;
to preserve state, economic and military secrets[70].

Similar obligations have been enshrined since 1955 in the rules of the Free German Trade Union organization *(Freier Deutscher Gewerkschaftsbund – FDGB):*

The trade unions imbue the working people with patriotism, love of their homeland, alertness against saboteurs and agents, and fulfilment of their duty to defend the socialist achievements of their workers'-and-peasants' state[71].

And in the 1972 Statutes we read that the unions

promote active participation by their members in social life; readiness to defend their workers'-and-peasants' state and their socialist achievements, and to exercise watchfulness[72].

Trade unionists are also exhorted to join the workers' Combat Groups.

Since the Party's intensive pressure had ensured at an early stage that almost the entire population belonged to one or another of the "organizations", men of an age to carry arms were under a virtually automatic obligation to take part in some form of military training.

In the first phase of rearmament, up to the end of 1951, it was still fairly simple to recruit the necessary numbers for the various armed police units. An inducement for voluntary entry into the People's Police was the superior food rations and high pay. Members of the armed units received 120 grams of butter or other fat a day, at time when normal consumers only received 29.5 grams.

In the same period political pressure was put on *ex-Wehrmacht* men, especially regulars, to make their military experience available. A part was played in this by the National-Democratic Party of Germany *(National-Demokratische Partei Deutschlands – NDPD)*, which was founded in the summer of 1948 – at the same time as the first garrisoned units of the People's Police – and addressed itself to the "middle classes, former Nazi party members, professional soldiers and officers". Numerous ex-servicemen who while POWs in the Soviet Union had belonged to the "Free Germany" National Committee, the League of German Officers and/or one of the "anti-fascist schools" were told when released to join the NDPD. They had been in the service of "criminal militarism", it was explained, and could now expiate their guilt by joining the new police forces.

The shortcomings of this recruitment method became apparent in late 1951 when a start was made with turning the cadre formations into full-strength military units, while at the same time labour shortages appeared. The recruiting commissions set up by the SED proved unable to attract sufficient men to the colours. It was clear that the army could not be built up without an efficient registration system.

On October 1, 1952, the job was entrusted to District, and over them Regional, Registration Departments, with a Recruitment Administration *(Verwaltung für Rekrutierung)* in overall charge at the headquarters of the Garrisoned People's Police. In 1956 the subsidiary bodies were renamed *Wehrbezirkskommandos (Bezirk =* region) and *Wehrkreiskommandos (Kreis =* district) respectively, and when the National Defence Ministry was set up it was made responsible for an Administration for Recruitment and Complementation *(Verwaltung Werbung und Auffüllung).*

Even this improved coordination of volunteer enlistment failed, however, to solve the problem. The campaign was now extended not only into the mass organizations but into the schools, state-owned factories and collective farms – wherever potential recruits worked, in fact – but despite this it was found necessary in 1959 to fix recruitment quotas for each district and parish. Even so, targets could only be met by increasing political pressures on able-bodied men of "volunteering" age. Admission to higher education was only granted on completion of military service. Young workers were threatened with relegation to lower wage grades, and skilled workers with loss of promotion prospects if they failed to "volunteer for honourable service in the armed forces". Others were tempted with the suggestion that impending political charges against their parents might be dropped.

Between 1950 and the introduction of universal conscription in 1962, the SED and FDJ repeatedly launched "all-out" recruitment campaigns which, like all other forcible measures, were reflected in refugee statistics. A considerable fraction of the age-groups in question tried to avoid service by escaping from the country. Between February 4, 1952, and December 31, 1959, a total of 234,157 men aged between 18 and 24 – the very groups the campaigns were aimed at – registered as refugees in West Germany or West Berlin.

The most vigorous effort of all began on August 28, 1961, just two weeks after East Germany was sealed off by the Berlin Wall and the tightening of the demarcation-line with the West. With six months to go before universal conscription was introduced, the FDJ announced a "fighting task" to win

In late August 1961, a fortnight after the GDR's almost hermetical sealing-off, the FDJ tried to win volunteers for the NVA in a mass recruitment campaign with slogans such as "Your fatherland calls you – protect the socialist republic!" "FDJ regiments" were formed.

volunteers with the emotional slogan: "Your fatherland calls you – protect the socialist Republic!" The "call to arms" by the FDJ Central Council was read out in every school, university, factory and urban or rural community. The campaign had all the trappings of mobilization for war. The younger generation was said to be "on the march"; detailed reports filled the daily press, and radio and television commentaries spoke of a "national event". The "volunteers" were given ceremonial send-offs in provincial towns with military bands in attendance; organized crowds jubilated and young girls handed over bouquets. A total of 253,000 young men were said to have answered the call[73].

The campaign was deliberately planned to prepare the public psychologically for the introduction of universal conscription. Toward the end of 1961 the press was full of reports of "working members of the public" demanding that the authorities finally introduce conscription, since it was everyone's duty to defend "the achievements of socialism and the fatherland". A few days after the Conscription Law was promulgated, Defence Minister Hoffmann declared that

> it is precisely this universal willingness of the young to defend the fatherland that provides the moral basis for the introduction of conscription for all[74].

After seventeen years of conscription, however, and twenty-five years of socialist military education, the younger generation's enthusiasm to serve in the forces is still insufficient for intensive recruitment and propaganda to be dispensed with.

National service, as the Youth Law puts it, "is highly esteemed by socialist society"[75]. The Law provides that those in positions of responsibility should

> keep in constant touch with young men in their areas who are performing their national service in the armed forces and look after the interests of their families. They should give support to NVA reservists when they resume their civilian jobs. Short-service and career soldiers who have completed their service with honour should be particularly assisted in their vocational work or studies.

The Defence Minister's "Regulations on Promotion" of February 13, 1975, call upon

> governmental and economic bodies, enterprises of all types, institutes, universities, higher, technical and general schools, social organizations and socialist cooperatives, all hereinafter referred to as enterprises, to engage in a large-scale operation to "promote NVA members who have been released from active military service"[76].

Similar encouragement is to be conferred on those who opt for voluntary service in the forces. "Vocational guidance"[77] is to start in the 7th grade at school, with the aim of persuading youngsters where possible to opt for a military career at the end of the 9th grade and apply in writing to their local *Kreis* recruiting office. Inside the schools help is given by staff responsible for recruiting new blood, and further details are provided by career advice centres and *Kreis* recruiting offices.

> Teachers and youth workers will give every attention to those young people who have manifested willingness to become NVA officers[78].

"Exacting political, military and technical demands" are placed on military cadres. In a socialist society, the military career has "very special status and importance"[79].

The NVA and socialist military education

It is in the National People's Army itself, that "nucleus of national defence", that "socialist military education" comes into full flower. Here, too, military training is only seen as one aspect of political training. Each will be dealt with in detail in a separate chapter below, along with the respective bodies within the army to which they are entrusted – the political organs and the army branches of the SED and FDJ.

The *NVA's civilian employees* are another target of socialist military education. Horst Glaeser, chairman of the Union of Civilian Employees of the NVA, explained, in March 1977, that

> it is of essential concern to all union officials further to improve political-ideological work and enable every member to cooperate still more intensively and effectively in enhancing the combat-readiness of detachments and establishments[80].

According to another spokesman, the "main thrust" of trade union activity in the NVA, "now as ever, is toward improving service and combat-readiness. The llth Session of the Central Committee of the Union of Civilian Employees of the NVA . . . left this in no doubt"[81].

There was no suggestion, at least in earlier years, that the unions should also represent the social interests of civilian employees. Only recently do we find calls for increased concern over the problems of working women – part-time employment, the health of working mothers or implementation of the Labour Protection Regulation No. 5[82].

An important part in socialist defence education is played by *NVA reservists,* both through their formal reserve service and in their other activities.

The terms of military service for the reserves were laid down by an order of the National Defence Council dated July 30, 1969[83]. The main provisions are as follows:

All men between the ages of 18 and 50 belong to the reserve if they are not on active service.

The NVA reserve falls into two classes:

Reserve I
– Officers up to the rank of captain, NCOs and other ranks up to the age of 35;
– officers from major upwards, to the age of 60;
– all men liable to service who have not been in the forces, up to the age of 35.

Reserve II
– Officers up to the rank of captain between the ages of 35 and 60;
– NCOs and other ranks between the ages of 35 and 50, or 60 in a defence situation;
– all men liable to service who have not been in the forces, between the ages of 36 and 50.

Left: Military ceremonial – the "Crescent" at the head of the military band. – Below: "Neues Deutschland" advertising the film "Scharnhorst", a five-part series on Prussian history for broadcast by the GDR television.

Reserve I constitutes the NVA's reserve for mobilization purposes, while in case of war Reserve II men would be called up for rear services.

Soldiers who have completed their conscript service continue to receive training by way of *Reserve Exercises,* to which all are summoned at intervals between two and four years, for maximum periods of three months per annum in the case of Reserve I and two months in that of Reserve II. The maximum total obligation is 24 months for officers of the reserve, 21 months for NCOs and other ranks. In addition to the normal exercises, reservists can also be called upon by order of the National Defence Council to submit to a brief "examination" of their readiness for service.

The reserve regulations also prescribe "social duties of ex-service reservists outside their actual reserve service". These duties consist of

> giving expert and effective support to state bodies and social organizations in the socialist military education of GDR citizens in the interest of continually enhancing the country's defences.

On the basis of the July 1969 decree the ex-service reservists' organizations were redefined in 1975 as Reservist Collectives and Reservist Groups respectively.

A *Reservist Collective* brings together ex-service reservists in state and economic bodies and other institutions, of all ranks and arms. *Reservist Groups* can be formed within the Collectives, which normally comprise from ten to a hundred men. The work of each collective is controlled by from three to five reservists, usually headed by an officer appointed by the local *Wehrkreiskommando* in consultation with the state authorities and SED enterprise branch. This officer in turn nominates the members of the controlling body of the Collective and, where necessary, the leaders and deputy leaders of the component Groups.

Special tasks are delegated to army formations and units for carrying out the various forms of cooperation with ex-service reservists. Commanders are responsible for

> – maintenance of close contact and cooperation with *Wehrkreis* and *Wehrbezirk* headquarters and with Reservist Collectives;
> – seconding officers as rapporteurs and lectors on military-political and technical questions, or to take part in reservist conferences and brains trusts;
> – ensuring close links between officers, NCOs and other ranks of the NVA with ex-service reservists;
> – inviting reservists, especially their officers and NCOs, to take part in exercises, training demonstrations and events organized on state holidays and the NVA's anniversary.

As has been mentioned, reservists are obliged to take part in other aspects of socialist military education than their regular reserve service. General Hampf, addressing Reservist Collective leaders in the Frankfurt a. d. Oder region, instanced the following commitments:

1. Undertaking effective military propaganda in the Reservist Collectives and among enterprise staff;

2. preparing young people in work brigades politically for military service; as instructors, exercise leaders and officials assisting the GST's basic and further pre-military training for NVA careers, as well as its sports activities;

3. in discharge of their honorary recruiting responsibilities at their foster-schools and in the FDJ recruiting brigades for military careers, lending an active hand in winning and supervising youngsters interested in such careers and reinforcing their will to pursue them.

In the process of discharging these various duties, or helping out with the Working Class Combat Groups and civil defence activities, or systematically improving their own performance in the "Eight Exercises Test" *(Achtertest)*, in the sports activities of their enterprise or their GST group, in military festivals *(Wehrspartakiaden)* and other such events, the reservists are at the same time complying in essence with the obligation to maintain their own combat fitness at the necessary standard[84].

The duties of reservists were once more stressed in the 1974 Youth Law:

> Reservists of the NVA will take active part in the socialist military education of the young. Their political and military knowledge and experience will fit them to be used in particular as propagandists, GST instructors, and work brigade and club leaders in the FDJ and the Ernst Thälmann Pioneer Organization[85].

"Effectiveness factors" in socialist military education

As Honecker put it in June 1978, "there is no sphere in the life of our society which is not permeated with defence concerns"[86]. That did not imply that every citizen lived up to the ideal of socialist military education, however great the efforts described in this chapter to make military awareness and an active role in national defence shibboleths of socialist identity. If we ask whether this education attains, or indeed can attain, its ends, we must first appreciate the fact that socialist military education has been repeatedly intensified whenever the SED felt it necessary to fasten its grip on the public in the wake of political events at home or abroad.

Thus the erection of the Berlin Wall in 1961 made it possible for universal conscription to be introduced the following year. At the same time Commissions for Socialist Military Education were created to give better guidance to the mass organizations which had been responsible for it since 1952.

When a grave crisis of confidence among the GDR public was caused by the invasion of Czechoslovakia in 1968, the SED Central Committee laid down the responsibilities of various sectors of society for socialist military education, which now became an integral part of the school curriculum.

When Willi Stoph, Chairman of the Council of Ministers of the GDR, in 1970 embarked on a rapprochement in the Erfurt and Kassel talks with West Germany's Chancellor Willy Brandt and so committed the SED to détente, pre-military training was tightened up and made obligatory as a twelve-day course for all 11th grade schoolchildren.

When the Final Act of the Helsinki Conference was signed in 1975, East Germany's civil defence system was completely militarized and put under the Defence Ministry.

When in 1978 the détente policy still appeared to be progressing, the SED leaders found socialist military education so important that they elevated the Central Committee's Working Group on Military Education to the status of an independent Department. A further consequence was the introduction of "military science" as a mandatory subject in the 9th and 10th grades of high schools.

Every shift, it can be said, in the direction either of tension or of détente, has been exploited by the SED leadership to intensify socialist military education. In the former case the stress would fall on the purely military side, in the latter – with its "softening-up" dangers – on ideology and discipline.

Apart from events on the broad political scene there are also factors ensuing from the general technological-social revolution that have their effect on military education. The Party is well aware of the inevitable civilizing effect of rising consumer expectations. But it seems to have found no answer to this problem so far, except to point out that socialist military education can be fun for the conscript who enjoys the machinery of war or trips to foreign countries – albeit, alas, only to "socialist" ones.

An article written in 1978 by Colonel Effenberger on "Sundry Effectiveness Factors in the Formation of Socialist Military Motives"[87] is of interest here. He pointed to two such factors which

> particularly at the present time have a wide significance for the individual's socialist defence-motivation. One is the influence of ten years of peace in Europe and the political détente process, while the other is the increasing satisfaction of essential material and intellectual needs in our society.

It would be a great over-simplification, says Effenberger, to suppose that

> increasing material prosperity and the satisfaction of spiritual and cultural needs by some automatic process bring about a high level of socialist defence morale or encourage, for example, the choice of a military career. Even when socialism has already won the day, it is far from true that favourable changes in the material conditions of life automatically produce analogous changes in mental awareness.

But what happens if people notice that life under "socialism" is worse than under "capitalism"? Or if they decide that though the arms training they receive in the course of "socialist military education" might be worth having if there were a real enemy around, what they are given much more of is propaganda, at great inconvenience, for a system that runs contrary to their personal interests? As the paramount feature of a system of all-pervasive tutelage of the citizen by the ruling party, socialist military education is a particularly oppressive burden in an age when the whole world is calling for more leisure time.

It is not beyond the bounds of possibility that socialist military education may one day have the opposite to its intended effect and that the East German public, precisely because of the vexations of socialist military training, will lose patience with the whole system of the "first German workers'-and-peasants' state" and decide to rely on the "Great Refusal".

Notes

[1] GDR Constitution of April 6, 1968, as revised in the Gesetz zur Ergänzung und Änderung der Verfassung der Deutschen Demokratischen Republik of October 7, 1974, quoted from *Neues Deutschland* of March 27, 1968, and September 28, 1974.

[2] Programme of the SED, quoted from *Neues Deutschland* of January 14, 1976.

[3] Militärlexikon, Deutscher Militärverlag, East Berlin 1971, p. 349.

[4] Militärlexikon, Militärverlag der DDR, East Berlin 1973, 2nd ed., p. 344.

[5] Marschall der Sowjetunion W. D. *Sokolowski* (ed.), Militär-Strategie, German translation from the 3rd, revised and enlarged, Russian edition, Köln 1969, p. 436 f.

[6] Borys *Lewytzkyj*, Die Marschälle und die Politik. Eine Untersuchung über den Stellenwert des Militärs innerhalb des sowjetischen Systems seit dem Sturz *Chruschtschows*, Köln 1971, p. 121.

[7] Reinhard *Brühl*, Militärpolitik für Frieden und Sozialismus. Zum 25. Jahrestag der SED, in: *Militärgeschichte*, East Berlin, 3/1971, p. 271.

[8] Militärlexikon, 1973, p. 344.

[9] Handreichung zur sozialistischen Wehrerziehung, ed. Karl *Ilter*, Albrecht *Herrmann* and Helmut *Stolz* for the Ministry for People's Education, Volk und Wissen Volkseigener Verlag, East Berlin 1974, p. 36.

[10] Ibid.

[11] Ibid.

[12] Cf. Geschichte der deutschen Arbeiterbewegung, vol. 6, East Berlin 1966, p. 286.

[13] W. *Ulbricht*, Die gegenwärtigen Aufgaben unserer demokratischen Verwaltung, in: W. *Ulbricht*, Zur Geschichte der deutschen Arbeiterbewegung, vol. 3, East Berlin 1953, p. 281 ff.

[14] Werner *Eltze*, Von der wehrsportlichen Interessengemeinschaft der FDJ zur Gesellschaft für Sport und Technik, in: *Militärgeschichte*, East Berlin, 1/1977, p. 37.

[15] Protokoll des IV. Parlament der FDJ, pub. by the Central Council of the FDJ, East Berlin 1952, p. 240.

[16] Address by Erich *Honecker* to the 2nd Session of the Central Council of the FDJ of August 14, 1952, in: *Tägliche Rundschau*, East Berlin of August 16, 1952.

[17] Protokoll der 2. Parteikonferenz der SED, East Berlin 1952.

[18] Die neue Lage und die Politik der SED, in Dokumente der SED, vol. 5, East Berlin 1956, p. 471.

[19] Toni *Nelles*, Der Aufbau und die Entwicklung der NVA – schöpferische Anwendung des Leninschen Militärprogramms durch die SED (1), in: *Militärgeschichte*, East Berlin, 1/1970, p. 28 ff.

[20] Militärlexikon, 1971, p. 299 (also in 1973 edition, p. 291).

[21] *Gesetzblatt der DDR*, pt. I, No. 11, September 16, 1964.

[22] Handreichung zur sozialistischen Wehrerziehung, p. 27 f.
[23] Vide chapter: Erziehung zum Haß auf den Feind, in: Soldat und Krieg. Probleme der moral-politischen und psychologischen Vorbereitung in der Sowjetarmee, ed. M. P. *Korobejnikow*, East Berlin 1972, pp. 116–118.
[24] Handreichung zur sozialistischen Wehrerziehung, p. 28.
[25] *Einheit*, East Berlin, 6/1971, pp. 690–702.
[26] Handreichung ..., p. 45 f.
[27] Ibid., p. 49.
[28] Ibid., p. 113.
[29] Ibid., p. 90.
[30] Ibid., p. 193.
[31] Statut der Freien Deutschen Jugend, in: *Junge Generation*, East Berlin, 7/1976, p.101.
[32] Admiral W. *Verner*, Head of the Main Political Administration of the NVA, in: *Militärwesen*, 8/1972, p. 9.
[33] DV-10/3 der NVA, January 1, 1963.
[34] Taschenbuch für Wehrpflichtige, East Berlin 1965, p. 60.
[35] Oberst Dr. W. *Butter* in: *Volksarmee*, East Berlin, 11/1967.
[36] Protokoll des VII. Parteitages der SED, vol. 4, East Berlin 1967, p. 285.
[37] Handreichung ..., p. 44.
[38] Ibid., p. 19.
[39] *Volksarmee*, 9/1971.
[40] Address by Günther *Teller* to the 10th Parliament of the FDJ on June 3, 1976, in: *Junge Welt*, East Berlin, June 4, 1976.
[41] Since the 4th Congress of the GST, September 12 to 14, 1968.
[42] Gesetz über die Teilnahme der Jugend an der Gestaltung der entwickelten sozialistischen Gesellschaft und über ihre allseitige Förderung in der DDR - Jugendgesetz der DDR, January 28, 1974. Issued in: *Gesetzblatt der DDR*, pt. I, No. 5 of January 31, 1974, pp. 45–49.
[43] *Pädagogik*, East Berlin 10/1966, p. 85.
[44] Handreichung ..., p. 39.
[45] Ibid.
[46] Ibid., p. 122.
[47] Hans *Beimler* was a commander in the International Brigade during the Spanish Civil War and fell in the Madrid fighting in 1936.
[48] Handreichung ..., p. 165.
[49] Zivilverteidigung 9 – Lehrbuch für Klasse 9, Volk und Wissen Volkseigener Verlag Berlin, approved for schools by the GDR Ministry for People's Education, East Berlin 1978. 255 pp.
[50] Ibid., p. 31.
[51] Sozialistische Wehrerziehung in der Berufsausbildung, East Berlin 1968, p. 26.
[52] Resolution of the Politburo of the SED Central Committee, the GDR government, the Federal Executive of the FDGB and the Central Council of the FDJ on December 7, 1976, in: Berufsbildung, East Berlin 1977, p. 57 ff.
[53] Sozialistische Wehrerziehung in der Berufsausbildung, p. 36.
[54] Ibid., p. 53.
[55] *Volksarmee*, 39/1968.
[56] Programm für die vormilitärische Ausbildung an den Universitäten, Hochschulen und Fachhochschulen der DDR, pub. by the Central Board of the GST, 1960. See also K.-H. *Gentsch*, „Zur Reservistenarbeit an den Hoch- und Fachschulen", in: *Militärwesen*, East Berlin, 3/1975, pp. 55–59.
[57] Jugendgesetz, vide supra Note 42, par. 22, p. 52.
[58] *Neues Deutschland*, September 9, 1968.
[59] Jugendgesetz, vide supra Note 42, par. 37, p. 55.
[60] Unter Führung der Partei der Arbeiterklasse – auf Kampfposition für die Erfüllung der militärischen Hauptaufgabe. An address by Major *Wittek*, Head of the Youth Department of the Main Political Administration in *Volksarmee*, Dokumentation, May 1971, p. 8.

61 *Volksarmee*, 36/1972.
62   do.   37/1972.
63   do.   36/1972.
64   do.   32/1976.
65 Taschenbuch für Wehrpflichtige, East Berlin 1965, p. 60.
66 Toni *Nelles*, op. cit., p. 30.
67 Dokumente der SED, vol. I, East Berlin 1951, p. 11 f.
68 Dokumente der SED, vol. V, East Berlin 1956, p. 92. In the 1976 SED Statutes
   there is a more general formulation that Party members have the duty and right
   "to protect and reinfore socialist property as the inviolable basis of the workers'-
   and-peasants' state, and the socialist order; and to strengthen the country's
   defences" quoted from *Neues Deutschland* of January 16, 1976. In more express
   terms, the Programme of 1976 makes it a task of the SED to "promote the
   readiness and ability of all citizens to effect the military defence of socialism".
   See Note 2.
69 *Junge Welt*, East Berlin, No. 134 of June 8, 1955, p. 3 ff.
70 FDJ Statutes, quoted from *Junge Generation* 7/1976, p. 103.
71 *Die Arbeit*, Monatsschrift für Theorie und Praxis der deutschen Gewerkschaften,
   pub. by the FDGB Federal Board, East Berlin 6/1955.
72 FDGB Statutes, passed at the 8th FDGB Congress of June 26 to 30, 1972, pub.
   Tribüne Verlag und Druckerei des FDGB, East Berlin, p. 4.
73 Cf. General Lieutenant Günther *Teller* in: *Sport und Technik*, pub. by the GST
   Central Board, East Berlin, No. 10/1974.
74 *Nationalzeitung*, East Berlin, January 28, 1962: Eine Frage bitte, Herr Minister.
   Telefonforum der 'Jungen Welle'.
75 Jugendgesetz,par. 24, p. 53.
76 Verordnung über die Förderung des aus dem aktiven Wehrdienst entlassenen Angehörigen der NVA – Förderungsverordnung, dated February 13, 1975, *Gesetzblatt
   der DDR,* pt. I, No. 13, March 13, 1975, pp. 221–229.
77 Handreichung . . . , p. 121.
78 Ibid., p. 189.
79 Ibid., p. 212.
80 Gewerkschaften in der NVA stärken Landesverteidigung – Konferenzen der Be-
   reichsgewerkschaftsorganisationen abgeschlossen, in: *Volksarmee*, 10/1977.
81 *Volksarmee*, 29/1976.
82 Irene *Bütow*, Vice-chairman of the Central Board of the Union of Civilian
   Employees in the NVA, in: *Volksarmee*, 9/1977.
83 Hereafter quoted from *Armeerundschau*, 6/1969, p. 72 ff.
84 Gemeinsam geht's schneller voran. Generalmajor Ernst *Hampf* sprach vor Leitern
   von Revervistenkollektiven im Bezirk Frankfurt/Oder über aktuelle Probleme der
   sozialistischen Wehrerziehung, in: *Volksarmee*, 10/1975.
85 Jugendgesetz, par. 25, p. 53.
86 *Neues Deutschland* of June 9, 1978.
87 Oberst Dr. W. *Effenberger*, Zu einigen Wirkungsfaktoren bei der Ausprägung sozialistischer Wehrmotive, in: *Militärwesen*, East Berlin, 8/1975, p. 7.

CHAPTER THREE

In the Service of Socialist Internationalism

After lengthy preparations the East Bloc countries agreed at their fourth conference to the Warsaw Pact, which was signed on May 14, 1955, and came into force on June 4 of the same year. Its full title is the "Treaty of Friendship, Cooperation and Mutual Assistance between the People's Republic of Albania, the People's Republic of Bulgaria, the People's Republic of Hungary, the German Democratic Republic, the People's Republic of Poland, the People's Republic of Rumania, the Union of Soviet Socialist Republics and the Czechoslovak Republic"[1]. Albania's adhesion was in abeyance from February 1, 1962, until she formally broke with the Pact on September 1, 1968.

The chief military provision of the Pact is its Article 4:

> In the event of an armed attack in Europe on one or several states that are signatories of the treaty by any state or group of states, each party to this treaty shall, in the exercise of the right to individual or collective self-defence in accordance with Article 51 of the U. N. Charter, render the state or states so attacked immediate assistance, individually and in agreement with other states that are parties to this treaty, by all the means it may consider necessary, including the use of armed force ...

The Warsaw Pact countries also reinforced the series of *bilateral treaties of friendship* initiated by the Soviets between 1943 and 1948 – with Czechoslovakia (1943), Poland (1945), Rumania, Hungary and Bulgaria (1948) – and due to run for twenty years, with a fresh series of bilateral agreements. The 1945 treaty with Yugoslavia, however, came to an early end when it was denounced by the U.S.S.R. on September 28, 1949.

The new system of treaties entered into between the middle sixties and 1972 between the Soviet Union and Poland, Bulgaria, Hungary, Czechoslovakia, Rumania and East Germany, and among these countries themselves, embraces as many members of the "socialist community of states" as possible, including the Mongolian People's Republic. It is thus a system with wider territorial coverage than the purely European Warsaw Pact, and larger in its content: it provides for "cooperation in all fields"[2].

The same applies in greater degree to a further series of *bilateral compacts between East Germany and the other socialist bloc countries,* concluded between 1975 and 1977. These reflect the "general drawing-together of the socialist nations and states". As Brezhnev put it at the 25th Congress of the Soviet CP:

As each socialist nation blossoms forth and the socialist states wax stronger in their sovereignty, so their mutual relations will become ever closer, more and more common elements will arise in their political, economic and social life, and their living standards will be gradually equalized[3].

The Soviets' hegemony over their allies is also subserved by the agreements on the *stationing of Soviet troops* concluded with some of the other countries of the "socialist camp" – Poland, the GDR, Rumania and Hungary – between December 1956 and May 1957. Only Rumania, where Soviet troops were obliged to leave in June 1958, has been able to dispense with the Soviet presence. But in 1968 Czechoslovakia also had to accept a treaty permitting the stationing of Soviet troops on her territory.

The military cohesion of the bloc in Europe, then, does not depend exclusively on the Warsaw Pact.

Under Article 9 the Pact allows for the accession of additional countries willing, "regardless of their social and state system", to help in guaranteeing the peace and security of the nations. This idea found early expression in the call for a European Security Conference. But it was stressed, and is still stressed, that the creation of the Pact

> marks at the same time a new political and military quality in the development of the socialist world system and of proletarian internationalism; it is also a step showing recognition in the military sphere of the natural law by which the socialist states merge ever closer together[4].

How seriously one can take the suggestion that the Pact is open to other countries *"regardless of their social and state system"* can be judged, however, by reading further in the same key statement of Army General Shtemenko, First Deputy Commander in Chief of the Pact's Joint Armed Forces.

> The Warsaw Pact is a reliable and effective instrument for peace and socialism ... The political basis of the socialist military bloc is the homogeneity of the social and state systems of the fraternal socialist countries[5].

It would be fair, then, to see the Warsaw Pact as the basis of an organization which formalizes a degree of military cooperation among the bloc states already provided for in other ways, but which also, in contrast to the numerous internal bloc functions of the bilateral treaties, serves as an *instrument of security for the bloc as a whole*.

The conclusion of the Pact in 1955 was not unrelated to the *Balkan Treaty* signed by Greece, Yugoslavia, and Turkey in the previous August – a Treaty which was not seen as aimed at Albania alone. But the Pact was still more relevant to Russia's relations with the other East Bloc states. Thus the coming into force of the *Austrian State Treaty* in May 1955 in consequence of the 1947 Peace Treaties would have obliged the Soviets to pull their troops out of Hungary and Rumania, where they were only supposed to be covering their lines of communication with their occupation troops in Austria. The Warsaw Pact, however, permits the *Soviet Union to maintain military units and commands in all the East Bloc countries* – even in Czechoslovakia, where there were none before, and in Poland, where there had been very few.

Command system and force strengths in the Warsaw Pact

The Pact's supreme organ is the *Political Consultative Committee,* on which each member-state is as a rule represented by the First Secretary of its Party's Central Committee, its Prime Minister, its Foreign Minister and, at least up to the 1969 reorganization, its Defence Minister. This body seldom meets; there was a two-year gap before its session in November 1978. It is chaired by representatives of the various member-states in turn.

Since early 1956 it has been assisted by a *Permanent Commission* charged with drawing up foreign policy recommendations, and a *Joint Secretariat* which is virtually the executive organ of the Pact. There are subordinate commissions for various subjects such as armaments and logistics which cooperate closely with *Comecon,* the Council for Mutual Economic Aid. The Secretariat is headed by the same Soviet general who is also Chief of Staff of the Pact's Joint Armed Forces.

The occupation of Czechoslovakia caused a convulsion in the socialist community which led to a partial reorganization in March 1969. The Soviet Union acceded to pressure from its allies for improved consultation and a larger voice in decisions, and some new directing organs were set up. A *Committee of Defence Ministers* was created to draft joint proposals for improving military efficiency. In judging the value of such a body one has to bear in mind that Warsaw Pact defence ministers are invariably soldiers and not, like most of their counterparts in the West, civilian politicians.

The reorganization also led to the formation of a *Military Council,* the appointment of *Deputy Commanders in Chief* to the Joint Armed Forces from the various allied forces, the attachment of senior officers to the *Joint Supreme Command* in proportion to each member state's financial and personnel share in the total forces, and the creation of a *Committee for Standardization of Military Technology.*

The *Joint Command* as the highest military authority with its seat in Moscow and also, since 1972, partly in Lwów in Poland, directs and coordinates the activity of the Joint Armed Forces. It is also responsible, with its staff, for preparing military plans in case of war and for deciding on the deployment of troops.

Among its main tasks are the coordination of plans for developing the national armed forces and improving their combat-readiness, as well as arranging mutual assistance in equipping these armies with modern technology and armaments[6].

Logistics and *air defence* are mainly provided by the Soviet armed forces, "since the Warsaw Pact organization does not possess the necessary capacity"[7]. This may have improved since 1975, but the Joint Armed Forces continue to be directly dependent on the Red Army.

The *Commander in Chief of the Warsaw Treaty Armed Forces* is a Soviet general, who being also *First Deputy Defence Minister of the Soviet Union* is directly subordinate to that minister. As the record shows, this Commander in Chief is always an outstanding soldier – Ivan Stepanovich *Koniev* (1955–1960), Andrey Antonovich *Grechko* (1960–1967), Ivan Ignatyevich *Jakubovsky* (1967–1976), Viktor Georgiyevich *Kulikov* (since 1977).

The First Deputy of the Commander in Chief is also *Chief of Staff of the Joint Armed Forces,* again always an experienced military man. The present incumbent is Anatoly *Gribkov.*

The Commander in Chief further holds the post of *Chairman of the Military Council,* which was set up in 1969 and meets ad hoc. As chief representatives of the various national forces the Council includes all the Deputy Defence Ministers in their capacity as Chiefs of Staff of their respective armies. Other members are the Chief of Staff of the Joint Armed Forces, the Commander of the Warsaw Pact Air Defence Troops, and the Commander in Chief of the Soviet Armed Forces Group in Germany.

The Pact's forces represent, according to an East German description, the *"strongest military power of the present day"*[8]. And the "mainspring of the Warsaw Pact armies' strength and invincibility", to quote a Soviet pen this time, is the "leading role of the communist and workers' parties in all questions of national defence and military build-up"[9]. An example is afforded by the Soviet Navy: "Only ten per cent of Soviet warships are now over 15 years old, and only one per cent over 20. The corresponding percentage for NATO is considerably higher – around fifty per cent, for example, in the case of the American submarine fleet."[10] The Soviet Navy today includes new-style Kiev-class aircraft-carriers, new outsize cruisers with long-distance missiles, landing vehicles for overseas operations, highly effective missile corvettes and hovercraft for naval operations in restricted areas, numerous conventional and nuclear-powered strategic and tactical hunter-killer submarines. "The national armies of the Warsaw Pact states have achieved a new and higher level of military effectiveness."[11]

Western sources agree that the offensive potential of the Warsaw Pact forces,

> and in particular of the Soviet forces, is increasing at an alarming rate. This is especially evident from the overall qualitative improvements arising from the deployment of new weapons systems and equipment of higher performance, and the continual development of still more up-to-date systems. Improvements in command and control, radio communications and infrastructure, as well as experience with distant deployment of naval and air forces, are also contributing to the process[12].

The members of the Warsaw Pact have also betrayed certain tendencies hard to explain in terms of *"growing partnership"*. But in contrast to what is normal in the West and elsewhere, differences of opinion are never revealed in the official "Declarations". At the November 22/23, 1978, session of the Political Consultative Committee *Rumania* adopted nonconformist standpoints on three issues – the Middle East, rearmament and defence organization. The Party leader, President Ceausescu, argued that since there was an adequate balance of forces as between NATO and the Warsaw Pact there was no need to devote additional resources to weaponry. His speech was followed by statements from the other member countries' representatives, emphatically endorsing greater efforts in the arms field.

In time of need all the forces of the Warsaw Pact states can be placed under the *Joint Supreme Command,* which is in any case *dominated by the Soviet Union.* In assessing the Pact's military potential, therefore, one has to take into account the entire military establishment of the East Bloc.

The Soviet forces, as estimated by the London-based International Institute for Strategic Studies, comprise 3,638,000 troops[13], to which some 750,000 uniformed civilians should be added; there are also 200,000 frontier troops under the KGB and 250,000 security personnel responsible to the Ministry of the Interior – both equipped with army weapons including tanks.

The other member states' forces comprise a total personnel of 1,094,000, with at least another 255,500 in the border guard and security services.

In peace time the Joint Supreme Command controls the *four groups of Soviet forces stationed in East Europe* outside the U.S.S.R., the entire *East German NVA,* and contingents from the other Pact countries. They amount to the following:

> – two Soviet armoured divisions in Poland – the *Northern Group* – with their HQ at Legnica;
> – ten Soviet motorized infantry divisions and ten Soviet armoured divisions in East Germany – the *Group in Germany* – with their HQ at Wünsdorf-Zossen near Berlin;
> – two Soviet motorized infantry divisions and two Soviet armoured divisions in Hungary – the *Southern Group* – with their HQ in Budapest;
> – three Soviet motorized infantry divisions and two Soviet armoured divisions in Czechoslovakia – the *Central Group* – with their HQ at Milovice near Prague; and
> – the *East German National People's Army* with its four motorized infantry divisions and two armoured divisions.

Of the sixteen Soviet tactical air armies, one each is stationed in the GDR, Poland, Czechoslovakia, and Hungary. Air defence authorities and troops are fully integrated in the *Warsaw Pact Air Defence* which covers the whole area with a dense network of command, observation and matériel stations.

The Pact's *Joint Naval Forces,* viz. the Soviet *Baltic Fleet* or Red Banner Fleet, the *Polish Navy* and the *NVA's People's Navy,* cooperate closely even in peace.

There are *Soviet medium range ground-to-ground missiles* and nuclear-capable aircraft stationed in Europe outside Soviet territory. Most of the other Pact states are also equipped with medium-range missiles, but there is no evidence that they control the nuclear warheads. Strategic missiles and aircraft are based on the Soviet Union itself.

According to an Austrian survey the *Warsaw Pact's land forces* in Northern and Central Europe comprise 68 divisions with 22,500 tanks and 2,700 aircraft, compared with NATO's 27 divisions, 6,100 tanks and 1,700 aircraft[14].

On February 16, 1979, West Germany's Foreign Minister Genscher gave the following figures:

> The Warsaw Pact has altogether 58 divisions in the GDR, Czechoslovakia and Poland. They face 28 western divisions in West Germany and the Benelux countries – in manpower terms, a difference of some 150,000 men. In tank numbers the ratio is about 3 : 1 to the disadvantage of the West, the Warsaw Pact having 19,000 against NATO's 6,500. In Central Europe, then, the Warsaw Pact has built up a considerable conventional superiority[15].

In regard to the "*grey area*" of weapons which because of their technical characteristics have not been dealt with either in the European "Mutual Balanced Force Reductions" talks in Vienna nor in the SALT negotiations on strategic arms, Genscher noted that it covered

> ... intermediate-range nuclear systems of strategic importance for Europe. In this area ... the Soviets have acquired a growing lead which is all the more significant because of the parity in strategic nuclear weapons.
>
> In the past few years the Soviets have begun to produce and put into service the new multiple-warhead mobile missiles known as the SS 20. With their Backfire bomber they have also introduced a new intermediate-range aircraft. Both systems are capable of reaching targets in West Europe from Soviet territory.
>
> These capabilities represent a strategic threat to Europe, against which there is nothing comparable on the western side.

"East Germany's contribution to the build-up, structuring and continuous enhancement of our collective military protection is especially apparent at historically points of intersection in the evolution of the NVA and the Warsaw Pact Organization."[16] This judgement was valid from the moment the Warsaw Pact was concluded, even if the Resolution of May 14, 1955, setting up the Joint Command said that

> the question of GDR participation in measures affecting the forces of the Joint Command remains to be discussed.

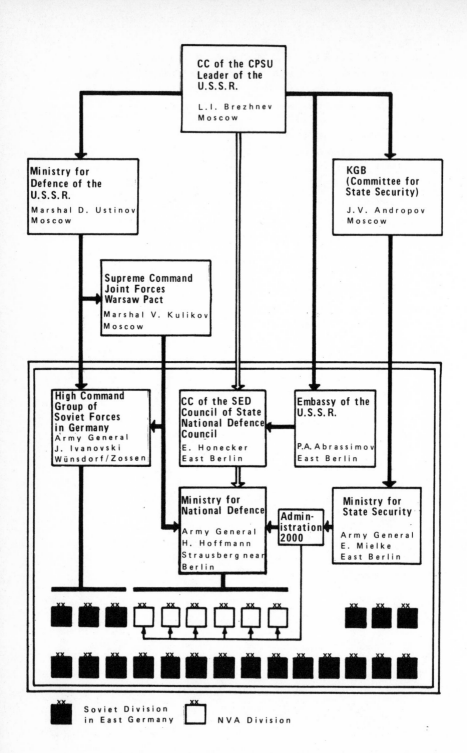

Soviet Division
in East Germany   NVA Division

78

Such a statement was needed for public consumption because, at the time the Pact was concluded, the GDR already possessed armed forces with the main characteristics of a regular army which had nevertheless to be disguised as "police": 70,000 Garrisoned People's Police, 18,000 Frontier Police, 11,500 Transport Police and 5,000 men attached to the State Security Ministry (December 1950 figures). It is significant that the GDR's representatives at the initial conference were Willi Stoph, Interior Minister and Chief of the Garrisoned People's Police, and his deputy General Hoffmann. No other country was represented by a Minister of the Interior or a police general.

It was decided at the January 28, 1956, session of the Political Consultative Committee in Prague that *all elements of the East German NVA should be included in the Joint Armed Forces.* Shortly before, on January 18, the People's Chamber had passed the Law on the Creation of the National People's Army, converting the Garrisoned People's Police into the NVA. NVA officers were appointed to positions of command in the Joint Armed Forces and provided, like the other countries, one of the Deputy Commanders in Chief.

Despite the formal entry of the NVA into the military organization of the Pact the assignment of major contingents to the Joint Armed Forces was not immediately practicable, though some units – as Defence Minister Hoffmann was to explain in 1968 – were seconded as early as 1956[17]. Not till May 24, 1958, was the entire NVA subordinated to the Joint Command.

Reasons of international propaganda lay behind this delay in a process which was not completed till the middle of 1960. For it was at this point of time that the West German Bundeswehr was assigned to NATO. The Warsaw Pact organization no doubt also felt the effect of the revolutionary events in Poland and Hungary during the autumn of 1956. From 1957 onwards it was utilized by the Soviets not only as a political forum, but also to an increasing degree as an instrument for

- control of the armed forces of all the East Bloc countries,
- political indoctrination of their troops,
- improvement and enlargement of these forces, and
- incorporation of the war potential of the other East Bloc states in their own military planning.

As we have seen, East Germany was during the sixties brought into the system of bilateral treaties between the members of the "socialist commonwealth". She concluded *Treaties of Friendship, Cooperation and Mutual Assistance* with the Soviet Union in 1964, and with Poland, Czechoslovakia, Hungary and Bulgaria in 1967. An agreement with Rumania, initialled on October 1, 1970, was not finalized until May 12, 1972. In 1975 all these bilateral treaties, which were to have run for twenty years, were replaced by a fresh series of Treaties of Friendship, Cooperation and Mutual Assistance as before. This "wideranging move to cement the GDR even more firmly into the socialist community of states"[18] was initiated on October 7, 1975, by a treaty with the U.S.S.R., followed by similar ones with Hungary on March 24, 1977, Poland on May 28, 1977, Bulgaria on September 14, 1977, and Czechoslovakia on October 3, 1977.

A further Treaty of Friendship and Cooperation between the GDR and the *Mongolian People's Republic,* dated May 6, 1977, also belongs to this series. In contrast to the treaties with the fellow-members of the Warsaw Pact there is no reference in the title to "mutual assistance", though the text by no means excludes this. But it belongs among the inter-socialist agreements in that Mongolia is territorially juxtaposed to the Soviet bloc and was the first Asian country – before Vietnam – to join Comecon.

In this same period East Germany took pains also to conclude Friendship Treaties with other socialist states not belonging to the Pact. These treaties, and the provisions for military cooperation that they contain, are dealt with later in this chapter.

The anxiety of the GDR to involve herself in the "socialist commonwealth" emerges clearly from Article 6 (2) of her revised Constitution dated October 7, 1974:

> The German Democratic Republic is an inseparable part of the socialist commonwealth of states. True to the principles of socialist international-ism, she contributes to the strengthening of that community, and fosters and develops friendship, overall cooperation and mutual assistance with all its member states[19].

To appreciate how the GDR and her army see themselves, however, the small print of Treaties and Constitutions is less revealing than the fact that they belong to a military coalition which, "under the leadership of the Soviet Union", is "the strongest in the world". "For German communists, to quote Ernst Thälmann, relationship with the Soviet Union has always been the acid test of proletarian internationalism."[20]

These words of Colonel General Kessler in 1978, occasioned by the "33rd anniversary of our people's liberation from fascism and imperialist war by the glorious Soviet Army", also celebrated the signature of the treaty with Russia on October 7, 1975, which had "conferred a new dimension on the partnership of our states". Eight years before that Kessler had said in a Red Army Day speech:

> The Soviet armed forces can boast a strength and combat-readiness enabling them to administer a withering rebuff to any adversary ... Together with their comrade-armies they provide sure conditions for building socialism and communism in the countries of the socialist com-monwealth and for further transforming the international power balance in favour of socialism ... Brotherhood-in-arms with the Soviet Army amounts to Leninism in action! There is nothing in the world that could breach this comradeship[21].

The NVA is indeed so *closely tied to the Soviet Army* that one cannot see how it could come any closer. There are several reasons for this. In the first place the NVA, unlike the other Warsaw Pact armies, is not the direct succes-sor of a national army but a newly created entity, in which former German *Wehrmacht* officers – largely Soviet prisoners during the war – played a part,

The Soviet Minister of Defence, Marshal of the Soviet Union D. F. Ustinov, and the Minister for National Defence of the GDR, Army General H. Hoffmann.

but only as military specialists while the principles and organization of the new East German "armed forces" were determined by the Soviet Army. Officer training was Soviet-designed from the outset.

As early as 1950 5,000 junior Garrisoned Police officers went *for training to the Soviet Union* in that year alone, and the process has continued undiminished. By 1975 1,000 NVA officers had graduated from Soviet military academies. In addition to weaponry and other specialist courses, land and air force officers of the NVA destined for general rank are given two or three years training at the Frunze Academy in Moscow, usually combined with attendance at the Soviet General Staff Academy. By November 1969 more than a hundred NVA cadres had attended the General Staff Academy and another twenty generals and admirals had been through the Senior Academic Course. For future People's Navy admirals, the services of the 1st Baltic Marine College in Leningrad and the 2nd Baltic Marine College in Kaliningrad are available.

Above all, the ever closer brotherhood-in-arms with Soviet troops sta-tioned in the GDR (afforded) the NVA invaluable assistance and support from the very first[22].

Especially during the early growing years of the GDR forces, *Soviet advisors* made their presence amply felt down to battalion level. Their influence continues today "through the activity of Joint Command representatives in the NVA"[23]. Since 1978 that activity has been directed by Army General Ivan Shavrov as Deputy Commander in Chief of the Joint Armed Forces with the NVA.

The *Soviet Forces Group in Germany*, under the command of Army General Yevgeni Ivanovsky, influences the NVA in many ways. It carries particular weight because of the large number of men assigned to it. With its ten armoured and ten motorized infantry divisions it represents the greatest concentration of power in a small space anywhere. It also has direct control of tactical air power, with over 1,000 combat planes at its disposal. These twenty divisions plus numerous other units, including the six divisions of the NVA, make East Germany the chief deployment area for the Pact in Central Europe, with half the country out of bounds for civilian purposes.

The preponderance of Soviet troops on East German territory inevitably determines their relationship with the country and its own army. GDR-based Russian troops, for example, enjoy freedom of movement in a much larger area than their opposite numbers in the other Pact countries. This is clear from a comparison of the Soviet-Polish stationing agreement of December 1956 with that signed by Moscow and East Berlin on March 12, 1957.

The Warsaw Pact text speaks in general terms of the need for "agreements between the signatory states" in regard to the "distribution of Joint Armed Forces bases" on their respective territories. Whereas the *Polish agreement,* however, states that any movement of Soviet troops outside their bases on Polish territory requires permission from the Polish authorities in each case, there is no such clear provision in the *stationing agreement with the GDR*[24]. Again, the treaty with Poland requires "special agreements" covering the size and deployment of Soviet contingents, whereas that with the GDR only mentions these subjects as "the subject of consultation" between the two governments.

Crucial importance attaches to Article 18 of the GDR treaty:

> In case of any threat to the security of Soviet troops stationed on GDR territory, the Supreme Command of Soviet Forces in the GDR may take measures to eliminate it in consultation with the GDR government and with due regard to the situation arising and to measures taken by the state authorities of the GDR.

This means that the Commander in Chief of the Soviet Force in Germany can declare a state of emergency throughout the country whenever he sees fit.

The fair conclusion that the treaty subjects East Germany to utter dependence on the Soviet Union is disputed by East German writers in terms of their own logic. "The basic principle of working class policy, effectively to defend socialist internationalism, mutual assistance, Warsaw Pact readiness and socialist achievements wherever they are threatened", cannot represent "any danger to the *sovereignty of the socialist states*"[25]. "Independence and sovereignty for a socialist state mean above all independence of capitalism, and the people's right to establish socialism and communism". "In social reality", again, there is "no such thing as sovereignty as such *(an sich)*; there is only the particular, class-related sovereignty of a given state as the power-lever of a particular class"[26]. The East German writer in question actually invokes the 1957 troop stationing treaty, which for him involves

> no diminution of sovereignty, but rather a comprehensive implementation and maximal underpinning and reinforcement of socialist sovereignty.

The *Soviet Forces Group in Germany*, then, is both the *largest agglomeration of Soviet troops outside Russia* and is stationed in that part of East Germany which represents the front-line deployment centre of the Joint Forces on land. Close cooperation between the Group and the NVA therefore goes without saying. At the same time *"brotherhood-in-arms"* has from the beginning amounted to a father-and-son relationship.

> The attitude of (the NVA's) officers, NCOs and other ranks and their determination to learn from the Soviet Army in all respects contributed significantly to the emergence of the NVA in the late fifties as, in essence, a modern socialist coalition army[27].

An analysis made in 1975 of 2,400 comparative efficiency tests carried out between the two forces in 1970 concluded that all these confrontations "helped the NVA to absorb the Soviet army's wealth of experience by personal contact"[28].

Close cooperation has developed into daily routine. "Close links with 'the regiment next door' should concentrate still more on exchanges of military experience and comparative tests, on joint training and close personal contact between troops."[29] As all such personal contacts, however, require strict control, it may be questioned how much strain they can take and how long they can last.

In political-ideological education, too, fraternization between the two forces plays a large role. In 1969 ninety per cent of all FDJ members in the NVA took part in organized study of Lenin's writings, by way of honouring the centenary of his birth. The 50th anniversary of the October Revolution and the Red Army, again, saw 1,300 "exchange-of-experience" meetings and 1,600 joint cultural and sports events.

Since 1968 a *"Week of Brotherhood-in-Arms"* has been organized each year for all NVA units. The 1970 celebrations led Army General Shtemenko, Chief of Staff of the Joint Armed Forces, to quote a saying of Lenin's inscribed in the entrance hall of the Joint Forces' headquarters:

> To you has fallen the great honour of defending our great ideas, weapon in hand, and putting into practice the international brotherhood of the peoples[30].

By 1967 the NVA had reached a level of efficiency permitting its full incorporation into the *First Strategic Echelon* of the Warsaw Pact organization. Its forces, in other words, belong to formations which would in case of war be *immediately involved in operations in Central Europe*.

The *NVA Land Forces* will either fight separately as a national army group or be assigned to higher Soviet formations. In either case the NVA will be deployed within a Soviet-led "front" or army group, available to march on to Federal German territory. Should the political situation persuade the Soviet leaders that they could achieve their political ends by limited military action, it is possible that the NVA would be thrown in on its own. But its logistic dependence on the Soviet Army would enable the latter to keep it on a short leash at all times.

The *NVA People's Navy* guards the Baltic even in peace time in close cooperation with the Polish Navy and the Soviet Baltic Fleet. In war time its purpose, again together with those two other navies of the Joint Forces, would be to secure the coastal flank of the invading communist armies and give them support from the sea, including amphibious operations and logistic aid.

The main tasks of the *NVA Air Force* lie in air defence, for which it is fully integrated into the Soviet air defence network. Apart from its numerous mis-

A member of the Group of Soviet Forces in Germany together with an NVA officer (right).

sile and AA units, the bulk of its operational aircraft would serve this purpose. To a limited extent it could also give support to the land offensive.

Joint manoeuvres and military displays

NVA commanders have from the outset been concerned to demonstrate *"German-Soviet brotherhood-in-arms"* in practice. As early as August 1957, NVA and Soviets troops were exercising together in the area between Berlin and the West German frontier. These manoeuvres, which also involved Air Force and Air Defence units, were held under the direction of Marshal Grechko, Commander in Chief of the Soviet Forces Group in Germany. For the NVA they were of "truly historic importance"[31]. NVA cadres from the staffs and units affected had been trained for their task in advance in Soviet institutions. It was made more demanding by the fact that the NVA had only a few months before been equipped with new technology, particularly the new medium battle tank. But the NVA was proud to find that its efficiency earned general recognition. New standards were set to ensure a continuous enhancement of the socialist military coalition in the following years.

> After evaluation of the joint manoeuvres, the Minister for National Defence and the Chief of the Main Staff of the NVA concluded that in addition to further work in mastering the offensive as the chief combat mode, still greater efforts would be needed in future to enable units to conduct resolute, yet mobile and active, defence operations[32].

Joint naval exercises with Poland took place in 1958, while in 1959 and 1961 there were fresh land exercises by NVA and Soviet troops in the GDR. The NVA also took part in manoeuvres in Czechoslovakia in 1961 and 1962.

In its own statements the NVA has always sought to establish a *causal link between its manoeuvres and international crises* or their elimination. Thus we read in connection with the early exercises:

> On August 13, 1961, the allied armies gave proof of their high degree of alertness and readiness by mounting a reliable guard and effective control over the GDR's frontiers with West Berlin and the Federal Republic, in accordance with a joint resolution of the Warsaw Pact governments. This demonstration of socialist military might showed the value of the socialist armed alliance, which kept the peace in Europe[33].

East German publicity draws a veil over the fact that the *Berlin Wall* and the barriers on the West German frontier were set up to stop *Republikflucht* ("desertion of the Republic"), in other words free movement within Germany. The official picture is as follows:

> In securing the GDR/FRG state border and, in particular, the hitherto open frontier with West Berlin by military means on the night of August 12/13, 1961, companies of the Working Class Combat Groups, with

units from the Frontier Police, NVA and other security organs supported by soldiers of the Soviet Army frustrated an act of aggression against the GDR planned by the West German imperialists. They smashed an attempt by revanchiste adventurers to incorporate our socialist state in the NATO power-bloc and resolutely prevented what might have been a worldwide conflagration[34].

Similar failure, we are told, met "the USA's aggressive policy toward revolutionary *Cuba*, thanks to the Soviet Union's firmness in preserving peace ... (The other Pact members' forces also) maintained a high state of readiness along with the Soviet Army for several weeks, thereby giving military support to the peace policy of socialism"[35]. Even the more serious analyses published in the GDR failed to mention that the USA was successful in pressing the U.S.S.R. to withdraw its missiles from Cuba.

Exercise *"Quartett"*, in which NVA units took part along with Soviet, Polish and Czechoslovak troops, was assessed in the GDR military press as the start of a new phase in "socialist comrade-ship-in-arms". It took place on GDR territory between September 5 and 15, 1963, under the guidance of Defence Minister Hoffmann. Marshal Grechko subsequently praised the NVA which was "now no different from our own armies"[36].

The naval exercise *"Flut"* in August 1963 was the first high point for the People's Navy in joint tactical operations and combat training with the Joint Armed Forces. It involved large contingents of the Soviet Baltic Fleet and the Polish Navy as well as the East German People's Navy, along with army units from the U.S.S.R., Poland and the GDR itself.

Exercise *"Zenit"* represented a similar first for the GDR Air Force and Air Defence, which had of necessity been intimately linked with Soviet air power from their inception.

The unexpected psychological success of these first big joint exercises with the GDR public as well as with the troops encouraged the leaders to hold the ambitious *"Oktobersturm"* manoeuvres in the Thuringian Basin between October 16 and 25, 1965.

They were preceded by a clearly political gesture in April of the same year, when NVA and Soviets troops conducted exercises to the *west of Berlin*, announced as a "test of training standards achieved during the winter programme". They were in fact a show of strength available for sealing off Berlin, involving particularly the air space over the west of the city. Admiral Verner, head of the NVA's Main Political Administration, remarked:

> The consternation of West German and West Berlin publications over the disturbance caused to the illegal session of the Bundestag in West Berlin requires the comment that this exercise by our troops clearly served to do more than test their combat readiness[37].

Headlines in the Party paper *Neues Deutschland* proudly announced that planes had flown low over West Berlin's *Kurfürstendamm* boulevard, and that traffic on "all through roads to Berlin" from the Western zones had been interrupted.

Only then came *"Oktobersturm"*, "the most important exercise yet held on German soil"[38]. This one also had a marked political purpose. As Army General Hoffmann said,

> it put the finishing touch to our policy of securing peace and mobilizing all peace-loving forces in West Germany ... At the same time it served to test the results of the 1964/65 training year in the armies of the First Strategic Echelon[39].

Never had so much publicity been accorded to a GDR manoeuvre. Press, radio and television were entirely dominated by it during October 1965.

Much political and psychological planning had gone into it. The very choice of the name "Oktobersturm" – no previous Warsaw Pact exercise had been named so demonstratively – was a *psychological* one. *Anti-West German propaganda* was stepped up long before the exercise was even announced officially. Bonn was described as the main enemy, an aggressive power only waiting to cross the border by force of arms. This, it was said, was what "NATO's agressive forward strategy" really meant.

For the officers and men of the Warsaw Pact the whole 1964/65 training period was a *preparation* for "Oktobersturm". Neither plans nor terrain, it is stated, were known to the commanders and troops involved beforehand; decisions had to be based on an independent assessment of the situation of both sides.

Units from the Soviet Forces Group in Germany, the NVA, Poland and Czechoslovakia all took part. Army General Koshevoy, who had commanded the Soviet forces in the GDR up to 1969, was in charge. The NVA's Major General Ernst commanded the "Blue" troops – one of the "parties to the conflict" – including a Soviet motorized guards division and a Soviet air corps; NVA Major General Poppe acted as umpire.

On six of the days a four-language newspaper was issued for those taking part, and an "Oktobersturm" army radio, using the opening bars of the "International" as its signature tune, broadcast reports from its own correspondents and multilingual commentaries throughout. Out of 27^1/$_2$ hours of broadcasting time, 12 hours were devoted to popular music and greetings. Every soldier received a folder of information in four languages – Russian, Czech, Polish and German. The main aim of this information was to justify the concept of the exercise, which was being fought out *"on enemy territory"*. One of the leaflets provided, bearing the title "No Quarter for the Enemy", ended with the words

> The enemy is planning and provoking an attack on our countries, attempting to destroy our socialist way of life. Our military assignment – to frustrate this intention and, in case of hostilities, to destroy the aggressor on his own soil – is thus profoundly just. We love socialism, we love our homeland. We are ready to sacrifice our lives for them. Today we are fighting for victory before the battle[40].

The style of "Oktobersturm" has been copied many times, for example in Exercise *"Moldau"* in Czechoslovakia, 1966. This was intended to rehabilitate the Hungarian People's Army, still discredited after the rising of ten years previously, and to encourage the under-developed "socialist defence morale" of the Czechoslovak population.

The basic operational concept of *"Moldau"* was similar to that of the previous year's exercise. Staffs and troops were to test the ability of the First Strategic Echelon "to deliver a massive counterblow against attempted aggression and to destroy the enemy on his own territory". Swift and well-covered troop movements over large distances were to be staged, to facilitate an "offensive smashing of West German aggression". The actual *combat exercises* were preceded by extended *combined foot and rail advances* from the troops' various home garrisons and repeated shifts of deployment, from September 17 on. The NVA troops started off with a 340 km day-and-night march in the wooded uplands, involving altitude differences of 600 m. Each motor vehicle in the NVA contingents had to drive some 760 km and each armoured vehicle 500 km. The Soviet troops were flown into the area over distances of up to 1000 km. The Hungarian troops also had to cover hundreds of kilometers in day and night marches to reach Czechoslovakia. In this respect *"Oktobersturm"* was left far behind. One of the most important characteristics of Exercise *"Moldau"* was the assumption of a *nuclear attack by the adversary* – neither in this nor nay subsequent exercise was the home side conceived as launching a nuclear first-strike. The units involved were obliged to move through the battle-theatre under the conditions of a nuclear engagement, and the logistic specialists had to provide supplies over difficult terrain. Finally, the employment en masse of airborne troops, helicopters and amphibious technology was to demonstrate a convincing "political and military success" on the part of the GDR's comrades-in-arms.

In the following year, 1967, *staff exercises* were held in East Germany, Czechoslovakia and Poland in March, late May and early June. Exercises of this kind have usually been conducted without the use of entire units. As their name implies they are designed to train commanding officers in their functions, usually at divisional level and above, and to ensure the smooth functioning of their staffs.

Two more troops manoeuvres including the GDR were conducted in August and September of 1967. In one case units of the NVA People's Navy, together with those of the Soviet Baltic Fleet and the Polish Navy, exercised off the Pomeranian coast under the direction of the Polish Defence Minister. In the second case contingents from the NVA and the Czechoslovak army exercised in Hungary, together with Hungarian troops and units of the Southern Group of Soviet troops stationed there.

A noticeable feature of the 1967 exercises was the special importance accorded, within a major operational area, to activities close to a frontier or sea coast. This casts an interesting light on the manoeuvre plans worked out by the Joint Supreme Command staff for the following year.

Czechoslovakia in 1968

As early as March, 1968, exercises took place in the south-east of the GDR and in Hungary to the accompaniment of powerful publicity campaigns. Movements of mixed-nationality formations were also tried out in East Germany and Poland in May and June.

Then from June 26 to July 12, Exercise *"Böhmerwald"* (in Czech šumava, the Czech name for the south-west Bohemian forest land) took place under the label of a *"staff exercise"*. On the assumption that the western enemy had launched an attack from the territory of the Federal Republic, an annihilating *counter-blow* was to follow from the eastern side. The latter was represented by troops from the Soviet Union, East Germany, Czechoslovakia, Poland and Hungary, all of which countries except Hungary were included in the exercise area. A key point in the plan was the "own situation assessment", according to which Czechoslovak troops were unable to provide sufficient protection for their own western border. The delay in the other participants' departure from Czechoslovakia at the end of the exercise – a week later the non-Soviet units had left, but only a negligible proportion of the Soviet troops – was an ominous sign of things to come.

This "staff exercise", to which the "staffs" had brought with them tanks, artillery and other unaccustomed elements, also featured the participation of NVA troops – though these were not allowed to leave their assembly area in the *Thüringer Wald*. Their commander Major General Ernst admitted in an interview with *Neues Deutschland*[41] that the exercise was directed against the reform movement in Czechoslovakia. Asked by the paper's correspondent what connection he saw between the exercise and the recent Dresden summit of Warsaw Pact leaders, at which increased pressure had been put on Czechoslovak representatives, he replied:

> The Dresden meeting of March 23 this year, like the sessions at Sofia and Moscow, was particularly important for the further strengthening of our commonwealth of peoples. The participants unanimously stressed their desire to take necessary steps toward a closer association of the socialist countries on the basis of Marxism-Leninism and proletarian internationalism. This also applied to cooperation between the staffs of our armies and to continued measures enabling our troops to carry out coordinated activities in the framework of the First Strategic Echelon with extreme precision and annihilating strength.

Soon afterwards, on July 24, a *rear services exercise* under the code-name *"Nyemen"* was started with great press publicity. At first this involved only Soviet forces from the western military districts of the U.S.S.R., but later on troops from Poland and the GDR took part. Lasting until August 10, this exercise was supposed to resolve supply, transport and other logistic problems. One important feature was the calling up of reservists. The exercise helped in fact to build up supply bases in the western U.S.S.R. in readiness for the invasion of Czechoslovakia.

Another manoeuvre held during these tense weeks was the *"Himmelsschild"* air defence exercise from July 25 to 31, in which further Soviet air force reinforcements were transferred to East Germany.

Immediately after *"Nyemen"* followed, from August 11 on, manoeuvres over an area extending from the western U.S.S.R. through Poland to the southern GDR. These comprised the *"Elektronik '68" signals exercise* which also helped to camouflage the movement of troops in Saxony, Thuringia and Hungary.

The simultaneous activity in Hungary was a deliberately planned component of a Warsaw Pact manoeuvre advertised as a "staff exercise with whole-unit participation". A glance at the map shows how the bulk of the interventionist armies, including full-strength NVA-divisions of Leipzig military district, were forming up in preparation for the August 21 *occupation of Czechoslovakia under the disguise of a manoeuvre* on that country's borders.

By their territorial range, extensive participation of allied contingents and successive choice of themes, the Pact manoeuvres of 1968 gave commanders, staffs and troops ample scope to put their theoretical knowledge into practice. But above all they proved to be a powerful instrument in the hands of the Soviet leaders for turning the "policy of strength" against a "fraternal" nation.

For the GDR and its National People's Army their part in the occupation of Czechoslovakia was a still more crucial event than it was for the Poles, Hungarians and Bulgars. Whether or not Ulbricht, as some Western observers believe, played a decisive role in persuading a hesitant Kremlin to launch an

August 1968 in the streets of Prague:
Military vehicles of the interventionist
forces set on fire by the
Czechoslovak people.

invasion, there is no doubt that the *East German leaders were among the first and strongest advocates of intervention.* What counted in the Kremlin was that Ulbricht had always gone along with every twist and turn of Soviet policy, however surprising. He had been the quickest and sharpest critic of every reform effort within the Eastern Bloc. Another important factor for Moscow was the apparent reliability of the NVA command. The military leaders in Poland, not to mention Hungary, had in various ways proved unreliable in their attitude to the Soviet Supreme Command. From East Germany's own point of view participation in the campaign was calculated finally to put her forces on an equal footing with the other national armies. For the creation of the NVA – as of the Garrisoned People's Police before it – had inspired considerable mistrust among the nations of Eastern Europe: these soldiers were after all still Germans, and wearing the same fieldgrey uniforms as Hitler's *Wehrmacht.* No sooner had World War II resentments faded than fresh doubts came to the fore. Gomulka and the Polish generals, like the other Warsaw Pact army leaders, were to learn that in August 1956 Ulbricht was offering Moscow military support for the suppression of the "Polish October". It caused the Soviets much trouble to weld the reluctant Poles and Czechs together with the Germans into an *"Iron Triangle"* – a phrase which was no longer to be found appropriate after 1968. But in any case it was necessary to involve East Germany in order to present as concerted an image as possible of the Pact's Joint Armed Forces.

On August 14 *Marshal Grechko,* the Soviet Defence Minister, arrived in East Germany, officially to inspect Soviet troops there. During the next few

"Ulbricht, what is the GDR Army looking for in ČSSR?" – A poster in Prague.

days West German and other western visitors were barred from entering certain areas of the GDR, including large parts of Thuringia and Saxony. Tourists who were already there had to leave their hotels overnight. The southernward movement of troops to the Czechoslovak border had begun.

The occupation troops were already on the march when, at 03.40 hours during that fateful night of August 20/21, 1968, all GDR radio stations carried an announcement that "Soviet military units ... together with units from the allied countries mentioned, have today entered the territory of Czechoslovakia".

Contingents from two of the NVA's six divisions took part in the operation. Units of the 11th Motorized Infantry Division from Halle were assigned to the Soviet 1st Armoured Guards Army, which advanced through Karlovy Vary and Plzeň as far as Budějovice. The 7th Armoured Division from Dresden provided contingents for the Russians' 20th Guards Army, which occupied Prague. The commanding officer, Army General Pavlovsky, had in addition brought into action a Polish army of four divisions which moved into northern Bohemia and Moravia through the Sudeten passes; five Soviet divisions to occupy Slovakia; 20 Soviet air regiments of the 24th Tactical Air Army from the south of the GDR to take over all the Czechoslovak airfields; two Hungarian divisions and parts of four Soviet divisions which penetrated into the south of the country from Hungary, and finally a strengthened Bulgarian regiment which reached the "manoeuvre area" by a highly devious route. Altogether 200,000 soldiers were involved, and in the course of 24 hours the whole of Czechoslovakia was occupied.

The importance of the operation was explained to the NVA in these terms:

> In this historic hour our comrades are today fulfilling their patriotic duty. It was indeed an historic test when the counter-revolution issued its deadly threat to socialism in Czechoslovakia. If troops had not marched forth from the five fraternal countries, the Czechoslovak people would inevitably have succumbed to a national catastrophe.
>
> As it was, however, we seized counter-revolution by the arm, just as it was raised to strike the decisive blow. This was a victory of historic importance, a victory for socialist internationalism[42].

Many of the occupation troops, however, were withdrawn from Czechoslovakia after a few days when their commanders had to admit that the troops were no longer to be relied on for suppressing the population. They were replaced by fresh Soviet units.

Within a few days East German troops were only being allowed to move around by night, otherwise remaining hidden in the Bohemian forests, and they were soon withdrawn anyway except for some small contingents. The chief reason for this was that world opinion saw the entry of NVA troops into Czechoslovakia as a repeat performance of Hitler's occupation in 1938/39. East German soldiers found themselves reading yard-high graffiti saying *"Wir wollen Eure Freundschaft nicht!"* ("We want none of your friendship!"). But there was a second reason for the hasty pull-back of NVA troops which must have weighed still more with the Soviet commanders. Many Czechs were familiar with developments in Germany and spoke German, whereas few of them knew Polish or Russian. In Soviet eyes far too many Czech-German discussions were taking place, and these could only damage their cause.

Further manoeuvres and demonstrations

The troops transports and test marches between the end of February and March 5, 1969 – when the Federal parliament opened its session in Berlin to elect a new President – were advertised as a joint Soviet Force Group/NVA exercise and again had a demonstratively political purpose. Soviet and NVA troops were moved along *main approach roads to Berlin,* evidently to a precise time-schedule. Observers had the impression that the same columns were seen marching up and down the same stretches several times. Nothing in the way of combat exercises took place, and the marches evidently served as an excuse for blocking the Berlin roads for tourist and goods traffic several times a day.

Between March 30 and April 4, 1969, NVA units took part along with Soviet troops and contingents from the Czechoslovak and Polish People's Armies in Staff Exercise *"Frühling 69"*. This was supervised by a Pole, Army General Chocha, and took place in Poland, East Germany and Czechoslovakia.

The high point of the 1969 training period was the autumn manoeuvre *"Oder-Neisse 69"*, lasting from September 21 to 28. An assessment drawn up four weeks later ran as follows:

> This manoeuvre, planned by the Joint Command and held in late September, surpassed all previous joint exercises in the area covered, the variety of elements involved and the multiplicity and difficulty of tactical variations tested. Large army and air force contingents, airborne and seaborne troops, territorial defence and frontier guard units operated together over terrain stretching from the Baltic coast to the Sudeten hilltops. Units of the Baltic Red Flag Fleet with its naval air force and of the GDR and Polish navies also took part.
>
> Notable features of this eventful high-speed operation were combat-confrontations involving a tough struggle to seize the initiative, the breaching of various water obstacles by motorized and armoured units, and tactical air drops. The highpoints undoubtedly included a precisely-timed air-and-sea landing to set up a major bridgehead on the Baltic coast, together with a mock-defensive operation to prevent it. Mass fighter-plane attacks and the use of helicopters for various purposes are also worth mentioning. In the course of the exercise fraternal forces brought into operation the latest weapon systems, e.g. new tactical and medium-range missiles, and other examples of modern military technology[43].

One important aim of the exercise was to test the control of troops by *electronic data-processing*. Defence Minister Hoffmann assessed *"Oder-Neisse 69"* as "a great triumph for our uniform Marxist-Leninist military policy and doctrine". It demonstrated, he claimed, the mature strength of the nations and armies allied in the Warsaw Pact, precisely in the spirit of the Moscow Conference which was at this time declaring the defence of socialism to be an international duty for all communists[44].

The third most ambitious test of the prowess of the Joint Armed Forces on GDR soil, after *"Quartett"* in 1963 and *"Oktobersturm"* in 1965, was the 1970 autumn manoeuvre *"Waffenbrüderschaft"* (Comradeship-in-arms). This was also the first time that *forces from all seven Pact members* were included with their staffs and troops. As a synthesis of previous exercises it was designed to afford a genuine opportunity to test, under complex conditions, the integrated command structures of the Joint Armed Forces as envisaged in the decisions of the Political Consultative Committee at its Budapest meeting of March 1969. The results of the exercise were said to have shown "the mature training standards of commanders and staffs, a high degree of combat-readiness and training efficiency among ground troops, air and naval units, skill in co-ordination and the ability to employ all weapons suited to modern combat"[45]. These were the first international manoeuvres to feature direct participation by East German *"Working Class Combat Groups"*, *People's Police* contingents and the entire *territorial defence organization*.

Soldiers of all seven Warsaw Pact forces at the end of the "Brotherhood-in-Arms" manoeuvre.

A striking note in the speeches made in connection with these manoeuvres was the favourable reference made to "the signing of the *treaty between the U.S.S.R. and the German Federal Republic*", while at the same time the Federal Republic came under renewed attack particularly from the East German side.

The Commander in Chief of the Joint Armed Forces, Marshal Yakubovsky, declared at a parade in Magdeburg that

> the signing of the treaty between the U.S.S.R. and the German Federal Republic, which is in the vital interest of all the nations of Europe, is a fresh expression of the policy of strengthening peace and international security[46].

The marshal did mention "forces of militarism and revanchisme in West Germany", but only to say that they were backed by the United States as the leader of "world imperialism".

Honecker, responsible at that time for security policy in the East German Party executive and an advocate of hardline policies, also mentioned the treaty

95

in his speech at the opening ceremony in Cottbus. But he painted it as the outcome of "a long fight, particularly on the part of the Soviet Union". He went on to say:

> No one, however, can overlook that West Germany is still being developed as the principal base for the accomplishment of America's global strategy. West Germany's system of state-monopoly tyranny provides a fertile field for the growth of right-extremist and neo-nazi forces. These forces are doing their utmost to pursue their revanchiste and expansionist aims[47].

At the conclusion of the exercise Ulbricht himself made a speech at Magdeburg, in which he only devoted one sentence to the Soviet-West German treaty, "whose ratification would help détente and the cause of peace", but spent more time on the "aggressive" nature of the West German *Bundeswehr*.

> What, then, is the situation in West Germany? The present West German army is following in the tradition of Hitler's. Many West Germans will object that there is a government in Bonn with a Social Democrat as Chancellor. Yes indeed, but the people of the GDR cannot for a moment forget that the West German state is an imperialist state whose arms monopoly pursues policies of domination . . . That is why the leaders of the Bundeswehr conduct experiments in new variants of aggression – clandestine warfare, deployment of commandos on "enemy territory" and suchlike[48].

In the following years the NVA took part in successive major Warsaw Pact exercises, viz. *"Herbststurm"* in 1971, *"Schild '72"*, *"Udar '73"* and *"Schild '76"*. These involved no innovation in venue or execution. *"Schild '72"*, for example, was devised as a "framework" manoeuvre with a number of fully-manned events being held for the most part on training-grounds. These events included role-reversal practice, combat with a mock-enemy, combat shooting and pure display numbers. Friction between "opposing" troops was to be avoided by intensive rehearsal.

Most manoeuvres have involved numbers of troops ranging between 40,000 and 60,000. *"Oder-Neisse"* in 1969 apparently used 100,000 or even more men. By contrast, some 200,000 troops took part in the large-scale *"Dyna"* exercise in Byelorussia on March 10 to 14, 1970, illustrating the relative preponderance of the Soviet Army inside and outside the Joint Armed Forces.

These large-scale *Grossmanöver* are almost always designed to make political points and, as the 1968 occupation of Czechoslovakia clearly showed, can be smoothly converted into surprise military operations. But for staff and troop training equal importance attaches to the regular exercises provided for in the *Joint Command's Combat Training Plan* and often conducted in strict secrecy. Every year, for example, joint command staff exercises are held, usually in the spring or summer, under this heading. There are as a rule separate ones for the Northern Group (East Germany, Poland, Czechoslovakia and the U.S.S.R.) and the Southern Group (Hungary, Bulgaria, Rumania and the

U.S.S.R.). In scope and number of exercises the Northern Group is several times more active than the Southern.

Publicity for manoeuvres in the East German mass media has considerably waned since 1973 and no joint exercises on a spectacular scale seem to have taken place meanwhile. This reticence is no doubt connected with the Helsinki talks and the MBFR negotiations in Vienna, for the actual number of minor manoeuvres involving only one or a few divisions, and largely conducted on training-grounds, has increased rather than decreased. While there were 16 such in 1972, for example, there were apparently 24 the following year.

It was the Warsaw Pact members who first, at the Bucharest meeting of the Political Consultative Committee in 1966, called for the *Conference on European Security and Cooperation* and they represented the Helsinki Final Act signed by 35 states on August 1, 1975, as their own achievement. Yet they sought at first to evade its provisions for mutual inspection of large-scale manoeuvres. The *exchange of observers* recommended at Helsinki was simply sabotaged. As early as the autumn of the same year, 1975, the West German government in announcing Exercise *"Grosse Rochade"* invited observers to attend. But this was ignored, and not even journalists turned up from the East Bloc. All the Helsinki signatories, again, were invited to watch Exercise *"Grosser Bär"* the following year, but no Warsaw Pact country sent representatives.

For the Warsaw Pact exercise *"Schild '76"*, involving land and air forces from the U.S.S.R., Poland, the GDR and Czechoslovakia, the Polish government – on whose territory it was to take place – issued invitations not to all Helsinki signatories but only to the neutrals – Finland, Austria and Sweden – and to a single NATO country, Denmark. These countries' observers, however, were not much the wiser. They were hardly in a position to recognize the various services and weapons involved, let alone to observe the operations from close at hand.

In the list of those "attending the exercise", published in the East German periodical *"Volksarmee"*, observers from neutral and western countries are included at the end. The first names are those of the First Secretary of the Polish Workers' Party, Edward Gierek, and the Chairman of the Polish State Council, Henryk Jablonski. After mentioning various Polish Party and government figures, the list then enumerates all the Warsaw Pact Defence Ministers, followed without a break by General Castro Ruz, Minister of the Cuban Revolutionary Forces; representatives of the command and staff of the Joint Armed Forces; and military delegations from the Warsaw Pact armies and the armies of Vietnam, Cuba, Mongolia and Yugoslavia.

One may rightly conclude that the efforts of the Warsaw Pact states to extend their military sphere of influence are indeed to be taken seriously. In these attempts to enlarge the "socialist commonwealth" East Germany and its NVA play an important role.

Military cooperation with the Third World

"Resolutely determined to help create favourable conditions for the continuation of the revolutionary process throughout the world, the fraternal socialist countries are fulfilling in the military sphere ... Lenin's call: 'Internationalism lies not in fine phrases, nor in oaths of solidarity, nor in formal resolutions, but in deeds'."[50] Thus the preamble to the Treaty of Friendship and Cooperation[51] signed by the GDR and the *People's Republic of Mozambique* on February 24, 1979, and it might have added that "internationalism" also lies in military cooperation, defined by a GDR source as comprising

- deliveries of weapons and equipment;
- training of military cadres;
- assistance in the creation of a domestic defence industry; and
- issue of licenses for weapons production and aid in setting up and training armed forces[52].

In this and other forms of aid, including secondment of instructors, auxiliary troops and so on for which there are no official data, East Germany and its army play a prominent role. Targets for this are not only *communist states* such as Vietnam, but also *non-aligned countries* and *national liberation movements*. All the continents except Australasia have been brought into this system of socialist military aid, the main emphasis for East Germany lying on Africa. In the view of a French military periodical, *TAM*, East Germany supplies far more military aid to the Third World than any other Warsaw Pact country, apart from the U.S.S.R.[53]. And according to another source[54] East German expenditure on military aid to African and Arab countries can be estimated at around 200 million marks per annum. A sum in excess of this was made available to Afro-Asian states and liberation movements in 1977 alone by way of "*solidarity supplies*". About a half of the 16,000 tons of goods thus distributed went to Africa. If one adds the extensive assistance given in training-specialists, the financial outlay of the GDR in aid of "anti-imperialist solidarity" must have greatly exceeded 500 million marks in value.

As early as the 5th Congress of the SED in 1958 Party leader Ulbricht had declared that

> our Party, and the government of the GDR, support peoples who are struggling for their independence ...[55]

When GDR Premier Grotewohl visited Egypt in January 1959 it was the first time a German head of government had been to Africa since World War Two.

Up to 1970 the main theme of East Germany's African policy was to contest Bonn's "*Hallstein Doctrine*" denying recognition to any country that accorded it to East Germany. Most African countries, however, defied the doctrine and established relations with the GDR during the seventies. East Berlin later shifted its aim to a joint policy "on the basis of Marxism-Leninism and proletarian internationalism". The military aspect assumed particular importance after the expulsion of Soviet advisors from the United Arab Republic on June 18, 1972. From that date the Warsaw Pact's arms programme for the Third World could no longer be left completely in Soviet hands.

The year before, in 1971, the GDR Party Central Committee and National Defence Council had instructed Defence Minister Hoffmann, in agreement with the Warsaw Pact organization,

> to take steps to raise military relations (with the Third World) to the same level as economic, scientific-technical and cultural relations, which are already intensively cultivated[56].

By October of the same year a GDR military delegation was already visiting *Iraq, Syria* and *Egypt.* Led by Defence Minister Hoffmann, it also included his deputies Admiral Verner, Head of the Main Political Administration, and Lieutenant General Fleissner, Head of Technology and Weaponry; Lieutenant General Streletz, Secretary of the National Defence Council; Lieutenant General Stechbarth, Head of the Land Forces; Major General Clement, and Colonel Winkler, who had led a delegation to the *People's Republic of the Congo* in the summer of 1970. The delegates, "whose visit will serve the further cementing of relations between the two friendly states and their armies, and their cooperation in the anti-imperialist struggle", stressed the "consistent attitude of the GDR toward Israeli aggression and its support for the Arab countries" and opined that in all three countries "military organization and structure, training and even equipment in many respects (resemble) those of our own armies"[57].

In June, 1972, another military delegation under Minister Hoffmann discovered "the same weapons as we use in our own NVA"[58] – this time in *Algeria*. (Other delegates were Colonel General Kessler, Chief of Staff; Admiral Verner; Colonel General Scheibe, Head of the SED Central Committee's Security Department; Vice-Admiral Ehm, Head of the People's Navy; Lieutenant General Poppe, Head of Rear Services, and Major General Günther Schmidt).

In October 1974 Minister Hoffmann, along with Lieutenant General Streletz and other officers, paid a visist to *Peru*. Both sides "expressed a wish to broaden and deepen friendly relations beween the GDR's NVA and the armed forces of the Republic of Peru"[59].

In January 1976 Hoffmann visited *India* with Generals Fleissner and Streletz and other officers. The delegation gained the impression that "conditions obtain for good, friendly cooperation in the military sphere"[60].

October 17 to 21, 1977, found Hoffmann leading a military party to the *People's Republic of the Yemen,* and on his way back he had a meeting in *Baghdad* with the Iraqi Defence Minister, Colonel Khairallah.

On May 1, 1978, Hoffmann embarked with military delegates on a 12,000 mile journey through Africa, visiting *Algeria, Guinea, Nigeria,* the *People's Republic of the Congo, Angola* and *Tunisia.* They remained for five days in the Congo and for six in Angola.

In early 1979 a military delegation led by the Inspector General of the NVA, Lieutenant General Borufka, visited the *Socialist Republic of Vietnam* and gave his "brothers-in-arms of the Vietnamese People's Army", as a present from the NVA, the training equipment for a technical NCOs college.

The end of May 1979 found Hoffmann leading a delegation – it included Generals Kessler, Stechbarth, Fleissner and others – to *Zambia, Mozambique* and *Ethiopia*. In the People's Republic of Mozambique, which enjoys a treaty of friendship with the GDR covering military cooperation, they stayed for six days.

Among the innumerable Third World military delegations to come to East Germany the highest-powered visitors were *"Vietnamese brothers-in-arms"* led by their Defence Minister *Army General Giap*. In April 1977 this delegation not only stayed in East Berlin but saw installations and troops in many other parts of the country. On this occasion, too, measures were taken "calculated to intensify cooperation between the NVA and the Vietnamese People's Army"[61]. Hoffmann gave an assurance that "the people and soldiers of Vietnam will always be able to rely on the solidarity of their class-comrades and brothers-in-arms in the GDR".

Two visits of special importance for the GDR's alliance policies were those paid by Party Secretary and Head of State Erich Honecker to *Korea* and *Vietnam* in December 1977, and to several African countries – *Libya, Angola, Zambia* and *Mozambique* – in February 1979.

Just as a "treaty of friendship and cooperation" between the GDR and *Mongolia* had been concluded in East Berlin on May 6, 1977, so Honecker's eastern trip in the same year produced a similar treaty with *Vietnam*[62] in Hanoi, on December 4, while his African tour yielded treaties with *Angola*[63], signed in Luanda on February 19, 1979, and with *Mozambique*[64] signed in Maputo five days later.

None of these agreements "on the basis of Marxism-Leninism and proletarian internationalism" contain provisions for military assistance, but they are formulated in a way – such as "overall cooperation and mutual aid" in the Vietnam treaty text – which leaves everything open. Only the treaty with *Mozambique* addresses itself to questions of military cooperation. Here we read:

> In pursuance of the fraternal friendship and cooperation between the two Parties and peoples, already forged during the armed national liberation struggle of the Mozambique people ... (Preamble)

> In the interest of strengthening the defence capabilities of the High Contracting Parties they will regulate their cooperation in the military sphere by bilateral agreements. (Article 5)

> Should a situation arise which threatens or violates the peace, the High Contracting Parties will immediately establish contact in order to coordinate their positions in regard to the danger in question or to restore peace. (Article 10)

On his 1979 visit to Africa Honecker also received leaders of *liberation movements* "still struggling for victory". The following movements were or are particularly favoured by the GDR:

– in *Portuguese Guinea,* the African Party for the Independence of Guinea and the Cape Verde Islands (PAIGC);

– in *Angola,* the People's Movement for the Liberation of Angola (MPLA), which was rescued by receiving three shiploads of arms, including heavy equipment, from the NVA;

– in *Mozambique,* the at first ideologically ambivalent Mozambique Liberation Front (FRELIMO);

– in *Rhodesia/Zimbabwe,* the African People's Union of Zimbabwe (ZANU);

– in *Namibia,* the South-West African People's Organization (SWAPO), the only active guerilla movement in the area since 1966;

– in *South Africa,* the African National Congress of South Africa (ANC), a body closely tied to the South African Communist Party.

– In the *Middle East,* the Palestine Liberation Organization (PLO) has received small arms since 1976.

GDR publications provide very few details of military cooperation with the Third World, and the following information is drawn from various western sources[65].

By early 1977, 22 African and Middle East states had received aid from the GDR either in the form of arms *(Morocco, Mali, Ghana, Libya, Lebanon, North Yemen, Bahrein)* or of arms and training *(Algeria, Guinea, Guinea-Bissau, Nigeria, Somalia, South Yemen, Syria, Iraq).* The East Berlin body responsible for arms aid is the *Büro Industrietechnischer Aussenhandel* ("Office for Technical Industrial Trade").

The first training assistance given to *Algeria* and *Iraq* was in military engineering, signals and logistics. In *Algeria,* which subsequently complained that GDR weapons and ammunition were unfit for use, there were at one time over 1,000 GDR soldiers.

In *Libya* NVA specialists constructed arms depots, signal systems and military hospitals for the Libyan army and did preparatory work on a military harbour near Benghazi.

In *Guinea-Bissau* the NVA, together with Cuban military, set up a regular army out of former guerilla units. GDR technicians put up a radar station near Bissau to monitor the sea approaches and the French naval base at Dakar.

Six hundred NVA personnel reorganized *Nigeria's* military communications system.

In *Tanzania* NVA engineers built two military airfields.

In *India* the NVA laid out three training-grounds.

In *Laos* it provided partial replacements after the withdrawal of American communications experts.

In *Angola* the NVA furnished a signals company and two engineer companies to put into running order, amongst other things, the country's ports and airfields. An NVA officer was at one time harbour-master in Luanda, the Angolan capital, and GDR pilots are still employed.

In *Mozambique* 430 NVA officers and NCOs were at hand from September 1976 to train guerillas then operating in *Rhodesia* in engineering and signals techniques.

Cooperation between the NVA and the Third World has not been without its setbacks, but the GDR was always quick to adapt to new situations. Only two months after a "cordial meeting" between Foreign Minister Fischer and General Teferi Benti, head-of-state of *Ethiopia* – a country with which East Germany maintains the closest relations – Benti was executed. *Neues Deutschland* greeted this as the liquidation of a "Trojan horse" and congratulated his successor Mengistu Haile Mariam, a man only able to maintain his position by terror. When Lieutenant Colonel Mariam flew into East Berlin on November 26, 1976, as Chairman of the Provisional Military Council of Administration of Socialist Ethiopia, Honecker was already at the airfield to embrace him. The government-sponsored *Ethiopian Herald* expressed gratitude for "the alacrity with which the GDR has responded to our appeal for support"[66].

In its efforts to win over the young states of the Third World the GDR leadership is well aware of the importance of their officer corps. Defence Minister Hoffmann has observed:

> Particularly in the armies of the so-called Third World there are ... many officers energetically opposed to colonial domination and the influence of foreign monopolies. In some cases they are also hostile to the semi-feudal and *grand bourgeois* class forces of their own countries, link their political strivings with socialist ideas and even favour the working class and its political vanguard. But frequently it is their connections with the bourgeoisie that prove to be the stronger. Once progressive officers will succumb to the influence of reactionary forces and switch to the counter-revolutionary camp. The ideological position ... of the army leaders in these countries therefore plays a significant role.

> The strength of the anti-imperialist forces in these armies and governments accordingly depends to a decisive extent on whether, and in what manner, they manage to sunder ties of pro-imperialist dependence, to establish links with the socialist commonwealth and to seek help from those quarters where military questions have long since been harmonized with social progress – the Soviet and other socialist armies[67].

Notes

[1] The full text of the treaty is given in: *Keesing's Contemporary Archives,* Bristol, vol. X, 1955–1956, p. 14250 f.

[2] Prof. Dr. J. *Krüger,* Akademie für Staats- und Rechtswissenschaften der DDR, Freundschaftsverträge – Wegweiser für die Annäherung der sozialistischen Staaten, in: *Militärwesen,* East Berlin 4/1978, p. 21.

[3] XXV. Parteitag der KPdSU, Rechenschaftsbericht des ZK der KPdSU und die nächsten Aufgaben der Partei in der Innen- und Außenpolitik. Report by L. I. *Brezhnev.* East Berlin 1976, p. 9.

[4] Hermann *Müller,* Einige Haupttendenzen der Entwicklung der Militärorganisation des Warschauer Vertrages, in: *Militärgeschichte,* East Berlin 2/1975, p. 147.

[5] Sergej Matwejewitsch *Schtemenko,* Die erfolgreiche Entwicklung des sozialistischen Verteidigungsbündnisses – entscheidender Faktor für die Erhaltung des Friedens, in: *Militärgeschichte,* 2/1975, p. 135 f.

[6] *Schtemenko,* loc. cit., p. 143.

[7] Lawrence T. *Caldwell,* The Warsaw Pact: Direction of Change, in: *Problems of Communism,* Washington, September/October 1975, p. 2.

[8] Hermann *Müller,* loc. cit., p. 147.

[9] *Schtemenko,* loc. cit., p. 143.

[10] Hermann *Müller,* loc. cit., p. 152.

[11] *Schtemenko,* loc. cit., p. 141.

[12] *For your file,* Brussels 1978. Information prepared by the News Section of the NATO International Military Staff for the ministerial meeting of 1977.

[13] The Military Balance 1978–1979, IISS, London 1978, p. 8 to 10.

[14] *Österreichische Militärische Zeitschrift,* Vienna 1/1977.

[15] Sicherheit und Entspannung, in: *Bulletin,* Federal Press and Information Office, No. 22, Bonn, February 20, 1979, p. 197.

[16] Karl *Greese* und Alfred *Voerster,* Über den Beitrag der NVA der DDR zum kollektiven militärischen Schutz der Warschauer Vertragsstaaten, in: *Militärgeschichte,* 2/1975, p. 160.

[17] Heinz *Hoffmann,* Interview: Nationale Volksarmee und Warschauer Vertrag, in: *Militärwesen,* 1968, p. 595.

[18] Prof. Dr. *Krüger,* loc. cit., p. 19.

[19] Verfassung der Deutschen Demokratischen Republik, East Berlin 1974, p. 12.

[20] Die Sowjetunion ist die Hauptkraft des Friedens, Festansprache des Mitglieds des Zentralkomitees der SED Generaloberst Kessler, in: *Neues Deutschland,* East Berlin, May 9, 1978.

[21] Colonel General *Kessler* at a celebration of the 52nd anniversary of the Soviet armed forces, in: *Neues Deutschland,* February 21, 1970.

[22] Waldemar *Verner,* Zur welthistorischen Bedeutung des Sieges der Sowjetunion und aller Völker der Antihitlerkoalition im Zweiten Weltkrieg, in: *Militärgeschichte,* 1/1975, p. 14.

[23] Ibid.

[24] Abkommen zwischen der Regierung der DDR und der Regierung der UdSSR über Fragen, die mit der zeitweiligen Stationierung sowjetischer Streitkräfte auf dem Territorium der DDR zusammenhängen, in: *Dokumente zur Außenpolitik ...,* vol. 5, East Berlin 1958, p. 677 ff.

[25] Hermann *Müller,* loc. cit., p. 151.

[26] H. *Kräger,* Der Klasseninhalt der Souveränität, in: *Deutsche Außenpolitik,* East Berlin 3/1972, p. 455. Quoted by Hermann *Müller,* loc. cit., p. 151.

[27] *Greese* and *Voerster,* loc. cit., note 16, p. 163.

[28] Ibid. p. 167.

[29] Waldemar *Verner,* loc. cit., p. 14.

[30] Unser Kampfbündnis ist unbesiegbar, in: *Neues Deutschland,* February 27, 1970.

[31] Karl *Greese,* Die Bedeutung der ersten gemeinsamen Übung von Truppen der NVA und der Sowjetarmee 1957 für die Entwicklung des kollektiven Schutzes der DDR und für die deutsch-sowjetische Waffenbrüderschaft, in: *Militärgeschichte,* 1/1968, p. 92.

[32] Ibid. p. 97.

[33] Hans *Höhn* und Ernst *Stenzel,* Das sozialistische Militärbündnis als eine Verwirklichung der Lehren der Geschichte, in: *Militärgeschichte,* 1/1975, p. 38.

[34] Generalmajor Gerhard *Lorenz,* Deputy Chief of the GDR Frontier Police and Head of its Political Administration, on August 13, 1961. Markstein in der Entwicklung unserer sozialistischen DDR, in: *Volksarmee,* East Berlin 33/1976.

[35] *Höhn* und *Stenzel,* loc. cit., note 33, p. 41.

[36] *Volksarmee,* East Berlin, special issue of October 11, 1963.

[37] *Neues Deutschland,* April 9, 1965.

[38] Mächtigste Militärkoalition der Welt schützt die sozialistischen Staaten, Ansprache des Genossen Walter Ulbricht auf der Großkundgebung der Waffenbrüderschaft, in: *Volksarmee,* Dokumentation – Manöver „Oktobersturm", 1965.

[39] *Volksarmee,* 47/1965.

[40] Radio DDR, October 18, 1965, 22,00 hrs.

41 Cf. Major General *Ernst* after Exercise *"Böhmerwald"* in *Volksarmee*, 28/1966.

42 *Volksarmee*, 40/1968.

43 Bündnis der Herzen und Waffen, Manöver Oder-Neisse 69 – Überzeugende Demonstration des sozialistischen Internationalismus, in: *Neues Deutschland*, October 25, 1969.

44 *Neues Deutschland*, September 29, 1969.

45 Mitteilung des Leitungsstabes des Manövers *"Waffenbrüderschaft"*, in: *Neues land*, October 19, 1970.

46 *Neues Deutschland*, October 19, 1970.

47 Ibid. October 13, 1970.

48 Ibid. October 19, 1970.

49 *Volksarmee*, 39/1976.

50 Oberstleutnant Dr. *D. Groll*, Friedrich Engels Military Academy, Die Rolle der Streitkräfte in der Nationalen Befreiungsbewegung, in: *Militärwesen*, 1/1977, p. 99.

51 For the text of the treaty see *Neues Deutschland*, February 26, 1979.

52 Cf. L. *Kruglow*, Über den militärischen Schutz der Errungenschaften des nationalen Befreiungskampfes, in: *Militärwesen*, 6/1975, p. 21 ff.

53 Militärhilfe für die Dritte Welt, in: *Österreichische Militärische Zeitschrift*, 2/1977, p. 150.

54 Henning von *Löwis*, Das politische und militärische Engagement der Deutschen Demokratischen Republik in Schwarzafrika, Ein Überblick von 1953 bis 1978, in: *Beiträge zur Konfliktforschung*, Köln, 1/1979, p. 46.

55 Walter *Ulbricht*, Der Kampf um den Frieden, für den Sieg des Sozialismus, für die nationale Wiedergeburt Deutschlands als friedliebender, demokratischer Staat. Address at the 5th SED Congress, East Berlin 1958, p. 11.

56 *Österreichische Militärische Zeitschrift*, 2/1977, p. 150.

57 *Volksarmee*, 43, 44 and 45/1971.

58 Ibid. 25/1972.

59 Ibid. 44/1974.

60 Ibid. 2 and 3/1976.

61 *Neues Deutschland*, April 9 and 10, 1977.

62 Text of treaty in: *Neues Deutschland*, December 6, 1977.

63 Text of treaty in: *Neues Deutschland*, February 20, 1979.

64 Text of treaty in: *Neues Deutschland*, February 26, 1979.

65 *Österreichische Militärische Zeitschrift*, 2/1977, p. 150; Henning von *Löwis*, loc. cit., pp. 5–54; Karl-Heinz *Woitzik*, Die Auslandsaktivität der sowjetischen Besatzungszone Deutschlands, Mainz o. J., 282 pp.

66 *Neues Deutschland*, November 27, 1978.

67 General *Hoffmann*, Streitkräfte in unserer Zeit, in: *Einheit*, East Berlin 3/1976, p. 358.

CHAPTER FOUR

Controlling Organs and Structure of the Defence Forces

The national defence system

The defence of East Germany is said to rest "on the political power exercised by the working class under the leadership of its Marxist-Leninist Party in alliance with the class of collective farmers, with the intelligentsia and with other actively employed citizens"[1]. The Defence Law goes on to say that national defence "has its firm basis in the socialist state-and-social-order, in its growing political and economic strength and in the public's political awareness and readiness to protect and defend socialist achievements". It is thus undertaken "in accordance with the right to individual and collective self-defence acknowledged in Article 51 of the UN Charter", in the Warsaw Pact and in the "Treaties of Friendship, Cooperation and Mutual Assistance" concluded with the U.S.S.R. and other countries in the socialist commonwealth. As the GDR military oath puts it, the country's whole military potential is also committed to the *defence of socialism* – which is in turn qualified in the various bilateral treaties quoted in the Defence Law, par. 1, as "based on Marxism-Leninism and proletarian internationalism". To speak of "national defence" is thus too narrow a concept.

Just who is in charge of the "national defence" effort is also somewhat vaguely stated on paper, but quite clear in practice. The *Constitution* contains no reference to a Socialist Unity Party of Germany *(Sozialistische Einheitspartei Deutschlands – SED)*, though in the military as in other spheres it is this body which makes all the decisions. What the Constitution does mention, in regard to every aspect of the GDR, is the "leadership of the working class and its Marxist-Leninist Party"[2]. In official eyes there is evidently no difficulty in reconciling the all-powerful role of the SED with Article 5 (3) of the Constitution, which says that "at no time and in no circumstances can any organs exercise state authority other than those provided for in the Constitution". Yet the Constitution makes no mention of the *Politburo of the SED Central Committee,* which makes the ultimate decisions.

The *National Defence Council* illustrates the cavalier fashion in which the East German leaders treat the "organs provided for in the Constitution" and arrange crucial transfers of power. For under the new Defence Law the Council has been given central prerogatives to which it had no legal title before.

The supreme command and control organs for the GDR's national defence are as follows:

– the *Politburo of the SED Central Committee,* whose Secretary General is Politburo member Erich Honecker;

Erich Honecker, Secretary General of the SED's Central Committee, Chairman of the Council of State, Chairman of the National Defence Council. Born in 1912, interned in Brandenburg prison during World War II, he was primarily concerned after 1949 with building up the FDJ organization and from 1957 was responsible within the SED leadership for Military and Security Policy.

Walter Ulbricht, Honecker's predecessor as SED leader up to 1971, was born in 1893 and died in 1973. In 1945 he returned from the Soviet Union to Berlin as Stalin's protégé. In the Party's top post since 1950 he encompassed, with the backing of the Soviet forces of occupation, the transformation of their zone of Germany into a communist state.

- the *Council of State*, whose Chairman is Erich Honecker;
- the *National Defence Council*, also chaired by Erich Honecker;
- the *Council of Ministers*, i.e. Cabinet, whose Chairman is Willi Stoph, another member of the Politburo; and
- the *Ministry for National Defence*, under Minister and Army General Heinz Hoffmann, also a Politburo member.

According to Article 48 of the Constitution the parliament or *People's Chamber (Volkskammer)* is the "supreme state authority" and the country's "sole constitution-making and law-giving body". To parliament are responsible both the Council of State, whose members it chooses (Article 66), and the National Defence Council. However, important rights in the military sphere belong also to these two bodies: the Council of State can declare a republic-wide *"state of defence"* and the National Defence Council can pass a resolution in favour of *partial or total mobilization.* In view of the mandatory nature of such decisions, once made, it is unlikely that the People's Chamber could subsequently change them.

Apart from the Ministry for National Defence, whose members contrary to Western practice are military men up to the top level, all the bodies we have enumerated are political instruments which not only maintain the primacy of politics vis-à-vis the military, but also exercise *"military leadership"* or "command" (Führung). This last is defined in the East German textbook *Das Moderne Militärwesen* as

the total sum of measures required to define targets for the activities of the military services and other armed organs of the state in protecting socialist achievements and destroying the aggressor in any armed confrontation that may arise, and to direct and steer those activities in accordance with the targets defined[3].

Given the structure of a communist state, paramount importance in "military leadership" attaches to the guidelines, instructions and orders of the SED Central Committee. Within the Committee, actual leadership inheres in the Politburo, which

- determines the role of the NVA at each stage within the system of national defence;
- checks and supervises the execution of its decisions by the armed forces; and
- gives their personnel ideological guidance.

Within the Central Committee Secretariat, the Secretary responsible for security is Politburo member Paul *Verner*.

In matters of detail the Committee's *Department for Security Questions*, headed by Colonel General Herbert *Scheibe*, carries responsibility. Since the command and control of the NVA by the Party are a specific feature of a communist state, these will be discussed in a later chapter.

It is no doubt of value in ensuring due respect for military concerns in overall SED policy-making that authoritative representatives of the military apparatus and other armed organs sit in the Central Committee.

SED Secretary General Erich *Honecker* can himself be rated a military expert, especially since he took over responsibility for the Politburo's Security Commission. As Chairman of the Council of State and of the National Defence Council he is automatically Commander in Chief of the NVA, even if this title has not so far been applied to him as it was to his predecessor Ulbricht. (It is, of course, only logical that in case of war the function would pass to the Commander in Chief of the Warsaw Pact's Joint Armed Forces, and thence to the Soviet Defence Minister or to the Generalissimo himself, i.e. the Soviet Party leader and Head of State.)

Another member of the 19-strong Politburo is GDR Defence Minister Heinz *Hoffmann*, Army General and academic military specialist. He belonged to the German Communist Youth League as early as 1926, fought in the International Brigade during the Spanish Civil War, and occupied leading positions from the start in the Garrisoned People's Police and NVA.

The present Premier, Willi *Stoph*, is also to be counted among the Politburo's military specialists. He joined the German Communist Youth League in 1928 (in 1939 he was however a *Wehrmacht* soldier) and as Interior Minister and Defence Minister in turn directed the expansion of the People's Police and NVA. He was Hoffmann's predecessor in the Defence Ministry and, like him, holds the rank of Army General.

Another Politburo member with a military science degree is the present Interior Minister and Chief of the German People's Police, Colonel General Friedrich *Dickel*.

Other Politburo members with military or police security experience are:

Minister for State Security Army General Erich *Mielke*, a Party member since 1925 and International Brigade man;

Alfred *Neumann*, who also served in the International Brigade;

Paul *Verner*, with International Brigade experience and now Central Committee Secretary for military and security matters; also Chairman of the relevant parliamentary committee.

All members of the Politburo are parliamentary deputies.

The *Council of State*[4], as a parliamentary organ, has the following duties in regard to "military leadership":

> – to ratify or terminate *state treaties* and other international legal instruments requiring such ratification – Article 66 (2);
> – to pass *basic resolutions* in matters of national defence and security, *organize national defence* with the help of the National Defence Council, *nominate members* of that body which is answerable for its activities to parliament and the State Council, and *determine military ranks* – Article 71 (1 and 2);
> – to establish state *Orders,* decorations and honorary titles, which are conferred by its Chairman – Article 75;

– in case of emergency to declare a *"state of defence . . .* if the situation should prevent the People's Chamber form convening or from assembling a quorum" – Par. 4 (2) of the Defence Law. (The Chairman of the Council of State can announce a state of defence, according to Article 52 of the Constitution, while Par. 4 (2) of the Defence Law further states that such an announcement can take any form, and be accompanied by any required declarations with international legal force.)

Set up in 1960, the National Defence Council was given wider powers by the 1978 Defence Law. Thus it can order *"total or partial mobilization"*[5] if it deems this "necessary in the interests of national defence because of a situation of jeopardy". Whereas the State Council Chairman (who is also Chairman of the Defence Council) can legally speaking only declare a "state of defence" by a State Council resolution, and without recourse to parliament, in cases of urgency, the National Defence Council can in practice function as an emergency government and dictate sweeping decisions:

> In carrying out mobilization, or acting in a state of defence, the National Defence Council is empowered and obliged, by dint of the tasks and authority deputed to it, to undertake all measures necessary for national defence and the protection of the socialist system, including measures which may require deviation from statutes and other legal prescriptions. The People's Chamber or the GDR Council of State, as the case may be, will pass the necessary resolutions on the activity of the National Defence Council at their next subsequent sessions respectively.

The new Defence Law makes equally clear how far the defence of the country is controlled in all important respects, even in peace time, by the National Defence Council:

> The GDR National Defence Council is responsible, on the basis and in pursuance of the laws and resolutions of the People's Chamber, for exercising central control of defence and security measures. In cooperation with other state organs it ensures the defence of the country and makes decisions necessary for that purpose, which are then binding upon all state and economic organs, manufacturing combines, enterprises, institutions, cooperatives, social organizations, associations, and individual citizens. To this end it issues legal prescriptions in the form of orders and decisions.

The National Defence Council is a kind of clandestine cabinet, of which only the Chairman, Erich Honecker, is known to the public. The other members, at least twelve in number, have never been openly named. They are, however, appointed by the Council of State and probably include the following: Paul Verner as Party Central Committee Secretary responsible for military and security policy; Willi Stoph as Prime Minister; Dr. Günther Mittag as CC Secretary for economic matters; Interior Minister Friedrich Dickel; State Security Minister Erich Mielke; Defence Minister Heinz Hoffmann;

State Planning Commission Chairman Gerhard Schürer; and Dr. Albert Stief, Chairman of the Workers' and Farmers' Inspectorate.

The Secretary of the National Defence Council is General Fritz Streletz, who is also a Deputy Minister for Defence and Chief of the Main Staff of the NVA.

The *Council of Ministers*, by contrast, merely "organizes the execution of the defence tasks entrusted to it". It also ranks below the National Defence Council in regard to the issuing of directives required for the implementation of the Defence Law.

The Ministry for National Defence (MND)

The highest military command and administrative organ of the NVA is the MND: the Minister since 1960 has been Army General Heinz Hoffmann. He holds supreme command within the NVA, even though Party leader Ulbricht while he was alive was occasionally referred to as Commander in Chief.

The MND "organizes and directs the land, air and sea forces of the NVA on the basis, and in implementation, of the laws, orders and decisions of the People's Chamber and Council of Ministers". The duties of the Ministry are "defined by the Council of Ministers". Such is the letter of the Law of 1956 establishing both the NVA and the MND[6]. But in the 1978 Defence Law, which attaches paramount importance as we have seen to the National Defence Council, the Defence Minister and his Ministry are only mentioned in two places: in connection with civil defence, and with the expropriation of land and buildings. The Ministry nevertheless enjoys considerable powers, as described for example in the chapter 8 below.

The Minister has a number of deputies at hand to help him run the NVA. The following names were published in the spring of 1980.

Each Deputy Minister is normally responsible for a particular sphere.

- Lieutenant General Klaus-Dieter *Baumgarten*, Chief of the Frontier Troops;
- Admiral Wilhelm *Ehm*, b. 1918, Chief of the People's Navy;
- Colonel General Werner *Fleissner*, b. 1922, Head of Technology and Weaponry;
- Lieutenant General Joachim *Goldbach*, b. 1929, Head of Rear Services;
- Colonel General Heinz *Kessler*, b. 1920, Head of the Main Political Administration;
- Lieutenant General Fritz *Peter*, Director of Civil Defence;
- Colonel General Wolfgang *Reinhold*, Chief of Air Force/Air Defence;
- Colonel General Horst *Stechbarth*, b. 1925, Chief of Land Forces;
- Colonel General Fritz *Streletz*, b. 1926, Chief of the Main Staff and Secretary of the National Defence Council.

Army General Heinz Hoffmann, Minister for National Defence.

The MND is organized in the main on the *Soviet pattern*. It recognizes, for example, no clear distinction between troop-commanding and administration. It is equally characteristic that all senior posts, including administrative ones, are filled by officers. Its headquarters in Strausberg just outside Berlin – a few officers are in East Berlin itself – employ over 3,200 army personnel and some 100 Soviet officers, against only about 1,000 civilians.

The MND is divided into a *Main Staff,* two *Main Administrations* – the Main Political Administration and the Main Administration for Civil Defence – and *Administrations* and *Departments* of various importance, size and independence. The Administrations and Departments are partly answerable to the Minister directly, partly to his various deputies or to the heads of service arms, main administrations, administrations and special services.

This complex structure of the top command is rooted in its Soviet prototype. Multiple overlapping of responsibilities was deliberately planned to prevent any element trying to act on its own. But the pattern also reflects contradictory tendencies in the growth of the NVA itself.

The MND's Administrations and Departments can be classified into several groups.

1. *Administrations and Departments responsible to the Chief of the Main Staff.*

The domain of the Main Staff covers all areas essential for the functioning of the *entire armed forces*. Although a separate Land Forces Command has existed for several years, its operational tasks are worked out at the top level by the Chief of the Main Staff. He has under him eight Administrations and five Departments.

The *Operations Administration* is responsible for planning the deployment of all NVA units within the Joint Armed Forces of the Warsaw Pact in accordance with the directions of their Commander in Chief.

The *Intelligence Administration* evaluates reports on foreign forces, corresponding approximately to NATO's G2 Service in its functions and methods.

The *Organization Administration* handles strength returns, disposition plans, equipment inventories and mobilization planning.

The *Replacement Administration* deals with recruitment of both conscripts and volunteers, and the listing and welfare of reservists.

The *Signals Administration* is responsible for all signals and communications in the NVA, ensuring their coordination and standardization according to Warsaw Pact guidelines. It also supplies troops with communications equipment and sees to its maintenance.

The *Military Transport Administration* deals particularly with the construction and military employment of railways.

The *Military Science Administration* collects and evaluates the work of military theorists, especially Soviet, and derives practical instructions for troop commanders from them.

Colonel General Horst Stechbarth, Chief of the NVA Land Forces, hands over "engraved daggers of honour" to graduates of the Ernst Thälmann Officers' College.

The *Administration for Mechanization and Automatization of Command* collects and assesses scientific research findings and converts them into practical instructions.

Of the various Departments answering to the Chief of Main Staff, mention may be made of

the *Commandant Service,* corresponding to military police in the West, but with responsibilities restricted to the MND and its seat in Strausberg; and

the *Data-processing Department,* which is fairly new and gaining importance with modern advances in military command and control. It gathers research findings and converts them into practical measures and facilities for the troops.

2. *Administrations and Departments responsible to the Heads of Technology and Weaponry, Training, and Rear Services.*

The *Planning Administration and Coordination Department* fall under this heading. Planning Administration coordinates matériel plans for all service arms and cross-references them with the relevant sectors of industry. The overall plan is agreed with the State Planning Commission and then passed to the Procurement Department, answerable to the Head of Technology and Weaponry.

3. *The Main Political Administration (Polithauptverwaltung).*

This is entrusted with carrying out and monitoring *all political work* within the NVA. Since the military performance and behaviour of every soldier can be regarded as a "political matter", the *Polithauptverwaltung* concerns itself with virtually everything. It affects the whole character of the NVA to a remarkable extent, and will be discussed in a later chapter along with other aspects of Party control.

4. *Administrations and Departments directly responsible to the Minister.*

These include Administrations handling *logistical planning,* requisitioning and distributing of supply goods for the individual service arms, and above all *training,* and also those handling services essential for all the forces, such as the military courts.

The Minister is also in direct charge of *espionage and counterespionage,* as follows.

The *Military Intelligence Administration* controls military espionage directed at West Germany, West Europe generally and other NATO countries. It is responsible for securing information on military capabilites and policy and on arms technology.

Administration 2000, the link with the State Security Ministry, is responsible for security matters throughout the forces. Its personnel includes officers employed by that Ministry but not recognizable as such, who are posted appropriately at all levels down to regimental staffs.

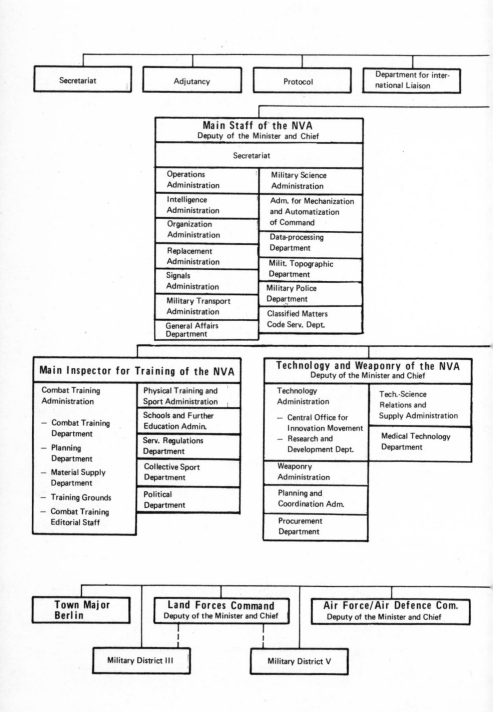

| Secretariat | Adjutancy | Protocol | Department for international Liaison |

Main Staff of the NVA
Deputy of the Minister and Chief

Secretariat

Operations Administration	Military Science Administration
Intelligence Administration	Adm. for Mechanization and Automatization of Command
Organization Administration	Data-processing Department
Replacement Administration	Milit. Topographic Department
Signals Administration	Military Police Department
Military Transport Administration	Classified Matters Code Serv. Dept.
General Affairs Department	

Main Inspector for Training of the NVA

Combat Training Administration	Physical Training and Sport Administration
— Combat Training Department	Schools and Further Education Admin.
— Planning Department	Serv. Regulations Department
— Material Supply Department	Collective Sport Department
— Training Grounds	Political Department
— Combat Training Editorial Staff	

Technology and Weaponry of the NVA
Deputy of the Minister and Chief

Technology Administration	Tech.-Science Relations and Supply Administration
— Central Office for Innovation Movement — Research and Development Dept.	Medical Technology Department
Weaponry Administration	
Planning and Coordination Adm.	
Procurement Department	

| **Town Major Berlin** | **Land Forces Command** Deputy of the Minister and Chief | **Air Force/Air Defence Com.** Deputy of the Minister and Chief |

| Military District III | Military District V |

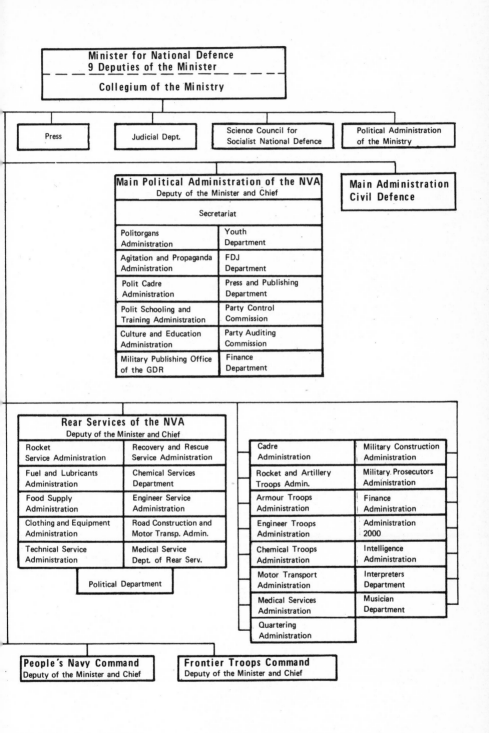

Minister for National Defence
9 Deputies of the Minister
Collegium of the Ministry

| Press | Judicial Dept. | Science Council for Socialist National Defence | Political Administration of the Ministry |

Main Political Administration of the NVA
Deputy of the Minister and Chief

Main Administration Civil Defence

Secretariat	
Politorgans Administration	Youth Department
Agitation and Propaganda Administration	FDJ Department
Polit Cadre Administration	Press and Publishing Department
Polit Schooling and Training Administration	Party Control Commission
Culture and Education Administration	Party Auditing Commission
Military Publishing Office of the GDR	Finance Department

Rear Services of the NVA
Deputy of the Minister and Chief

Rocket Service Administration	Recovery and Rescue Service Administration
Fuel and Lubricants Administration	Chemical Services Department
Food Supply Administration	Engineer Service Administration
Clothing and Equipment Administration	Road Construction and Motor Transp. Admin.
Technical Service Administration	Medical Service Dept. of Rear Serv.

Political Department

Cadre Administration	Military Construction Administration
Rocket and Artillery Troops Admin.	Military Prosecutors Administration
Armour Troops Administration	Finance Administration
Engineer Troops Administration	Administration 2000
Chemical Troops Administration	Intelligence Administration
Motor Transport Administration	Interpreters Department
Medical Services Administration	Musician Department
Quartering Administration	

People's Navy Command
Deputy of the Minister and Chief

Frontier Troops Command
Deputy of the Minister and Chief

A number of other, more conventional posts are also directly responsible to the Ministry, such as the *Protocol Department* and the *Attaché Department* for international liaison, as well as bodies unique to the NVA like the *Sport and Technology Society Department* which liaises between that pre-military training organization and the Ministry for National Defence.

The Land Forces

These are under the orders of the *Land Forces Command* in Potsdam, through Military Districts III and V. A *Military District* is defined in the NVA as "a superior military-administrative territorial grouping of formations, units and military facilities of the various arms, special troops and services"[7]. The troops and services within a Military District constitute an Army Corps.

The Land Forces comprise

- two armoured divisions;
- four motorized infantry divisions;
- army troops and army schools.

The two kinds of divisions have the same basic structure as in the Soviet forces.

The actual breakdown of the Land Forces is as follows:

- MND or Land Forces Command, disposing of
2 engineer regiments,
1 signals regiment,
3 training regiments for training reservists,
1 training regiment for railway personnel and railway engineers, other army troops, and
officers' colleges and other training institutes under their direct control;

- Military District III, Leipzig, disposing of the
4th motorized infantry division, Erfurt,
11th motorized infantry division, Halle,
7th armoured division, Dresden,
plus its own army troops;

- Military District V, Neubrandenburg, disposing of the
1st motorized infantry division, Potsdam,
8th motorized infantry division, Schwerin,
9th armoured division, Eggesin,
plus its own army troops.

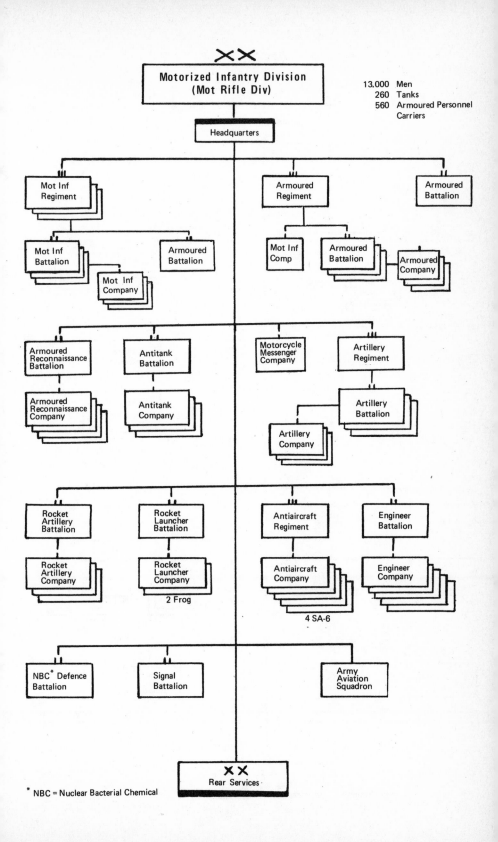

XX

**Motorized Infantry Division
(Mot Rifle Div)**

13,000 Men
260 Tanks
560 Armoured Personnel
Carriers

Headquarters

Mot Inf
Regiment

Armoured
Regiment

Armoured
Battalion

Mot Inf
Battalion

Mot Inf
Company

Armoured
Battalion

Mot Inf
Comp

Armoured
Battalion

Armoured
Company

Armoured
Reconnaissance
Battalion

Antitank
Battalion

Motorcycle
Messenger
Company

Artillery
Regiment

Armoured
Reconnaissance
Company

Antitank
Company

Artillery
Battalion

Artillery
Company

Rocket
Artillery
Battalion

Rocket
Launcher
Battalion

Antiaircraft
Regiment

Engineer
Battalion

Rocket
Artillery
Company

Rocket
Launcher
Company

Antiaircraft
Company

Engineer
Company

2 Frog

4 SA-6

NBC* Defence
Battalion

Signal
Battalion

Army
Aviation
Squadron

XX
Rear Services

* NBC = Nuclear Bacterial Chemical

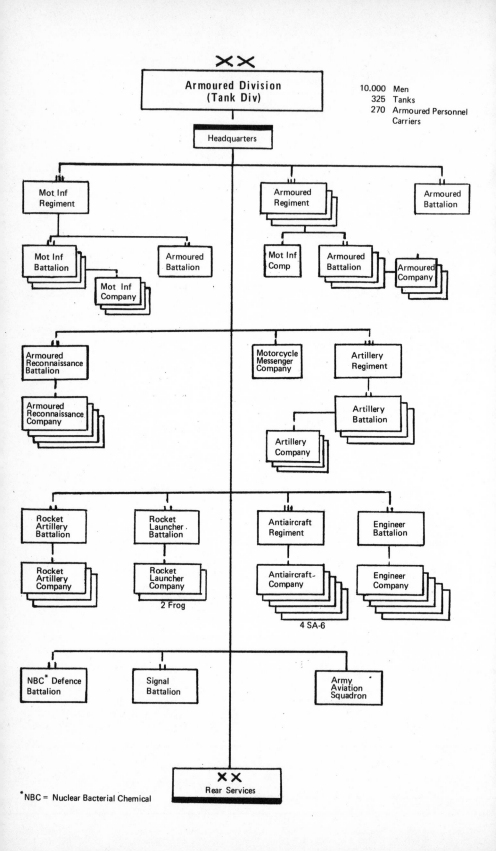

Armoured Division (Tank Div)

10.000 Men
325 Tanks
270 Armoured Personnel Carriers

Headquarters

Mot Inf Regiment
- Mot Inf Battalion
  - Mot Inf Company
- Armoured Battalion

Armoured Regiment
- Mot Inf Comp
- Armoured Battalion
  - Armoured Company

Armoured Battalion

Armoured Reconnaissance Battalion
- Armoured Reconnaissance Company

Motorcycle Messenger Company

Artillery Regiment
- Artillery Battalion
  - Artillery Company

Rocket Artillery Battalion
- Rocket Artillery Company

Rocket Launcher Battalion
- Rocket Launcher Company

2 Frog

Antiaircraft Regiment
- Antiaircraft Company

4 SA-6

Engineer Battalion
- Engineer Company

NBC* Defence Battalion

Signal Battalion

Army Aviation Squadron

Rear Services

*NBC = Nuclear Bacterial Chemical

Strengths and ratios in the Land Forces are approximately:

15,500 officers	= 13 %
21,000 NCOs	= 18 %
83,500 other ranks	= 69 %
120,000 men	= 100 %

Frontier Troops

The supreme authority here, under the MND, is the *Frontier Troops Command* in Pätz. As they are formally distinct from the NVA and have many special features, these "Frontier Troops of the GDR" will be discussed in the following chapter.

Their total establishment, including training units and schools runs to 50,000.

Air Force/Air Defence (Luftstreitkräfte / Luftverteidigung)

The *Air Forces/Air Defence Command* at Eggersdorf controls

- 2 fighter divisions, Cottbus and Neubrandenburg;
- 1 fighter training wing, Bautzen;
- 1 transport wing, Dessau;
- 2 helicopter wings, Brandenburg-Briest;
- 6 AA missile regiments;
- 1 signals regiment;
- technical battalions, ground supply facilities, and schools.

Establishments are approximately:

8,000 officers	= 22 %
8,500 NCOs	= 25 %
18,500 other ranks	= 53 %
35,000 men	= 100 %

Their main task is to prevent penetration by enemy aircraft or missiles of GDR air space. The Air Defence division and AA missile troops are fully integrated into the Warsaw Pact air defence organization, forming since 1962 part of the so-called *Duty System (Diensthabendes System),* which includes corresponding Soviet, Polish and Czechoslovak units. The Duty System commands and personnel are always at a high level of alert and are designed as the initial defence against surprise attack.

The People's Navy (Volksmarine)

The *People's Navy Command* at Rostock controls some 300 ships and boats, the Coastal Frontier Brigade, a signals unit and supply units.

The *breakdown* is as follows:

1st task force, Peenemünde, with its
– minelaying and minesweeping divisions,
– landing craft divisions,
– submarine chaser division, and
– auxiliary vessel division;

4th task force, Warnemünde, with its
– coastal defence division,
– minelaying and minesweeping divisions,
– submarine chaser division, and
– auxiliary vessel division;

6th task force, Bug, comprising
– missile patrol boats and motor torpedo boats;

Coastal Frontier Brigade, Rostock, with
– eight groups of boats plus land forces to the tune of 12 battalions and training units;

the Karl Liebknecht People's Navy Officers' College and other naval schools with motor boat units.

There are in addition signals and supply units, a shipbuilding instruction division, a testing centre and helicopter forces.

Establishments are approximately:

3,200 officers	=	17 %
5,700 NCOs	=	30 %
10,100 other ranks	=	53 %
19,000 men	=	100 %

The breakdown and command structure of the People's Navy shows its great dependence on the Soviet Navy, which emerges also from its officially defined task: "The GDR People's Navy exists to protect the sea-frontier of the GDR from any attack in cooperation with all elements of the NVA and in loyal brotherhood-in-arms with the Baltic Red Banner Fleet and the Polish Navy". It is thus a component part of the United Baltic Navy.

The structure of military command

The general character and special features of the GDR forces are strongly influenced by the *ratio of officers to NCOs and other ranks*. Quality of command and, even more, military reliability are enhanced by the number of well-trained commanders. Something similar applies to the level of political reliability, though to a lesser extent since factors external to the forces are involved in that case.

In all the Warsaw Pact forces there is a surprisingly high proportion of senior ranks, and the NVA is no exception with its total approximate strength of

26,700 officers	=	15 %
35,200 NCOs	=	20 %
112,100 other ranks	=	65 %
174,000 men	=	100 %

Thus to every two privates or ratings there is a soldier of higher rank to lead and control them.

The particularly high ratios of officers to men in the air and sea forces can be explained by their very large requirements for technical specialists who have longer service and may also occupy higher ranks for social and proficiency reasons. The fact that nearly half the establishment in these services occupies positions of control must tend to reinforce military reliability.

Notes

1 Gesetz über die Landesverteidigung der DDR (Defence Law) of October 13, 1978, *Gesetzblatt* pt. I. No. 35, 1978, p. 377.
2 GDR Constitution of April 6, 1968, as given in the Gesetz zur Ergänzung und Änderung der Verfassung der DDR of October 7, 1974, quoted from *Neues Deutschland* of September 28, 1974.
3 *Das moderne Militärwesen,* East Berlin 1968, p. 459.
4 GDR Constitution, loc. cit. note 2, Section III, Chap. 2, Arts. 66–75.
5 Defence Law, v. note 1.
6 Gesetz über die Schaffung der NVA und des Ministeriums für Nationale Verteidigung, quoted from *Neues Deutschland,* January 19, 1956.
7 Militärlexikon, Militärverlag der DDR, East Berlin, 2nd ed. 1973, p. 231.

CHAPTER FIVE

Frontier Troops and their Employment

The line which has divided Germany and the German nation for over a generation is in East German terms the *"State Frontier West" (Staatsgrenze West)* with a special separating purpose to fulfil. The troops stationed on its eastern side are performing what Defence Minister Hoffmann has called "front-line service in peacetime"[1]. And "since they are engaged continually on combat tasks, they require leadership in combat terms"[2]. The reason was set forth in the conscripts' handbook *(Taschenbuch für Wehrpflichtige)* as early as 1965:

> The two states existing in Germany today illustrate the fact that a small group of imperialists and militarists in the country are irreconcilably confronted, on the other hand, by the great mass of peace-loving forces throughout Germany. The Bonn state is the power-instrument of the imperialists and militarists, an enemy of the German nation; while the GDR is the fatherland of all peace-loving and progressive Germans. The state frontier of the West German Federal Republic, which extends for 1,381 kilometers from the Baltic to the Fichtelgebirge, is also one of the crucial dividing lines between socialism and imperialism in Europe. And in the midst of the GDR there is a 164 kilometer state frontier running round the special territory of West Berlin, which the imperialists have developed into a NATO base and spy centre[3].

The NVA textbook *Das moderne Militärwesen,* published in 1968, after a more specific analysis of the "imperialist" threat but with no mention of the frontier's function vis-à-vis the GDR's own population, draws the following conclusions.

> In socialist states bordering on imperialist ones, border control cannot be limited to police measures. The forces of imperialism make systematic attempts to permeate the frontiers of socialist countries and use them as a target for provocation. Aggressive actions staged by these forces in the border areas, and demands for frontier changes, are calculated to serve as excuses for launching aggression against the socialist states ... Socialist states must therefore expect their imperialist adversaries, at the outset

Right: On August 13, 1961, the GDR began building the Berlin Wall to seal off West Berlin. The top photograph shows the Brandenburg Gate, with Combat Group members in the foreground and Alert Units of the People's Police behind them. Below, an NCO of the NVA Frontier Troops escaping to West Berlin on August 15, 1961 – a snapshot that was reproduced throughout the world.

of a war and immediately before it, to pour masses of subversive elements, unchecked, across the frontiers. The deployment of such elements is an integral part of the theory and practice of clandestine warfare. Socialist states like the GDR, which have key frontiers to guard between imperialism and socialism, therefore need a soundly organized military system of frontier protection as part of their national defences. The GDR Frontier Troops are a military body directly answerable to the Ministry for National Defence. They carry a high responsibility for the preservation of the peace in Europe[4].

Nothing has changed in this estimate of the situation or its consequences. Thus we read in the Party Central Committee's greetings to the Frontier Troops on their thirtieth anniversary, December 1, 1976:

The powerful onward march of socialism, as well as the undiminished aggressiveness of imperialism, its headlong rearmament and obstinate attempts to undermine the process of détente, all go to increase the responsibilities of the GDR Frontier Troops. Increasingly provocative moves against our state frontier during 1976 and the massive efforts to damage the sovereign rights of the GDR show yet again the need for a high level of fighting power and combat readiness, as well as continual class-conscious revolutionary alertness[5].

Two basic reasons can be adduced for the continued evolution of the Frontier Troops from a police into an army-type organization capable of "active combat to protect the inviolability of the state border"[6]:

– the construction right along the border, especially since 1966, of strong and effective installations which in time, and with further sophistication, will eliminate the need for huge numbers of men to guard it;
– the requirement felt by the country's leaders that these troops, as combat-capable units, should be available to the Warsaw Pact's Joint Command in even more versatile roles than before.

The change of name on January 1, 1974, from *NVA Frontier Troops* to *Frontier Troops of the GDR* has not affected their military character; both before and after the change they were directly responsible to the MND. The purpose may well have been to exclude them from any international agreements on the reduction of armed forces.

The evolution of the Frontier Troops

When the so-called *German Frontier Police* first appeared in 1946 alongside Soviet troops they were at first concentrated, because of their still small numbers, at the border crossing points and on alternating patrol duties in the huge surveillance zone.

In a review of their history on the occasion of their 30th anniversary, the Chief of the Frontier Troops gave this justification for their creation in 1946.

> In violation of internationally binding agreements, a democratic revolution in the Western zones was frustrated. Ever more patently the imperialistic occupation forces demanded the restoration of the power of German monopoly capital with all the divisive intentions that went with it. The consequent unleashing of the "cold war" began to take effect ever more markedly along the demarcation line. For those responsible for guarding the border, this meant increasing concern with the struggle against political provocations directed by imperialist agencies, against economic acts of sabotage and against other wrecking operations aimed at the anti-fascist democratic order[7].

The aims of the "anti-fascist democratic revolution" emerge from the description of the Frontier Police in the same survey.

> This meant that the Frontier Police, set up in late November 1946 on the soil of what was later the GDR in accordance with the objective needs of the class war, had from the very first a class character that initially bore the stamp of the first stage of the uniform revolutionary transition from capitalism to socialism[8].

By 1952 the GDR felt strong enough to extend its *sealing-off measures* considerably. At this period the Frontier Police closed 174 through roads, including 3 *autobahns,* and thousands of public and private paths. The extensive east-west *waterways* system was declared out of bounds in both directions except for goods transport on the *Mittelland Canal* and the *Elbe river.*

The next major step was an agreement on Soviet-East German relations concluded on September 20, 1955, which nominally – to demonstrate the GDR's full sovereignty – conferred on her sole responsibility for *"guarding and controlling the state frontier,* including personnel of the Western occupying powers" and involved an increase in the strength of the Frontier Police. (In fact the U.S.S.R. continued to reserve a decisive proportion of sovereign power for itself.)

The developments that followed were summarized on the occasion of the NVA's tenth anniversary:

> In response to the requirement that units should be completely combat-capable, the German Frontier Police were given a thoroughly military structure from the top command downwards. Units were taken off strength in turn to be retrained on army lines, and border guards on the pattern of military pickets were introduced.
>
> The German Frontier Police were to a large extent relieved of responsibility for checking traffic on the state frontier with the West German Federal Republic and the Berlin West Ring, and crossing-points passed under the supervision of what was then the "Office of Customs and Freight Control".

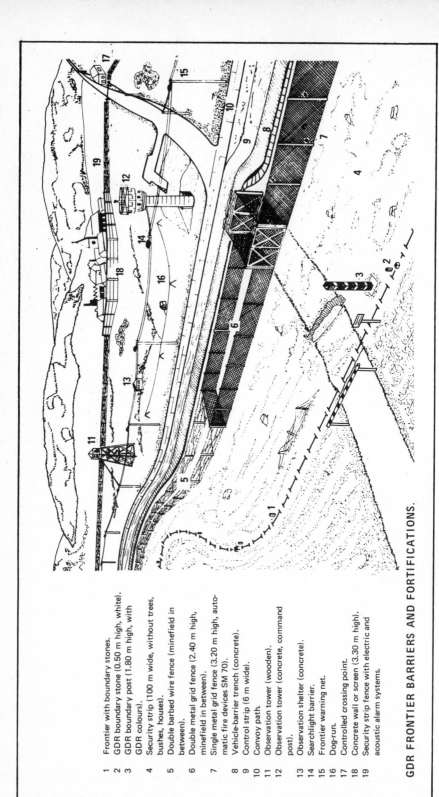

1   Frontier with boundary stones.
2   GDR boundary stone (0.50 m high, white).
3   GDR boundary post (1.80 m high, with GDR colours).
4   Security strip (100 m wide, without trees, bushes, houses).
5   Double barbed wire fence (minefield in between).
6   Double metal grid fence (2.40 m high, minefield in between).
7   Single metal grid fence (3.20 m high, automatic fire devices SM 70).
8   Vehicle-barrier trench (concrete).
9   Control strip (6 m wide).
10 Convoy path.
11 Observation tower (wooden).
12 Observation tower (concrete, command post).
13 Observation shelter (concrete).
14 Searchlight barrier.
15 Frontier warning net.
16 Dog-run.
17 Controlled crossing point.
18 Concrete wall or screen (3.30 m high).
19 Security strip fence with electric and acoustic alarm systems.

GDR FRONTIER BARRIERS AND FORTIFICATIONS.

Members of the GDR Frontier Troops working on the demarcation line, the elaborately fortified and secured frontier facing the Federal Republic of Germany.

The deployment of the German Frontier Police to guard the state border in the autumn of 1961 proved to be its decisive test of efficiency as a frontier force[9].

The operation of August 13, 1961, referred to here, with the subsequent construction of the *Berlin Wall*, meant the complete sealing-off of West Berlin as a "NATO base and hotbed of *revanchisme*".

From September 15 of that year, under National Defence Council Order No. 1/61, the entire German Frontier Police were transferred from the control of the *Minister of the Interior* to that of the *Defence Minister*. With this the "actual history of the Frontier Troops" began[10].

Under their new control the Frontier Troops were radically transformed. The changes helped to give them the character of a frontier force in the

Members of the GDR Frontier Troops searching for floated mines in the dead branch of a small river; in the foreground, members of the frontier guard of the Federal Republic of Germany.

full sense, and made for more effective protection of the border. The most important measures were as follows:

– The Frontier Troops were strengthened with cadres from other elements of the NVA and the training standards of their officers were raised.

– A uniform structure was introduced on the western frontier.

– A change to border surveillance was made on the frontiers with the Polish People's Republic and Czechoslovakia.

– Border guard weaponry and technology were modernized and measures toward motorization were introduced.

– Engineering works were completed on the GFR frontier.

– Political and military directives of the NVA were adopted[11].

On August 23, 1962, a City Garrison Headquarters was set up in East Berlin and frontier police units in the city subordinated to it.

Re-equipment with more modern weapons, concentration of training effort in specialized units, massive construction of border defence installations and a changeover from the use of volunteers to personally selected and carefully tested conscripts has produced a high level of polish and efficiency.

After a top-level restructuring in 1970/71 the changes of September 1974 saw the rechristened "Frontier Troops of the GDR" separated from the NVA while still remaining subordinated to the Defence Ministry.

Structure, duties and frontier regulations

Supreme control, under the Defence Minister, rests with the *Frontier Troops Command* in Pätz near Königswusterhausen, to which are responsible *Frontier Command North* in Stendal, *Frontier Command Centre* in Berlin-Karlshorst and *Frontier Command South* in Erfurt. For over 15 years, up to June, 1979, the Chief of Frontier Troops was Lieutenant General Erich Peter; he was then succeeded by Major General Klaus-Dieter Baumgarten. This officer is also a Deputy Defence Minister.

Frontier Commands North and South are responsible for "State Frontier West" bordering on the Federal Republic. Each command disposes of 6 *Frontier Regiments* and 2 *Training Regiments*.

Each Frontier Regiment consists as a rule of 3 *Frontier Battalions,* and each of these has 4 *Frontier Companies.* The total establishment of a battalion is here 408 men.

In normal conditions each company is on border guard duty for 8 hours at a time over its battalion sector, which is anything from 20 to 30 kilometers long according to the terrain.

Surveillance of the GDR's coastal *Three-mile zone* is undertaken by the frontier guard forces of the *People's Navy* in Rostock. These control 4 *Groups of Vessels* with a total of 18 Kondor-type patrol boats. *The Dömitz Boat Section* (which is independent of the People's Navy) disposes on the Elbe altogether of 21 short-patrol and 3 long-patrol boats, of which 4 or 5 are on duty every day. On the Elbe, the Frontier Troops are assisted by the GDR *Water Police,* equipped with 4 short-patrol boats, of which one is a hydrofoil.

Directly responsible to the Frontier Troop Command are the 2 *Independent Regiments* on the frontiers with Poland, at Frankfurt-on-Oder, and Czechoslovakia, at Pirna.

Frontier Command Centre in East Berlin controls the regiments and units whose personnel constitute the *"Ring round Berlin".* These are 6 *Operational* and 2 *Training Regiments,* with a further special regiment responsible for the border crossing-points. The regiments belonging to Frontier Command Centre are differently structured from the others, consisting of a Staff, Staff Company, 5 Frontier Companies of 4 Platoons, each of 3 Squads, a Boat Company where appropriate, one company each for Signals, Transport and Supplies, and Engineering, and Artillery units. A *"GÜST Regiment"* (*Grenzübergangsstelle* = border crossing point) consists of 8 Companies. The 2 Training Regiments comprise Staff, Staff Company, Transport and Supplies Company, 5 Training Companies, Signals Company and Anti-tank and Mortar Sections of 3 batteries each.

The total strength of the GDR Frontier Troops is 50,000, of whom some 32,000 are in the 12 western frontier regiments, about 12,000 in the "Ring round Berlin" and about 3,000 in the People's Navy frontier forces. The total also includes training units, staffs and schools in the interior, among them the *Rosa Luxemburg Frontier Troops Officers' College* in Plauen. About 12 per cent of the personnel are officers (6,000), 16 per cent NCOs (8,000), and the 36,000 or so other ranks make up the remaining 72 per cent.

The Frontier Troops, according to the "Military Lexicon", "include various arms, special troops and services and possess maritime and airborne capabilities appropriate to their requirements"[12]. Their *weapons* include pistols, automatics, light machine guns and the RPG-7 anti-tank *Panzerfaust* – all of it equipment common to motorized infantry units. They have tractors, dozers of various sorts and earth-drills available. Their vehicles include the "*Grenztrabant*", a military version of the civilian "*Trabant*"; this is the standard vehicle for frontier patrolling. Ranks and uniforms are as in the NVA land forces, just as the Frontier Guard Units of the People's Navy, and the Boat Companies of the Frontier Commands Centre and North, share the Navy's blue uniform.

The Frontier Troops are closely associated in the areas where they operate with volunteer "*Frontier Auxiliaries*" (Grenzhelfer), "*Frontier Security Activists*" (Grenzsicherheitsaktivs), and the *People's Police*. The "Frontier Auxiliaries", numbering about 2,000 at present and including ex-members of the Frontier Troops, are controlled by their local Frontier Company. They wear civilian clothes and are distinguished by an armband printed with the words *Grenzhelfer Kodo Grenze*. They assist the Frontier Troops by monitoring the border areas, checking traffic on roads leading to the no-entry zone, identifying suspicious persons and detaining border-violators.

The "Frontier Security Activists" consist of politically trusted individuals who because of their professional or social standing are particularly suited for checking up on residents of the border areas.

The *People's Police* cooperate with the various posts of the Frontier Troops, mainly in the coordinating and organizing of border surveillance.

The "defence education" efforts of the Frontier Troops are particularly focussed on that part of the population living near the western and Berlin frontiers with the aim of mustering their support for border security measures – a process which "naturally cannot be left to its own devices"[13].

The Frontier Troops' responsibilities in the border areas have grown continually greater over the years. The following "peaceful tasks" are listed for those on the western frontier:

> – to guard frontier-sealing and security installations in their own area;
> – to prevent escapes from the GDR;

Soldier of the Frontier Troops.

- to ensure public order and safety in the border areas in cooperation with other bodies and with local residents;
- to prevent illegal border-crossing into the GDR;
- to reconnoitre the border areas;
- to deal with frontier incidents on their own initiative;
- to observe shipping inside and outside territorial waters;
- to protect fisheries in coastal frontier waters; and
- to provide military defence of the frontiers in case of war.

In this last event, they are committed to the "defence of the GDR's Western frontier" until the arrival of other forces.

The Frontier Decree of March 19, 1964, laid down comprehensive *regulations* for the various border regions and territorial waters[14], and empowered the appropriate ministers to issue orders in accordance with the special features of each region covering

- security strips, control zones and border zones;
- approach and through roads;
- registration procedures and entry and residence permits;
- special rules for closing hours, hunts, swimming, fishing, use of crossing-points and penalties for their infringement.

This decree was superseded on June 15, 1972, by a fresh order from the Minister for National Defence and the Minister of the Interior and Chief of the German People's Police[15]. This subsumes a number of regulations issued in the interim and is related to improvements in the security installations and intensified surveillance of the areas behind the border. It enables the number of escapes to be reduced by restrictions on freedom of movement among the populace and by closer observation, and hence enables the use of firearms to be curtailed. It thus imposes fresh hardships on the great majority of border residents while bringing alleviation to a small number whose homes are now excluded from the "border areas".

No special registration or entry regulations were introduced for the areas bordering on Czechoslovakia (460 kilometers of frontier) or Poland (450 kilometers).

The Order of December 30, 1961, on the Protection of the GDR Sea Frontier was re-issued in a new version by the Ministry for National Defence on March 19, 1964, to comply with international Conventions on Territorial Waters and High Seas[16]. This was also incorporated in the 1972 Frontier Order. It includes regulations of particular importance for coastal units charged with frontier protection, and deals with the coordination of fixed points for the determination of the base-line and the demarcation of territorial waters from inland sea areas.

Barriers and fortifications

The 1,378.1 kilometer long frontier between West and East Germany, whose precise course has been settled since 1974 by a joint commission representing the two territories, has been systematically converted by East Germany over the past quarter-century into a barrier equipped with a deeply zoned network of obstacles and fortifications sealing the territory off from the West.

Since the governmental order of May 26, 1952, the entire frontier and in addition since 1962 the coast of Mecklenburg and West Pomerania has been marked off with a five kilometer deep *control zone*, from which "unreliable" residents have been removed for resettlement further inland. Other residents have their identity cards stamped to confirm permission to remain there. All public events, meetings and so on within this zone have to end by 10 p. m.

Beyond this zone there still remains a *security strip* about half a kilometer wide which can only be entered with special permission at prescribed "control passing points". All inns except those run by enterprises, all cinemas, rest homes, boarding houses and hotels in the security strip have been closed. Over long distances the strip is sealed off with a fence linked in parts to an electric alarm system. In certain sectors anyone touching the fence thereby alerts Frontier Troop personnel so that countermeasures can be taken against a fugitive who is still 500 meters away from the actual frontier.

Over the past years vision over the security strip has been improved by tree-felling, earth-removal and rasing of farmsteads or hamlets, thus affording an excellent field of fire to the forces guarding the frontier on the GDR side.

At the same time *concrete walls* and *screens* about 3.3 meters high have been erected to impede any observation of buildings close to the border from the Western side.

Progress has also been made with the installation near villages and in areas difficult to keep under surveillance of powerful intermittent *searchlights*, partly linked with *acoustic alarms*, as another form of barrier. In particularly *"escape-prone"* sectors of the strip both acoustic and optical alarm systems, well camouflaged, have been installed; they are set off by *trip-wires* and incorporate very light ejectors and sawn-off pistols firing blank cartridges. At many points in the control zone, too, there are *electric alarm systems*, like those on the security strip fence, which alert the nearest frontier company when the wires are touched. Other gaps in the line are closed by the use of specially trained *guard dogs* on running leashes giving them a beat of up to 200 meters.

Particularly rapid progress has been made over the last few years in extending the concrete *convoy-path* which enables the motorized elements of the Frontier Troops to move rapidly along the border.

Between the convoy-path and a 1–2 meter wide *vehicle-barrier trench* there is a *security strip* some six meters across which is continually harrowed and kept free from weeds so as to show any tracks or footprints. The whole strip is generally checked by a patrol for signs of disturbance every day.

The final barrier, nearest to West Germany, is a *fence* whose nature is not everywhere the same. Over some stretches there still exists the double fencing

Automatic fire device fixed at the metal grid fence at the frontier facing the Federal Republic. When detonated, the 100 g explosive charge propels a total of 90 jagged iron fragments in a cone-shaped pattern.

of concrete sets and barbed wire with a *minefield* in between, as laid down after the Berlin Wall was built in 1961. Over much the greater length of the frontier, however, this has been torn down and replaced with a double (and partly mined) or, latterly, a single but higher metal *grid-fence,* furnished over long stretches with *SM 70 automatic fire and alarm devices.*

The firing elements in the system are placed at various heights on every fourth set, i.e. at ten meter intervals, on the East side of the grid-fence. They are linked with tension wires, contact with which actuates the firing mechanism and sends a signal via an electric cable to the local frontier company, which is alerted both acoustically and by a visual display showing the exact spot where some fugitive is trying to breach the barrier. The firing barrels, fixed parallel to the fence, shoot in the same direction with a certain angle of scatter, the shot consisting of numerous sharp-cornered splinters effective, much like a fragmentation-mine, up to a distance of 25 meters.

By the end of 1979 the extent of the barrier along the frontier with West Germany was as follows:

length of metal grid fence	1,281 km,
length of security strip fence	1,041 km,
length of minefields (number of mines 900,000)	292 km,
length of sections equipped with SM 70 system (number 39,300)	393 km,
length of concrete walls or screens	24 km,
length of vehicle-barrier trench	808 km,
– including concrete-lined part	551 km,
length of convoy-path	1,313 km,
– including concrete-surfaced part	1,215 km,
number of earth shelters	900,
number of observation towers, concrete	583,
number of observation towers, wooden	82,
length of dog-runs	97 km,
number of guard-dogs	996,
length of sections equipped with searchlights	271 km.

In October 1964 NVA engineer units also began constructing new fortifications along the *Berlin wall* erected three years previously, in August 1961. These were designed to rule out any escapes into West Berlin from East Berlin or the GDR. Publicized as a *"modern frontier",* the system was completed in 1970. With an average depth of fifty meters the barrier features a wall of concrete slabs along the front- edge and a deer-fence along the rear edge. By the end of 1979 this 164.1 kilometer long ring around West Berlin comprised the following:

Concrete slab wall, 3.5 to 4 meters high, armed with iron and in most places surmounted with steel tube, 102 km;

metal grid fence, 3 to 4 meters high, close-meshed and sharp-edged, toothed on top, no oblique through-view, 55 km;

vehicle-barrier trench, 3 to 5 meters wide and deep, 107 km;

security strip, average breadth 15 meters, sanded and swept to show any tracks;

front boundary of patrol area, marked as a rule in three colours on lamp standards or poles, 30 to 40 meters from frontier line;

convoy-parth – a 3 to 4 meter wide concrete or tarmac road for motorized patrols or alerted troops, 123 km;

security-trap zone with 247 observation towers, 135 shelters, 260 dog-runs or rails and numerous trip-wires actuating acoustic or optical alarm signals;

contact-fence, about 2 meters high, which switches on an observation-tower lamp when touched, 122 km;

wire-mesh deer-fence, about 2 meters high, to prevent unnecessary triggering of the alarm system on the adjacent contact-fence.

By continually intensifying frontier security measures the GDR has succeeded in reducing the volume of *attempted escapes* further and further. In 1973, 380 civilians and 28 uniformed members of the forces managed to cross the border into West Germany; by 1979 the respective figures had sunk to 74 and 12. But the fact that some escapes still succeed – like the group of eight persons who made it in September 1979 in a balloon sewn together from sheets – shows that the frontier is still not hermetically sealed.

Rewards in cash or kind, and paid leave, are offered for each case of "frustrated frontier breakthrough". Typical prizes are 200 to 300 Marks for a detachment leader and 150 to 200 Marks for a ranker, possibly with a gold-watch and one or two days' additional leave as well.

Use of firearms

Every soldier on frontier duty is required to prevent breakthroughs, if necessary by *use of arms*. Paragraph 62 of the June 1972 Frontier Decree states that "use of firearms by members of the Frontier Troops is only permitted in accordance with military regulations issued by the Ministry for National Defence." But General Hoffmann, the minister in question, told Berlin Frontier Troops on May 25, 1965:

> What you are protecting is the most humane system that history has known. We are therefore deeply convinced that your hand must never falter when you have your sights on an enemy.

Hoffmann has continued to make similar statements. An edition of his speeches and essays put out in February 1971, for example, contains this passage:

> We must ensure through our ideological work that it becomes second nature for every member of the Frontier Troops to see that any frontier-violator – in whichever direction he is trying to cross – is acting as an

enemy of our Republic or at that moment becomes an enemy in that he is deserting to the imperialist camp and thereby providing the extremists with fresh material for agitating and slandering our Republic[17].

... A soldier must realize that for friends there are control pass-points provided on the state frontier. But whoever tries to cross the border of our sovereign state illegally ... is an enemy, and will be treated as an enemy ... Exercising forbearance towards traitors means acting against the interests of the whole nation[18].

In regard to the use of arms against frontier violators the *Handbuch für Grenzsoldaten* ("Handbook for Frontier Soldiers")[19] explains:

Pursuit of frontier violators is the border soldier's most positive tactical action, aimed at their preliminary detention or destruction as the case may be.

If we turn to the NVA Service Regulations, DV-10/4, we find as No. 314 the following:

Use may only be made of firearms
a) by order of the Minister for National Defence in operations to protect the GDR;
b) by order of the commanding officer, duty sentry or patrol leader during attacks on units, guards or patrols, where the use of firearms is necessary in self-defence and other means no longer suffice, or to determine the extent of armed resistance;
c) in combat on the decision of a superior, in order to overcome open disobedience or resistance by a subordinate to the restoration of military order and discipline;
d) on the decision of guards, sentries and patrols or other temporarily or permanently armed personnel, if other means are insufficient or no longer sufficient, in order
— to prevent activities clearly aimed at treason toward the workers'-and-farmers' state; or effectively
— to prevent or deflect an immediately impending or already existing attack on installations of armed authorities and other state-owned, social or economic facilities, or on oneself or on other persons, in accordance with legal provisions relating to self-defence and states of emergency[20].

Judging by official statements and sentences passed on escapees and those convicted of abetting escape, "activities clearly aimed at treason towards the workers'-and-farmers' state" must be taken as including all attempts to escape the country. And the phrase "immediately impending or already existing attack on installations of armed authorities" covers any damage to barbed wire or alarm systems inevitably associated with an attempt at flight.

As a rule, aimed fire must be preceded by a *warning order and a warning shot*. But No. 318 of the service regulations allows *aimed fire without warning* if, for example, an immediate danger would arise for the life of third parties, for the soldier's own life, or for installations of the armed authorities or for other state-owned, social or economic facilities, which cannot be averted by other means[21].

There is a further regulation applying to frontier guard duty which has been several times modified. (DV-30/9 of 1963 came into force in a new version on May 1, 1967, only to be replaced on September 1, 1972, by Frontier Sentry Regulation DV-10/00/0/0013.) This is kept highly confidential.

According to Frontier Guard Regulation DV-30/9 the duty of a patrol is

to act as a scout, track down and preliminarily detain frontier violators and, where necessary, to take action in accordance with the regulations on the use of firearms.

In regard to concealed sentries, the regulation goes on:

the deployment and camouflage of concealed sentries must ensure surprise operation aimed at luring frontier-violators and provocateurs into ambush and denying them the possibility of armed resistance or flight.

Longwinded as the regulations about the use of arms by sentries are, at critical points the wording is remarkably vague. What precisely is meant by activity "clearly aimed at treason toward the workers'-and-farmers' state"? What is an "immediately impending attack on installations of the armed authorities" which can make "aimed fire" essential? How does one "deny someone the possibility" of flight or armed resistance? The GDR authorities have the opportunity here, and it might be said the duty, to provide definitions proof against misinterpretation and abuse, if they wish to show that their frontier control regulations are no different from those of other countries.

According to official statistics published in West Berlin on November 19, 1976, 70 persons had by that date been *killed* trying to escape across the "ring round Berlin" alone. The number of lives lost in attempts to cross the GDR's western border is harder to establish with certainty because of the greater complexity of the terrain. It is known, however, that 101 persons fell victim to automatic installations or use of force by GDR personnel on that frontier between August 13, 1961, and December 31, 1976.

According to a *Volksarmee* statement in 1976, 18 members of the GDR Frontier Troops were "victims of armed attacks and provocations on the GDR's borders with West Germany and Berlin" between August 1949 and December 1975[22]. Referring to the same period, Defence Minister Hoffmann declared: "Twenty comrades, twenty young human beings murdered by the class enemy, laid down their lives in the defence of our state frontiers!"[23]

Special features of the Frontier Troops

There are other features of frontier duty than the rigorous firing regulations which make it *unpopular in the rank-and-file,* viz.

– exhausting conditions of service with 8-hour duties day and night,
– accommodation in remote villages where the civilian residents are virtually subject to emergency laws;
– scarcity of cultural facilities, and of girls.

In a statement on the 30th anniversary of the Frontier Troops it was stressed that

> frontier service remains a particularly responsible class-duty for the working-class and all other employed persons. It is service for the well-being of the entire people, and more than ever it demands a high level of awareness, class-consciousness and willing self-sacrifice[24].

The chief problem is to find candidates who are *reliable in the official sense* and to train them in unconditional discharge of their duties when the nature of those duties affords them better opportunity to escape than any other soldiers. Ceaseless political brainwashing and uniquely strict application of disciplinary penalties are used to instil total obedience.

Thus from the moment when the first Frontier Police units were formed in November 1946 it was a matter of policy

> to throw the most experienced communists into the most complex class-struggle sectors. It is surely of more than historical interest that from the very start until now the proportion of working-class officers has always oscillated between 75 and 85 per cent[25].

As with the land, air and sea forces of the NVA, recruits for the Frontier Troops are signed on every spring and autumn but remain for the first six months in special training units. Here they are given basic military training, preliminary frontier-work training and intensive political schooling. Their political reliability is checked with particular care, by State Security agents among others. Only then are recruits assigned for normal duties to the individual frontier companies or special units such as engineers and signals.

A special officers' training school was opened in Plauen in December 1963 which, along with all others, was raised to *Hochschule* status in 1974 and became the "Rosa Luxemburg" Officers' College for the GDR Frontier Troops. In Perleburg the Frontier Troops have an NCOs College, named after Egon Schultz, which offers "frontier training" and courses in driving, signals, defence and engineering. There is a special College for Frontier Troop Ensigns in Nordhausen. Any other training required is done at the regular army schools.

Judging from the training programmes alone, the Frontier Troops can be seen to function as border-sealing and security units rather than as frontier police in the western sense.

Notes

[1] Heinz *Hoffmann*, address to graduates of the Rosa Luxemburg Frontier Troops Officers' College on August 26, 1965, in: Sozialistische Landesverteidigung, Aus Reden und Aufsätzen 1963–1970, East Berlin 1971, p. 286.
[2] Heinz *Hoffmann*, report to Frontier Troops' Commanders Conference, November 17, 1964, in: Sozialistische Landesverteidigung, v. note 1, p. 201.
[3] Taschenbuch für Wehrpflichtige, East Berlin 1965, p. 191.
[4] Das moderne Militärwesen, East Berlin 1968, p. 385 f.
[5] *Volksarmee*, 49/1976.
[6] Heinz *Hoffmann*, report to Frontier Troops' Commanders Conference, November 12, 1965, in: Sozialistische Landesverteidigung, v. note 1, p. 326.
[7] Lieutenant General E. *Peter*, Deputy Minister for National Defence and Chief of the GDR Frontier Troops, 30 Jahre zuverlässige Sicherung der Staatsgrenze der DDR, in: *Militärwesen*, Militärverlag der DDR, East Berlin, 12/1976, p. 5.
[8] Ibid., p. 4.
[9] Lieutenant Colonel *Vogt*, Über die Entwicklung der Deutschen Grenzpolizei zu einer Grenztruppe, in: *Volksarmee*, Dokumentation, November 1965, p. 20.
[10] Wilfried *Hanisch*, Militärwissenschaftliche Konferenz in Vorbereitung des 30. Jahrestages der Grenztruppen der DDR, in: *Militärgeschichte*, Potsdam, 1/1977, p. 90.
[11] Lieutenant Colonel *Vogt*, loc. cit.
[12] *Militärlexikon*, Militärverlag der DDR, 2nd ed., East Berlin 1973, p. 147.
[13] Lieutenant Colonel H. *Fritzsche*, Einige Erfahrungen aus der wehrpolitischen Erziehungsarbeit der Grenztruppen der DDR in der Öffentlichkeit, in: *Militärwesen*, 2/1979, pp. 70–72.
[14] Verordnung zum Schutz der Staatsgrenze der DDR, March 19, 1964, *Gesetzblatt* pt. II, p. 255 ff.
[15] Anordnung über die Ordnung in den Grenzgebieten und den Territorialgewässern der DDR (Grenzordnung), June 15, 1972, *Gesetzblatt* pt. II.
[16] *Gesetzblatt* pt. II, March 19, 1964.
[17] Heinz *Hoffmann*, report to Frontier Troops' Commanders Conference, November 17, 1964, loc. cit., p. 198.
[18] Ibid., p. 199.
[19] Handbuch für Grenzsoldaten, East Berlin, 1964, p. 43.
[20] Ibid., p. 41.
[21] Ibid., p. 42.
[22] *Volksarmee*, 34/1976.
[23] Heinz *Hoffmann*, 30 Jahre Schutz unserer Grenzen, Ansprache auf der Festveranstaltung zum Jahrestag der Grenztruppen der DDR in der „Volksbühne" zu Berlin, November 30, 1976, *Neues Deutschland*, December 1, 1976.
[24] Wilfried *Hanisch*, loc. cit., p. 91.
[25] Ibid., p. 90.

CHAPTER SIX

Other National Defence Agencies

In addition to the National People's Army, controlled by the Ministry for National Defence, there are numerous other agencies in East Germany which subserve the purposes of national defence including, that is to say, defence of the "socialist system". In this connection Defence Minister Hoffmann has said:

> The GDR system of national defence is a complex of multifarious agencies and institutions, conditioning and complementing one another. They include the NVA as the keystone of national defence, the territorial and civil defence forces, the instruments for the economic underpinning of defence, the social organizations for socialist military education, the command organs and much else[1].

The official Military Lexicon defines socialist national defence as "the inwardly and outwardly organized armed protection of a socialist state or coalition of states against imperialist aggression"[2].

And in respect of the GDR it states that

> national defence also includes the ensuring of domestic security, which is the responsibility of agencies of the Ministry for State Security and the Ministry of the Interior[3].

We shall deal in this chapter with

— the armed agencies of the *Ministry of the Interior,* particularly insofar as they form part of the GDR's *territorial defence;*

— the armed agencies for the *Ministry for State Security;*

— *Civil Defence;*

— the *Working Class Combat Groups* as a component of territorial defence, and

— the *Society for Sport and Technology* as a pre-military training body.

The armed agencies of the Ministry of the Interior

The Ministry of the Interior is

> the central state agency of the GDR Council of Ministers responsible along with other government bodies, particularly those concerned with jurisdiction and security, for ensuring public order and safety[4].

The Minister of the Interior since 1963 has been Colonel General Friedrich Dickel, former Deputy Minister for Defence. Born in 1913, a veteran communist and member of the SED Central Committee since 1967, a "Hero of the GDR" since 1975, Dickel is simultaneously *Chief of the German People's Police.*

The German People's Police (*Deutsche Volkspolizei – DVP*), whose members are supposed "because of their common class mission"[5] to enjoy close comradely links with the NVA and with "their Soviet comrades in the regiment 'next door' "[6], were told in 1977, the 60th jubilee of the October Revolution, that their main task was

> further to reinforce the fighting strength and combat-readiness of our units through the high quality and efficiency of the service, the continuous strengthening of its political awareness, its keen military discipline and cohesion, and thereby to show ourselves worthy of our models, mentors and friends above all in this jubilee year of Red October[7].

In a *Neues Deutschland* article written for the 1979 Day of the DVP, Minister Dickel declared:

> Our acceptance of Party leadership ensures that we do our share in shaping the socialist revolution in our country and that we successfully cope with all problems and tasks arising in the effective protection of the workers'-and-farmers' state ... Our comrades are cementing their ideological steadfastness, knowing well that their daily work is intimately connected with the worldwide class struggle in the interface between socialism and capitalism, between the alliances of the Warsaw Pact and NATO, in the arc of tension where war and peace are decided. They make their contribution to the strengthening of our system of government and society, to the enhancement of the authority of socialist state power and the furtherance of socialist justice by practising high revolutionary alertness, giving exemplary service, raising the quality and efficiency of their work and continually improving their knowledge and skill. Our People's Police take a Party-inspired and responsible view of their rights and duties, as laid down in the Law of June 1, 1968, on the Tasks and Powers of the DVP[8].

The agencies of the Ministry of the Interior, who are all subject to strict military discipline and have corresponding rank designations, include also the fire brigades and the prison service. The militia-type Working Class Combat Groups are another body responsible to the Ministry of the Interior for training, equipment, and supplies.

The police are supported by some 135,000 *volunteers* who assist it in their spare time. More than 264,000 men and women are active in the *Transport Safety Collectives,* and the number of *fire brigade volunteers* runs to about 460,000.

The Ministry runs a number of institutes for training senior cadres, with the *Karl Liebknecht German People's Police College* as the most advanced, and including the *Wilhelm Pieck Ministry of the Interior Officers' School* and the *Heinrich Rau* and *Hermann Matern Technical Schools*. Some officers also do their training at NVA institutes.

The highest control agency of the DVP in the Ministry is the Main DVP Administration *(Hauptverwaltung der DVP)*, which is in direct charge of

— the 14 DVP Regional Authorities *(Bezirksbehörden der DVP)*,
— the Wismut Karl-Marx-Stadt DVP Area Command in Siegmar-Schönau, responsible for the protection of the Wismut enterprise, and
— the DPV Presidium in East Berlin, with its 9 Police Inspectorates and 1 Waterways Police Inspectorate.

There are also 21 People's Police Alert Units *(Bereitschaften)* in battalion strength answerable, along with other formations, both to the Ministry and to the above-mentioned Commands.

People's Police Alert Units

For the army, the members of the Alert Units are "fellow-soldiers in green uniform"[9] whose Interior Ministry training, like their own, is designed to *"create political and military qualifications for optimum combat-readiness"*.

> Service in the DVP Alert Units is military service. Our men are organized in squads, platoons and companies. The training year is divided into semesters as in the NVA. There is no lack of inspections, mock-alarms and operational exercises. How often in our units do we hear the command "On with battle-dress!" All that distinguishes the "Greens" then is their dark green epaulettes and helmets[10].

The special demands put on them are described as follows:

> Operational training is daily routine. It covers tactics, firing practice — first-shot-on-target being a matter of duty — seeking out and frustrating lawbreakers, protecting premises and installations, and patrolling. In short, our comrades learn everything they need to enable them to secure public order and safety in the GDR.

With a total strength of some 18,000, the 21 Alert Units are all uniformly equipped and trained. Normally there is one Alert Unit to each of the GDR's fourteen regions *(Bezirke)*, but the key industrial regions of Leipzig, Halle and Magdeburg with their large working-class population have two Units each, while the East Berlin People's Police Presidium disposes of three, quartered in Basdorf. The government evidently has a poor opinion of the political reliability of the "workers" as defined by the communists and, particularly in view of the *17 June 1953 rising*, expects disturbances to occur primarily in these areas.

In general an Alert Unit comprises

- two motorized companies,
- one armoured personnel carrier company,
- one mortar company,
- one staff company with signals platoon, engineer platoon, chemical platoon, reconnaissance platoon, transport platoon, supply section, control section and medical section.

The Alert Units wear grey-green uniform and carry light and medium-weight infantry weapons. After their 18 months of basic service their members are often assigned to other branches of the police.

Officers do their training at the Arthur Becker Officers' College at Dresden, afterwards at the Friedrich Engels Academy. NCOs attend the Kurt Schlosser NCO School at Dresden.

Other branches of the DVP

The German People's Police are adjured to perform their function "as a defence and security agency of the people and a power-lever of the revolutionary working class" in "brotherly, fighting, cooperation with the other armed agencies of the GDR"[11]. On the occasion of their 25th anniversary in June 1970 *Volksarmee* wrote that the DVP had proved its worth in two revolutions – the *anti-fascist democratic revolution* and the *socialist* one[12].

The *Main Administration of the DVP* in the Interior Ministry includes Main Departments for the various functional branches of the police. A list of these branches shows that the DVP structure differs somewhat from Western police forces in its size and range of duties. Thus we have:

- the regular *Schutzpolizei*, the main DVP element for public duties, including Ward Commissioners *(Abschnittsbevollmächtigte)* responsible for protection of enterprises, leave arrangements etc. in their own areas.
- Traffic Police *(Verkehrspolizei)*, whose members are all charged with "ensuring the security and smooth flow of road traffic" though their various duties are indicated by such titles as Traffic Monitor, Traffic Controller, Traffic Instructor or Driving Test Examiner, Traffic Technician, Accident Inspector or Vehicle Specialist.
- Criminal Police *(Kriminalpolizei)*, responsible for the whole complex area of crime fighting and prevention. Their activities extend to every sphere of social life; they are supposed to prevent, discover, investigate and elucidate penal offences.
- The Transport Police *(Transportpolizei)* are trained in various specialities, all related to the railway system. They supervise rail passenger and goods safety as well as rail freight matters.
- Passports and Registration *(Paß- und Meldewesen)*. This branch deals with all police registration documents. Its members issue identity cards, process applications for travel abroad and monitor compliance with legal requirements for police registration.

– Volunteer police assistants *(Freiwillige Helfer der VP)*. Organized in platoons and squads, these are for the most part recruited and assembled by the Ward Commissioners mentioned previously. They assist for example in running the Commissioner's consulting periods, controlling traffic at peak hours, checking logbooks, patrolling, and various crime-prevention routines, and are active in the "social organizations". They have the authority and duty "to intervene in breaches of public order, to explain the requirements of orderly behaviour to the public and to issue warnings in cases of minor infringements of the law", but they are not empowered to pronounce penalties for breaches of order[13]. They give support in addition to the Waterways, Traffic and Transport Police.

From a military point of view the most important branch after the Alert Units is that of the *Transport Police*, whose Main Department controls Operational Companies *(Einsatzkompanien)* in each of the Transport Police Wards covering the same areas as the respective Railway Directorate Districts *(Reichsbahndirektionsbezirke)* of East Berlin, Cottbus, Dresden, Erfurt, Halle, Magdeburg, Pasewalk and Schwerin. These companies, 150 strong, are equipped with light and heavy machine guns as well as pistols, carbines, automatics and anti-tank launchers (RPG-7). They wear dark blue uniform. Service in these companies is legally equivalent to military service.

The armed agencies of the Ministry for State Security

The *Ministerium für Staatssicherheit (MfS)* is defined as "the state's central agency under the Council of Ministers for organizing defence and counter-measures against counter-revolutionary assaults on the socialist government and society of the GDR"[14].

The *Minister for State Security* since 1957 has been Army General Erich Mielke, whose association with this "special agency of the dictatorship of the proletariat"[15] goes back to 1950 when it was set up with himself as Deputy Minister. Born in 1907, Mielke has been a member of the Party Central Committee since 1950 and of its Politburo since 1971. Like Defence Minister Hoffmann and Interior Minister Dickel he was made a "Hero of the GDR" in 1975. In August 1931 this veteran communist was involved in the assassination of two Berlin police captains.

The Ministry's agencies, committed like others to "defending the workers'-and-farmers' state", celebrated its 25th anniversary on February 8, 1975, "jointly with the public"[16].

> On the basis of SED resolutions and documents, in cooperation with the other armed organizations, and relying on its firm bond of trust with the GDR public and countless unnamed underground fighters, the soldiers, NCOs, officers and generals of the Ministry for State Security and the Felix Dzierzynski Guard Regiment have waged a hard and uncompromising struggle against the enemies of peace and socialism. Inspired

by the ideas of proletarian socialism and in cooperation with all fraternal organizations of the socialist commonwealth, especially with the glorious Soviet Cheka, they have successfully and honourably fulfilled the tasks assigned to them[17].

While thus congratulating the Ministry on its 20th anniversary in 1970, the SED Central Committee simultaneously called upon it to continue its good work.

The MfS had a particularly crucial role to play at the time when the first GDR armed units were being set up, just as its Soviet equivalent had done. Since February 1957, however, when the Alert Units, Frontier Police and Transport Police passed into the control of the Interior Ministry, the only armed force at its disposal has been the Guard Regiment named after Felix Dzierzynski, founder of the Bolshevik secret police or Cheka.

This regiment, with a total strength of over 6,000 men, was set up to protect government buildings and personnel. It consists of four operational battalions, a heavy battalion and a training battalion. Training and equipment are like those of the DVP Alert Units, the latter including light tracked vehicles, armoured personal carriers, mortars, recoilless anti-tank guns and AA machine guns. Individual soldiers carry pistols, rifles or automatics. Great emphasis is put on the political reliability of the regiment, whose members serve for at least three years.

Among other MfS agencies mention should be made of the Main Administration for Reconnaissance *(Hauptverwaltung für Aufklärung)*, the main channel for espionage directed at the West German army in particular.

"Civil defence - the concern of every citizen"

Civil defence is regarded as "an inseparable part of national defence"[18], and the new Defence Law confirms the description. Its purpose is there defined as

> organizing the protection of the public, the economy, vital facilities and cultural values against the effects of military aggression and especially agents of mass destruction, and against the effects of natural catastrophes. Civil Defence also has the duty to prepare and deploy manpower for rescue, salvage and urgent repair work and to execute measures to help maintain state, economic and social activities[19].

The *Minister for Defence* is responsible for Civil Defence through the *Director of GDR Civil Defence.* This is Lieutenant General Fritz Peter, a former NVA liaison staff officer in the Warsaw Pact's Joint Command. His authority is dependent on resolutions of the *Council of Ministers,* which prescribes all basic civil defence measures at national level. These are in turn derived from resolutions of the *National Defence Council.*

The various ministers (apart from those of the armed forces), the directors of other central state agencies, the chairmen of local councils, the directors of economic bodies, industrial combines, enterprises and institutions, and the chairmen of cooperatives are all in charge of civil defence within their own spheres of responsibility.

Thus the *chairmen of local councils*, in their capacity as directors of local civil defence, are entitled to give instructions to, and require services from, other civil defence directors and members of the public within their own territory. Considerable involvement of social organizations and of all private persons is envisaged.

Compulsory service can be introduced to cope with civil defence tasks if needed, covering all men between the ages of 16 and 65 and women up to 60.

The Civil Defence Law of September 16, 1970, replaced the Air-raid Defence Law of February 11, 1958, and was superseded in turn by the new Defence Law of November 1, 1978.

Even when civil defence, however, was a responsibility under the old legislation of the Interior Minister, it was the Defence Minister who inspected its state of efficiency. Thus in March 1977 General Hoffmann held consultations with local council chairmen and civil defence directors for the region of Halle "concerning topical questions of military policy and GDR civil defence tasks in the wake of the 9th SED Conference". He praised the "outstanding performance of hundreds of thousands of employed persons" whose "work in the commands and units of civil defence" had "achieved a conspicuous improvement of efficiency"[20].

The Civil Defence personnel also fulfils some of the functions of *territorial defence*, supporting the armed forces for example by ensuring their operational freedom of movement inside the GDR. There are *Civil Defence Staffs* under military command in the country's 15 regions, 27 urban and 191 rural districts. These are manned by Civil Defence officers and NCOs, mostly recruited from the NVA, People's Police and SED officials. The strength of this active core of officers and NCOs amounts to about 3,000, but there are several hundred thousand civilians, including many women, who can be called upon.

An *Institute of Civil Defence* was set up in Beeskow in June 1979 with the status of a teaching academy. Civil Defence officers are here qualified as college instructors, while cadres from state and economic bodies and social organizations, along with honorary cadres from Civil Defence staffs and units, are given basic and advanced training at a higher level.

Priority allocations for Civil Defence construction works have been made, or at least authorized, for Party and government bodies and for the Civil Defence agencies themselves, down to district level. But shelters for the public and for industry, key locations apart, are few in number and poor in quality. No doubt shortages of material for construction generally are the main obstacle.

The Working Class Combat Groups

"The Combat Groups hold trusty watch at the side of the NVA, Frontier Troops and other armed agencies."[21] They "play an important role in civil defence as part of the home-ground forces"[22]. "As the direct *armed instrument of the working class* they have the special task of protecting enterprises and installations from diversionary forces and from any counter-revolutionary elements who might infiltrate, to guard important transport and supply facilities and so forth."[23] Their *close fraternal association with the NVA* also means that they can be used for rear security and similiar support tasks; they are reckoned with in the overall planning of the *socialist alliance* as their close contact with Soviet forces in the GDR demonstrates. In the *Waffenbrüderschaft* Warsaw Pact manoeuvres of autumn 1970, Combat Groups took part for the first time. "On the very first day they proved themselves, along with DVP Alert Units, by smashing an airborne unit dropped by 'the enemy' well behind their own defence lines."[24]

At the time they were set up in 1953, the Combat Groups – originally "Factory Combat Groups" *(Betriebskampfgruppen)* – were designed purely as *Party troops for a civil war*. Meanwhile, with more than 500,000 members, they have increasingly taken on the character of a *territorial army*, of which about a half could be called upon at any time. The motorized battalions, at least, are mobile units with their own signals and supply systems and could be deployed beyond their home areas. They have not only light infantry weapons but heavy machine guns, light and medium mortars, trucks, anti-tank rifles, anti-tank and recoilless artillery, AA machine guns, 37 mm twinbarrel AA guns and 76 mm cannons. Armoured reconnaissance and staff cars and armoured infantry cars are being continually added to their inventories.

As their full name "Combat Groups of the Working Class" implies, they correspond to the old Marxist concept of a *"working class under arms"*, and they claim to continue the tradition of various armed communist organizations in the early Weimar Republic, 1918 to 1923, and the *Roter Frontkämpferbund* of 1924 to 1933. Compared with the militias of other Warsaw Pact states the Combat Groups are of considerable military value.

According to a chronological account published by the *Institut für Militärgeschichte*, Combat Groups were from July 1953 onwards "set up in major socialist enterprises, state administrations and other institutions. They consist of volunteers organized in hundred-companies *(Hundertschaften)*, platoons and squads, and their material requirements and training are provided by the Main Administration of the German People's Police"[25].

The SED first displayed its Combat Groups in East Berlin and other cities when they joined the 1954 May Day parades, still unarmed at that time. The *Kämpfer* (Fighters), as their members were called for short, wore blue overalls with the traditional red armband of the Red soldiers in 1918. During the first years they consisted almost entirely of SED members or candidate-members. Not till about April 1954 did the Party, which approved new "fighters" and appointed their commanders, start recruiting non-Party men to cope with the shortage of suitable candidates in its own ranks. Some 10 to 15 per cent of workers and employees in state factories, administrations and other workplaces are said to belong to the Combat Groups. "Political fitness" has always taken priority over military qualifications, though the latter are likely to have been tested already through pre-military training in the Society for Sport and Technology or in conscript service.

In 1955 the Combat Groups underwent reorganization. As a Warsaw Pact member the GDR undertook "to increase defensive preparedness by enlarging the nation's armed forces". A resolution on "the organization and training of the Combat Groups" passed by the Party Politburo on May 31, 1955, declared: ". . . Within the framework of these measures the Party's Combat Groups need to be turned into an effective instrument of homeland defence . . ." Local Party leaders were adjured to remember that all Combat Groups must be operationally competent, strictly organized, armed units.

Further steps in the militarization of the Combat Groups resulted not from any exacerbation of the international scene but from *détente*, ushered in by the preparations for a Geneva conference in the spring of 1955. For in case there were East-West agreements on the scaling down of regular armies, the SED was anxious to retain a force which would not be affected, because it

Members of the "Working Class Combat Groups" being trained with a recoilless 82mm gun (RG 82mm).

would be excluded as a Party organization from international military statistics. The training, arming and operational command of the Combat Groups were accordingly entrusted, not to the NVA, but to the People's Police.

Official comments continually mention the Combat Groups in the same breath as "the lessons of recent international events". At the SED Central Committee's 29th Session of November 12 to 14, 1956, for example, following the "counter-revolutionary putsch in Hungary", it was made a Party aim to "increase the strength of the Combat Groups of the GDR Working Class, take all measures to improve its armament and equipment, and provide it with thoroughgoing training"[26]. Again, the Combat Groups played an important role during the erection of the Berlin Wall on August 13, 1961, and they were standing by when Warsaw Pact units entered Czechoslovakia in August 1968.

Another reason for the enlargement of the Combat Groups was the fact that regular garrisoned forces could only be expanded to a limited degree for *economic and manpower reasons*. The mustering of hundreds of thousands of workers and white-coloured employees into the Combat Groups who remained in their factories, collective farms, offices and so on meant that a military organization was being built up without any need for barracks, without any loss of production hours – training was always done in spare time, especially after the introduction of the five-day week in August 1967 – and without any further requirement of military or technical equipment, since use could be made of stocks already held by the People's Police or the factories. The Combat Groups, in fact, do not cost the Party a penny.

By the autumn of 1959 the Combat Groups had already reached their present level of organization.

All basic instructions and decisions affecting the Groups are made in the *SED Central Committee*. The Politburo's National Security Commission, and in matters of detail the Security Department of the Central Committee, have two lines of command to the Combat Groups:

1. through the *Interior Ministry* and its surbordinate People's Police authorities, largely in matters of training, equipment and deployment; and

2. through the *SED Regional Committees* and their District Committees for personnel and political purposes.

The *Party's First Secretaries* at district and regional level are also chairmen of the "operational directorates" *(Einsatzleitungen),* to which the commanders and commissioners of all military and police units in the district or region belong. These First Secretaries are in any case themselves in command of the Combat Groups.

The *Battalion Commanders* are appointed by the Party branch in the battalion's patron factory *(Trägerbetrieb)* subject to confirmation by the *Party's District Committee,* to which regular reports have to be rendered on training standards and operational experience. Commanders can only order deployment of units in agreement with the appropriate Party bodies.

150

"Fighters" undergoing anti-gas training.

The manpower base of the Combat Groups lies in the *factories*. Here, at their own places of work, it is much easier for Party officials to contact and keep check on individual members of the Combat Groups than it is for Party branches in residential areas to control other members of the public. The military structure of the Combat Groups only corresponds to the organization of a factory where the latter is large enough to sustain a whole unit. Otherwise several small factories will band together to run a single Combat Group unit.

The basic unit in the Combat Groups is the *Hundertschaft* (100 fighters), which like a company in the army is composed of three *platoons*, each of three *squads*. Since 1958 between three and five "hundreds" have been combined to form a *Combat Group Battalion*, whose staff comprises a Commander, a Deputy Commander for Political Work (*Politstellvertreter*), a Deputy Commander for General Duties, a Chief of Staff, a Deputy Commander for Supplies, a Weapons and Instruments Officer and two orderlies.

The *Regional Reserve Battalion* is not a battalion of reservists, but a military reserve for the First Regional Secretary of the Party. All the hundreds in these battalions are fully motorized, and their 3rd or *Heavy Hundreds* are particularly well armed and equipped.

Membership of the Combat Groups is supposed to be voluntary, and the voluntary principle was officially maintained even after the introduction of general conscription on January 24, 1962. But there are legal and other provisions for maintaining recruitment levels and reminding the *Kämpfer* of their duty.

Recruitment is in the hands of Party branches in the factories. Their committees are supposed to keep reserve lists so that as soon as one *Kämpfer* goes he can be replaced by another. By a Politburo resolution of May 31, 1955, Combat Group members have to be men between 25 and 60; younger age groups are taken into the Society for Sport and Technology. This means that for 35 years of his working life – including the five last years in the reserve, whose members can only be used in their own factories – a man is compelled, in addition to his own job and to all the other calls on his leisure which a totalitarian state can impose, to render a considerable quantity of service for what is largely an unpopular cause. On top of this he has to take part in a combat exercise almost every month.

According to the oath devised in 1959 the right to give the Combat Groups instructions pertains only to the Party and not, as the NVA oath specifies, to a state authority such as the "workers'-and-farmers' government". The text runs:

> I am willing as a Working Class Fighter to follow the instructions of the Party, to defend the German Democratic Republic and its socialist achievements at all times, weapon in hand, and to lay down my life for her. This I solemnly vow.

The Society for Sport and Technology

The *Gesellschaft für Sport und Technik (GST)* is defined as "a socialist mass organization of the GDR, whose whole activity is aimed at developing the defence-readiness and competence of the public, and particularly of the young"[27].

> Its main task is to prepare young people of pre-conscript age for their military service in such a way that they come to see this as a class duty and acquire the necessary skills in their pre-military training.
> As an integral part of the GDR's national defences the GST thereby serves as a school for preparing young people directly for their term of service in the armed forces.

The Central Board of the GST reported to the organization's 6th Congress in 1977 as follows:

> By helping to educate defence-conscious socialist patriots and proletarian internationalists, and by popularizing the concept of defence-readiness,

defence-efficiency and defence-potential maintenance among the workers and all sections of the public, the GST has turned itself into the socialist defence organization of the GDR[28].

Since the GST held its 5th Congress in 1972 nearly 200,000 young men have won its certificate *"For Pre-military and Technical Proficiency"* each year. It has provided basic training for future *army specialists*. 450,000 young people have qualified for its *Driving Permit*. Forty per cent of its *Training and Defence Sport Centres* have been set up since 1971, and in these GST members have undertaken voluntary work worth over 40 million marks[29]. It boasts 175,000 honorary officials, instructors, exercise leaders, trainers and combat umpires. Since September 1977 a large number of these, however, have received remuneration.

When this *"socialist defence organization"* was created 25 years ago it was designed, as its name suggests, to have the image of a body fostering civilian sparetime activities of a general nature. Once the U.S.S.R., however, had come out in favour of permitting "domestic national armed forces in Germany" in its note of March 10, 1972, to the Western allies, the SED introduced pre-military training. In particular the Free German Youth organization, which had in most respects followed an outwardly pacifist line, was now encouraged to promote weapons training, and its May 1955 Statutes commit all its members to "preparedness for defending peace and the homeland".

The GST, set up as a public corporation by order of the government on August 7, 1952, was charged with the pre-military training of young people of both sexes in the age groups 14 to 25[30]. The GST is also acknowledged in the Youth Law of January 28, 1974, which mentions support for the GST by state and government officials, and by teachers, as a means of preparing the young for the defence of socialism[31].

The GST takes as its model the Soviet *DOSAAF* (Voluntary Society for Cooperation with the Army, Air Force and Navy) which has 75 million members (sixty per cent of the adult population) and over 40,000 vehicles[32], and is headed by no less an officer than Alexander Pokryshkin, Marshal of the Air Force and threefold Hero of the Soviet Union.

The *Ministry of the Interior,* as the body originally responsible for setting up military units in the GDR, was also at first in charge of the GST. Both training and financial planning, however, passed into the hands of the *Ministry for National Defence* when that was created in January 1956.

With its 450,000 or so members, seventy per cent of them active ones, the GST is divided into a Central Group and 14 Regional Groups *(Bezirksverbände)* corresponding to administrative areas. There is a *Central Board (Zentralvorstand)* to execute decisions of the GST's highest body, its *Congress;* this used to convene once in four years and now does so once in five. The seat of the Central Board is at Neuenhagen near Berlin and its chairman is Colonel General Günther Teller. He and all the other senior members of the Board's secretariat are active or reserve officers of the NVA.

The *Regional Groups* in turn break down into *District Groups,* and these

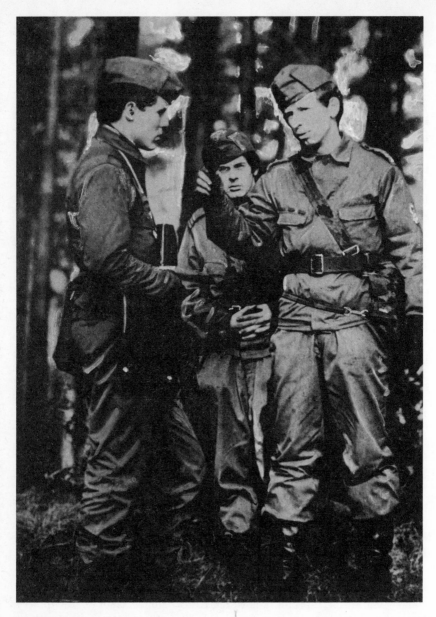

GST leaders during an exercise.

into over 15,000 *Basic Units (Grundorganisationen)* based on state-owned enterprises, collective farms, schools or residential areas.

A single basic unit may consist of a *squad (8 to 25 members), a three-squad platoon,* or one or more *"hundreds"* of three to four platoons each. The size of the basic unit depends on the number of members in the factory, school etc.

For training purposes, each unit is divided into *Sections* for the various sporting categories. At least eight members have to opt for a particular sport to entitle them to a section. Sections are also classified under *Special Disciplines; Motoring,* for example, is subdivided into *Automobile Sport* and *Motorcycling.* GST members working in small enterprises where there is insufficient support for a particular section may be able to transfer to a neighbouring unit.

Training and education are controlled by the unit's executive committee, to which up to three members per squad, five per platoon and seven per "hundred" belong, according to the sizes of the various elements.

The four-year pre-military training course run by the GST is divided into *basic training,* and *training for NVA careers.* The GST has agreements with the Central Council of the Free German Youth organization, the People's Education Ministry and the State Office for Vocational Training to "ensure effective coordination of measures in the schools and in society for the education and training of the young in the years prior to conscript service"[33].

The basic training course, covering the first year, takes in 11th grade students from the "extended secondary schools" (*Erweiterte Oberschulen)* and Special Schools, and first-year apprentices. The second year of the course is intended for second and third-year apprentices and other youngsters working in industry or on the land.

The basic training involves at least 85 hours in the year, with various competitive events on top. Training is regarded as complete when participants have taken part in at least 80 per cent of the course and have qualified in rifle-practice and in at least five disciplines out of the eight included in the *Achtertest.* They then receive the badge conferred *"For Pre-military and Technical Proficiency", Grade One.*

A small-calibre sporting gun is the main weapon used in the basic training. Along with practice in the use of this, and of airguns, instruction is also given during pre-military training in the use of hand weapons current in the NVA itself.

All GST members wear uniform, and new "GST defence sport clothing" was introduced in 1979. This consists of track suit, T-shirt and peaked cap, in a different colour for each sport.

The GST shooting-practice regulations are exactly like those in the NVA. After having the weapons explained to them, the young GST members are coached in behaviour and safety on the range, learn the various military rifle-drill movements and undergo the principal types of shooting practice – including night firing – used in NVA basic training.

The qualifying tests are usually taken during the 10 to 14 days of annual holiday at a GST training camp. Until the late fifties these were mere tented camps; now, however, they have not only training facilities but permanent accommodation with sickrooms and ambulances, canteens large enough to feed up to 1,800 trainees.

The final field tests include compass marches, obstacle courses, first aid, field cookery and various cross-country and combat events.

The course of "training for NVA careers" is a more demanding one, and its increasing importance was stressed at the GST's 6th Congress. As a result of the basic emphasis on military requirements, those sports which have little or no significance for the armed forces were taken off the GST training programme years ago – horseriding, for example, and dog and pigeon racing. Model aeroplane and model ship building, however, were retained as sources of considerable technical knowledge, though they now play only a minor role in GST activities.

GST Branches now include the following Sections, for which equipment and weapons are available:

- Shooting, with rifle and pistol;
- Motor sport, divided into Motorcycle and Automobile disciplines;
- Signals Sport, comprising radio, field telephony and telegraphy;
- Aviation Sport, comprising flying and gliding, parachuting and model plane flying;
- Naval Sport, including sailing, diving and model ships.

All the Sections hold national and even international competitions, with championship events, publicity for winning results and score tables, and old-style competitions at national level, and multi-disciplinary competitions against other Warsaw Pact military organizations at the international level.

Successful completion of this special training, which also lasts two years and is usually given to boys – and girls – between the ages of 16 and 18, brings with it the badge *"For Pre-military and Technical Proficiency", Grade Two*. Qualifications achieved are then entered by the military authorities in the trainee's military records.

Any member of the public can take a GST driving test, for mopeds at 14 and for Class 1 vehicles at 15. Those who take the NVA Careers course for army drivers can obtain the Class 5 vehicle driving license.

At its 6th Congress in Karl-Marx-Stadt, June 1977, the GST was given the Gold Medal of the Fatherland Order of Merit. Defence Minister Hoffmann, whose address was hailed as the "high point" of the Congress[34], had this to say:

> Your work can be rated "good" if a young man attends training regularly and achieves, say, "good" or "very good" marks in Defence Sports. It can be considered "excellent" if the same man does morning exercises for twenty minutes every day off his own bat, or runs obstacle courses regularly without anyone having to stand behind him every time and tell him to, but simply out of awareness and a personal need to keep himself healthy for his own sake and at the same time to make himself fit for what will be expected of him when he joins the colours.

In their Statement of Intent to the SED Central Committee, the Congress delegates undertook on behalf of the "GDR's socialist defence organization"

> to prepare the young for military service in such a way that they will see the defence of socialism as the supreme political and moral consequence of socialist patriotism and proletarian internationalism; be ready and able to prove themselves as steadfast and disciplined defenders of socialism in the ranks of the NVA and Frontier Troops of the GDR; strive for high achievements in pre-military training and defence sports; and through an attractive and varied programme of defence sports to give large numbers of the public a chance to enhance and maintain their defence capabilities[35].

Notes

[1] Das moderne Militärwesen, East Berlin 1958, p. 6.
[2] Militärlexikon, Militärverlag der DDR, East Berlin 1973, p. 201.
[3] Ibid., p. 202.
[4] Ibid., p. 261.
[5] Ibid., p. 68.
[6] Die Volkspolizei, East Berlin 4/1977.
[7] Ibid.
[8] Im Dienst der Werktätigen für Ordnung und Sicherheit, Colonel General Friedrich Dickel, SED Central Committee member, Minister of the Interior and Chief of the German People's Police, in: Neues Deutschland, June 30/July 1, 1979.
[9] Volksarmee, East Berlin 26/1970.
[10] Volksarmee, 26/1975.
[11] Volksarmee, 26/1970.
[12] Ibid.
[13] Die Volkspolizei, 6/1977.
[14] Militärlexikon, note 2, p. 261.
[15] Volksarmee, 6/1975.
[16] Volksarmee, 7/1975.
[17] Volksarmee, 7/1970. The Cheka – a Russian abbreviation for the Extraordinary Commission for Combatting Counter-revolution and Sabotage – was set up in 1917, renamed GPU in 1922, and succeeded in turn by the NKVD, MVD and KGB (Committee for State Security).
[18] Gesetz vom 16. September 1970 über die Zivilverteidigung in der DDR – Zivilverteidigungsgesetz. Gesetzblatt I, No. 20, p. 289.
[19] Gesetz über die Landesverteidigung der DDR (Verteidigungsgesetz) vom 13. Oktober 1978, II. Abschnitt, Zivilverteidigung, Gesetzblatt I, No. 35, p. 378 f.
[20] Einsatzbereitschaft der Zivilverteidigung gewürdigt, Neues Deutschland, March 26/27, 1977.
[21] Neues Deutschland, August 14/15, 1976.
[22] Militärlexikon, note 2, p. 167.
[23] Cols. Willi Effenberger and Werner Elze, Wofür du deine Waffe trägst (III), in: Der Kämpfer, Organ der Kampfgruppen der Arbeiterklasse, SED Central Committee, East Berlin, October 1968.
[24] National-Zeitung, East Berlin, October 16, 1970.
[25] Chronologie 20 Jahre Militärgeschichte der DDR (Teil I: 1949–55), in: Militärgeschichte, East Berlin 1/1969, p. 123.
[26] Chronologie 20 Jahre Militärgeschichte der DDR (Teil II: 1956–59), in: Militärgeschichte, 2/1969, p. 219.
[27] Militärlexikon, note 2, p. 133.

[28] *Neues Deutschland*, June 18/19, 1977.

[29] Ibid.

[30] *Gesetzblatt I*, No. 108, August 14, 1952, p. 712 ff.

[31] Gesetz über die Teilnahme der Jugend an der Gestaltung der entwickelten sozialistischen Gesellschaft und über ihre allseitige Förderung in der DDR – Jugendgesetz der DDR. *Gesetzblatt I*, No. 5, January 31, 1974, p. 53.

[32] *Sport und Technik*, pub. GST Central Board, East Berlin 3/1977.

[33] *Volksarmee*, 48/1969.

[34] *Sport und Technik*, note 32, 7/1977.

[35] *Neues Deutschland*, June 20, 1977.

CHAPTER SEVEN

Political Organization within the NVA

Ever since the NVA was created it has been continually repeated, in almost identical phraseology, that "the *further strengthening of the Party's leading role in the army* is a decisive precondition"[1] for the fulfilment of its military tasks. Indeed the Statutes of the SED themselves make this claim, with all that it implies in the field of organization.

> The strength of the armed agencies resides above all in the fact that they are led by the Party of Marxism-Leninism. Hence the growing role of Party organizations in all spheres of socialist national defence[2].

Again, "the principle first established by Lenin of the leading role of the Marxist Party has always been consistently applied in the GDR"[3]. As early as the First Delegates' Conference of SED Party organizations in the NVA, held in March 1956, the political executives and Party organizations of the SED were given the task of bringing their weight to bear on the ideological education of all army personnel. This notion was reflected in such Central Committee documents as the "Directives for the Work of the NVA Politorgans", i.e. political executives, issued on May 21, 1957, and the "Instructions for the Work of SED organizations in the NVA". On January 18, 1958, there followed the Politburo resolution "On the Role of the Party in the NVA". As a result of these directives

> a system of political leadership and organization had been set up in the NVA by the late fifties which ensured the implementation within it of the Party's leading role. The system was based on a Party structure which measured up, not only to the military requirements of peacetime service, but to the complex demands of war and armed combat[4].

Over the years the Politburo has repeatedly, and often in detail, concerned itself with the aims and organization of political work in the armed forces. In December 1976, for example, the Politburo put out "instructions for the executive Political organs *(Politorgane)* and SED Party basic organizations *(Parteiorganisationen)* in the NVA and the GDR Frontier Troops".

> This new edition incorporates not only requirements arising from resolutions of the SED 9th Congress, in particular from the Programme and Statutes approved by it, but also experience derived from political work among the NVA and GDR Frontier Troops as well as among the fraternal armies, especially the Soviet Army[5].

The "key factors in the Party's leading role in our armed forces", as Defence Minister Hoffmann put it[6], were described at the 1976 9th Congress by Secretary General Honecker as follows. This role, he explained,

> depends on clear guidance by the Central Committee, on the growing vigour of the Party organizations and on the example set by communists with in the military units, as well as on skilled leadership by commanders and Politorgans[7].

The effectiveness of the Party's work, Hoffmann said in the following year, must "to an increasing degree" be measured by its *real influence on all aspects of command*, viz. by the way the Party helps

- to reinforce individual leadership,
- to analyse in depth what has been achieved in education and training,
- to understand and implement troop leadership as socialist leadership of human beings, and
- attentively to assess the effects of commanders' decisions on the thinking and behaviour of the soldiers[8].

In order to exercise its claim to leadership in the NVA, the SED has created a complicated apparatus which guides and controls every soldier via four different channels:

- the Politorgans,
- the Party organizations,
- the Free German Youth organization (FDJ), and
- SED officials within the officer corps.

The "Politorgans" in the NVA

The highest NVA Politorgan is the Main Political Administration *(Politische Hauptverwaltung*, PHV). This was set up by the first Party directive of May 21, 1957, originally as the *Politische Verwaltung*. It controls a large network extending from the *Defence Ministry* down to company level, both horizontally and vertically throughout the whole army. Within the Ministry is has the authority of a Party Central Committee Department and, as such, is directly responsible to the Central Committee.

It is headed by a Deputy Minister for Defence, who since January 1979 has been Colonel General Heinz Kessler, till then chief of the NVA Main Staff and (like Admiral Verner, his predecessor in the years 1959 to 1979) a Central Committee member.

Right: Colonel General Heinz Kessler (above), Chief of the NVA's Main Political Administration, and Admiral Waldemar Verner (below), his predecessor until January 1979.

The PHV is charged with the *direction of all political work within the NVA*. This includes on the military side the coordination of political task-formulation, political education of the army and Party schooling of SED and FDJ members, the boosting of military morale, verification of compliance with orders, involvement in all personnel matters and keeping cadre files.

The chief agent of political work and director of the politorgans is the *Political Officer (Politoffizier)*, an offshoot of the tradition of *Red Army commissars*. During the Russian Civil War of 1917 to 1921 the commissar had a higher status in the units of the "Red workers' and peasants' army" than the military specialist, who had usually served in the tsarist forces. At a later stage commissars and commanders were put on an equal footing, until in 1942 the commissar was downgraded as a *Deputy Commander for Political Affairs* and made clearly subordinate to his *commanding officer*.

Following the February 1955 appointment of Marshal Zhukov as Soviet Defence Minister, and the 20th Party Congress of the year after, the standing of Party cells in the Soviet army was reduced and the untrammelled authority of commanding officers in all spheres re-emphasized. Since that time the principle of individual command *(Einzelleitung)* has been adhered to.

The GDR's army, relatively young as it is, has undergone similar vicissitudes, especially since the number of *ex-Wehrmacht officers* in the NVA during its first years was comparable with the proportion of ex-tsarist officers in the Soviet forces – a topic increasingly taboo in NVA propaganda and historiography.

Up to 1961 political officers were trained at the Berlin-Treptow *Politschule* in the following manner for the job of giving political instruction and keeping an eye on both men and officers.

Volunteers for the political officers' course were given purely political instruction for three years, and had military crash courses in the officers' schools of the service they were intended for. Officers promoted from the ranks would be given two years training at Treptow to become political officers and then, after several years' service in the ranks, would be recalled to Treptow for their qualifying courses.

In an effort to make the Politorgans more effective, the tasks of political officers were from 1961 assigned only to officers who had satisfactorily completed their service in the ranks. The separate preliminary training thus appeared superfluous, and was replaced by specialists' courses.

In view of new requirements, however, the *Politschule* was soon reopened. On March 3, 1970, the "Defence Ministry School for Further Training of Political Cadres" was promoted with the title of *"Wilhelm Pieck Military-Political Academy"*. To mark the occasion Defence Minister Hoffmann gave its staff the task of

> training political officers capable of independently grasping the spirit of Party resolutions and basic military documents, creatively deducing from them the needs of their daily work in ideological education, and ensuring

the full effectiveness of the system of ideological work in their own area of activity. Graduates of this Academy should excel in such paramount socialist soldierly virtues as boldness and courage, fight selflessly to fulfil the tasks assigned them and set an example both in their personal and their army life[9].

With the new emphasis on comradeship-in-arms with the Soviet Army, brought about by the crisis that followed the August 1968 occupation of Czechoslovakia, political work in the NVA was in many ways aligned directly with that in the *Soviet Army*. A programme of joint measures was signed in January 1971 by Admiral Verner as head of the NVA Main Political Administration, and by General Maltsev as head of the identically-named body in the Soviet Forces Group in Germany[10]. It was proposed not merely to cooperate on special occasions but to organize "exchanges of experience" between Party and youth officials in the two armies, and such agreements have since become a routine affair.

In June 1978 the "exchanges of experience" between the politorgans of the GDR and Soviet forces were enlivened by a visit to the GDR from a delegation of the *Main Political Administration of the Soviet Army and Navy,* led by its head, Army General Alexei Yepishev. For several days the Soviet officers inspected units and instruction centres of all parts of the NVA and made themselves "fully familiar with the responsible work of politorgans, Party cells and FDJ organizations in the NVA"[11]. As the weekly *Volksarmee* wrote:

> Our partners in the discussions stressed continuous education of army personnel in the spirit of socialist patriotism and proletarian internationalism as an urgent topic for ideological work[12].

The Soviet delegation leader is said to have been very critical after this inspection of political work in the NVA. There were, of course, no public reports of this, but it can be guessed that his criticism was directed at the insufficient relevance of political work to military preparedness. It is not clear whether the replacement of the 64-year old Admiral Verner as head of the HVP by the 58-year old Colonel General Kessler was connected with this, or was really due to "reasons of health"[13]. However, it is significant that none of the generals with years of political service behind them was chosen to succeed Verner, whereas Kessler, though as one of the founders of the FDJ he must always have been interested in political matters, had been primarily responsible for "combat-preparedness" both as Chief of the Air Force/Air Defence and then as Chief of the NVA Main Staff.

The PHV is divided into *Departments* and *Subdepartments,* of which the most important in its range of functions is the Propaganda and Agitation Department. It also features a *Party Control Commission* and a *Party Auditing Commission* with between 11 and 13 members each, nominated by the head of the PHV subject to confirmation by the Central Committee's *Zentrale Parteikontrollkommission* and *Zentrale Parteirevisionskommission* respectively.

The Director of the Party Control Commission (PKK), though responsible to the head of the PHV, has direct contact with the Party's central PKK and with the Commissioner of the State Security Service.

The PKK itself is responsible for

- conducting all Party proceedings against Party members of Commander or similar rank, and against members of politorgans;
- supervising subordinate PKKs;
- supervising compliance with Party statutes;
- monitoring fulfilment of Party resolutions, and
- observance of the Party's general policy.

The Defence Ministry's *"Administration 2000"*, which liaises with the *State Security Ministry,* keeps an eye on the entire NVA including the PHV and its agencies. The activity of the PHV, again, is not restricted to the NVA, since it maintains numerous links with other government and Party offices.

Worthy of special mention is the Defence Ministry's "Independent Department" *(Selbständige Abteilung).* This receives instructions from the head of the PHV and is responsible for agitation in, and infiltration into, West Germany. Its targets are servicemen, young people liable to conscription and ex-members and officers of the *Bundeswehr;* in former years it was particularly aimed at veterans' associations.

To carry out its NVA work down to company level the PHV controls a network of

- Political Administrations *(Politverwaltungen)* in the various Military Regions and in the Command offices of the land, air and sea forces, the Frontier Troops and Civil Defence organization; and
- Political Departments or Deputies for Political Work in the military units, training schools and other bodies.

The politorgans are not elected by anyone; they are simply set up on the recommendation of the head of the PHV and the directors of the lower political administrations of the Military Regions *(Militärbezirke),* People's Navy, Air Force/Air Defence, Frontier Troops and Civil Defence.

The Directors of Political Administrations in Military Regions and equivalent levels are simultaneously Deputy Chiefs for Political Work there. They are also First Secretaries in the Executive of the respective Party District in the NVA. The Deputy Directors of Political Administrations, in turn, are Second Secretaries in the corresponding Party body.

Directors of Political Departments in units, training schools etc. are Deputy Commanders of those bodies; they are also First Secretaries of SED District Executives, while their Deputies are Second Secretaries.

Numerous officers are employed in the political Subdepartments, with the functions of

- Director of the Political Department,
- Deputy Director of the Political Department,
- Senior Instructor for Party Work,

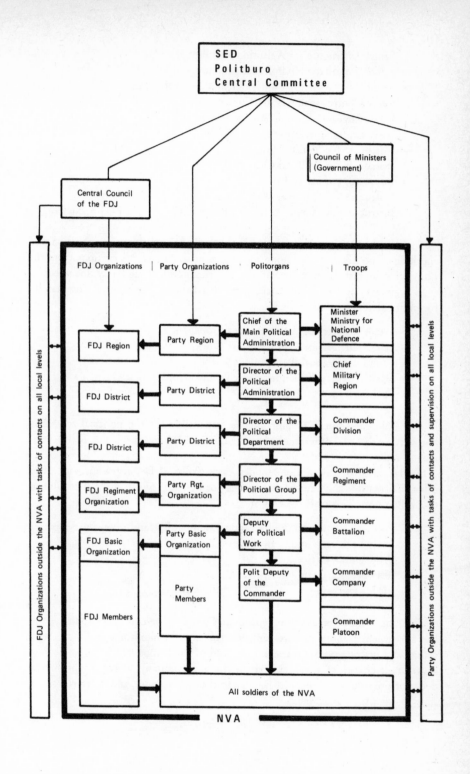

- Senior Instructor for Agitation and Propaganda,
- Senior Instructor for Political Schooling,
- Senior Instructor for Political Schooling in the Ranks,
- Party Control Commission Chairman,
- Party Revision Commission Chairman,
- Assistant for Youth Problems (FDJ),
- Instructor for Youth Work,
- Instructor for Political Cadres,
- Instructor for Party Information,
- Instructor for Cultural Mass Work,
- Instructor for Personnel Record Keeping (Party and FDJ documents).

The job of a Political Department is primarily to supervise the execution and checking of political work among the troops according to instructions from the Political Administration of its Military District, and to issue Party documents.

In regiments and the equivalent, there is a Deputy Regimental Commander for political Work, assisted by a

- Senior Officer for Agitation and Propaganda,
- Senior Officer for Cultural Mass Work,
- Club Leader and Librarian,
- SED Secretary (full-time, elected), and
- FDJ Secretary.

This Political Deputy Commander is responsible for the political schooling not only of NCOs, other ranks and SED and FDJ members, but of his regimental fellow-officers too.

Similar, each Battalion Commander has a Political Deputy who, with three other officers to assist him, is responsible for political work in the battalion or equivalent unit. This staff consists of

- Political Deputy to the Battalion Commander (and immediate superior in charge of every soldier in the unit),
- Propaganda Officer,
- SED Secretary (full-time, elected), and
- FDJ Secretary.

The Commander of every independent Company or equivalent unit, again, has a Political Deputy to give him political advice, monitor compliance with orders and instructions, and check the mood of the troops. He is the immediate superior in charge of each serviceman. In any company whose establishment does not provide for a Political Deputy to the Commander, the latter is responsible for that function himself.

SED Party Organs in the NVA

In addition to the military politorgans imposed from above, and the local civilian Party executives who watch over the execution of Party resolutions by units stationed in their area, soldiers and above all officers are under the surveillance of the pseudo-democratic *Party organizations,* and analogous *FDJ organizations, inside the NVA* itself. By as early as 1956 some 99.2 per cent of all officers, 42.8 per cent of NCOs, 7.2 per cent of other ranks and 37.7 per cent of the army's civilian employees were members or candidate-members of the SED[14].

In the GDR's virtually one-party system the SED is entitled to have organizations in the armed forces, whereas the other, puppet, parties enjoy no such right[15].

The NVA organizations are charged with *schooling all servicemen* – not only SED members and candidates – in politics and ideology on Marxist-Leninist lines. They also have the duty to encourage Party members and candidates in the conscientious fulfilment of their purely military tasks. They have to exert influence on the Marxist-Leninist education, and the theoretical military training, of officers and to monitor their effectiveness. They have the right to make suggestions to commanders on training and education, and on the choice and promotion of new officers.

NVA Party organizations derive their legitimacy from the Party Statutes, where in the 1976 version we read:

> Party organizations in the NVA, Frontier Troops, German People's Police and railway personnel work to special instructions confirmed by the Central Committee.
> Their Political Departments and Executives are obliged to maintain close contact with local Party Executives[16].

In December 1976, for example, the Central Committee issued instructions on the need to implement resolutions of the Party's 9th Congress.

Immediately below the *Central Committee* itself stands, in the hierarchy of Party organizations in the army, the Defence Ministry's *Main Political Administration.* This carries the equivalent authority of a Party Regional Executive and, as such, directs all Party activities in the NVA.

Following a Party directive of November 1963 aimed at "strengthening the collective principle in consultations about basic questions of Party work in the NVA" a *Secretariat* was set up in the Main Political Administration[17]. Its First Secretary is at the same time head of the Administration, an arrangement which ensures the unity of the politorgans working on military lines, and the army's Party organizations working on SED lines.

At levels below *Party Region,* the army's SED organizations are classified as *Party Districts, Party Basic Organizations (Parteigrundorganisationen)* and *Party Groups.*

Examples of Party Districts are the organizations in the Defence Ministry, the Political Administrations of the two territorial Military Regions and equivalent agencies of the Commands of the various services, and Political Departments in the NVA's units, training schools and the like.

The most important Party organizations in the NVA, where the grassroots activity occurs, are the three thousand and more *Party Basic Organizations*.

The establishment of a Party Basic Organization requires confirmation by the appropriate Politorgan. The Executives of these organizations, subject to some important qualifications, are elected by the members. Before an election, candidates for positions on the Executive must be checked by a Party Control Commission. Party organizations of staffs, units and other bodies with several basic organizations hold delegates' conferences or members' meetings where they elect for a two-year period a Central Party Executive *(Zentrale Parteileitung – ZPL)* which ranks above the unit Basic Organizations, and reports both to the conferences or meetings, and to the superior Politorgans.

This arrangement, laid down in a Party directive of November 14, 1967, was intended to establish clearer relationships between the various Party organizations and the Politorgans.

As far as possible, *Party executives* are expected to include the appropriate *commanding officers*. Where a commanding officer or his Political Deputy does not enjoy the "confidence" of the Party organization in question, its Executive can request the Executive at the level above it to procure his removal. In practice this is only likely to happen if the officer in question is due to be replaced anyway and the Executive is given a tip-off from higher up.

A serviceman can only join the Party basic organization in his own unit. The basic organization decides after a year's probation whether a candidate is finally accepted; if so, according to SED Statutes he has all the rights and duties of a Party member except that of voting or being elected. Once a full member, he has virtually no means of leaving the Party.

Party dues amount to anything between a half and three per cent of a member's income or pay. In the NVA Party members are expected to show exemplary behaviour by Party standards and to *achieve military standards above the average*. If they get into trouble, members must reckon with Party punishment as well as military proceedings. Party sanctions, in order of increasing severity, are classified as reprimands, severe reprimands, and expulsion from the Party. Penalties for minor offences are classified as "criticism by fellow members", "disapproval" and "warning" – all regarded as devices for "Party education". No penalties take effect, however, until confirmed by the relevant Party Control Commission or, in the case of expulsion, by the Commission at one level higher.

Party proceedings against officers of the rank of battalion commander or deputy commander upwards are normally carried out by a Party Control Commission.

In practice, any military offence by a Party member can be treated as a violation of Party discipline as well.

Free German Youth Organizations in the NVA

The third channel by which SED policies are brought to bear on young servicemen is via the *Freie Deutsche Jugend (FDJ)* organizations, to which about 80 per cent of them belong. As the state's youth organization, the FDJ serves exclusively the *interests of the Party* to which it is beholden. The *SED Statutes* state:

> As the GDR's socialist youth organization, the FDJ is the active assistant and fighting reserve of the Party.
> It helps the Party in its communist training of the young in the spirit of Marxism-Leninism, socialist patriotism and proletarian internationalism.
> It recruits the young for conscious and active participation in forming an advanced socialist society, defending the GDR as their socialist fatherland and creating conditions for the gradual transition to communism[18].

And again:

> The FDJ acknowledges the leading role of the Party of the working class.

Or as the *Statutes of the FDJ* itself put it:

> The FDJ works under the leadership of the SED and regards itself as the Party's active assistant and fighting reserve[19].

These Statutes repeat in detail the obligations of FDJ organizations in the services. They have to observe both the Statutes of the FDJ and any special instructions confirmed by its Central Council *(Zentralrat)*. And it is their duty to educate "all servicemen who are not FDJ members into being socialist patriots and proletarian internationalists in accordance with their military oath"[20] .

Further obligations are as follows:

> FDJ organizations in the armed services will maintain close links with local branches in the neighbourhood. They will give these branches special support in socialist defence education for the young. They will regard it as a prime task to imbue young servicemen with a willingness, once their active service is over, to work in key sectors toward the creation of an advanced socialist society and to be active both in the socialist defence education of the young and as honorary instructors in the Society for Sport and Technology[21].

In its directive of November 5, 1963, the SED Central Committee called for the creation of "youth commissions" in the politorgans. These are intended to help the Party Executives

> to guide FDJ organizations in the NVA in encouraging the initiative and activity of FDJ members and other young servicemen, to give them more responsibility and to lead them toward exemplary fulfilment of all tasks

designed to ensure a constant high level of combat-readiness and toward the acquisition of first-rate political, military, scientific/mathematical and technological qualifications[22].

From battalion level upwards there are officers in the politorgans who deal with youth questions on a full-time basis.

Among the SED agencies which have their fingers in the NVA mention must be made of the *NVA Trade Union Organization,* which embraces thousands of the NVA's civilian employees. Its officials work closely with commanders, directors, politorgans and Party organizations. A typical resolution passed at a delegates' conference of NVA trade union organizations declared in brief:

> All out for continual strengthening of the NVA's fighting power! All out for its permanent combat-readiness[23]!

SED officials in NVA officers' uniform

The question of who gives orders in the NVA, the military commander or the politofficer – the *politruk,* as his Soviet equivalent is called – was settled long ago. The commanding officer is responsible both for military decisions and for "political work". On various occasions Defence Minister Hoffmann, when defining the "leading role of the Party in the forces", has laid paramount stress on the importance of the commander.

> The leading role of the Party in the armed forces requires and signifies, quite consistently, the unconditional implementation of individual leadership as the unity of political and military command[24].

Hoffmann sees the training of commanders as "individual leaders" *(Einzelleiter)* in these terms:

> True, our commanders who took charge of newly-created units when the NVA came into being were loyal members of the Party of the working class. Yet hardly any of them at that time had the requisite practical experience, or theoretical knowledge, for socialist troop leadership. Yet to be a commanding officer in a socialist army means to act and make decisions as a political official responsible to the Party of the working class, and as a military specialist at the same time. It means possessing undivided right of command and responsiblity over hundreds or thousands of class comrades, having the right to decide on one's own – but also the duty to consult with the collective and to respect its opinion. Our commanders had first to learn all this, and to impart it to their subordinate officers. By upholding them in their efforts to see all commands unconditionally obeyed and strict military discipline and order maintained, Party members helped to reinforce the authority of their

commanders; they implemented, and continue to implement, the leading role of the Party as the source of effective fighting power.

Party political workers, even when they have officer rank, have thus retreated to an increasing extent into the role of assistants vis-à-vis their commanding officers. As Hoffmann put it in 1977:

> In the past training year, and particularly since the 9th SED Congress, Politorgans, Party and FDJ organizations have carried out intensive political work. During this period they have had extensive experience and gained many new insights.
>
> One of the most important of these, I think, is that it has proved very valuable to tighten the relationship between ideological work in all its forms and methods, and military life, and to be even more consistent in putting them to the service of effective fighting strength and combat-readiness[25].

A year later, Hoffmann was saying:

> Our officer cadres and politorgans, our Party and FDJ organizations, must devote most of their time and the best of their efforts to increasing the fighting strength and combat-readiness of our units, to creating confidence in our Party, government and military leaders, creating awareness of the victory of our just cause[26].

For in the last resort, politorgans and Party organizations in the NVA are of value only to the extent that they can win the troops over in a human sense.

> Most of our Party organizations and groups are ideologically consolidated Party collectives. From their theoretical political grounding – and in the case of older comrades from their Party experience too – their members are fully qualified to fulfil the tasks before us, collectively and well. What we still need more of is radiated power, impact on the masses by Party organizations and by veteran communists. That is the underlying sense of the Politburo resolution of May 18, 1977, on forthcoming tasks for the Party's political mass-work. And that is also the decisive requirement, so that the influence of Party organizations can be enhanced in all spheres of military life[27].

The effectiveness of political agencies in the NVA can only be assessed in a broader context, viz. whether the SED leaders can succeed, under the conditions of greater freedom of information as accepted by both West and East since the Helsinki Final Act of 1975 – conditions rendered unavoidable by the continuous improvement of communication techniques – in training the kind of officials who possess enough human "radiation" to win unconditional receptiveness for all the Party's demands. The hectic activity of the Politorgans in recent times, albeit oriented as far as possible now to the narrow field of "realities" – such as "combat-readiness" and "economic underpinning" – shows that the leaders of the SED are at least able to read signs of the times.

Notes

1 Beschlüsse und Dokumente der 14. ZK-Tagung und der Berliner Konferenz im Mittelpunkt einer Kommandeurstagung der NVA, in: *Volksarmee,* East Berlin, 52/1970.

2 Programm der SED, in: Protokoll der Verhandlungen des IX. Parteitages der SED, May 18 to 22, 1976, vol. 2, East Berlin 1976, p. 257.

3 Toni *Nelles,* Der Aufbau und die Entwicklung der NVA – schöpferische Anwendung des Leninschen Militärprogramms durch die SED (I), in: *Zeitschrift für Militärgeschichte,* East-Berlin, 1/1970, p. 29.

4 Gerhard *Lux* and Toni *Nelles,* Der Aufbau und die Entwicklung der NVA – schöpferische Anwendung des Leninschen Militärprogramms durch die SED (II), in: *Zeitschrift für Militärgeschichte,* East Berlin, 6/1970, p. 664.

5 Major General H. *Brunner,* Für weitere Fortschritte in der Qualität unserer Parteiarbeit, in: *Militärwesen,* East Berlin, 3/1977, p. 5.

6 Heinz *Hoffmann,* Aus dem Referat zur Auswertung des IX. Parteitages der SED vor dem Parteiaktiv der Landstreitkräfte der NVA, June 28, 1976, quoted in H. *Hoffmann,* Sozialistische Landesverteidigung, Aus Reden und Aufsätzen 1974 bis 1978, Militärverlag der DDR, East Berlin 1979, p. 366.

7 Erich *Honecker,* Bericht des ZK an den IX. Parteitag der SED, May 18, 1976, Reden und Aufsätze, vol. 4, East Berlin 1977, p. 475.

8 Heinz *Hoffmann,* Wir verwirklichen die Beschlüsse des IX. Parteitages, *Militärwesen,* January 1977, reprinted in Heinz *Hoffmann,* Sozialistische Landesverteidigung, v. note 6, 1979, p. 403.

9 *Volksarmee,* 10/1970.

10 Do. 2/1971.

11 Do. 28/1978.

12 Ibid.

13 *Volksarmee,* 3/1979.

14 Lieutenant Colonel G. *Lux,* GDR Institute of Military History, Die Entwicklung des Aufbaus der Politorgane und Parteiorganisationen der SED in der NVA, in: *Militärwesen,* 6/1974, p. 77.

15 In addition to the SED there are four other parties in the GDR, all explicitly acknowledging the "leading role" of the SED, viz. the Christian Democratic Union, the Liberal Democratic Party of Germany, the National Democratic Party of Germany and the Democratic Farmers' Party of Germany.

16 Statut der SED, Abschnitt IX, Die Parteiorganisationen in der NVA, den Grenztruppen, der Deutschen Volkspolizei und im Eisenbahnwesen, in: Protokoll der Verhandlungen des IX. Parteitages der SED, loc. cit., note 2.

17 Quoted from Lt. Col. G. *Lux,* loc. cit., note 14, p. 78. (Party Directive of November 5, 1963, p. 17).

18 Protokoll ... loc. cit., note 2.

19 Statut der Freien Deutschen Jugend, in: *Junge Generation,* East Berlin 7/1976, p. 100.

20 Ibid., p. 115.

21 Ibid.

22 Lt. Col. G. *Lux,* loc. cit., note 14, p. 78.

23 3. Delegiertenkonferenz der Gewerkschaftsorganisationen der NVA, in: *Volksarmee,* 23/1970.

24 Heinz *Hoffmann,* Unsere Errungenschaften sind zuverlässig geschützt, in: *Einheit,* September 1974, quoted in Heinz *Hoffmann,* Sozialistische Landesverteidigung, loc. cit., note 6, 1979, p. 60.

25 Heinz *Hoffmann,* loc. cit., note 8, p. 399.

26 Heinz *Hoffmann,* Ideologische Probleme zur Sicherung hoher Kampfkraft im Ausbildungsjahr 1977/78, *Militärwesen,* January 1978, quoted in Sozialistische Landesverteidigung, loc. cit., note 6, p. 527.

27 Ibid., p. 531.

CHAPTER EIGHT

The Supply System of the NVA and the Economic Support of National Defence

The NVA has no term fully comparable to *logistics*[1], as used in NATO, embracing all military supplies and infrastructure. But the ground is adequately covered in other language. Thus the system of supply, *Versorgung*[2], is seen as that part of the material underpinning which deals on a continuous basis with the planning, procurement, stocking, issuing and auditing of matériel. The various types of supply are ensured by service units of the arms, special forces and rear services and are functionally subdivided into munitions supply, fuel-and-lubricant supply, food supply and clothing-and-equipment supply.

While *Supplies* are largely the responsibility of the NVA leadership, the *Economic Support of National Defence (Ökonomische Sicherstellung der Landesverteidigung)* is a top-priority function which, as a key element of national defence in general, belongs par excellence to the political leadership, i.e. to the supreme organs of the Socialist Unity Party of Germany and those of the East German state. This function is exercised in the economic and military spheres alike and includes the following important elements:

— military-economic planning as a component of overall social planning, and hence in particular of the military and economic planning required by a socialist state or a socialist alliance;

— scientific and technological research and development of direct or indirect relevance to defence;

— production of goods for defence purposes;

— procurement of military equipment and its delivery to the forces;

— military-economic stockpiling;

— organizing and executing the industrial implementation of military technology;

— provision for military transport and communications;

— military construction works;

— military-economic measures in the financial, agricultural, commercial and other fields;

— maintenance of the efficient functioning of key sectors of the economy in time of war[3].

Both the NVA supply system and the economic support of national defence are far more closely tied up with the civilian economy than in western countries, because of the totalitarian nature of the state and the centralized planning and management of the economy. A further reason, however, is that the technology required and used by the forces "is often similar or identical in its make-up and function from that employed in manufacture and other social spheres, albeit with a different social purpose"[4]. Nowadays, we read, there "hardly exists a single sector or branch of the economy which is not directly or indirectly related to the defence of the country"[5]. It becomes "ever more apparent that combat-readiness depends to an increasing degree on economic preconditions. The revolution in military methods requires of society an ever greater outlay on modern arms and equipment and the products of the economy"[6]. In education and training too, then, military-economic exercises are accorded precedence, along with politics and ideology, before general military instruction[7].

Legal framework and organization

Central responsibility for defence and security measures belongs to the National Defence Council "in pursuance of the laws and decisions of the People's Chamber and of the decrees of the Council of State"[8]. The same applies to the "economic support".

The new Defence Law of 1978, referring to the tasks of the economy, states:

(1) The economy shall be so managed and planned as to provide an economic underpinning of the national defence at all times.
(2) Ministers and heads of other central institutions of the state, and chairmen of local councils will prepare for the conversion of the economy in accordance with central decisions to meet the requirements of the defence situation and will implement it when so instructed[9].

An analogous passage in the Five Year Plan Law 1976 – 1980 for the development of the GDR economy runs as follows:

The tasks of general economic support of national defence, and of domestic safety and order, are an integral part of the socialist state's economic policy. By meeting them the GDR makes a valuable contribution towards the defensive strength and military protection of the community of socialist states, and to guaranteeing peace. State and leading economic institutions will firmly incorporate the resultant tasks in their management and planning[10].

The body with paramount responsibility for elaborating the pronouncements, regulations and decisions of the National Defence Council for the economic support of national defence is the State Planning Commission, working closely with the GDR Research Council and the specialist ministries in the various economic sectors. The State Planning Commission includes a Special Department for the NVA, headed by a general who is one of the Commission's vice-chairmen.

In its executive function of securing adequate supplies of weaponry, technology, equipment, and goods to the NVA, the Defence Ministry reaches into every detail of the economy. The NVA representatives in the factories, the

174

Militärabnehmer, have considerable authority. Quality-checking is one of their chief tasks. Factory managers are under a general obligation to create and maintain conditions for the fulfilment of any requirements laid down by the military customer.

During a "defence situation" or defence readiness exercises, "contributions will be made by national and economic bodies, industrial groups, factories, institutions and cooperatives in accordance with planned expenditure, including the use of basic resources"[11]. In preparation for such contributions "information can be required, and obligations set out, at any time to ensure that items which might be requisitioned will be in the condition desired"[12].

The provisions of this Defence Law with its scope for mobilizing every enterprise into arms production even in peacetime mean that the GDR has achieved precisely that "militarization of the economy" which its party propagandists often impute to the West. The definition of that phenomenon given in the East German *Militärlexikon* could well be applied to its country of origin:

> Militarization of the economy embraces all sectors (industry, agriculture, construction, transport and communications, trade, traffic) and involves not only arms manufacture but such things as
> – structural and proportional changes throughout industry;
> – orientation of research and development to warlike purposes;
> – expansion of the state-monopoly apparatus of direction and control to meet the needs of a war economy[13].

Organization of supply within the NVA

The NVA's overall supply system is organized on Soviet lines. Ultimate responsibility lies with the Defence Minister. Within the Ministry, the subordinate commands of the service arms and the various staff levels responsibility is split into two areas:

– The Deputy Defence Minister and *Head of Technology and Weaponry* is also in charge of military Research and Development and central procurement. Supplies for special arms and services, such as artillery and rocket troops, armour, motor transport, chemical services, engineers, construction etc., fall to the Chiefs of Administrations for Special Arms and Services, who are likewise directly answerable to the Minister.
– The Deputy Defence Minister and *Head of Rear Services* is in charge of general supplies, such as fuel, equipment and clothing, foodstuffs and sanitation.

The supply offices of the rear services and the special supply services of the arms are subdivided down to the staffs of lower commands as far as battalion level.

Great attention is paid to the rear services. In March 1979 the late Head of Rear Services in the NVA, Lieutenant General Helmut Poppe, quoted a saying of the Soviet Marshal Bagramian, based on his World War II experiences: "The rear services are half the victory and a bit more!"[14]

General Poppe had this to say of the rear services' functions:

> Their sphere of activity extends from the physical comfort of the troops and their provision with uniforms and equipment to the uninterrupted supply of fuel and lubricants, the proper maintenance and repair of all kinds of arms and equipment, the smooth running of military transport, medical welfare and purchasing. It is the soldiers of the rear services who, in the most severe conditions, furnish our men with whatever they need for victorious combat ...
> Every new weapon naturally requires a more and more complex system of supply and servicing. The rear services, then, will remain as indispensable as ever. It is up to them, with minimum use of personnel and resources, to make a maximum contribution to the fighting-strength and readiness of our army[15].

An important role in the supply system of the NVA is played, as in civil planning, by the *norm*. Consumption and reserves of ammunition and fuel are laid down, and made the subject of orders, by tactical commanders. According to Soviet doctrine the "principle of availability" as applied to the supply system should guarantee rapid mobility on the field of battle. The standard Soviet textbook *Military Strategy* says of the rear services:

> They comprise a variety of detachments, workshops, depots and offices responsible for the material and technical underpinning of troops in battle. In peacetime only the rear services of those formations and units will be kept at full strength which are expected to be operational in the initial phase of warfare, along with the full range of spare-parts depots. Rear services detachments and offices of the armies, fronts and fleets, however, will for the most part only be staffed or brought to full strength when mobilization occurs.
> The increasing need must be stressed for local resources on enemy territory to be exploited in the course of an offensive. Leaders of the rear services must be particularly prepared for this[16].

The personnel strength of the NVA supply troops can be fairly rapidly expanded by calling up reservists. Civilian employees of nationalized enterprises, e.g. in haulage, who are already subject to call-up can be used to reinforce the corresponding supply formations. Under the Defence Law "every able-bodied citizen, in the event of a defence situation, can be required to

Right page: Guided surface-to-air missile SA-2 in firing position. – Since 1962 the NVA has possessed surface-to-air missiles of a kind known in the West as SAM (Surface-to-Air Missile) or SA. The SA-2 (Nato codename: Guideline) achieved marked success at first in the Vietnam war.

SA-3 (Nato codename: Goa) surface-to-air missile.

SA-4 (Nato codename: Ganef) surface-to-air missile.

SA-9 (Nato codename: Gaskin). This surface-to-air missile was first shown by the NVA at a parade on October 7, 1979.

lend a personal hand in or beyond his place of residence"[17]. Even in peacetime the rear services employ large numbers of civilians, nearly 70 per cent of them women.

Because of the technological revolution, however, the rear services are faced with the difficult problem of performing their enhanced tasks with scarce *"labour capital"*. An expert from the Friedrich Engels Military Academy has touched on this, preferring to quote exact figures from Western forces, but then conceding that conditions are much the same in the socialist forces:

> The proportion of army personnel charged with underpinning functions has gone up. In 1964 the NATO contingents of the US army had some 56 per cent of their men in the rear services. Today 13.5 per cent of the entire US army is devoted to motor and gear maintenance alone. Though proportions are different in the Soviet army, Soviet military specialists often repeat that the rear services today constitute a vast army on their own[18].

For the Soviet Army we know that between 1940 and 1953, covering the initial years of the revolution in military methods, the number of engineers went up by 200 per cent and of technicians by 50 per cent. In the Strategic Rocket Troops of the U.S.S.R. the proportion is particularly high, with 72 per cent of all officers being engineers or technicians.

To show the role of "labour capital in the socialist armed forces", attention is drawn to the lengthening periods of training for specialists.

> The interchangeability of labour is at the same time decreasing. It is becoming more and more difficult to transfer personnel to other posts

or duties even in the same unit or crew. To apply the principle of mutual replaceability needs increasing effort and initiative, and these often play a cardinal role in socialist competition[19].

The NVA regards the *transport system* as especially important for the operational efficiency of the armed forces, including rail and road networks, pipes and waterways. NVA troops and conscientious objectors' construction brigades are used to repair railways, roads and bridges, and pipeline construction units are trained in shifting mobile fuel-lines to provide quick supplies for armoured and mechanized troops.

All improvements in the road network are planned from the military standpoint with the aim of increasing military carrying capacity, a consideration which may have helped to secure the GDR's agreement to the construction of *Autobahnen* between the Federal Republic and West Berlin. With 100 km of roads per 100 square kilometres East Germany has the highest road density of all Warsaw Pact countries. The GDR rail network has the same density as that of West Germany. An elaborate waterways system of canals and rivers extends over all parts of the GDR, affording a floating stockpile of, for example, fuel, so that large quantities can be transported and delivered where needed with consequent relief for road traffic.

Modernization of *military and postal communications* has furnished the armed forces with a diversified system of wire, radio and relay communications for military purposes. The addition of data-processing and transmitting facilities will further enhance the efficiency of communications between commands.

The NVA's air transport capacity[20] – two transport squadrons with 20 Il-14, 3 Tu-124, 8 Tu-134 and six helicopter squadrons with 46 Mi-1, 18 Mi-4, 40 Mi-8 – is sufficient for assault and special operations on a tactical scale and for major supply tasks.

NVA *stockpiling* distinguishes between

– mobile reserves of ammunition and fuel transported by units of the land forces in their own carriers, or available to the air force at airfield depots or held by the navy on board ships; and

– military and civilian warehouse reserves of mass consumption or specialized goods kept in NVA or industrial depots.

These reserves are sufficient for the NVA's land, air and naval forces in the initial phase of a war.

The arms industry and socialist economic integration

The NVA's *rear services* maintain a large number of *workshops and facilities* of many kinds intended purely for carrying out repair work, and that only on a limited scale. This function, however, is an increasingly important one, both for reasons of economy and for military preparedness. Those non-military enterprises which in fact work exclusively for the NVA and other armed services are grouped together in the *Vereinigung volkseigener Betriebe Eisen, Blech und Metall* (Union of People's Enterprises in the Iron, Sheet-Iron and Metal Sectors) in Karl-Marx-Stadt and are directly controlled by the Administration for Technology and Weaponry in the Defence Ministry. The combine includes the Peene Dockyards at Wolgast and a number of industrial repair enterprises, explosive factories and ammunition works.

Apart from handguns and other small-calibre automatic weapons the GDR itself makes few end-products for warfare. Its heavy weapons and equipment are imported from the *Soviet Union*. It does, however, produce components for heavy weapons, as well as light and medium military aircraft and naval vessels up to minelayers, anti-submarine boats and landing craft, and all the uniforms and personal equipment needed for its own troops. Mention may also be made here of engineering vehicles and equipment and of the high-grade products of the GDR's electronic and optical industries which are discussed elsewhere.

There are several reasons why East Germany, compared with other Soviet bloc countries, produces few conventional armaments. One is that, even before the war, the area contained far less heavy industry than Western Germany, and the dismantling of factories and removal of plant to the Soviet Union immediately after the war made domestic armaments production unthinkable in the early period of GDR rearmament. Again, *Czechoslovakia* had an established armaments industry of a high standard which had supplied German needs during the war and from 1948 was available to supply the communist armies. Partly under Soviet license Czechoslovakia produces heavy equipment, military aircraft, armoured vehicles and heavy artillery, and was developing the large Tatra transport truck. When the *Korean War* began in 1950 and the Soviet Union drew the European satellites into its own armament manufacture, *Polish* industry was diverted to arms production on a large scale, contrary to original plans. A similar change for East Germany would have been inopportune not so much for economic as for political reasons: the Potsdam Agreement forbade any German rearmament. The revival of the *aircraft industry* around Dresden that was started in the early fifties was suddenly interrupted on Soviet instructions despite its initial spectacular success. Whether the decisive factor was fear of competition, doubts about East German reliability or a new Soviet plan remains unclear.

On the question of East German rearmament Defence Minister Hoffmann stated in 1964:

> (The NVA) is specifically organized and armed for tasks within the framework of the Joint (Warsaw Pact) Forces and to protect the sovereignty of the German Democratic Republic. We neither need nor possess strategic missile forces or bombers or ocean-going naval vessels ... We do not propose to make all the technical instruments of war for ourselves. We are only developing and producing such weapons and equipment as we have accepted responsibility for under Warsaw Pact

arrangements, in addition to such items as can be manufactured by any country[21].

The fact that most weapons used in the NVA, as in the armies of the other Warsaw Pact members, are of Soviet origin facilitates a degree of standardization which makes equally good sense economically and militarily. In 1969 the Warsaw Pact's Political Consultative Committee, meeting in Budapest, decided not only to reorganize the structure of the Pact generally but to set up a *Committee for Coordination of Weapons and Technology*. Accordingly the 25th Comecon session of July 1971 prescribed military-economic integration as a *Complex Programme* for all economic sectors with a view to speeding up arms production. This was to apply not only to industry but to agriculture, transport, post and communications, the health system and building.

NVA publications make much of the superior *standardization* of armaments in the Warsaw Pact compared with NATO. Thus in 1975 we could read:

> According to latest reports the "Atlantic Alliance" is using 15 different types of tank. Our own armies have to be "content" with a mere four, three of which come from the same stable (the three T-models and the PT-76).
>
> The principal infantry weapons – automatic rifles and machine-guns – are represented in NATO by 17 machine-gun types and 8 automatic rifle systems. We use just the Kalashnikov submachine gun, the light machine gun derived from it and the single heavy machine gun. As against four different NATO rifles, we have the one kind from Tula[22].

The rationale for Comecon economic coordination is that it "increases the economic potential of all the Comecon countries and thereby of the whole socialist community. This is bound, directly and indirectly, to enhance the defensive strength of the Comecon countries . . ."[23]

New advances in the socialist division of labour in production and research are claimed, viz.

> – step-by-step integration of Comecon resources in raw materials, intermediate products, labour, investment, production and research capacity on the basis of state-organized socialist ownership, amounting to an increase in the inter-state mobility of production forces;
> – step-by-step creation of inter-state production complexes, starting with raw-material exploitation, building and the production and utilization of common systems of machinery and tools. Research and production in close association;
> – continuous improvement in the adaptation of economic structures, which as they achieve perfection will gradually constitute components of the unified socialist structure of a community of socialist states[24].

The same article states proudly that

> the Warsaw Pact's industrial potential is nowadays almost double that of the EEC, which constitutes the economic basis of the aggressive NATO

bloc in Europe. "With their 360 million population the members of the socialist alliance make up the world's largest industrial complex, quite capable of jointly solving the intricate problems of its own development and collective defence. It boasts one-third of the world's industrial production and 27 per cent of the world's GNP." (I. Mazlennikov, Die ökonomischen Grundlagen für die Verteidigungskraft der Warschauer Vertragsstaaten, quoted in *Presse der Sowjetunion,* Berlin, vol. 11, 1974, p. 6.)[25]

This extraordinarily high estimate of the Soviet bloc's own economic and military potential cannot be dismissed as a mere fanfare for the "international example of socialism". There are western voices which say the same thing, albeit from different motives. General Haig, as Supreme Commander of NATO forces in Europe, told the US Senate Armed Services Committee on March 1, 1977:

> Today, that determined effort has procured for the U.S.S.R. a military posture quantitatively superior to that of the West in many key areas, and constantly increasing in technological sophistication to the point where the West's traditional qualitative advantage is rapidly evaporating. Most important, the emergence of these capabilities has been accompanied by the development of a modern, expanded production base capable of fielding military hardware in greater quantities, and of greater sophistication, than we have ever previously observed . . .[26]

In their testimony before the same Committee on January 24, 1977, Senators Sam Nunn and Dewey F. Bartlett observed:

> Serious consideration should be given to establishing within each ministry of defense powerful bureaucratic constituencies committed solely to achieving standardization and interoperability . . . Ultimately, however, progress will require discarding of the notion that logistics should be exclusively a national responsibility . . .[27]

It is true that among the Warsaw Pact forces the "supply" system is also a national responsibility of each country, but it is so committed to supporting the "socialist community of states" that there is no question of independence. For on that side it is the Soviet Union which "carries the main burden of implementing the Complex Programme of socialist economic integration and of securing territorial defence economically . . ."[28] The same applies to Comecon, which now comprises ten states – the U.S.S.R., Bulgaria, Cuba, Czechoslovakia, East Germany, Hungary, Mongolia, Poland, Rumania and Vietnam – with their very disparate contributions to the expansion of economic potential.

The GDR, having become "one of the world's ten most powerful industrial nations"[29] and risen to the second position in the communist bloc, is for military-economic purposes tied to the Soviet Union not only by the Warsaw Pact and Comecon but also, specifically, by its *Treaty of Friendship, Cooperation and Mutual Assistance* of October 7, 1975.

In pursuance of agreements reached by Honecker and Brezhnev at their Crimea meeting in the summer of 1978 for the elaboration of a *Programme of Specialization and Cooperation* between their two countries in the period up to 1990, various details were settled, on June 21, at the 23rd session of the Joint Governmental Commission for Economic and Scientific-Technical Co-operation. These included cooperation in *satellite exploration of the world's natural resources* as a sequel to the Interkosmos Programme and outer space experiments, and further development of "multispectral photography as a prime technique in aerocosmic exploration of the world for economic purposes". The same session reached agreements on *machine-tool and processing machine construction* and on a major re-equipment of the East German *electrical engineering industry*[30].

In connection with the 30th anniversary of Comecon in 1979 Honecker had this to say of East Germany's performance:

> She has made a notable contribution to the material-technical basis of socialism in the other Comecon countries by exporting the products of her engineering and chemical industries[31].

On the same occasion Comecon celebrated its ten-year old policy decision to embark on the Complex Programme as a "truly historic decision"[32], and defined the aim of joint efforts in the decade to come as

> accelerating scientific-technical progress in all respects, meeting rational requirements of raw materials, fuel, energy, machines, equipment and modern technologies, improving the public supply of food and consumer goods and developing an efficient, up-to-date transport network for the Comecon countries in harmony with the heavier demands of their economies and their mutual cooperation.

At a Comecon session in Moscow, in June, 1979, the East German premier Willi Stoph declared, as head of his country's delegation, the government's willingness to sign "a series of agreements on future cooperation in the production of equipment for *nuclear power plants, industry and transport ...*"[33] He particularly emphasized multilateral specialization and cooperation in producing nuclear plant, going on to say that

> most of the increase in electricity output in the DDR after 1980 will be assured by the installation of nuclear power stations.

Soviet premier and delegation-leader Kosygin likewise stressed areas in which the GDR could make a signal contribution and which are at the same time significant for the military economy: *mechanical engineering, energy economics – especially nuclear –, and transport*[34].

Although, incidentally, in stressing the importance of delivery dates and quality standards Stoph also spoke of the need to "guarantee a high degree of operational safety" in plant to be delivered by East Germany, the question of damage to the environment from nuclear power plants remains taboo in the GDR. A Soviet specialist's report on "Nuclear Plants in the Comecon Countries"[35] published in June, 1978, by *Volksarmee*, omitted reference to the safety theme which had bulked large for years in the public debate in West Germany, crippling construction schemes and threatening to split political parties. Meanwhile the total output of Comecon nuclear power stations is put by Soviet sources at over 10,340 megawatts.

The *electrical* and *electronic,* especially *microelectronic,* industries are intended to play a key role in enhancing East Germany's economic capacity. Their expansion was the subject of the SED Central Committee's 6th meeting, at the end of June, 1977. In the context of the "implementation of the Central Committee's decisions in the field of electrical engineering and electronics" the June 25–26, 1977, weekend edition of *Neues Deutschland* devoted three whole pages to a speech by the minister responsible for this area and another page-and-a-half to the Committee's resolution the following day.

There can be no doubt that because of the decisive importance of electronics, chemistry, optics and so on for modern armaments, the GDR, with its high standing in these fields, has become by dint of socialist economic specialization and cooperation the foremost military production partner of the Soviet Union within the communist bloc. Though she manufactures little by way of conventional weaponry for herself or for export to the Third World, certain key products in the economic underpinning of communist bloc defence put her in second position after the Soviet Union, well ahead of all others.

This has brought East Germany an inevitable access of prestige and a share in decision-making, albeit in the No. 2 role. For the country's own economy her commitments to the Warsaw Pact, Comecon and the U.S.S.R. have meant an *enormous additional burden* that can only be borne at the price of extreme *thrift.* As Stoph explained in justifying the 1979 Economic Plan in the People's Chamber, a "national plan for socialist rationalization" had been drawn up for the first time which was designed to achieve uniform management and rationalization of the country's entire economy[36]. At the end of April, 1979, Honecker made a speech demanding "greater efforts" and spelling out "long-term factors and requirements".

> With the strengthening of the GDR in view we must take fundamental account of major changes affecting our economic growth, arising from changes in the world market. Nobody today can doubt that we are dealing with a long-term, continuous process. Prices of essential raw materials and energy sources which had already reached a high level in past years are continuing to go up. We cannot overlook this . . .
>
> We have to consider new orders of magnitude in expanding the GDR's economic performance by efficient all-round housekeeping, we have to consider the use we make of the end-product and the mobilization of all our efforts to increase it . . .
>
> In these circumstances it has become a matter of unconditional priority to strengthen the material-technical basis of the economy . . .
>
> We must use ideology to create a climate in which this task is appreciated by the public as one of life-and-death . . .
>
> In world terms, a hard struggle is being currently enacted . . . to develop and utilize the most up-to-date technology. This is part of the class conflict in which we cannot afford to fail[37].

This appeal was launched at a time in which not only priorities for the "most up-to-date technology" were being set, but *unfulfilled planning targets, shortages, low harvest yields and high indebtedness* – about 60 billion dollars in the Comecon case according to Western estimates in 1979 – could no longer be concealed.

The NVA has itself been deeply affected by this pressure for extreme economy. At a seminar for senior NVA cadres, held in May, 1979, under the chairmanship of Defence Minister Hoffmann to discuss SED economic policy, the Politburo's economic specialist Günter Mittag – exactly echoing Honecker's words of the month before – stated that "it has become a matter of unconditional priority to strengthen the material-technical basis of the economy"[38].

Like other cardinal matters in communist countries these two developments – the demands made of certain key industries in the GDR at Soviet behest on the one hand, and on the other hand the resultant strain on the economy in meeting both domestic needs and military demands – are hardly ever published in concrete figures.

In June, 1979, Stoph supplied the following information about the "increasing cooperation" between the GDR and the rest of Comecon. The GDR's trade turnover with her Comecon partners had reached about 14 billion roubles, compared with 10 billion in 1975. The Comecon share in East Germany's foreign trade had at the same time risen from 66 to 69 per cent. The share of specialized and coproduction engineering items in the total export of machinery and plant to Comecon countries had grown between 1975 and 1978 from 26 to 44 per cent [39].

But it is nowhere stated how much of this export figure is due to the state trading concern *Ingenieur-technischer Außenhandel* (Engineering Foreign Trade), which is responsible to the Defence Ministry for the import and export of weapons and other military ware. Not that information on this, or on arms exports to the Third World, would be particularly illuminating since key products destined for direct or indirect military use are in any case not included in military expenditure.

The East German *defence budget* is for the same reason equally unhelpful. Only since 1968 have certain military expenditure items been shown clearly and separately in the state budget. Up to 1977, resources were said to be allocated "*for national defence and security*"; after that date there were two separate items: "*national defence*" and "*public order, jurisdiction and frontier protection*". The planned share of the military budget in 1977 was about 9 per cent of the total budget. Planned expenditure for 1979 on "national defence" was 8,674 million marks, and on "public safety, jurisdiction and frontier protection" 3,474 million – 12,148 million marks in all[40]. The London-based International Institute for Strategic Studies has put the GDR's 1977 military outlay at 11,020 million marks compared with a GNP of 54,600 million[41].

There is some evidence that the expansion of East German industry in sectors producing *inter alia* high-grade arms material, though enhancing the overall potential of the Soviet-led bloc, is more of a hindrance than an asset to the military technology of the East German forces themselves.

Whereas in earlier years it used to be asserted that "the technology and armament of the NVA meet all our requirements for the country's defence"[42], or "we have all we need in the way of modern weaponry"[43], there are now more and more *signs of bottlenecks*. Colonel General Fleissner, Deputy Defence Minister and Head of Technology and Weaponry, when asked in 1977 "how the supply of modern military equipment to the NVA had fared in the last few years", replied that it had been possible "to a large extent" to utilize the "results of scientific-technical progress and the advantages of the socialist system"[44]. In communist terminology "to a large extent" implies "not very much". The General went on to say:

> Our army personnel are continually exercised to catch up with the latest technology. That is basically a good sign: far be it from me to criticize the itch to innovate, or to congratulate those who are loth to abandon the old and familiar. But sometimes our people, especially the young ones, overdo it and would prefer to throw away the so-called older equipment, which naturally requires more effort to use and look after. That is an attitude no country can afford. Even in modern armies there will always be found the latest fighting material alongside older weapons and equipment, and the task will always remain to ensure that they both work together in combat.

In 1978 another expert, equally concerned to stress the need for technological propaganda in socialist army training, declared:

> Some members of the public have been pointing to weapon models and systems, and technical equipment, both in the NVA and frontier guard units – especially defensive devices – which strike them as "antiquated" when compared with the very latest. Our military-technical propaganda needs to point out, therefore, that the combat-readiness of our troops has at every stage maintained the necessary standard while using technology of different generations[45].

In the journal *Volksarmee*[46] it has even been said that "whether a weapon is modern or not, depends not on its year of manufacture but on combat conditions." Or again: "Experience teaches that the introduction of new military technology does not automatically produce greater fighting efficiency and combat-readiness". Which is obviously true, if the troops do not master the new skills at the same time.

The specialist periodical *Militärtechnik* has gone more deeply into certain aspects of weapon modernization. A contributor has described the headlong advance of science and technology as the root cause of "rapid loss of enthusiasm for weapons and equipment". The succession of generations in a weapons system, he argues, is fundamentally a function of its performance.

> The length of service of a weapons system is also influenced, however, by its cost-effectiveness. For if it is still regarded as adequate, and yet the expense, say, of its maintenance exceeds a certain amount, such as the cost of replacement, then one of the possible deadlines for a new system has been reached[47].

What is needed, to an increasing extent, is to upgrade the weapons and equipment already in service. The same author invokes Marshal Grechko[48]:

> ... There is accordingly a very timely trend in scientific-technical advances in the military field toward modernizing the equipment with which an army has long been furnished and giving it, so to speak, a second life, provided this is militarily as well as economically justifiable ...

The process of giving things a *"second life"* involves new costs, of course, as well as savings.

> (It) requires numerous modifications and new series in all components of the system in question. It means keeping a larger stock of gauges and test equipment. It means more working space, more tools and jigs. A bigger range of spare parts and to some extent of expendable materials is needed. The necessary technical documentation for servicing, activation and maintenance grows enormously, in the case of a modern fighter aircraft, for example, it may amount to some ten thousand sheets even without the manufacturing paperwork[49].

If every weapon system or indeed every weapon has to be given a "second life", which usually means revival in a more specialized form, there is not much "standardization" left. The task of maintaining service-ability involves not only the armed forces, and in particular the rear services, but also industry.

As usual in East Germany, the "political awareness" of those involved is called upon to solve the problem, and this applies to the soldiers as well as to the scientists, engineers and workers. This means an increased burden for the strategic sectors of East German industry, and the immediate withdrawal of resources form other sectors. For the NVA, the *Complex Programme* amounts to heightened pressure toward "economic thinking" in the sense of more work and less to work with.

Notes

[1] A GDR commentator explains "logistics" as follows: "The increasing supply-dependence of the imperialist armed forces on their economic base has led to the emergence of a separate, third area of military art. Alonside strategy and tactics we now have logistics – a state-monopoly mechanism linking the capitalist economy and the forces of aggression." (Siegfried *Börngen*, Neue Forschungsergebnisse zur Entwicklung der Ökonomie der sozialistischen Streitkräfte, in: *Militärgeschichte*, East Berlin, 2/1976, p. 226.)

[2] Militärlexikon, Deutscher Militärverlag, East Berlin 1971, p. 393.

[3] Ibid., p. 287.

[4] Das moderne Militärwesen, Deutscher Militärverlag, East Berlin 1968, p. 57.

[5] Colonel Prof. Dr. habil H. *Einhorn* und Colonel Dozent S. *Schönherr* of the Friedrich Engels Military Academy, Militärökonomie und militärischer Klassenauftrag, in: *Militärwesen,* East Berlin, 3/1977, p. 60.

[6] Major General G. *Storbeck*, Effektiver Einsatz der materiellen und finanziellen Mittel sowie der Zeitfonds des Panzerdienstes erhöht die Kampfkraft und Gefechtsbereitschaft, in: *Militärtechnik*, East Berlin, 4/1979, p. 169.

[7] Cf. *Einhorn*, loc. cit. p. 60.

[8] Gesetz über die Landesverteidigung der DDR (Defence Law) of October 13, 1978. *Gesetzblatt*, Part. 1, No. 35, p. 378.

[9] Ibid., Section III, Ökonomische Sicherstellung und weitere Maßnahmen für die Landesverteidigung, par. 7, Aufgaben der Volkswirtschaft, p. 379.

[10] From the Gesetz über den Fünfjahrplan für die Entwicklung der Volkswirtschaft der DDR 1976–1980, in: *Neues Deutschland*, East Berlin, December 17, 1976.

[11] Defence Law, loc. cit. par. 8, p. 379.

[12] Ibid., par. 9, p. 379.

[13] Militärlexikon, Militärverlag der DDR, East Berlin 1973, p. 244 f.

[14] Was Marschall Bagramjan sagte, spornt uns heute an, Tribüne sprach mit Generalleutnant Helmut Poppe, in: *Tribüne*, East Berlin, March 9, 1979.

[15] Ibid.

[16] W. D. *Sokolowski* (ed.), Militär-Strategie, German translation of the 3rd, revised and enlarged Russian edition, Cologne 1969, p. 422.

[17] Defence Law, loc. cit., par. 11, Persönliche Arbeitsleistungen, p. 379.

[18] Lieutenant Colonel Dr. K. *Lehmann* of the Friedrich Engels Military Academy, Einige Aspekte der Entwicklung und effektiven Nutzung des Arbeitsvermögens in den sozialistischen Streitkräften, in: *Militärwesen*, 2/1977, p. 91.

[19] Ibid., p. 92.

[20] International Institute for Strategic Studies, Military Balance 1978–1979, London 1978, p. 14.

[21] Heinz *Hoffmann*, Grundfragen der Militärpolitik der SED, lecture to the Karl Marx Party High School, March 4, 1964. Quoted in his: Sozialistische Landesverteidigung, Aus Reden und Aufsätzen 1963–1970. Part 1, East Berlin 1971, p. 135.

[22] Lieutenant Colonel K. *Erhart*, Trümpfe, in: *Armeerundschau* – Soldatenmagazin, Militärverlag der DDR, East Berlin, 5/1975, p. 7.

[23] Colonel Grad. Soc. Sc. G. *Leuteritz* and First Lieutenant Grad. Ec. Sc. R. *Bresch* of the Wilhelm Pieck Military-Political University, Sozialistische ökonomische Integration und die Stärkung des sozialistischen Verteidigungspotentials, in: *Militärwesen*, 2/1975, p. 14.

[24] Ibid., p. 14 f.

[25] Ibid., p. 15.

[26] Wireless Bulletin from Washington (USIS Bonn), No. 42, March 2, 1977.

[27] NATO and the New Soviet Threat, Report of Senator Sam *Nunn* and Senator Dewey F. *Bartlett* to the Committee on Armed Services, U. S. Senate, Washington 1977.

[28] *Leuteritz* et al., loc. cit. p. 16.

[29] Erich *Honecker*, closing address at the SED Central Committee's 10th Session, quoted in: *Neues Deutschland*, April 28/29, 1979.

[30] Ökonomische Beziehungen zur Sowjetunion weiter verstärkt. Press communiqué of the 23rd Session of the Joint Government Commission for Economic and Scientific-Technical Cooperation between the GDR and U.S.S.R., *Neues Deutschland* June 22, 1978.

[31] *Neues Deutschland*, June 25, 1979.

[32] Do., June 30/July 1, 1979.

[33] Do., June 28, 1979.

[34] Ibid.

[35] Prof. Dr. Nikolai *Sinew*, Vice-chairman of the State Commission for the Use of Nuclear Energy in the U.S.S.R., Kernkraftwerke in den RGW-Ländern, in: *Volksarmee* 6/1969.

[36] *Neues Deutschland*, December 16/17, 1978.

[37] Do., April 28/29, 1979.

[38] Do., May 15, 1979.

[39] Do., June 28, 1979.

[40] *Gesetzblatt*, Part 1, No. 42, December 21, 1978, p. 463.

[41] International Institute for Strategic Studies, loc. cit. p. 14.

[42] Title of an unsigned article in: *Militärtechnik*, 9/1974, p. 391.

[43] Heinz *Hoffmann*, speech at the 7th Conference of delegates from SED Party organizations in the NVA, June 8, 1969. Quoted in his: Sozialistische Landesverteidigung, p. 833.

[44] Interview with Lieutenant General W. *Fleissner*, Deputy Defence Minister and Head of Technology and Weaponry, Hohe Gefechtsbereitschaft verlangt meisterhafte Beherrschung und gewissenhafte Wartung der Kampftechnik, in: *Militärwesen*, 6/1977, p. 3.

[45] Lieutenant Colonel Grad. Soc. Sc. G. *Wohler* of the Friedrich Engels Military Academy, Militärtechnische Propaganda – Bestandteil der sozialistischen Wehrerziehung, in: *Militärwesen*, 4/1978, p. 39.

[46] Colonel Dr. *Wünsche*, Moderne Kampftechnik bedingt modernes Denken, in: *Volksarmee*, 32/1976.

[47] Colonel Grad. Eng. *Ullmann*, Einige Aspekte der Modernisierung von Waffensystemen, in: *Militärtechnik*, 9/1976, p. 385.

[48] Marshal of the Soviet Union A. A. *Grechko*, Die Streitkräfte des Sowjetstaates, quoted by Colonel *Ullmann*, loc cit., p. 385.

[49] *Ullmann*, loc. cit., p. 387.

CHAPTER NINE

Weapons and Major Equipment

Most of the NVA's weapons and equipment come from the *Soviet Union;* some are supplied by Czechoslovakia and Poland, partly made there under Soviet license. Only in the *electronic, land vehicle and shipbuilding fields are* there notable domestic products.

GDR commentators have from an early stage described the NVA's equipment as *"modern"*, befitting the "class requirement to protect the German people's first socialist state"[1]. In January 1976, on the eve of the NVA's twentieth anniversary, it was declared that

> the range and effectiveness of the NVA's weaponry has increased ten-fold since 1956. In the air force, fighter plane speeds have quintupled since that year and flight ceilings trebled. In the People's Navy, the range of vulnerable targets has more than doubled over the same period, with increased strike accuracy and greater effectiveness per strike[2].

Between the 8th and 9th SED Party congresses, in 1971 and 1976 respectively,

> the combat effectiveness of troops was enhanced in all parts of the services, whatever the weapons. The chief contributing factor was the introduction of Soviet weapon systems, increasing the firepower and mobility of troops and ships[3].

GDR Defence Minister Hoffmann drew this contrast with NATO:

> The Warsaw Pact armies are not only uniformly provided with modern, largely Soviet, weapons and vehicles, but the latest Soviet weapon systems have moreover superior performance parameters to those of NATO[4].

Western reports similarly abound with comments on a *striking improvement in Warsaw Pact conventional armament*. Thus we read in testimony given to the US Senate Armed Forces Committee on January 24, 1977, under the heading NATO and the new Soviet Threat:

> It is the central thesis of this report that the Soviet Union and its Eastern European allies are rapidly moving toward a decisive conventional military superiority over NATO. This trend is the result of NATO's failure to modernize and maintain its conventional forces in response to the Warsaw Pact's build-up and modernization of conventional forces[5].

> Against a background of strategic nuclear parity with the United States and substantial advances in their tactical nuclear capability, the Soviets

have provided their non-nuclear forces deployed opposite Western Germany an ability to initiate a potentially devastating invasion of Europe with as little as a few days warning. This is evident in a growing emphasis upon firepower and readiness of ground forces and in the dramatic transformation of Soviet tactical aviation from a defensive force into a hard-hitting air armada of extended reach[6].

It is probable, then, that Warsaw Pact forces would already be on the Rhine by the time NATO decided to use tactical nuclear weapons. As key factors permitting a *blitzkrieg* advance by the Warsaw Pact forces, the same report adduces the following:

> The T-72 main battle tank has been introduced into the Group of Soviet Forces in Germany. This improvement in tank quality has been coupled with an increase of 60 to 80 tanks in the standard inventory authorised for their 16 motorised rifle divisions in East Europe. Together, these improvements have greatly strengthened Pact armour, which today outnumbers NATO's by almost three to one.
> The replacement of armoured personnel carriers with the BMP-60 mechanized infantry combat vehicle. This has granted Soviet infantry an ability to fight without dismounting – a capacity denied to almost all of NATO's mechanised infantry (German infantry being the sole exception). For the most part, NATO is still tied to the technologically obsolescent armoured personnel carrier.
> The shift from towed to self-propelled artillery, which permits artillery to keep pace with advancing armour, thus significantly enhancing the tank's survivability. This shift has been accompanied by an estimated expansion of at least 50 per cent in the number of Soviet artillery tubes in East Europe in recent years.
> The proliferation throughout Soviet ground forces of a formidable array of tactical air defence systems. Better air defence could result in a severe loss of NATO aircraft during the stages of hostilities.
> The impressive growth of Soviet ability to neutralise NATO's anti-tank capabilities[7].

The rapid introduction on a large scale of a host of longer-range, heavier-payload aircraft and assault helicopters – the MiG-21 J, K and L, MiG-23, SU-17, SU-19, Backfire bomber and Mi-24 – greatly reduced NATO's traditional advantage in tactical air power. According to 1977 US estimates, the Soviets have increased their deployment of new fighter-bomber aircraft in East Europe by 200 per cent in the last two years[8]. Moreover, recent Pact air exercises appear to be focussing more and more upon simulated long-range strikes against vital NATO military targets.

The latest West German White Book also takes it for granted that the Warsaw Pact forces, unlike those of NATO, are structured for offensive use.

> In Central Europe and on NATO's flanks the Warsaw Pact's conventional forces, especially its ground forces, enjoy a clear superiority. Tak-

ing into account reinforcement capability on both sides, the proportion of tanks as between NATO and the Warsaw Pact is about one to three. The extent of the threat exceeds this ratio, for in NATO's defensive doctrine the measure of the threat from the Warsaw Pact's superiority is NATO's own anti-tank capability ... The other part of the comparison rests on many, still more imponderable, factors ... That of quality has for many years played a large part in estimates of the East-West power balance. With its technological lead and superior weapon quality, NATO was able to compensate for the Warsaw Pact's numerical advantages. The latter relied more on large numbers of weapons in standardized series. However, the East is catching up with Western technical advances, in recent years ever more rapidly ... Less and less can NATO outweigh quantitative weaknesses with qualitative strengths[9].

Naturally we find *no critical comments on Soviet weaponry either in Soviet or in East German publications;* they would be felt as incompatible with the aim of "using the armed forces as political instruments in every situation"[10].

In serious *Western evaluations, however, we do occasionally find qualified assessments of Soviet equipment.* Friedrich Wiener, an Austrian military specialist, wrote for example in 1974:

> Since the unfortunate experience of the October 1973 Yom Kippur war, there must be considerable doubt whether the newer T-62 tank represents a great gain as a replacement for the earlier T-54 and 55. It displays many technical defects and was stopped in large numbers by Israeli fire. It was striking how quickly it burnt up even after a relatively light hit. The chassis, too, was inferior to that of all Western types[11].

Wiener concludes that the Soviet attempt to use the T-62 to draw even with the West's Leopard, AMX-30 and Chieftain tanks was a failure[12]. And no more T-62s are being made. The T-70/T-72 main battle tank is designed to fill the gap.

The Soviet Union's inventory of main battle tanks, conservatively estimated at 42,000 (of which over 15,500 are deployed in East Europe), is alone of sufficient magnitude to absorb a very high loss rate, perhaps even higher than that sustained by both sides during the Yom Kippur war[13].

Christoph Bertram, Director of the International Institute for Strategic Studies in London, noted in April, 1977 that

> the direction and momentum of the trend is hardly in dispute. In the last thirty years the U.S.S.R. has improved its military potential in almost every respect – on land, at sea and in the air ... Of paramount importance is the resultant shrinking of the West's military options, while those of the East have grown[14].

To appraise the NVA's arsenal one needs to realize that none of the Warsaw Pact's armies are so tied to that of the Soviet Union as the East German one. It could not join the Soviet army in forming the front line of the First

The standard infantry weapon is the "Kalashnikov" submachine gun; in front, an anti-tank launcher (RPG–7).

Anti-tank guided missile as individual weapon.

Strategic Echelon if its degree of mechanization, for example – tanks, artillery and infantry alike – were below that of the Soviets.

After the NVA parade in East Berlin on October 7, 1979, and the simult-aneous People's Fleet display in Rostock for East Germany's 30th anniversary, the future trend of rearmament became clear. The new T-72 battle tanks were shown, along with 152 mm howitzers and the new anti-aircraft rocket systems. Assault helicopters made their first appearance at the parade. It is these elements which may well receive growing emphasis in the years to come. Newer models may be coming into service with the air force to replace the old fighters – battle-tested Soviet third generation machines like the MiG-27 suggest themselves. In the NVA's People's Marine units, new series of coastal de-fence frigates may be added to the existing *Rostock* and *Berlin* classes, and similarly with the large landing craft of the *Frosch* class. Successors must be found for the *Hai* class submarine chasers and *OSA* class guided missile patrol boats. An extension of helicopter capability for the marines is not to be excluded.

The following enumeration of current NVA weapons and vehicles makes no claim to completeness; a full review would have to include many variants in use. The list is mainly derived from GDR sources.

I Land Forces

Infantry weapons

Makarov pistol (PM) – This semi-automatic pistol introduced in the Soviet Army in the early fifties as a personal combat weapon has an effective range of 50 m and a rate of fire of 30 rounds per minute (rpm). The magazine capac-ity is 8 rounds, calibre 9 mm, weight 0.810 kg with fully loaded magazine.

Dragoonov rifle (SWD) – This has replaced the older *Mosin-Nagant rifle (Mod. 1891/1930)*. A semi-automatic with single-shot fire, it has an adjust-able ring sight and telescopic sight and is designed as a sniper's weapon. The sight range extends to 1,200 or 1,300 m. It can be used with or without a bayonet. Practical rate of fire 30 rpm. The magazine holds 10 7.62 mm rounds. Weight without bayonet and rounds, 4.3 kg. Standard equipment of a motoriz-ed infantry company. .

Simonov self-loading carbine (SKS) – Semi-automatic hand gun with single-shot fire, wooden stock and folding bayonet. Also used with telescopic sight as a sniper's weapon. It employs the short M-43 7.62 mm round, the uniform Warsaw Pact ammunition, and is standard motorized infantry company equip-ment.

Kalashnikov submachine gun, modernized (AKM) – This fully automatic hand gun for single-shot and continuous fire is made in East Germany on the lines of the Warsaw Pact's standard Soviet-made *Kalashnikov (AK),* from which it differs in the plastic stock and pistol-grip and pressed steel housing, which make it lighter and handier to use. Its magazine takes 30 short 7.62 mm rounds; total weight about 4 kg, length 87 cm. Bayonet and infra-red sight can be attached. The effective single-shot range is 400 m, with a rate of fire of 40 rpm; with short bursts at 100 rpm the effective range is 300 m. The rounds retain their penetrating power up to 1,500 m. A standard motorized infantry squad weapon.

Kalashnikov light machine gun (RPK) – This fully automatic pneumatic-loading weapon has a folding bipod and is designed for single-shot or continuous fire. It can be used with any of three different magazines: a curved 40-round box magazine, a 75-round barrel magazine or the AKM's 30-shot curved box magazine. It fires the short 7,62 mm round and with full magazine weighs 5 or 7 kg. Every motorized infantry spuad possesses one.

Kalashnikov light machine gun (RPK) – This fully automatic pneumatic-used with a folding bipod carriage (Mod. PK) or – for anti-aircraft purposes – with a tripod (Mod. PKS); also in battle tanks (Mod. PKT) and personnel carriers (Mod. PKB). The belt-ammunition is the old M-08 7.62 mm rifle round. The effective rate of fire is up to 250 rpm and total weight about 9 kg with the bipod, 16 kg with the tripod. Most effective range for ground and air targets up to 1,000 m. This is another motorized infantry squad weapon.

Anti-tank launcher (Panzerbüchse) (RPG-7) – This recoilless weapon, common to all the Warsaw Pact forces, features a 40 mm diameter tube on the end of which is fitted an 84 mm wing-stabilized hollow-charge shell, projected mechanically. The shell has an armour-piercing warhead with electrical impact detonator. The most effective firing-range is about 150 m and armour up to 200 mm thick can be penetrated. For distances of up to 150 m an open leaf-sight is used, for up to 500 m an optical sight. The maximum practical rate of fire is 4 to 6 shells per minute. Weight 4.1 kg unloaded, 6.35 kg loaded. An infra-red target-finder can be fitted. This is a standard weapon of every motorized rifle squad, for close-up tank fighting.

Hand grenades – Various Soviet grenades are in use among the Warsaw Pact forces. Offensive grenades include the *RGD-42* and *RGD-5*, with effective fragment radius of 25 m and 15–20 m respectively. Fragments of the egg-shaped *F-1* defence grenade are effective at distances of up to 200 m. The *RKG-3, RKG-3M* and *Az-58-K-100* are special anti-tank grenades capable of penetrating any military vehicle armour.

Armoured personnel carriers

40 P Armoured personnel carrier (BRDM) – A light armoured, fully enclosed amphibious combat vehicle with four-wheel drive and two adjustable auxiliary axles. Weight 5.1 t, length 5.7 m, width 2.25 m, height 1.9 m. The 90 HP six-cylinder petrol engine gives it a maximum speed on land of 90 km/h; in water it attains 10 km/h with water-jet propulsion. It has a cruising range of 500–700 km and climbing gradient of up to 30 per cent. It is equipped with an infra-red device for night operations and holds a crew of six in addition to the driver. Armament consists of a 7.62 mm heavy machine gun mounted on the forward hull wall. This model has been used by reconnaissance units since the 1960s and also finds employment as a command vehicle. Modified versions have retractable launchers for various types of anti-tank shells. This, and the 60-P carrier, represent the transition from group-transport vehicle to group-combat vehicle.

40 P-2 Armoured personnel carrier (BRDM-M-1966) – A light armoured, fully enclosed amphibious combat vehicle with four-wheel drive. Weight 7 t, length 5.75 m. The armament is housed in a revolving turret and consists of one 14.5 mm and one coaxial 7.62 mm heavy machine gun. Propulsion is by a 140 HP rear engine and a water-jet motor; top road speed 100 km/h. This was evolved in 1966 from the 40 P carrier and was for a time the most advanced reconnaissance vehicle.

152 Armoured personnel carrier (BTR-152) – Light armoured three-axle wheeled carrier with open troop compartment carrying up to twelve men. Weight 6.7 t, length 6.55 m, width 2.35 m, height 2 m. The 110 HP Zis-123 engine permits a speed of 75 km/h. Cruising range 600 km, climbing gradient 30 per cent. Armament consists of a 7.62 mm heavy machine gun mounted on the forward hull wall. In earlier times a standard infantry transport vehicle, it is no longer up to modern combat standards; it has been replaced in the NVA by more modern equipment and handed over to other forces.

50 P Armoured personnel carrier (BTR-50 P) – Light armoured amphibious carrier with the same tracks as the PT-76 amphibious tank and with open or closed troop compartment. With room for 18 men, it weighs 13 t, length 7 m, width 3.1 m, height 2.3 m, infra-red driving light. The armament, a 7.62 mm heavy machine gun, is mounted forward. The six-cylinder diesel engine of 240 HP gives the vehicle a speed of 50 km/h on dry land and 10 km/h in the water. The cruising range is 350 km and climbing gradient 38 per cent. Standard equipment in the infantry units of the tank divisions, it is also used as a command vehicle.

60 P Armoured personnel carrier (BTR-60 P) – A light armoured eight-wheel amphibious carrier, open on top. A 7.62 mm heavy machine gun, mounted forward, provides the firepower. It is driven by two 90 HP six-cylinder petrol engines, attaining a land speed of 80 km/h and a water speed of 15 km/h. It is equipped with water-jet propulsion and infra-red driving light and sight. Length 7.76 m, width 2.83, height 2.3 m. The wheels are shod with low-pressure tyres that can be regulated while driving, even if the vehicle is slightly damaged.

60 PA Armoured personnel carrier (BTR-60 PA) – A new generation, developed from the original 60 P in 1965, with closed troop compartment. Weight 10.2 t, lenght 7.56 m, width 2.82 m, height 2.08 m. Armament: a 7.62 mm heavy machine gun mounted on the forward hull wall. Two six-cylinder engines, each of 90 HP, permit a land speed of 80 km/h and water speed of 10 km/h.

60 PB armoured personnel carrier.

60 PB Armoured personnel carrier (BTR-60 PB) – In this further development of the 60 P series, the troop compartment is enclosed in armour up to
13.5 mm thick and hermetically sealed against radioactive and chemical sub-
stances and bacteriological warfare agents. The armament, enclosed in a revolving turret, consists of one 14.5 mm and one coaxial 7.62 mm heavy machine
gun. Weight 10 t, length 7.56 m, width 2.83 m, height 2.31 m. The crew of
anything from three to nine infantrymen can fire through side ports, making
the vehicle a "mobile fortress". Two GAZ-49 90 HP B-engines permit a speed
of 80 km/h on land and 10 km/h in the water. Cruising range 500 km, climbing gradient 30 per cent. It is also used as a radio vehicle.

BMP Armoured personnel carrier – It is claimed to be "the world's first
fully effective carrier". Using the PT-76 amphibious tank's chassis, this
represents the current compromise between a light battle tank and an APC. It
possesses formidable on-board armament – 76 mm anti-tank gun, 7.62 mm
machine gun, and anti-tank rockets – so that it is effective in combat against
armour. Weight 14 t, lenght 6.6 m, width 3.2 m, height 2 m. A rear hatch gives
access under cover for the crew of three plus eight infantrymen. A 280 HP six-
cylinder diesel engine permits a land speed of 65 km/h and water speed of
15 km/h. Cruising range 350 km. The BMP is a very sensitive vehicle and
highly demanding in control and servicing.

MT-LB multi-purpose towing and transport vehicle – This latest Soviet-
manufactured gun-towing vehicle in the Warsaw Pact armies has a net weight
of 12 t, a load ceiling of 2 t, towing power of 2.5 t and accommodation for
crew of two plus eleven men. Length 6.45 m, width 2.85 m, height 1.86 m.
The revolving-turret armament is a 7.62 mm machine gun. A fully-enclosed

tracked vehicle that affords protection both for its own personnel and that of the towed vehicle, as well as of any further load, from infantry fire and shrapnel, and can drive over contaminated terrain. Weapons can be fired through the ports. The eight-cylinder, 240 HP diesel engine permits the following top speeds: with towed vehicle, 47 km/h; without, 62 km/h; in water, with own track propulsion, 5–6 km/h.

Tanks

PT-76 Amphibious tank – This fully armoured amphibious combat vehicle, developed in the early 1950s, ranks as a light tank in weight terms – 14 t. Length 6.91 m or 7.65 m including gun barrel; width 3.14 m, height 2.2 m.

BMP armoured personnel carrier.

T-54 medium battle tank.

T-55 medium battle tank.

Its armament consists of a 76 mm mounted cannon and 7.62 mm coaxial heavy machine gun. The 240 HP diesel engine permits a land speed of 45 km/h; in water 15 km/h is attained by water-jet propulsion. Cruising range 350 km, climbing gradient 30 per cent. With its crew of three, the PT-76 is standard equipment for reconnaissance companies and battalions.

T-54 (T-54 A, T-54 AM) Battle tank – This 36 t tank, developed in the early 1950s, is by Soviet weight-classification the ancestor of the modern medium tank. Length 6.4 m or 9 m including cannon, width 3.27 m, height 2.4 m. Armament consists of a stabilized 100 mm mounted cannon, a coaxial 7.62 mm machine gun, another 7.62 mm forward machine gun, and a 12.7 mm anti-aircraft machine gun on the turret. The twelve-cylinder diesel engine develops 520 HP permitting an average speed of 50 km/h. Range 400 km, climbing gradient 30 per cent. There are infra-red night-driving light and sight, and a snorkel for underwater operation. Crew of four. This tank, several times improved over the last few years, is standard equipment in the tank battalions of motorized infantry and armoured regiments.

T-55 Battle tank – This medium tank is a further offshoot of the T-54, with modifications affecting mainly the interior. In addition to its 100 mm cannon, stabilized in two planes, it also has a coaxial 7.62 mm heavy machine gun. The front-mounted and AA machine guns of the T-54 are dispensed with. The standard equipment includes a snorkel for underwater operations, infra-red night driving light and sight and a more ample supply of ammunition. The cruising range also exceeds the T-54's. Like the T-54 it is standard equipment for the armoured regiments.

T-62 Battle tank – This third generation medium tank is a descendant of the T-55. Weight 36.5 t, length 6.55 m or 9.5 m including cannon, width 3.37 m, height 2.18 m. Armament: 115 mm smooth-barrel cannon, 7.62 mm machine gun and on some models 12.7 mm anti-aircraft machine-gun, too. For firing in the dark the T-62 possesses infra-red observation equipment and night-sight. The twelve-cylinder 580 HP diesel engine permits a speed of 50 km/h. Cruising range over 500 km. It can operate over contaminated terrain, submerge when crossing water barriers and destroy targets with the first shot. Much praised in advance during the early 1960s, this tank has been meanwhile improved on, or overtaken, because of its defects in firepower, armour and manoeuvrability.

T-72 Battle tank – Experience with the T-62 led to this model, which has superior technical equipment on the whole and a completely new chassis with six track wheels instead of the T-62's five. Weighing about 40 t, better armoured and somewhat shorter and wider, it is armed with a 125 mm cannon, one 12.7 mm AA machine gun and one 7.62 mm AA machine gun. The automatic loading, automatic targetting for first-shot strike, and twelve-cylinder 700 HP diesel engine giving the tank a speed of some 70 km/h, lend it improved combat effectiveness. It requires a crew of three, not four as with the T-62, and has a cruising range of some 500 km. Like all Soviet tanks it is equipped with a snorkel and infra-red night driving light.

The modern T-72 medium battle tank, a descendant of the T-62.

Anti-tank weapons

Anti-tank guided missile (PALR = Panzerabwehrlenkrakete) – These small solid-fuel rockets are available in the NVA in various calibres and on a variety of carrier vehicles – ZP-26, SPW-40 P, SPW-40 P 2, SPW-BMP – or as individual weapons. One model well-known in the West under the NATO codename *Snapper* is a meter long, with a calibre of 140 mm and some 25 kg in weight. Its range extends to 2,000 m. Wire-guided; the warhead will penetrate armour 500 mm thick. PALRs can be mounted in clusters of three, four or six. They are relatively cheap and almost indestructible, but rather slow in flight at 115 m per second. The newer generation includes longer-range, still heavier rockets which take up less room in the launching-vehicle – plane, tank or helicopter. Radio-guided PALRs, though easier to control, are also more vulnerable than wire-guided missiles.

57 mm Self-propelled anti-tank gun – This anti-tank artillery piece on its single-axle, split box-trail carriage is driven by a 22 HP petrol engine, permitting an average speed of up to 45 km/h. Two ammunition boxes for 57 mm grenade cartridges are fixed on the trails. Firing range 8.5 km; armour-penetration capability 100 mm at 1,000 m. The gun is drawn by a truck or APC, its own power being used for changing position when deployed. Standard equipment of the motorized infantry battalion.

85 mm Self-propelled gun – This anti-tank weapon on its single-axle, split tube-trail carriage is driven by a 22 HP gasoline engine, giving it a speed of 25 km/h. It uses 85 mm shells which can penetrate 130 mm armour at 1,000 m. It can be drawn by truck or APC, and moved for short distances on its own power. It is operated by a crew of five men. Standard equipment of the motorized infantry regiment.

100 mm cannon – The long barrel is held in a cylindrical cradle and has a muzzle brake. It is carried on a split-trail carriage. It fires 100 mm shells with high-explosive and armour-penetrating warheads. Penetration power 170 mm at 1,000 m. Maximum firing range 20 km, rate of fire 10 shells per minute. Standard equipment of artillery regiments in the motorized infantry divisions.

Anti-aircraft weapons

14.5 mm AA machine gun (ZPU) – The 12.7 mm calibre, formerly used both as field and AA machine gun, has been replaced by this standard ZPU. The twinned version ZPU-2 is also mounted on the PTR-40 and BTR-152 armoured personnel carriers. The ZPU-4 squad version is found mounted on a two-axle cruciform carriage. Effective range for air targets 2,000 m, for ground targets 2,500 m. Rate of fire from each barrel 600 rpm. Single man crew.

23 mm twin AA cannon (ZSU-23-2) – Two fully automatic AA guns mounted coaxially on a 360° revolving platform. This weapon, used in all the services, rests on three footplates when in firing position or on two tyred wheels for the march; for firing, these wheels are folded against the carriage. The gun fires 23 mm shells, effective against low and fast-flying aircraft at up to 1,500 m and against ground targets to 2,000 m. Maximum range 7 km. Effective rate of fire 200 rpm from each tube. With its carriage the weapon weighs barely one ton and can be dropped by parachute. It is towed by truck or APC at up to 70 km/h. Standard equipment of motorized infantry regiments.

Triple anti-tank guided missile on a 40-P armoured personnel carrier.

23 mm quad AA cannon self-propelled carriage (ZSU-23-4) – Four fully automatic AA guns with electronic targetting, housed in superimposed pairs in an enclosed, light armoured revolving turret with radar antenna. Fires 23 mm shells. This light armoured, tracked weapon mounted on a PT-76 as prime mover is effective against aerial targets to a height of 1,500 m or ground targets to a distance of 2,500 m. Maximum range 7 km. With all four barrels the rate of fire is up to 3,400 rpm. Crew of four. With its 240 HP diesel motor this 15 t AA tank attains a speed of 45 km/h. Cruising range 250 km, length 6.85 m, width 3.14 m, height 2.4 m without antenna.

57 mm M-50 AA cannon – A fully automatic gun resting on a two-axle tyred-wheel cruciform carriage that can be lowered to the ground, with swing-out trails. Fires 57 mm shells. With radar equipment aerial targets can be engaged to a height of 6,000 m, with optical sight up to 4,000 m. Maximum range for ground targets 12,000 m, with a penetration capability of 100 mm at 1,000 m. The gun is operated by a crew of seven, weighs about 5 t, can be towed by truck or tractor and is standard equipment in the AA battalions of armoured and motorized infantry divisions.

57 mm twin self-propelled AA gun carriage (ZSU-57-2) – This fully automatic twin gun is mounted on the T-54 light armoured self-propelled tracked carriage. Length 6.2 m, width 3.5 m, height 2.75 m. The turret can be swivelled round 360°. It uses 57 mm shells effective against aerial targets to a height of 8,800 m and ground targets to a distance of 12,000 m. Rate of fire per tube is 100 rpm. Elevation and traverse effected electro-hydraulically. Operated by a crew of seven. A 520 HP diesel engine enables this 28 t AA tank to travel at 60 km/h. Its cruising range is 350 km.

100 mm M-49 AA cannon – This was introduced in the NVA when the 85 mm cannon was no longer adequate. Weighing 10 t in firing position, it can be mounted on a solid-tyre limber barrow, and towed by a ZKW M-1954 tractor. Effective AA range 12,000 m with a maximum range of 15,000 m against aerial targets, 21 km against ground targets. Rate of fire 15 rpm with a 16 kg shell. Part of the equipment of the AA regiment in a territorial defence district.

Anti-aircraft guided missiles

SA-2 – Since 1962 the air defence and ground forces of the NVA have possessed surface-to-air missiles known in the West as SAM (or SA plus code-number) and in the Soviet Union as V 750 VK, or complete with radar and generators as the V 75 SM system. The SA-2 is a two-stage rocket, the first stage with solid fuel and the second with liquid. The missile is 10.7 m long, with a starting weight of 2,300 kg. It is fired from a fixed position. Carried on a ZIL-157 truck, the SA-2 has a vertical range of 18 km and a slant range

Left: Army anti-aircraft guns of various calibres, in the foreground a 23mm anti-aircraft cannon self-propelled carriage (ZSU-23-4), below: 57mm anti-aircraft cannon.

of 40 to 50 km. Guidance is by command, radio, and homing. An SA-2 battery carries six launching rails and twelve missiles, all of which can be set off in less than fifteen minutes. The SA-2, which exists in several versions, has been exported to the Third World and enjoyed initial success in Vietnam.

SA-3 – Displayed in the Soviet Union as far back as 1961, this missile was first shown in the GDR on May 1, 1976. It is a twin rocket, again carried on a ZIL-157 truck and erected by it into firing position, and is the army's AA weapon for medium and low altitudes. Its vertical range is 15 km, slant range 25 to 30 km. There are beam and homing guidance systems. Both stages are solid-fuelled and the length of the missile is 6.7 m.

SA-4 – Another twin missile, shown in Moscow since 1964 and in East Berlin since 1975, self-propelled on its own armoured carriage. Vertical range 24 km, slant range 80 km. It can engage high-flying targets. Its first stage has four solid-fuelled boosters. Total length 8.8 m. Further missiles are carried on another vehicle and crane-hoisted on to the launching-rail, which can be rotated around 360°. An SA-4 battery consists of a command vehicle, eight launching-rail carriers, two fire-control vehicles and a vehicle with other radar equipment, along with several further transporters.

SA-6 – This missile, first displayed in Moscow in 1967, was used in the 1973 Arab-Israeli war where it met with success in the first phase. A 6.3 m long triple rocket mounted on a self-propelled armoured carriage, it is controlled by a combination of command and homing guidance. The launching-rail can be turned round 360° and is highly mobile; rail and fire-control equipment are carried on separate vehicles. The composition of the SA-6 battery is similar to that of the SA-4.

SA-9 – This newest model in the NVA, known since 1975, is quad-mounted on a four-wheeled vehicle, namely the 40 P-2 APC which also carries the launching rail and electronic equipment. For firing, the 360°-traverse frame can be raised with its four rocket-containers; for the transport mode these rest on the wheeled vehicle. Target acquisition and identification as well as guidance are readily achieved by various systems. An army AA weapon particularly suited for engaging low altitude targets, with a range of 8 km.

Artillery

Mortars are classified under tube artillery in the Warsaw Pact armies, being smooth-bore, high-angle guns of simple design. Up to 120 mm calibre they have no breech and are muzzle-loaded. From 160 mm upwards calibre they are loaded from behind like other guns.

82 mm mortar models M-1937, M-1941 and M-1953 are used in the mortar platoons of the motorized infantry divisions. The weapon weighs 56 kg, with a tube length of 1.28 m, range of about 3 km and crew requirement of three.

120 mm M-1953 mortar – When in firing position, the 1.65 m tube rests on a 1 m diameter base-plate and a shock-absorbing bipod, and is operated by

The 122mm self-propelled howitzer (122mm-SFL) was first seen in 1974 (above), however, not yet in the NVA; the 152mm self-propelled howitzer (152mm-SFL) was first shown to the public in 1976 and for the first time to be seen in the NVA in 1979 (below).

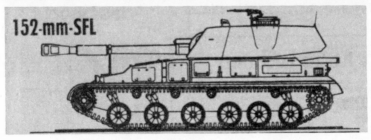

five men. It weighs 275 kg and for transport is towed by truck or APC on a single-axled, pneumatic-tyred trailer. It fires 120 mm shells producing shrapnel and smoke. The range is about 6 km, the rate of fire 9 rpm. Standard equipment of mortar batteries in the motorized infantry regiments.

160 mm M-1943 mortar – This provides a cheap means of considerably increasing artillery firepower. The piece weighs 1,300 kg, has a tube-length of 2.5 m and a range of 8 km. The projectile weighs 40 kg. It requires a crew of six and is transported, hitched at the muzzle, on a carriage.

122 mm M-1938 howitzer – With a total weight of 2.5 t, this high-angle gun with its conventional barrel-cradle is mounted on a single-axle split-trail carriage. It fires 122 mm cartridge shells; maximum range is 12 km and rate of fire 5 to 6 rpm. Like all artillery, the howitzer can also be used to fire armour-penetrating ammunition. It requires a crew of seven and is towed by truck. Standard equipment of an artillery regiment in both armoured and motorized infantry divisions.

122 mm D-30 howitzer – This modern Soviet-made gun, first shown by the NVA in 1974, has a muzzle brake and can be turned through 360° on its base-plate. This in turn rests in the firing position on three trails splayed forwards and sideways, and in the travel position on a single-axled carriage. The muzzle brake also provides a towing hitch, so that the whole piece can be towed, with trails and barrel pointing forward, by a single truck – the Tatra 813 or Ural 375-D. It fires 122 mm high-explosive and armour-penetrating shells, with a maximum range of 15 km. Its aim is exceptionally precise and it is standard equipment in the artillery regiments of motorized infantry and armoured divisions.

122 mm self-propelled howitzer (122-mm-SFL) – This example of the new generation of self-propelled artillery was first displayed in Poland in 1974. The external characteristics of this amphibious howitzer are the chassis, similar to that of the PT-76 but with seven instead of six track-wheels; a pontoon-shaped hull; driving-wheel in front, motor front right, driver's port on the left; revolving turret – quite novel for self-propelled artillery – with two exit ports; modern infra-red targetting and observation devices; large muzzle brake and ejector in the front third of the 122 mm barrel. The turret facilitates mobility in fire control. With this weapon, too, the principle is applied that a self-propelled howitzer should be of larger calibre than the tanks it provides support for.

152 mm howitzer M-1943 (D 1) – Already in use during World War II, this gun uses the same carriage as the 122 mm M-1938 and possesses a muzzle brake. It uses 152 mm cartridge shells with high-explosive and armour-penetrating warheads; rate of fire 3 to 4 rpm. Maximum range about 12 km. Weighing 3.5 t, it is hitched to a tractor for transport and is standard equipment in the artillery regiment of every territorial defence district.

152 mm M-55 gun howitzer (D-20) – This modern Soviet-made weapon, first shown by the NVA in 1974, has a muzzle brake and two hauling-cylinders over the barrel and rests on a single-axle split-trail carriage, which is furnished with folding pivot-rollers and a support plate. It fires cartridge shells with fragmentation, high-explosive, armour and hollow-charge warheads. Maximum range around 17 km, rate of fire 4 rpm. Weighing 6 t, the gun is towed by tractors such as the Tatra 813 or Ural 375-D; on good roads it attains a speed of 60 km/h, cross-country 15 km/h. Standard equipment in the artillery regiment of every territorial defence district.

152 mm self-propelled howitzer (152-mm-SFL) – The NVA first put this Soviet new-generation piece of heavy self-propelled artillery on display for the GDR's 30th anniversary on October 7, 1979. It has a heavy chassis with six medium-sized track wheels and four small track return rollers, a pontoon-shaped hull, front drive, revolving turret and long barrel with muzzle brake and ejector, and modern targetting and observation equipment and infra-red devices. The turret has side-ports and an AA machine-gun mounted on the right side. This howitzer can travel in water.

100 mm cannon – See above under anti-tank weapons.

130 mm cannon – This muzzle-brake gun is held in a traditional barrel-cradle and rests on a splay-carriage with wheel-supported limber. It fires 130 mm high-explosive and armour-penetrating cartridge shells. Maximum range 27 km. Weighing 8 t, it is towed by a Tatra 813 tractor. With its crew of eight, it belongs to the artillery regiment equipment of each territorial defence district.

Rocket launchers and ground-to-ground guided missiles

122 mm BM-21 rocket launcher – Developed in 1964, this 13 t multiple launcher is transported, up to 75 km/h, on an Ural-375 D truck. There is a turntable carriage to which four banks of ten launching tubes are fixed. They fire three-meter long 122 mm calibre projectiles to a distance of up to 20 km. These are detonated either from the BM-21's own cabin or by distant control up to 60 m away. With its forty tubes, this is among the area fire weapons of the motorized infantry division's artillery regiments.

240 mm BM-24 rocket launcher – Introduced into the NVA in 1963, this multiple rocket launcher carried on a ZIL-175 truck has its launching rack on a turntable carriage for twelve rockets, mounted in two superimposed ranks of six, each of 240 mm calibre. The warheads can be filled with explosive or chemical agents. Maximum range 12 km. This area fire weapon is held by the artillery regiments of motorized infantry divisions. In 1975 the NVA showed a new version with a forty-tube launching rack, mounted on a Ural-375 D or Tatra-813 Koloss truck.

Tactical rocket on self-propelled tracked carriage – The unguided ground-to-ground solid-fuel rocket known in NATO as FROG 4 (FROG = Free Rocket Over Ground) is launched from a single rail mounted on a light armoured self-propelled carriage of the PT-76 amphibious tank series. The rocket, which can

Unguided tactical ground-to-ground rocket (Nato codename: Frog-4, Free Rocket over Ground).

Unguided tactical ground-to-ground rocket Frog-7.

Guided operational-tactical ground-to-ground missile (Nato codename: Scud-A).

Guided operational-tactical ground-to-ground missile Scud on a four-axled tractor truck.

carry a nuclear warhead, is propelled by two boosters to engage targets as distant as 45 km. Standard equipment of rocket battalions in motorized infantry and armoured divisions.

Tactical rocket on eight-wheeled self-propelled carriage – This unguided ground-to-ground solid-fuel rocket – NATO codename FROG-7 – is launched from a rail mounted on a ZIL-135 eight-wheeled self-propelled carriage. The one-stage rocket, which can take a nuclear warhead, can reach targets as far off as 60 km. Held by rocket battalions of both motorized infantry and armoured divisions.

Medium range missile on self-propelled tracked carriage – This guided ground-to-ground missile – NATO codename T-7A SCUD-A – is launched from a rail mounted on a heavy tracked self-propelled carriage of the same design as the JS battle tank. The one-stage missile, using liquid fuel and accommodating a nuclear warhead, is launched vertically from a horseshoe-shaped platform and achieves ranges of 150 km. This system is held by the rocket brigade of each territorial defence district.

Operational-tactical missile on eight-wheeled self-propelled carriage – This guided ground-to-ground missile – NATO codename T-7B SCUD-B – rests on a launching rail mounted on an MAZ-543 eight-wheeled self-propelled carriage. The missile body, which uses liquid fuel and can be fitted with a nuclear warhead, has a range of 250 km. Standard equipment of a rocket brigade in each territorial defence district.

Engineer equipment

P2 S amphibious truck – This four-wheel drive amphibian is an East German imitation of the small Soviet MAV amphibious truck in the GAZ-46 series. The two-axled, solid tyre truck is 5.1 m long and weighs 1.96 t; it is driven by a four-cylinder petrol engine. On the road it reaches a speed of 95 km/h, in water it can manage 10 km/h with its propellor. An all-purpose vehicle of the first amphibious generation, it holds four men. No longer in the inventory of engineer units.

BAV medium amphibious truck – A six-wheel drive, three-axled amphibious truck designed on the ZIL-485 series. Length 9.5 m, width 2.5 m, height 2.6 m. The six-cylinder petrol engine develops 110 HP and gives the seven-tons vehicle a road-speed of 80 km/h and a water-speed of 10 km/h. Cruising range 500 km. It will carry loads of 2.5 t on land and 3 t in the water. Capacity 28 fully equipped men or one artillery piece, such as a 122 mm howitzer. At the rear it has a loading flap and capstan. Once standard equipment of the pioneer battalion in both motorized infantry and armoured divisions, but subsequently withdrawn.

K-61 large amphibious truck – With a weight of 9.5 t, this heavy tracked vehicle is 9.15 m long, 3.15 m wide and 2.15 m high. It will carry payloads of

3 t on land or 5 t in the water, with room for a 152 mm howitzer, a truck or 40 men with their equipment. Driven by a 135 HP diesel motor, it can travel at 35 km/h on land and 10 km/h in the water. Cruising range 260 km. Standard equipment of landing and rivercrossing units in engineer battalions of both motorized infantry and armoured divisions.

PTS-M heavy amphibious truck – A 17.7 t heavy tracked amphibian, 11.5 m in length, 3.3 m in width and 2.65 m in height. An improved version of the K-61; it will hold 70 men and carry a payload of 5 t on land and 10 t in the water. Land speed up to 40 km/h, water speed up to 15 km/h. The enclosed cabin provides protection from nuclear radiation. An infra-red searchlight facilitates night travel. Standard equipment of engineer battalions in motorized infantry and armoured divisions.

Self-propelled tracked ferry (GSP) – A heavy ferry constructed from components of the PT-76 and K-61 amphibious trucks. It has a tractive power of 50 t and reaches a speed of 30 km/h on land and 10 km/h in the water.

AT-T heavy tracked artillery tractor – A specialized vehicle held by engineer units since 1958 and using the T-54 tank chassis. Net weight 20 t, road and cross-country payload 5 t, towing capacity 25 t. Length 7 m, width 3.2 m, height 2.85 m. The twelve-cylinder A-401 diesel motor develops 415 HP. Speed 5–35 km/h, cruising range 700 km, climbing gradient up to 58 per cent.

PMP pontoon bridge equipment – This is part of a construction set carried in its entirety on 18 transport vehicles. The individual river and shore pontoons are laid on the water and raised up again by lifting tackle installed on the transport vehicles. Once the parts have been assembled in the water they make a pontoon bridge 120 m long with a six-meter roadway. Parts of the set can also be assembled as ferries with a load capacity of 100 t, and propelled by power boats. The pontoon set is held by engineer battalions in the motorized infantry and armoured divisions, and in the territorial defence districts.

TMM heavy treadway bridge – The two-part bridge, carried on a KrAZ truck, has its own laying equipment. Each treadway is 1.5 m wide. Unfolded, the bridge is 4 m wide and 11 m long and will carry a load of 60 t. It takes about forty minutes to erect. A set comprises four such bridges and is standard equipment for engineer units in the motorized infantry regiments, and in both motorized infantry and armoured divisions.

MTU bridge-laying tank – The 3.5 m broad, 14 m long treadway bridge is mounted on a T-54 tank chassis. The whole span can be pushed forward horizontally, laid in position and picked up again by the prime mover. It will sustain a load of 50 t. The MTU was for a long time the main bridge-laying tank in the Warsaw Pact forces.

BTU tank dozer – Every battle tank can be fitted with a dozer blade for removing obstacles or levelling covering trenches.

BLG-60 – This bridge-layer is an East German variant based on the T-55 tank. Weighing 37 t, it has remarkable driving performance and its 21 m long,

3.2 m wide folding bridge has a high load capacity of 50 t. Like all its predecessors this vehicle shares the perfomance details of the T-55.

PT-55 mine clearing equipment – Comprising two sets of four rollers, this can be fixed with appropriate attachment to every battle tank.

PMR-3 mine layer – This consists of a chute with ploughshare and earthing-over brushes at the end; mounted on a single-axle, it can be hitched to an APC. It is single-manned and lays mines while travelling at about 15 km/h.

E-305 W truck dozer – An earth-moving machine mounted on a KrAZ truck chassis. Equipped with dozer blade; high-level and low-level shovels and draw bucket; grab, and crane. The equipment is driven by a 48 HP motor separately from the prime mover. Digging rate up to 60 cubic meters per hour.

DOK-M universal engineer machine – This specialized vehicle of Czechoslovak manufacture is designed for road and emplacement construction, barricade clearing and vehicle salvaging (cable-winch) and cutting angle-steel (electro-welder). The air-cooled twelve-cylinder diesel motor develops 255 HP and runs a generator (for four electric driving motors and the winch-motor) as well as a set of hydraulic pumps. It also provides a source of current for welding and metal cutting. Earth-moving capacity 150 cubic meters per hour.

BAT-M road-building machine – This is a full-track AT-T artillery tractor fitted with a 4–5 m wide dozer blade for various earth-moving jobs. It can dig large trenches at a rate of 150 to 450 cubic meters per hour, scurf a 10 cm layer of top-soil at 4 to 5 km/h and lay paths for transport columns at a rate of from 1.5 to 10 km/h. Its crane can carry 2 t and its net weight is 27.5 t. In travel posture it is 7.05 m long, 4.5 m wide and 3.75 m high. Road speed 22 km/h.

BTM-3 ditching machine – An improved version of the Soviet BTM series, this bucket-wheel ditcher mounted on the full-track AT-T artillery tractor can move about 800 cubic meters of earth an hour. It can dig ditches in any pattern 1.5 m deep, even in frozen soil.

Miscellaneous wheeled vehicles

ES 250 A medium-weight motor cycle – This single-seater with its single-cylinder two-stroke air-cooled petrol engine, developing 14.25 HP at 5,100 rpm, was superseded in 1963 by the 16 HP ES-250/1/A model. The following *ES-250/2/A* built from 1968 onwards has a 17.5 HP engine; with this model the top speed was increased to 105 km/h and cruising range to 390 km. Since 1973 this series has been gradually replaced by the more modern *TS-250/A/19* HP cycles made in Czechoslovakia.

P 3 car – This multi-purpose cross-country vehicle produced in East Germany during the 1960s has a payload capacity of 0.75 t. Its differential-gear limiters and low-pressure tyres enable it to negotiate terrain with poor bearing quality. It has seven seats and is powered by a 75 HP six-cylinder four-stroke petrol engine. Maximum speed 95 km/h, cruising range 540 km, climbing gradient 65 per cent. It is used as a command, signals and repair squad vehicle.

GAZ-69 car – Based on Soviet products of the 1950s, the GAZ-69 has a stable bucket design and rear seats positioned lengthwise. Length 3.85 m, width 1.85 m, height 2.03 m. Net weight 1,535 kg, load capacity 425 kg, towing capacity 750 kg, two plus six seats. Four-stroke four-cylinder petrol engine, developing 65 HP. Maximum speed 90 km/h, cruising range 340 km, climbing gradient 55 per cent. It is used as a command car, a prime mover for anti-tank guided missiles, an anti-parachutist squad vehicle or a mortar and light rocket-launcher tractor.

UAZ-469 car – This multi-purpose cross-country car, a replacement for the GAZ-69, has a net weight of 1,380 kg, hard-surface payload of 500 kg, towing capacity of 850 kg. Length 3.96 m, width 1.77 m, height 1.93 m. The four-cylinder petrol motor develops 72 HP. Maximum road speed 100 km/h, cruising range 450 km.

Robur truck (LO-1800 A) – This cross-country truck of East German manufacture is used for transport, for traction, as a cable-laying squad vehicle or as maintenance workshop with or without open roof. From the basic model there were evolved a box (Type 1) and specialbox (Type II) model, as well as a box Type III with side-flap. The Robur uses a 70 HP air-cooled four-cylinder petrol engine; it has a top speed of 80 km/h, range of 590 km, climbing gradient of 45 per cent. There are four plus twelve seats.

ZIL-157 truck – This Soviet-made three-axle multi-purpose vehicle is driven by a 104 HP six-cylinder petrol engine. It has three seats plus fourteen to twentyeight. The low-pressure tyres and tyre regulation mechanism permit the negotiation of terrain with poor bearing quality. It is used for transport and traction. A closed-in variant is made for special built-in accessories.

G-5 truck – This three-axle, all-wheel-drive multi-purpose vehicle with a payload of 5 t and towing capacity of 8 t is of domestic GDR manufacture. It is used for transport and for traction. In addition to the standard model there is the G-5 with all-weather roof, the special closed model, the G-5 tanker, the breakdown truck and so forth. The six-cylinder diesel engine develops 120 HP. Maximum speed is 60 km/h, range 585 km and climbing gradient 42 per cent.

Ural-375 D truck – This Soviet-made three-axled eight-ton lorry is used for transporting (5 t capacity) or towing (10 t capacity) heavy loads and troops. It has low-pressure tyres and pressure-regulation capability. The eight-cylinder petrol engine develops 180 HP. Top speed 75 km/h, range 600 km, climbing gradient 65 per cent.

KrAZ 214 truck – This Soviet-made three-axled heavy lorry of 12.5 t carries a payload of 7 t and has a towing capacity of 50 t on roads and 10 t cross-country. The six-cylinder diesel engine develops 205 HP. Maximum speed 55 km/h, range 530 km, climbing gradient 55 per cent. The steering is power-assisted. Used for transport and traction of heavy loads.

Tatra 813 (Kolos) tractor – This all-wheel-drive multi-purpose tractor, specially adapted for engineer units and as a prime mover for rocket-launchers, is produced in Czechoslovakia. Net weight 14.4 t, payload 8 t, trailer capacity 100 t on roads, 15 t cross-country. Length 8.8 m, width 2.5 m, height 2.7 m. The tractor has eight wheels and two individually steered axles; driven by an air-cooled twelve-cylinder diesel engine of 250 HP, it attains on its own the fairly high speed 85 km/h. Range 1,000 km, climbing gradient 65 per cent. The driving-cabin, sealed against ABC weapons, has room for eight.

II Air Force / Air Defence

The following types of aircraft and of other weapons, not dealt with in the preceding section, are employed in the NVA's Air Force/Air Defence.

MiG-15 – This was the earliest of the jet planes with backswept wings to be designed by the Soviet aircraft builders Mikoyan and Gurevich – hence MiG – from 1946 onwards, and was introduced into the NVA in 1956. Having proved its worth in the Korean War, the MiG-15 was then overtaken as a fighter craft, but is still used for training because of its similarity to succeeding models. The jet engines give it a maximum speed of 1,050 km/h. It has a range of 1,300 to 1,800 km and reaches an altitude of 15,000 m. Its armament consists of two 23 mm and one 37 mm guns which can fire 30 23 mm and 6–7 37 mm shells per second.

MiG-17 – This single-jet fighter-bomber is an improved version of the MiG-15. Introduced as the air arm's standard fighter, it is now used only in the fighter-bomber role. Vaunted as the "crowning achievement of subsonic fighter construction", it attains a speed of 1,000 km/h at 3,000 m. Under normal conditions the operational radius is 1,200 km. It can be fitted with two reserve fuel tanks under the wings, enabling it to fly for two-and-a-half hours. Operational ceiling 15,000 m. Armament consists of two 23 mm and one 37 mm gun, together with two containers each holding 16 unguided 57 mm air-to-ground rockets. The F version is fitted with a WK-1F afterburner which shortens take-off-distance to 350 m instead of 590 m.

MiG-17 PF – This version is equipped for night and all-weather combat with an Isumrud-1 radar sight which acquires targets at 12 km and enables them to be engaged at 2 km with the three 23 mm guns.

MiG-21 (MiG-21 F-13) – This single-jet, single-seater high performance fighter with delta wings was first displayed in the Soviet Union in 1956 and is the standard fighter in the GDR. It reaches a maximum speed of 2,000 km/h (Mach 2) at 12,000 m. Operational radius between 1,500 and 2,000 km, ceiling over 20 km. It is made in several versions, one with two 37 mm guns and air-to-air missiles, another, with somewhat superior performance, armed with missiles only. Two-seater variants have also been made for training. New

MiG-17.

service models are provided with radar sights for all-weather operation, a recognition device and a wide range of other electronic equipment.

MiG-23 – The first swing-wing aircraft from Mikoyan's drawing board, it reached the East German air force in 1978. A single-seater interceptor, also used as a fighter-bomber, it has a length of about 17 m, a wing-span – according to posture – of 8 or 14 m, and a weight of between 12,700 and 15,000 kg.

MiG-21.

MiG-23.

It attains the high velocity of 2,450 km/h at an altitude of 10,000 m. Operational ceiling around 18,000 m and radius over 1,000 km. By way of armament it carries a 23 mm twin-barrel gun and air-to-air rockets, as well as free-fall bombs, if required. The large forepart of the fuselage, with the nosecone tapering into the pitot boom, contains distant-scanning radar. The electronic equipment of this all-weather fighter is more comprehensive than in previous types.

MiG-27 – This fighter bomber, also with swing wings, differs externally from the MiG-23 mainly in the forepart of the fuselage. On the underside it is flat as far as the nose and of the same width as the rear, while its side view presents a flat downward slope from cabin to nose. The pitot boom is positioned on the starboard side of the nose. Maximum speed about 1,300 km/h, operational radius between 500 and 1,400 km according to the armament carried, which comprises a six-barrel 23 mm gun, air-to-ground rockets and free-fall bombs. Like all swing-wing aircraft, the MiG-27 and its complex technology place severe demands on both pilot and service and supply personnel.

IL-28 – This machine, made by the Soviet aircraft designer Ilyushin, has been turned out in large numbers since 1950. A light tactical bomber, it is a high-wing monoplane with two jets and carries a crew of three – pilot, navigator

20 mm guns, and free-fall bombs. It is still used to tow aerial practice targets.
radius 2,500 km, ceiling 12,500 m. Armament consists of two 23 mm and two
and rear-gunner. Maximum speed at 10,000 m around 900 km/h. Operational

IL-14 – This plane is used to transport medium-weight cargo (up to 5 t) and
troops and to drop parachutists (24 men). With its two 1,900 HP double-radial
engines, this low-wing monoplane has all-weather capability and reaches a
speed of 400 km/h at an altitude of 2,000 m. The normal operational radius is
800 km and ceiling 7,000 m. This aircraft was built during the 1950s under
license in the GDR.

Tu-124 – Designed by Tupolev for civil flying, this machine is used by the
NVA as a short distance transport plane. The length is 30.5 m, wing span
25.7 m, height 8.1 m. Maximum take-off weight 38,000 kg including a load of
7,450 kg. Speed 825 km/h, ceiling 11,700 m, operational radius with maximum
load 2,320 km or with maximum fuelling 2,930 km.

Tu-134 – Used as a passenger plane by the Soviet Aeroflot line since 1967,
it is in the NVA inventory for short and medium distance transport. Given at
first the codename Tu-124-A, it has a length of 31 m, wing span of 29 m and
height of 9 m. The maximum take-off weight is 44,200 kg including load of
9,250 kg, while that of the *Tu-134-A* model, in service since 1970, is 47,200 kg
with a load of 9,980 kg. At the ceiling altitude of 11,000 m the speed is 870
km/h; operational radius with maximum load 2,830 km, or with maximum
fuelling 4,350 km (4,570 km for the Tu-134-A).

MiG-27.

An-2 – This biplane, used for liaison in all the communist air forces, is driven by a 1,000 HP radial engine. Length 12.4 m, wing span 18.18 m, take-off weight up to 5,500 kg. It can accommodate ten parachutists and is used for training all pilots in paradropping.

L-29 Delfin – An advanced jet trainer of Czechoslovak manufacture. Production of this much-used model ceased in 1974 when another, also Czechoslovak, system, the *L-39 Albatros*, was developed for introduction in all Warsaw Pact forces. The L-39 – with which are associated the TL-39 flight simulator, NKTL-39 catapult training device and K-39 semi-automatic control console – is powered by a Soviet AL-25 TL turbojet engine. At 5,000 m it attains a speed of 750 km/h. Service ceiling 11,300 m, range 1,000 km, rate of climb 22 m per second. Two-man crew. The instrumentation corresponds closely to that of a combat aircraft.

Mi-1 – This four-seater multipurpose helicopter was produced by the Soviet designer Mil in 1949 and introduced into the NVA in 1957. It is used as a liaison and ambulance plane; for the transport of wounded men basket-like containers can be fitted to the outside of the fuselage. It is powered by a single radial engine, has a top speed of 180 km/h and range of 580 km. Service ceiling 3,000 m. A version imported from Poland is called the *SM-1*.

Mi-2 – Built under Soviet license in Poland for the past few years, this version has replaced the Mi-1/SM-1 in the NVA. With two turbojets instead of a single piston engine, the Mi-2 has a superior performance, viz. greater safety, higher speed – 210 km/h – and larger take-off capacity – 3,550 kg instead of 2,290 kg. The equipment is also improved, with a wider range of armament: guided anti-tank missiles, guns and machine guns aft, and traversing machine guns in the cabin.

Mi-4 – Used as a transport helicopter but also adapted for minelaying. In addition to its two-man crew it can accommodate 16 fully armed men or a corresponding weight of vehicles and weapons up to 5,220 kg. The forward position of the 1,700 HP radial engine leaves the rear part of the fuselage available for rapid access. The first of the NVA's helicopters, it has a top speed of 210 km/h, a normal range of 400 km and service ceiling of 5,300 m. It is armed with a 12.7 mm mounted machine gun. The *Mi-4MÄ* variant, with searchlights forward and accommodation for submarine detection and combatting equipment, is also in the People's Navy inventory.

Mi-8 – This has the same dimensions as the Mi-4 – length 25 m, rotor diameter 21 m – but its two engines, each of 1,500 HP, give it enhanced capability: top speed 250 km/h, take-off weight 11,000 kg in place of 6,950 kg, range 500 km. It enjoys greater flight safety, especially over water, and carries four containers for 57 mm unguided air-to-ground rockets. The NVA now has

a modified version serving as a multi-purpose armed plane, carrying 192 57 mm unguided air-to-ground rockets in six containers to the left and right of the fuselage, anti-tank rocket launching-rails on top of these containers, and a traversing machine-gun in the nose. Movable devices on the cabin windows also enable marksmen inside to engage ground targets from the air with their automatics.

Mi-24 (also designated A-10) – The GDR's 30th anniversary parade of October 7, 1979, saw the introduction of a new assault helicopter into the NVA, with slim fuselage, retractable front undercarriage, forward gun, and stump wings for carrying the rocket containers and anti-tank rocket launching-rails. This Mi-24, flown by a Soviet woman-pilot in 1975 at a record speed of 334/464 km/h, is a highly manoeuvrable plane, having little in common with the Mi-8 as regards lift and propulsion.

III People's Navy

The ships of the People's Navy are classified according to battle function into various categories and sub-categories. The categories comprise: *Coastal Defence Ships*, similar in size and purpose to frigates in the West German navy; *Patrol Boats*, subdivided into *Guided Missile Patrol Boats, Large Torpedo Boats* and *Small Torpedo Boats; Submarine Chasers* with sub-categories *Large* and *Small; Clearing Seacraft* with sub-categories *Seagoing Minesweepers (MSR)* and *Coastal Minesweepers (R); Landing Craft*.

Fast Attack Craft form the nucleus of the People's Navy units.

The navy's inventory includes, in addition to the categories mentioned, *Auxiliary Craft* such as *Supply Ships, Tankers, Tugs, Rescue Ships, Fire-Fighting Craft, Diving Vessels* and *Torpedo Recovery Boats*.

Helicopters are the only People's Navy aircraft.

Coastal Defence Ships

At the beginning, between 1957 and 1978, these consisted of Soviet guard ships of the *Riga* type built from 1950 to 1953. These had a displacement of 1,100 t, three 100 mm universal guns, four paired 37 mm guns, a twin torpedo tube, depth charge projectors and runways and elaborate targetting, radar and sonar equipment. Their speed was 25 to 30 knots. They bore the names *Karl Marx, Friedrich Engels, Karl Liebknecht* and *Ernst Thälmann*. None of them is now in service.

In July 1978 the Soviet-built *Rostock* coastal defence ship was commissioned, representing a new generation. According to Defence Minister Hoffmann it possessed "tactical-technical parameters" exemplifying the "summit of scientific achievement" and equal to the "demands of maritime warfare in the present state of the art"[15]. Another ship of the same class, the *Berlin*, entered service in May, 1979. Both ships belong to the Soviet *Koni* type and are armed with anti-aircraft guided missiles.

Some of the most up-to-date ships of the People's Navy: The coastal defence ship "Rostock" (above), the minesweeper "Tangerhütte" (below).

Fast Attack Craft

The People' Navy possesses three different types, providing its main attack capability: *Guided Missile Patrol Boats, Large Torpedo Boats* and *Small Torpedo Boats,* of which the first two are of Soviet, the second of East German manufacture.

Guided Missile Patrol Boats – These are small, fast, handy craft carrying four launching rails on their upper decks for sea-to-sea or sea-to-ground aerodynamic rockets. They have a displacement of 200 tons. They carry radar-guided AA weapons to engage aerial targets. Their four guided tactical rockets enable them to attack any other ship, or suitable land target, without running into enemy fire. Fully automatic radar-guided guns give protection against aircraft or other patrol boats.

The Soviet *Osa* type introduced in the People's Navy has a displacement of 165 t and a length of 40 m. It is driven by three diesel engines and develops a speed of 35 knots. Its armament comprises four launchers and four 30 mm guns. The GDR navy has fifteen boats of this type.

Large Torpedo Boats – These, the People's Navy's main torpedo vehicles, have similar dimensions to the guided missile patrol boats. They have a displacement of 130 t and carry up to four tubes with a corresponding number of torpedos, with electronic equipment to suit. They can travel at over 40 knots. In addition to their torpedos they possess automatic machine guns and can carry light anti-submarine weapons.

The Soviet *P-6* class, built in 1952–53, has a displacement of about 70 t, length 27 m, diesel propulsion, speed about 42 knots and crew of fifteen. Armament: four 25 mm AA guns, two torpedo tubes, twelve depth charges. None of these ships is now in service.

The *Seeteufel* type is East German built. Displacement 150 t, speed about 35 knots. Armament: two 57 mm AA guns and two tubes.

Small Torpedo Boats – The *Forelle* type *Iltis* class of light torpedo boats, also home-produced, have been in the People's Navy since 1963. Main data: displacement of some 55 t, speed 40 knots, armament consisting of two torpedo tubes. No vessel of this type is now in service.

Experience with these light torpedo boats led to the introduction of the *new Small Torpedo Boats* with an additional 23 mm double mount gun for self-defence. Their radar equipment permits more accurate navigation and combat under all conditions of visibility. These boats are true surface-skimmers, starting to ride when 50 or 60 per cent of their full speed is attained. With only half the engine power they have a higher maximum speed, similar armament and better equipment than the earlier light torpedo boats.

Left: "Hai"-class submarine chaser (above), "Osa"-type guided missile patrol boat (below).

Submarine Chasers

Large and small submarine chasers – Their main armament comprises projectors, depth charges and other anti-submarine equipment. Sonar devices enable them to locate, pursue and attack submarines. Semi or fully automatic machine guns provide defence against aircraft and permit them to engage minor surface targets. Displacement up to 400 t, speed 25–30 knots.

The *Hai* class submarine patrol boats built in the GDR in 1962 have a displacement of 300 t, length 57 m, diesel engines, speed of 25 knots. Complement of forty-five men. Armament: four 30 mm AA guns, four times five anti-submarine rockets.

Clearing Craft

The old *Minelaying-and-Minesweeping Ships (MLR-Schiffe)* had a displacement of up to 800 t and were equipped to set up, or remove, mine barriers. They had a top speed of 15 knots. Vessels of this sub-category were also used for other off-shore purposes, for which they carried anti-submarine weapons, artillery and other appropriate equipment. They are all out of service.

One of the most up-to-date of the People's Navy's Seagoing Minesweepers *(MSR-Schiffe)* is the *Tangerhütte* which left the stocks on February 11, 1972, and entered service the same year. Up to October 1977 it had gained the "best ship" title ten times, i.e. in every possible six-month period since it was commissioned.

The older *MLR* and *Minesweepers (R-Boote)* have now been taken out of service. These include the *Habicht I* class built in East German shipyards in 1952–54, the *Habicht II* class (GDR) of 1954–56, and the *Krake* class (GDR) of 1956–58, together with Minesweepers of the *Schwalbe I* class (GDR) of 1953–54 and *Schwalbe II* class (GDR) of 1954–58. Only one *Schwalbe* remains in service.

The mine-section of the People's Navy is nowadays dominated by the *Kondor* class *Coastal Mine-Detectors*. These entered service in the late 1960s and early 1970s. They are some 50 m long with a displacement of about 400 t. Diesel-powered, they can run at over 20 knots. They carry a complement of some twenty-three men and three twin 25 mm AA guns. – The shorter version *"Frontier Ships" (Grenzschiffe)* have only one twin 25 mm AA gun.

Landing Craft

In this category there have also been considerable changes. The *Labo* class and other *Small Landing Craft* of 100 to 200 t, made to carry one, or two, armoured vehicles and their crews, have been taken out of service. The same applies to the *Medium Landing Craft* such as the *Robbe* class, which with a displacement of around 600 t could move and disembark five tanks and a motorized infantry company with all its vehicles.

A "Frosch"-class landing craft being loaded outside a port installation.

Practically all that remain in the People's Navy are the Landing Craft of the *Frosch* class, displacing 1,900 t. Diesel-powered, they can travel at about 18 knots, and are armed with four 30 mm and four 57 mm AA guns, two anti-submarine projectors and mine laying devices. They are constructed to transport troops over long distances (sleeping accommodation).

Because of their fairly deep draught these cannot be used for landing in shallow waters. They are therefore restricted to carrying amphibious tanks and APC, or to transferring their vehicles on to Small or Medium Landing Craft while still in deep water.

Landing craft, as well as their nominal function, can also be used for transporting matériel or laying mines.

Other vessels

One of the largest ships in the People's Navy is the 1,750 t *Wilhelm Pieck Training Ship*, built in the Polish shipyard of Gdansk in 1976. It is 72 m long, 12 m wide and draws 4 m. Propulsion is by two 1,800 HP diesel engines and three 270 HP auxiliary diesel engines. Its armament consists of four twinned 25 mm guns on a double carriage and four 30 mm guns on twin turrets. From May 19 to July 3, 1979, the *Wilhelm Pieck* went on a 10,000 nautical mile voyage that took it as far as the Black Sea. It was escorted by another Polish-built ship, the *Otto von Guericke Salvage and Rescue Ship*. This highly seaworthy ship can also be used as a *Seagoing Tug* and as a mother-ship for diving operations. Polish sources give the following details: standard displacement 1,561.3 t, length 72.2 m, width 12 m, draught 4 m, speed 17.5 knots. Operational range, at an economic speed of 12 knots, 3,000 nautical miles.

Notes

[1] Klaus *Krumsieg*, a German Army Museum specialist, Die Landstreitkräfte der NVA, motorisiert, gepanzert, feuerstark, in: *Armee-Rundschau*, Magazin des Soldaten, East Berlin, 7/1969.

[2] Lieutenant Wilfried *Hanisch* of the GDR Institute of Military History, Armee des Volkes. Zur 20jährigen Geschichte der Nationalen Volksarmee. In: *Volksarmee*, Militärverlag der DDR, East Berlin, 4/1976.

[3] Army General Heinz *Hoffmann* at the 9th SED Party Congress, quoted in: *Volksarmee* 22/1976.

[4] General Heinz *Hoffmann* at the 10th Delegates' Conference on the theme: Überlegenheit des Sozialismus – Weil die Partei uns führt, quoted in: *Volksarmee* 15/1976.

[5] NATO and the new Soviet Threat, Report of Senator Sam *Nunn* and Senator Dewey F. *Bertlet* to the US Senate Committee on Armed Services, January 24, 1977, p. l., US Government Printing Office, Washington 1977.

[6] Ibid., p. 4.

[7] Ibid., p. 4 f.

[8] Ibid., p. 5.

[9] 1979 Weißbuch zur Sicherheit der Bundesrepublik Deutschland und zur Entwicklung der Bundeswehr, pub. for Ministry of Defence, Bonn, September 4, 1979, p. 118 f.

[10] Friedrich *Wiener* (pub.), Taschenbuch der Landstreitkräfte, vol. 2, Die Armeen der Warschauer-Pakt-Staaten, München 1974, p. 42. First English edition 1976, tr. William J. *Lewis*, Vienna 1976.

[11] Ibid.

[12] Ibid., p. 250.

[13] NATO and the new Soviet Threat, v. note 5, p. 14.

[14] Christoph *Bertram*, Warum rüsten die Sowjets? Moskau kann sich allein mit Waffen weltweite Hochachtung verschaffen, in: *Die Zeit*, Hamburg, April 8, 1977.

[15] *Volksarmee*, 31/1978.

CHAPTER TEN

Political-Ideological Education and Training

Political education and training play a *prominent role* in the armed forces of all the communist countries. In the East German services, we read, "*political-ideological education is the heart of socialist troop-leadership*"[1]. Ideology is increasingly

> recognized, and comprehensively applied, as the decisive motive force toward good performance in military service ... How could it be otherwise, since everything we seek to accomplish is achieved by way of human thoughts and feelings, by way of consciously aimed activity under the guidance of the Marxist-Leninist party? And the further we progress in creating an advanced socialist society and the greater the responsibility of the socialist armies for the protection of socialism and peace, the greater also the challenge in the theoretical field and the greater the importance of the mass-effectiveness of socialist ideology ...[2]

Since "political and moral steadfastness is unthinkable without a Marxist-Leninist view of the world"[3], servicemen are enjoined to realize such truths as these:

> The Marxist-Leninist view of the world provides a motive and stimulus for the readiness and endeavour of servicemen to strive, side by side with the Soviet Army and the other fraternal socialist armies, to achieve a high level of fighting strength and combat-readiness in aid of the military defence of our fraternally linked commonwealth of states, and in case of war to secure victory over the aggressor.
>
> It implants socialist relationships in the military collectives, thus decisively influencing the inner stability of the socialist armed forces.
>
> It imbues the actions and behaviour of servicemen with the necessary partisanship and assurance of victory.
>
> Adoption of a Marxist-Leninist view of the world is therefore the most important theoretical precondition for fulfilling our military class-duty and acquiring the forms of thought and behaviour necessary to that end.

For the purposes of ideological education, this means that we must

- impart the specific lessons of Marxism-Leninism to all servicemen, and imbue them with the communist convictions that derive from them;

– foster in all servicemen a profound loyalty and trust toward the working class and its Party, and toward our own socialist state;

– equip all servicemen with comprehensive knowledge of the challenge posed by the struggle to tilt the balance of forces further in the direction of socialism, and of the revolutionary class-mission of the socialist armed forces;

– make clear to all servicemen the unity of proletarian internationalism and socialist patriotism, and instil into them firm internationalist attitudes toward the fraternal socialist states (especially the Soviet Union) and their armed forces;

– give all servicemen a clear picture of the aggressive nature of imperialism and a vivid impression of the enemy, and enhance their capacity for offensive ideological argument; and

– prepare all servicemen for the political-ideological, moral and psychological demands of modern warfare[4].

Though the terms "ideology", "*Weltanschauung*" and "Marxism-Leninism", and equally the terms "training", "education" etc. are often used without clear distinctions, two things stand out:

1. that the "*political-ideological*" *part dominates the overall programme of NVA training*, and
2. that the topic, far from standing on its own, is *interwoven with everything else and is judged by its contribution to combat-readiness.*

The vast importance attached to political ideology emerges, for example, from the definition in the East German Military Lexicon of *Ausbildung* (i.e. the completed process of training, *Bildung)*:

Ausbildung: the unitary process of functional, planned and organized political and military education and training, carried out under the guidance of finishing instructors (*Ausbilder*) with the aim of preparing servicemen and socialist combat collectives in all respects for armed combat.

In the course of this instruction servicemen acquire both general and specialized knowledge and skills, and those moral, intellectual and physical capabilities and qualities are brought out, or perfected, which are required for the fulfilment of the particular duties their service imposes, under all the conditions of modern armed conflict. As a pedagogic process, *Ausbildung* is characterized by a synthesis of education and training, a synthesis of teaching and learning and a synthesis of personality development and development in the collective.

The synthesis of education and training is primarily reflected in *Ausbildung* by its purposeful infusion with ideology, and by the exploitation of every thematic and methodological opportunity to create firm class attitudes among servicemen and to strengthen socialist combat collectives[5].

It is also continually emphasized that political education can only be judged successful if it promotes *combat-readiness.* On this point Colonel General

Heinz Kessler observed in April 1976 at the 10th Delegates' Conference of SED Organizations in the NVA and Frontier Troops:

> In whatever stage we find ourselves in the implementation of the Party Programme and other decisions of the 9th Congress, the struggle for a high level of fighting power and combat-readiness will always be at the centre of the ideological work of communists and SED organizations among the NVA and Frontier Troops[6].

According to another writer, the aim of ideological work in the NVA is "to shape all servicemen into selfless warriors for the cause of socialism, politically and morally steeled and ready to fight at any time"[7]. It is as important to train "socialist soldiers" as "military collectives".

This *"personality of the socialist soldier"* which is always cropping up in socialist military education is defined in the Military Lexicon as follows:

> The socialist soldierly personality *(sozialistische Soldatenpersönlichkeit)* is one which
>
> – is loyally devoted to the working class and its Marxist-Leninist Party and contributes, in the spirit of socialist internationalism and socialist brotherhood-in-arms as well as of love for the socialist fatherland, to the military strengthening and safeguarding of the GDR and the socialist commonwealth;
>
> – is ready and able, in accordance with the military oath and the duties laid down by the Constitution, to fulfil every command of the Party and state leadership; is obedient and disciplined out of political conviction; accepts all the hardships of service; behaves in comradely fashion and strives after military expertise in the combat collective so as to be better prepared for war than the aggressor;
>
> – is deeply imbued with hatred toward imperialism and its hirelings, able at any time correctly to assess the most rapid and fundamental changes in the political and military situation and to fight steadfastly, and win, under the conditions of any possible war. The socialist soldierly personality is among the most decisive factors in the superiority of a socialist army over every imperialist aggressor. It evolves in the course of military activity[8].

Following Engels' axiom that "everything which men set in motion must pass through their heads"[9], paramount importance is accorded in ideological education to *awareness (Bewußtsein)*. But the need is also stressed to appeal to the *emotions*. "Those emotions have to be brought into play which are important for establishing conviction, e.g. desire to survive in order to complete a difficult task."[10] It is essential to achieve "a synthesis of the rational and the emotional in the ideological education of servicemen". And so the commander, too, is responsible for the soldier's "political-moral and psychological preparation"[11].

Methodologically, ideological training is supposed to work by well-aimed impact on the serviceman's consciousness and character whether on or off duty. For this purpose the NVA makes use of the disciplines of "military education theory" *(Militärpädagogik)* and "military psychology", whose beginnings go back to 1957[12]. The foundations were laid by Soviet textbooks that in their day dominated the whole field of education and psychology in East Germany. The NVA made particular use of Colonel Yegorov's "Psychology", the German translation of which was entitled *Militärpsychologie.* Military education and psychology were then taken up in a big way in the East German officers' colleges, and intensive courses on both subjects, run in cooperation with the East Berlin Humboldt University, started in 1960. In the middle sixties the NVA went over to independent empirical research, centred on the Friedrich Engels Military Academy, and a university-level part-time course on military education and psychology was introduced. At present the declared aim is "to enlarge the ideologically instructive function of these sciences and their contribution to forming and intensifying Marxist-Leninist world attitudes among all servicemen, especially commanders and instructors"[13], and to conduct an "offensive confrontation" with "modern bourgeois notions and 'theories'."

On the theoretical side, ideological education in the services is now concentrated on Political Schooling courses for conscript NCOs and other ranks, and Advanced Social Science Courses for officers and career NCOs.

Political Schooling and Advanced Social Science Courses

Political Schooling embraces all "functional ideological training for NVA NCOs and other soldiers based on a long-term programme. Essentially, it is Party schooling..."[14]. By contrast officers and career NCOs, Party and FDJ officials, group leaders in the Political Schooling courses and all soldiers concerned with "political mass-work" attend the *Advanced Social Science Courses (Gesellschaftswissenschaftliche Weiterbildung – GWW)* in various groups.

For both areas new instructions were laid down in a *Political Schooling Directive* based on a Politburo resolution of November 7, 1972, entitled "Agitation and Propaganda Tasks in Implementation of the Decisions of the 8th SED Congress". A survey carried out three years later had this to report on the new system as applied in the People's Navy[15]:

> – At the level of the Political Administration and of Political Departments in the units, the *monthly consultations* with appropriate Politorgan members on the current content of individual GWW and Political Schooling topics has proved its worth. The previous practice, by which discussions in the Political Departments were often concerned only with administrative arrangements, has been superseded in the People's Navy.

> – *Preliminary Schooling* has now become the key to further improvement in Political Schooling. A useful step here has been the formation of special GWW study groups by Political Schooling instructors.

The same survey admits to certain persistent defects, however:

- unjustified exemption from Political Schooling;
- holding courses at times when, because of leave and other reasons, participation is very low;
- lack of coordination of monthly Political Schooling topics with political mass-work;
- unjustified coincidence in time of GWW sessions for staff officers with Political Schooling courses in the units.

Since most of the Political Schooling group leaders are young officers in the first or second duty-grades, who have many other military jobs to do, older officers and staff officers are urged to help them out. Under the "individual leadership" principle, the *commander of a unit is responsible for its Political Schooling;* in practice decisions are made by his deputy, the Political Officer *(Politoffizier).*

Both GWW and Political Schooling courses are large based on guidances from the Main Political Administration, which supplies large quantities of training material. There are tape-recorded lectures, lantern-slides and display charts to enliven lessons, but army students are also encouraged to use their own facilities – films, radio and TV, maps, diagrams, wall-charts, wall-newspapers and so on.

A 1974 report on the "high level of political-ideological work"[16] in the Air Force/Air Defence lays stress on the following aspects of Political Schooling for the future:

1. The starting-points for content planning are the *achievements of socialism in practice (realer Sozialismus),* the value of defending it, and its growing might and superiority as the decisive factor in the worldwide revolutionary process.
2. A more profound awareness should be inculcated of the *dialectics of the class war in the new phase of confrontation* between socialism and imperialism and its impact on the military class-mission.
3. The nature of the *imperialist system must be unmasked.* Its forces "are to be found not just somewhere across the Big Water, but also right on our doorstep in the German Federal Republic".
4. The *"growing historic responsibility of the socialist armed forces"* needs a still more forceful and convincing theoretical exposition.

Four hours a week are set aside in units and staffs for the Political Schooling of NCOs and other soldiers. In addition to the instructor's presentations it includes short talks by individual soldiers. Twenty-minute briefings are given before the start of duty hours as an addition to the regular schooling.

A fixed scheme is also laid down for the officers, career NCOs and Political Workers *(Politarbeiter)* taking part in GWW courses.

Political Schooling in the army is not to be confused with the Party Schooling which SED members undergo in their spare time. This consists, in the NVA, of a monthly meeting conducted by the Company's part-time Party Secretary. The Company's FDJ Secretary similarly holds an FDJ meeting once a month. Finally, special political lectures are held for all servicemen, usually out of hours, every two months or so, with officers or guests from civilian Party organizations as the speakers.

A further device for intensifying Political Schooling is the tightening up of inspection by the Politorgans.

The NVA has learnt from experience that the men are most open to discussion of political events during military exercises, particular just before a climax. Political Officers regular make use of such moments, therefore, to hold meetings of an informational nature.

The "battlefield meeting" *(Kampfmeeting)*, a political training device employed in peace time during major manoeuvres, features visits by senior officers and high Party officials to address the ranks or talk over problems with them. Delegations from the "fraternal armies" are often invited, or veteran workers and Party members may be introduced.

Tradition and example

In the "worldwide confrontation between socialism and imperialism", we read, *"growing importance attaches to history, memories of past events and old traditions"*[17]. These accordingly occupy a big place in ideological instruction. As Colonel Heider of the Friedrich Engels Military Academy goes on to explain,

> the cult of tradition *(Traditionspflege)* does not amount merely to passing on facts about historic events and processes. More than any other form of ideological work it is aimed directly at the encouragement of moral norms and conduct, at bringing people to act and behave in the socially relevant manner when grappling with present or future tasks. To cultivate tradition means to expose the historic meaning of past actions by progressive individuals and class forces, and to present them in a way that strengthens the will and provides motivation... The fostering of military tradition thus contributes to the development of socialist soldierly personalities.

Traditionspflege in the NVA, according to the Military Lexicon, derives from "resolutions of the SED Central Committee and the GDR government, as well as the research findings of Marxist-Leninist historiography. It is characterized by partisanship and scholarliness"[18].

Tradition-fostering in the NVA takes such forms as

- presentation of banners and oath-taking ceremonies,
- meetings with working-class veterans,
- visits to historic sites and the GDR Army Museum, and
- anniversary commemorations.

Strands in the "progressive military tradition" include

- the struggle of the German working class and its revolutionary Party,
- the part played by German patriots and internationalists in other countries' national and social liberation movements, the impact of progressive forces on the history of the German people,
- the achievements of the NVA in the military safeguarding of the GDR's socialist construction, and
- the consolidation of brotherhood-in-arms with the allied armed forces, especially the Soviet Army.

Further *progressive elements in history,* we learn, are

the centuries-long self-sacrificing struggle of the popular masses to have an army of their own for securing and protecting the interests of the working folk, and the demand for a general arming of the people as the keystone of the working class's revolutionary military programme in its struggle against capitalist exploitation and militarism[19].

The *unity of army and people* enshrined in the National People's Army is another historic achievement which Defence Minister Hoffmann stressed in an article written in 1975.

In 1956 there arose a German army which has continued in the progressive traditions of German military history: the traditions of the Peas-

Delegates at an NVA Party meeting.

ants' War and the Wars of Liberation, of the workers' defence forces of 1918/19, of the Red Army of the Ruhr, of the German International Brigade fighters and the Anti-fascist warriors. And this was the first professional socialist army of liberated workers and farmers to come into being in a country which had brought forth not only outstanding bourgeois military men – a Scharnhorst or a Clausewitz – but also a theoretical military genius of the working class, Friedrich Engels[20].

Another writer declared in 1976 that

> the many millions who fell in the Second World War remain in the memory of the GDR people. We distinguish clearly enough between soldiers who were misused for imperialist purposes, and the fascist potentates with their 'last-drop-of-blood' generals... And so the eternal flame that flickers in the memorial in our capital, Berlin, to recall the victims of fascism and militarism, commemorates the Unknown Anti-fascist Resistance Fighter as much as the Unknown Soldier[21].

It may, of course, be thought that the NVA soldier, seeing that "eternal flame", must have some difficulty in supposing that it honours his father who fell in Russia, when during his compulsory reading of Soviet war literature he is expected to be enthusiastic over descriptions of "fascist mercenaries" being ruthlessly slaughtered.

After an initial period of silence about *German history, "national tradition"* began to be approved again at the 2nd SED Conference of July 9/10, 1952, when the writing of national history was elevated to a Party policy. However, only slow progress was made in putting the new directives into practice. Not till 1956 were the *uniforms* of the Garrisoned People's Police, hitherto similar to those of Soviet soldiers, replaced by others resembling those of the *Wehrmacht*. In 1961 monuments were erected once more to the *Prussian generals* Blücher, Gneisenau and Scharnhorst. In 1963 the NVA celebrated the *Völkerschlacht* of Leipzig, and since 1968 an NVA guard of honour has stood at Gneisenau's grave.

It is now some time since the SED reached the conclusion that the GDR need not be ashamed of its *revolutionary tradition* vis-à-vis the other socialist countries. The highest proletarian authorities can be quoted for its revolutionary past. Friedrich Engels, for example:

> The German people also has its revolutionary tradition. There was a time when Germany was bringing forth men who could be set beside the best revolutionaries of other countries[22].

Despite this testimony it remains difficult to discover a clear pedigree for the NVA. Though scholars and writers have striven for decades to present a *consistent historical picture,* there are still many blank patches. At irregular intervals the NVA soldier learns from his army press of new names and events on which to base his sense of "tradition".

There is another, ideological obstacle in the way of the tradition-makers, namely the view that *only the popular masses are capable of achieving historic progress.* But since it is clearly impossible to link a military tradition with anonymous crowds, the NVA is repeatedly forced to justify exceptions to the rule.

> We are well aware – and it is our duty to go on explaining this to officers, NCOs and other ranks – that it is the popular masses who are the authors of all progress in history. But at the same time we must stress that, in order to do justice to their decisive historic role, they themselves produce outstanding personalities who ... devise and formulate the policies of their class, their state or their Party, who organize the implementation of those policies and guide the activities of thousands and millions of human beings[23].

The various *traditional elements* can be grouped under these headings:

- glorious feats of arms in the service of progress,
- examplary class warriors,
- great soldiers and military politicians,
- exemplary socialist fighting groups,
- exemplary NVA units,
- exemplary NVA soldiers,
- German-Russian brotherhood-in-arms,
- socialist brotherhood-in-arms, and
- military traditions due for rejection.

All these categories are being continually supplemented and revised. Under the first heading we have

- 1525 the Great Peasant War,
- 1813 the heroic freedom struggle against Napoleon,
- 1848 the revolution in Germany,
- 1918 the November revolution in Germany,
- 1919 the Bavarian Soviet Republic,
- 1920 the communist rising in the Ruhr,
- 1921 the communist operations in Central Germany,
- 1923 the communist rising in Hamburg,
- 1936 the International Brigade's part in the Spanish Civil War, and
- 1961 the building of the Berlin Wall on August 13, by which the NVA "preserved the peace".

The list of *exemplary class warriors* is particularly prone to expansion. It includes all communist officials who were executed or died in concentration camps in the Nazi era. Then come deceased SED officials, Party poets and so forth; here a special effort is made to establish their fame, since they are mostly quite unknown people who lived in anonymity before 1933 and so lend themselves admirably to the creation of legends. Units and barracks are named after them, so that their inclusion in the cult of tradition is assured. Among the better known "exemplary class warriors" are August Bebel, Karl Liebknecht, Rosa Luxemburg, Franz Mehring, Ernst Thälmann, Richard Sorge, Otto Grotewohl and Wilhelm Pieck.

The roll-call of great soldiers and military politicians is also continually added to. The well-known personalities here include Florian Geyer, Götz von Berlichingen, Thomas Münzer, General Clausewitz, Major von Lützow, Major von Schill, Field Marshal Blücher, General von Scharnhorst, General von Yorck, General von Gneisenau, Theodor Körner and Friedrich Engels.

Here, too, there is a constant effort to squeeze in unknown names in order to celebrate revolutionary military virtues. Suitable candidates for the process are those German deserters like Fritz Schmenkel who fought in *communist partisan groups* during the last war, and German communists like Ernst Schacht who fought in the *Red Army*.

The SED daily *"Neues Deutschland"* has provided the following data to qualify Fritz Schmenkel as a great soldier:

While a corporal in the 186th Artillery Regiment he decided in the late autumn of 1941 to leave his unit. He fell ill, found his way to a Russian peasant hut behind the lines and was there nursed back to health by a peasant woman. He joined a partisan group. His qualifying test was "to shoot a fascist officer before the eyes of his comrades". He became a member of the "Death to Fascism" unit. Wearing German uniform, he ambushed a German supply transport. He was given the code-name Ivan Ivanovich. Schmenkel fell "into the hands of fascist myrmidons and perished, like a brave communist, from the assassins' bullets". "In the darkest night of fascism, patriots like Fritz Schmenkel rescued the honour of the German working class. Fritz Schmenkel, Hero of the Soviet Union, remains unforgotten!"[24]

Of the "great soldier" Ernst Schacht we learn the following: He was born in 1904, the son of German emigrés in Switzerland. In 1918 he joined the Communist Youth Association, in 1922 the Office of the Communist Youth International in Berlin. In 1924 he emigrated to Moscow, in 1926 he entered the Communist Party of the Soviet Union and was trained at the Borisoglebsk Flying School. In 1928 he flew against the counter-revolutionary Bazmachi in Central Asia; in 1936 he took part in the fighting in Spain and earned the Order of Lenin; in 1937 he became a Hero of the Soviet Union, in 1938 a Major-General and Commander of the Soviet Union's Advanced Tactical Flying School; in 1941 he was shot on the instructions of Beria as an alleged agent of the German General Staff. "Ernst Schacht, Soviet general of German nationality, Hero of the Soviet Union, helped to forge the world's first socialist air force. Even after he had fallen he remained in the ranks of the fighters, for Soviet pilots who had been his pupils went on to smash the fascist foe!"[25]

The most obvious candidates for the label of *"exemplary NVA soldier"* are those who have lost their lives in Frontier Troop service along the Berlin Wall or the western border. It matters little whether those in question had just committed a breach of duty, like Captain Rudi Arnstadt on August 14, 1962, or like two East German servicemen who in 1976 were shot by another NVA member escaping to West Germany. All were in truth victims of the frontier conditions created by East Germany, and in particular of the "Shoot to kill" directive.

Zealous NVA soldiers, however, can win the "exemplary" epithet without dying. Defence Minister Hoffmann – himself the first (1975) "Hero of the GDR" – has commended Lieutenant Colonel Biermann, commander of an armoured regiment, as an *"exemplary NVA soldier"*:

> Already as a cadet Comrade Biermann had marked himself out by his consistent Party-mindedness in thought and action, his perseverance in learning, his ardour in overcoming difficulties, his respect for the collective and his initiative in carrying out all orders. As a member of the Party Executive in the Officers' Academy he always bore in mind our Party's advice that an officer can only meet the exacting demands of a socialist army if he acts above all as a teacher toward the troops under his command and has the ability, by word and deed, to guide the creative energies of the whole collective toward the solution of its political and military tasks. By his example and his diligence he contributed decisively to the way in which the soldiers, NCOs and officers of his unit took the initiative in rallying mass support among soldiers, NCOs and officers of the NVA to honour the 15th anniversary of the foundation of the GDR[26].

Not only individuals but whole units can be singled out as exemplary. The following rank as *"exemplary socialist fighting formations"*:

- the People's Navy Division (which existed from November 11 to December 25, 1918, in Berlin),
- the Red Army of the Ruhr (1921),
- the Proletarian Hundreds (1923),
- the Red Front-fighters' League *(Roter Frontkämpferbund – 1924 to 1933),*
- the Thälmann Brigade in Spain (1936), and
- the "Free Germany" National Committee in the U.S.S.R. (1943 to 1945).

Here again additions are being continually made. In 1976, for example, the periodical *"Militärgeschichte"* wrote of the "international character, build-up and activity of the illegal military organization in the Buchenwald concentration camp". According to this account it featured a strict military hierarchy from "Director of the international military organization" down to "Group leader", and some of the units were called "battalions". "The military cadres were in general recruited from among communists, whose reliability, steadfastness and ability to keep silent had been tested a hundred times. In a few cases other anti-fascists were brought in."[27]

There are already *"exemplary units" in the NVA,* for the leaders are naturally concerned to establish a tradition within the new army. Articles in the military press, publications, TV and radio broadcasters are always on the look-out for "examples" to hold up. The number and nature of "latter-day models of heroism in the performance of duty" knows almost no bounds.

The theme of *German-Russian brotherhood-in-arms* is very prominent in the NVA's cult of tradition. It is regarded as dating from the Convention of Tauroggen on December 30, 1812, when the Prussian general Count Ludwig Yorck (later von Wartenburg) at first agreed on the neutralization of the Prussian troops with the Russian general Dyebich. Their subsequent coopera-tion in fighting the imperialist Napoleon is celebrated as the cradle of Russo-German comradeship.

Since the 50th anniversary of the October Revolution in 1967, the participa-tion of former German POWs in the Red Army's actions between 1917 and 1921 has been hailed as a further milestone in this brotherhood-in-arms, of which the "Free Germany" National Committee and the German deserters who fought with Soviet partisans in World War II are seen as a logical contin-uation.

Among still further milestones in the present era the Warsaw Pact man-oeuvres, from *Quartett 1963* to *Schild 76,* are given as examples. Indeed the autumn exercise in 1970, where for the first time all seven Warsaw Pact armies took part, bore the name *Waffenbrüderschaft.*

This same "brotherhood-in-arms" has been eulogized in countless poems and manifestos, such as the Oath of Buchenwald *(Schwur von Buchenwald),* and in 1967 a *Waffenbrüderschaft Order* was established.

Within this socialist military fraternity the leading role of the Soviet Union goes without saying, and the exploits of the Red Army occupy a corresponding place in NVA traditionalism.

> The heroism of the glorious Soviet Army and of the whole multinational Soviet people in their uncompromising struggle with fascist German imperialism and Japanese militarism is a model for us in our class edu-cation[28].

The NVA's partial recourse to German traditions of soldierliness requires constant care in distinguishing those traditions considered "revolutionary" from the other ones.

We are told that "it is the commanders and officer cadres above all on whom the revolutionary tradition of the socialist army rests"[29]. As for the content, methods and practical challenges of tradition-fostering, these have to be based on "resolutions by leading Party bodies, the standing Orders on Tra-dition-Fostering *(Traditionspflegeordnung)* and commands and instructions issued for the current training year"[30]. The GDR Institute for Military Hist-ory, set up in Potsdam in 1953, has a large hand in developing the required traditions.

According to the standing orders referred to, "a Tradition Circle is to be set up in every unit to research into revolutionary and progressive traditions, nur-ture them and popularize them in a worthy form. Its main research activity should be directed toward the life and impact of revolutionary prototypes, the military traditions of its own unit in conjunction with those of its Soviet foster-unit, the history of the working class and youth movement in the locality and the evolution of the unit's garrison town"[31].

The *Tradition Circles* are supposed to play a prominent role in the activity of the FDJ organizations. Each Circle – in a Frontier Troop garrison, say – has from 7 to 10 permanent and 10 to 20 temporary members. The permanent members include a Leader, Club Council Chairman, Photography Section Head, Graphic Artists, Painters and others with special skills. The floating members are given the jobs of collecting and processing material and ensuring the safety of the Circle's property. The Central Tradition Circle of a unit directs or assists its other Circles; it will include a member responsible for popularizing the traditions attached to the unit's – and its garrison's – name; an editorial group; an archive group; a member responsible for cooperation with the Soviet foster-unit; a photography group; various hobby groups; a member responsible for contact with local tradition-cult groups, veterans etc., and a member responsible for cooperation with the local SED History Commission.

Military ceremonial and discipline

In the field of ideological education respect for tradition is closely linked with military ceremonial and the cultivation of military discipline. *"Iron discipline in the army is, so to speak, the holiest of holies"*[32], as the Soviet leader Kalinin put it in a phrase often quoted in NVA circles. Discipline has to be directly related to the requirements of military service and of actual combat. The observance of ceremony and other outward forms is also deeply interlinked with operational service, and is by no means to be dismissed as a formality.

According to the NVA's Standing Orders on Ceremonial, this is "part and parcel of military *Traditionspflege* in the NVA". Ceremonial "demonstrates that revolutionary and progressive traditions, especially those of the German and international workers' movement, are firmly rooted in the NVA"[33].

The importance the NVA attaches to outward forms is brought home to the young soldier as soon as he joins up – at the oath-taking ceremony.

Since April 30, 1956, every NVA unit has had its own *banner*, which remains with it at all times and in a "defence situation" must be kept in the area of the unit's combat operations. Every member of the unit is under an obligation to defend the banner stalwartly at all costs and to prevent it falling into the enemy's hands. If it is lost, the unit commander and all soldiers directly to blame are called to account, and the unit is dissolved. The "holiness" of the banner is taken so seriously that the unit is not allowed to repair any tears in the material itself.

Army units were among the recipients of *Banners of Honour* conferred by the SED Central Committee for outstanding performance in the "socialist competitions" held in honour of the 9th Party Congress. These are made of particularly costly material and rank among the highest of all banners.

> Traditional ceremonies are infused in the NVA with fresh content. They include parades, Great Retreat, Garrison Reveille, guards of honour at the Memorial to the Victims of Fascism and Militarism with their elaborate mounting ceremony, and so forth[34].

The Parade, as the "highest demonstration of military respect", consists of "an assembly and march-past of troops with music, accompanied by an aviation fly-past or naval review". It is designed to "give the public an idea of the state of training and equipment of the armed forces, as well as of their fighting power". As well as parades of honour there are field parades at the end of troop exercises – and other strict rules govern the conduct of flag parades and parades for the dead[35].

Garrison Reveille (Großes Wecken) involves a band and a guard of honour. *Great Retreat (Großer Zapfenstreich)* features an enlarged band, banner commando, guard of honour and torch-bearers. In East Berlin and other major cities several bands, commandos and torch-bearers, and two guards of honour, take part on these occasions.

Whenever possible, a *Großer Zapfenstreich* should be introduced by a Salute, for which an artillery battery is brought in. For encamped troops, the duty officer orders the bugler to sound the signal *Locken* (First Post) a quarter-of-a-hour before the *Großer Zapfenstreich* begins.

The *Mounting of the Guard* has been re-established as a tradition on the *Unter den Linden* boulevard in East Berlin. A permanent armed guard has been posted since May 1, 1962, in front of the Memorial to the Victims of Fascism and Militarism, the *Neue Wache* built by Schinkel in 1818, and every Wednesday a band and guard of honour march up to it. Numerous spectators gather to watch the double picket being changed in parade-ground step to the sound of General Yorck's March.

The NVA allows no anniversary, exercise or other service function to go by without a display of the prowess of the "first German workers'-and-farmers' army". By this frequent exposure of its members to public view, the NVA's leaders hope to foster pride and esprit de corps among the population as well as the ranks.

Singing on the march is also seen as a valuable educational device in the following ways.

> – It has an organizing function, keep the marching troops in time and maintaining discipline. Marching songs, it is said, make the individual "aware of his place in what is going on around him". They „strengthen the soldier's confidence, courage and willingness to perform the task that lies ahead".

Defence Minister Hoffmann decorating a banner with the "Karl-Marx-Order".

– It has an ideological function with a special role in the class struggle as an instrument for "agitation". The soldier identifies with the ideas and standpoint expressed in the song. Thus there is justification even for songs that celebrate "the sunny side of life" and express nothing but pleasure and the joy of music. However, they must not be allowed to "depart from basic Party principles or descend into tasteless banality";

the "relation between the individual's interests and society's" must always be kept clear.

– Singing on the march has, finally, an emotional function, with words and melody combining to evoke feelings. The important thing is that those feelings should serve an educational purpose. The *Thälmann-Lied*, for example, evokes "feelings of hatred for the hero's torturers", and is aimed at "the most reactionary forces in West Germany". The song *Schwer mit den Schätzen des Orients beladen* (Laden with Treasures from the Orient), by contrast, awakes feelings of "longing for the exotic, of sentimentality and *Weltschmerz*". And these are "not merely useless but positively harmful for the purposes of our training efforts".

The NVA makes use of "positive" emotional situations to remind the soldier of his *personal status*. Thus "if a serviceman is personally congratulated or thanked by a superior in the course of duty, he should answer: 'I serve the German Democratic Republic' ". And if a superior expresses thanks to a unit, the whole unit should give the same answer[36].

Every NVA unit maintains a *Roll of Honour*, designed to assist it in creating its own tradition by listing the names, with photographs, of all men and NCOs who have especially distinguished themselves in the performance of their military duty. The record is kept in a special place of honour and should be accessible to all.

The other ways in which the NVA accords credit are equally designed for their *emotional effect*. They include

– camera shots taken in front of the unit's banner,
– notification of exemplary performance to parents or previous employers, and
– public conferment of "Exemplary Soldier" certificates.

Education through competition

NVA service is characterized by incessant *competitiveness*, a feature adopted from the Soviet system and widely applied to civilian life as well.

The basic instructions were laid down in 1964[37]: the aim and content of socialist competition in the NVA were to be determined by its forms and methods, the most important forms being

– the Championship Movement *(Bestenbewegung)*,
– the Innovation Movement *(Neuererbewegung)*, and
– Contests *(Wettkämpfe and Wettstreite)*.

"*Complex competitiveness*" in the army is a concept embracing the combined efforts of servicemen, civilian empoyees, subordinates and superiors, units and staffs, to fulfil priority tasks on the model of socialist cooperative labour.

It is the SED Party organizations that direct the socialist competition system in the NVA from above. They check the qualitative fulfilment of competition tasks, dragoon the mass organizations into taking part, lead the "struggle against formalism and bureaucratism", uncover reserves and ensure the exemplary performance of their own members and candidate-members. In socialist competitiveness the various forms of competition are practised side by side, so that Party members more than any other servicemen must strive, over and above normal training targets, to achieve others of different kinds as well.

According to an account given in 1974, socialist competitiveness can be defined as

> that field of activity in a modern socialist army where officers, NCOs and other ranks can give full rein to their creative potential in the interest of fulfilling high-priority military tasks. The object basis for this is provided by socialism, which for the first time makes it possible to "apply the competitive system on a mass scale, truly to guide the majority of working people into an area of activity where they can excel, develop their skills and manifest those talents which the people pours forth like an inexhaustible spring" (V. I. Lenin, *Wie soll man den Wettbewerb organisieren?* How to Organize Competition, in vol. 26 of Lenin's Werke, Berlin 1961, p. 402)[38].

Socialist competition, here justified as a means of developing the personality, was never regarded in the NVA as an end in itself, but according to the Standing Orders on Competition of February 7, 1972, is a decisive condition for "*successful fulfilment of top-priority military tasks* set by Party and government leaders"[39]. Responsibility for conducting it is "one of the most important concerns of ideological work among the troops"[40], in the words of Admiral Verner, Head of the NVA's Main Political Administration, in 1973. Already in the sixties commanders, Politorgans, Party and FDJ organizations were elevating competition to an "indispensable tool of leadership"[41]. Though it is carried out by Party and FDJ agencies, the commander "must not leave competition to run itself"[42].

Within the system of socialist competition an important role falls to the *Championship Movement*. In this "soldiers, NCOs and officer cadets vie individually and collectively for 'good' or 'excellent' marks in all branches of training and in the fulfilment of combat tasks, throughout the training year"[43]. The Championship Movement is aimed at the implementation of Party and State resolutions and is linked to significant peak points in political and social life.

The form that the Championship Movement took in 1958 was called the Compass Movement *(Kompaßbewegung)*. Every participant receives an exercise book with a compass printed on the cover and pages inside headed with various dates. The soldier has to write in a series of self-imposed undertakings, usually attached to particular days. These Days of Commitment *(Tage mit Selbstverpflichtung)* may involve such ambitions as

- winning a sports badge,
- taking part in Construction Economy,
- regular attendance at an FDJ Circle,
- additional FDJ work in his unit,
- achieving the "excellent" grade for discipline,
- getting higher scores in rifle practice,
- acquiring another military qualification,
- earning a marksman's lanyard,
- exemplary care of weapons,
- study of an approved political book,
- recruiting subscribers for the army newspaper, or
- recruiting subscribers for the Party daily.

A comparative assessment of results takes place each quarter, and marks are given according as deadlines were kept or not. Officials work out which were the best units and sub-units, and these receive banners, certificates or cups in recognition.

The extent to which training is dominated by the Championship system is clear from the statistics. During *Operation 70* 95 per cent of all People's Navy personnel took part in their Championship Movement, and over two-thirds of these qualified. In 1970 4,380 members of the People's Navy were marked, and 2,574 marksmen's lanyards were awarded. Of the Navy's FDJ members, 72 per cent won the proficiency badge "For Knowledge", 952 of them in gold. In nine stages between the 8th and 9th Party Congresses more than 340,000 champion's badges were conferred on individual members of the NVA and Frontier Troops, many individuals receiving more than one. Before the introduction of new Standing Orders on December 1, 1976, Defence Minister Hoffmann declared that the most valuable and comprehensive form of socialist competition was the Commitment Movement, and called for it to be encouraged more than ever. "Not everyone can be champion, but everyone must in principle have the chance to take part."[44]

In the *Innovation Movement,* which is again modelled on Soviet practice, all soldiers and civilian employees are invited to make suggestions for the improvement of service equipment or procedures.

The "constant increase" of participation is much proclaimed in the military press. As early as 1961 the number of suggestions handed in reached 4,403 in that year alone, to a total estimated value of 4.4 million Marks; in 1963 this figure was put at 10.8 million.

At the 9th Party Congress Hoffmann claimed that 60,000 suggestions had been submitted since the previous one. Some 10,000 had been exhibited, he said, at the so-called *"Masters-of-the-Future Fairs" (Messen der Meister von morgen),* and about 7,000 had been of direct use for military purposes.

It was publicly admitted, however, that disagreements had arisen. The paper *Volksarmee* reported in 1976 that on the basis of the Innovation Order of

December 22, 1971, the minister had issued a "standing instruction for the encouragement of innovators and inventors". There were indications, the report said, that innovation agreements had been concluded in excessively vague terms, deadlines for processing and confirming had not been kept and remuneration had not taken place. The army's legal officers had to institute proceedings[45].

As for the types of contest called *Wettkampf* and *Wettstreit*, a Ministry for Defence document explains:

> *Wettkämpfe* and *Wettstreite* mobilize servicemen and civilian employees of the army to develop their creative powers in the solution of specific tasks in the units, schools, enterprises, workshops and camps of the NVA. They are primarily organized in army units to cope with priority tasks in operational training, and are designed to secure fulfilment of the NVA's main mission[46].

Wettkämpfe and *Wettstreite* are concerned with rigidly defined areas of military training. They involve competition in every field of daily military routine, from shooting practice to barrack-room decoration, from saluting to boot-polishing. There have been Cultural Contests, Contests to find the Strongest Man in the Army, Contests to win the Sports Badge, 4,000 meter cross-country running races, contests in regular attendance at sports training and many other kinds.

Contests are not restricted to NVA units. On May 1, 1965, there was a *GDR-Soviet encounter* for the first time between "members of the People's Navy *Heinecke* Unit, and comrades from the Red Banner Fleet". In 1969 People's Navy units made 18 "Friendship" and "Foster" Agreements for competition with Soviet units. Similar activities go on between the GDR land forces and Soviet troops stationed there – the so-called "regiment from next door".

Other aids to training

Ideological indoctrination also includes "*aesthetic education and training*", which was in fact made a priority task for political instruction in connection with the GDR's 20th anniversary.

As Major General Lange said:

> The young company commander must not be a mere expert consumer of art and literature ... He should be in a position to evolve intellectual and cultural life within his unit ... It must be seen to everywhere that intellectual and cultural activity is regarded as an indispensable component of the soldier's life and of socialist competition[47].

Whatever may be thought of the NVA's "expertise in art and literature", it is true that the army's energies are from time to time mobilized to stress some ideological differentiation from the West, e.g. by denouncing dissidents. Thus we hear that "numerous members of the NVA and Frontier Troops, including artists, writers and folk-art craftsmen ... have rejected the campaign launched by West Germany in connection with the cancellation of Biermann's GDR citizenship"[48].

The *military press* is an important adjunct of ideological training in the NVA. Army papers were at first set up in Military Regions and Divisional Areas in close imitation of Soviet models, but in 1961 the divisional, and the following year the regional, periodicals were abandoned.

Since 1962 *Volksarmee* has been the only army paper. Established on September 1, 1956, it now appears in a 16-page edition once a week, though at one point it was put out more frequently. It is the official organ of the Defence Ministry but is described as having a "universal character" and regularly contains political schooling supplements.

The magazine *Armeerundschau*, which first appeared on November 1, 1956, is a more popular product, printed monthly and partly in colour. Its content is complementary to that of *Volksarmee*. Both are more widely read and attractively set out than the run of GDR newspapers or periodicals.

Militärwesen, "the military policy and military theory monthly", has appeared in 128-page editions since March 1, 1957, and is intended for officers at battalion command level and above as well as readers in leading government circles and social organizations.

Another periodical with élite pretensions is *Militärgeschichte*, published since 1961 by the GDR Institute of Military History in Potsdam. It runs to 128 pages every second month.

The special magazine *Militärtechnik* (nine times a year), which first came out on March 1, 1961, is mainly addressed to technical personnel in all the services. One of its aims is "to provide evidence from military technology of the superiority of the socialist defence coalition and its forces over the imperialist armies"[49].

There is a *Zeitschrift für Militärmedizin* which appears six times a year.

Certain other periodicals are only obtainable within the NVA, such as the Party political series *Parteiarbeiter* and *Im Klub*.

The series *Wissen und Kämpfen* – Knowledge and Fighting – produced in various editions for rank-and-file, NCOs, cadets, officers, and trainee NCOs and trainee officers, is another adjunct to political schooling.

The *Militärverlag* der DDR publishing house (originally *Deutscher Militärverlag)* issues a wide selection both of light and specialist literature. Up to 1970 it had put out 2,700 titles in nearly 90 million copies. In addition it has printed 12 million or so copies of 330 Soviet works, including almost 40 volumes of memoirs.

The *NVA Book Club (NVA-Buchgemeinschaft)*, set up in 1963, offers works at very modest prices. It was stated in 1976 by the director of the East-Berlin distributing agency for NVA books and periodicals that the army ran 70 bookshops of its own. Bestsellers in 1975 were *Geschichte des Luftkrieges; Schützen, Kanoniere, Kommandanten;* a two-volume account of the Russian campaign in the last war, *Der Grosse Vaterländische Krieg;* a translation of Polevoy's "896 Kilometers to Berlin"; Vol. II of General Shtemenko's Memoirs; Neutsch's *Der Friede im Osten;* and at the other extreme a collection of jokes, *Wer lacht da?* The social sciences account for about 40 per cent of the output[50].

Another institution run by the Defence Ministry is the NVA's *Army Film Studios* at Potsdam-Griebnitzsee. These turn out army educational films with the main stress on political indoctrination, also shown in public cinemas and on TV. Founded in 1960 these studios shot in 15 years over 180 documentaries, over 140 training films and over 200 newsreels, and produced dubbings of 135 army films from other Warsaw Pact countries[51].

The NVA's *military museums* are another important prop for ideological education. Following reorganization in the early seventies there are now three major ones.

The *Dresden Army Museum,* opened in 1972, has an exhibition area of 77,000 square feet. Its main stock was at first the collection of small arms and swords from the former Saxon Army Museum, returned by the Soviet Union in 1958/59, together with items from the naval section of the Berlin *Museum für Meereskunde.* The largest military museum in East Germany, it is supposed to demonstrate "the complexity of the historic confrontation in terms of military history – the struggle between progress and reaction in the military history of Germany".

The *Army Museum in Potsdam's Marble Palace* dates from 1961. Its display area is far smaller – some 10,700 square feet. Rearranged in 1975, it bears the imprint of the ruling dynasty – it was in its time the property of the kings of Prussia, and then of the German emperors – as well as of the history of Potsdam in the "era of Brandenburg-Prussian militarism", not to mention that of "the struggle of the best elements of the German people against the forces of militarism". The Potsdam Museum alone brings in some quarter-of-a-million visitors a year.

With its mere 4,300 square footage, the *Königstein Fortress* near Dresden is the smallest of the NVA's central museums, featuring a permanent exhibition of "Military Technology and the Social System". This is meant to show visitors that "imperialist war is a prime source of profits for the imperialist monopolies".

Every serviceman is expected to visit one of the major NVA museums at least once during his service – in his spare time, committed though it is to other ideological activities.

The devotion of one's *free time to socialist education* is a requirement that the SED imposes equally on civilians. The FDJ slogan "Wherever we are missing, the enemy is at work!" *(Wo wir nicht sind, arbeitet der Gegner!)* leaves the NVA member merely to choose which of the available activities he spends his leisure on.

Short-service and regular soldiers are equally well provided for. They have *special recreation centres,* e.g. in the Uckermark and on the island of Rügen, where they can spend their leave with their families almost cost-free. In addition to restoring their bodies they are naturally expected not to neglect the "ideological steeling" process. For specially suitable men, leave trips to other communist countries are organized. They go in civilian dress but remain under strict military discipline and control.

In earlier years this political sollicitude outside duty hours aroused bitter complaint, but the more relaxed regime introduced subsequently, plus more interesting and better presented programmes, has led to a certain acquiescence.

How far the NVA soldier identifies with his leaders' ideological aims, however, remains uncertain. In a population which votes by over 99 per cent in general – albeit not secret – elections in favour of the ruling system, the army, it might be argued, must be totally convinced of that system's justice and invincibility. Such, for example, is the tenor of an article by Colonel General Streletz, Deputy Defence Minister and Chief of the Main Staff, which appeared on March 1, 1979, for the NVA's 23rd anniversary.

> The long-term military policy of the Party leadership and of the whole SED, as coordinated with the communist parties of the Soviet Union and other Warsaw Pact states, has determined and continues to determine the politically conscious and well-disciplined behaviour and high level of operational preparedness and military competence of all servicemen[52].

One notes the word "all". But a more cautious note is sounded by the Minister himself in an article, published in January 1979, for a more restricted public.

> The fact that *most* members of the NVA have openly opted for socialism and are at heart convinced of the justice and invincibility of our social order, of the strength of our socialist commonwealth and of the leading role of our Party – all these positive attitudes must be guided even more purposefully to the point of personal commitment by every serviceman to accept wittingly the tough military consequences: in a word, to be a socialist soldier[53].

Notes

[1] Commander W. *Rickert,* Lecturer in Marxism-Leninism, Erfahrungswerte der politischen Schulung in der Volksmarine, in: *Militärwesen,* East Berlin, 1/1975, p. 103.
[2] Major General E. *Hampf,* Zur ideologischen Arbeit in der NVA und in den Grenztruppen der DDR bei der Durchführung der Beschlüsse des IX. Parteitages der SED, in: *Militärwesen,* 9/1976, p. 5.
[3] Die weltanschauliche Erziehung – Grundlage der politisch-moralischen Standhaftigkeit, in: *Militärwesen,* 7/1977, p. 101.
[4] Ibid., p. 102.
[5] Militärlexikon, Militärverlag der DDR, East Berlin 1973, 2nd ed., p. 36.

Mounting of the guard at the "Unter den Linden" memorial in
East Berlin.

6 *Volksarmee,* East Berlin 15/1976.
7 Colonel R. *Dietzsch* and Lieutenant Colonel L. *Beck,* Für ein höheres Niveau der
  politisch-ideologischen Arbeit in den LSK/LV, in: *Militärwesen,* 9/1974, p. 103,
  quoted in: *Parteiarbeiter,* East Berlin, Sonderheft IX. Delegiertenkonferenz, February 1, 1974, p. 9.
8 Militärlexikon 1973, p. 343.
9 Friedrich Engels, Ludwig Feuerbach und der Ausgang der klassischen deutschen
  Philosophie, in: *Marx/Engels,* Werke, vol. 21, East Berlin 1962, p. 298. Quoted
  by Lieutenant Colonel G. *Semmler* of the Friedrich Engels Military Academy,
  Politisch-pädagogische Aufgaben zur Leitung von Erziehung und Bildung im
  Truppenteil (I), in: *Militärwesen,* 1/1974, p. 42.
10 Lieutenant Colonel H. *Friedrich* of the Friedrich Engels Military Academy, Zur
  Einheit von Rationalem und Emotionalem in der politischen Schulung, in: *Militärwesen,* 9/1976, p. 52.
11 Major General A. *Seefeldt,* Die Verantwortung des Kommandeurs für die politisch-
  moralische und psychologische Vorbereitung der Armeeangehörigen; in: *Militärwesen,* 5/1977, p. 3.
12 Colonel K.-D. *Uckel* of the Friedrich Engels Military Academy, Zur Entwicklung
  der Militärpädagogik und Militärpsychologie in der NVA, in: *Militärwesen,* 10/
  1974, pp. 52–62.
13 Ibid., p. 62.
14 Militärlexikon 1973, p. 297.
15 Cf. Commander W. *Rickert,* loc. cit. note 1, pp. 103–108.

[16] Colonel *Dietzsch*, loc. cit. note 7, p. 104 ff.

[17] Paul *Heider*, Militärgeschichte und lebendige Bewahrung der revolutionären Traditionen in der Klassenauseinandersetzung unserer Zeit, in: *Militärgeschichte*, East Berlin, 4/1975, p. 389.

[18] Militärlexikon 1973, p. 243.

[19] Paul *Heider*, loc. cit. note 17, p. 391.

[20] *Neues Deutschland*, East Berlin, March 1/2, 1975.

[21] Johannes *Streubel*, Zur musealen Gestaltung militärischer Traditionen, in: *Militärgeschichte*, 5/1976, p. 595.

[22] Quoted from: *Volksarmee*, 16/1969.

[23] Admiral Waldemar *Verner* in: *Militärwesen*, 2/1962, p. 168 ff.

[24] *Neues Deutschland*, November 28, 1964.

[25] *Volksarmee*, 49/1964.

[26] *Volksarmee*, 24/1965.

[27] Günter *Kühn* and Wolfgang *Weber*, Internationaler Charakter, Aufbau und Tätigkeit der illegalen militärischen Organisation im Konzentrationslager Buchenwald, in: *Militärgeschichte*, 4/1976, pp. 427–439.

[28] Siegfried *Mai* and Werner *Thiel*, Sowjetische Kampftradition – ein Mittel zur klassenmäßigen Erziehung in der NVA, in: *Militärgeschichte*, 1/1976, p. 33.

[29] Waldemar *Verner*, Aus dem Bericht . . . an die X. Delegiertenkonferenz der Parteiorganisationen der SED in der NVA und in den Grenztruppen der DDR, in: *Parteiarbeiter*, April-Sonderheft, 1976, p. 30.

[30] Wolf *Gerhardt*, Erfahrungen aus der Arbeit der Traditionszirkel in Truppenteilen der NVA und der Grenztruppen der DDR, in: *Militärgeschichte*, 2/1975, p. 213.

[31] Ibid.

[32] M. I. *Kalinin*, Über kommunistische Erziehung und militärische Pflicht, East Berlin 1960, p. 135, quoted by Lieutenant Colonel A. *Bendrat* in: *Militärwesen*, 3/1975, p. 46.

[33] Cf. Sport und Technik, 3/1976, p. 11.

[34] Wehrdienst – Warum? Wann? Wo? Wie? 125 Antworten, ed. by a collective under the leadership of Colonel Rolf *Leuschner*, Militärverlag der DDR, East Berlin 1974, p. 34.

[35] Militärlexikon 1973, p. 289.

[36] Dienstvorschrift DV-10/3, No. 29.

[37] Anordnungs- und Mitteilungsblatt des Ministeriums für Nationale Verteidigung, pt. I, 1964, No. 22, Blatt 2.

[38] Alfred *Voerster*, Über den Platz des sozialistischen Wettbewerbs in einer „Geschichte der NVA der DDR", in: *Militärgeschichte*, 1/1974, p. 63.

[39] Loc. cit. note 37, pt. I, 1972, No. 6, Blatt 1.

[40] Quoted from Alfred *Voerster*, loc. cit. note 38, p. 64.

[41] Dietrich *Richter*, Erfahrungen des sozialistischen Wettbewerbs in der Volksmarine in den 60er Jahren, in: *Militärgeschichte*, 6/1976, p. 706.

[42] Alfred *Voerster*, loc. cit. p. 64.

[43] Loc. cit. note 37, pt. I, 1964, No. 22, Blatt 2.

[44] *Volksarmee*, 45/1976.

[45] *Volksarmee*, 6/1976.

[46] Loc. cit. note 37, pt. I, 1964, No. 22, Blatt 2.

[47] *Volksarmee*, 34/1969.

[48] *Volksarmee*, 48/1976.

[49] *Armeerundschau*, East Berlin, 9/1974, p. 52.

[50] *Volksarmee*, 8/1978.

[51] *Volksarmee*, 4/1976.

[52] *Volksarmee*, 9/1979.

[53] Army General Heinz *Hoffmann*, SED Politburo member and Defence Minister, Zu einigen Führungs- und Erziehungsaufgaben im neuen Ausbildungsjahr, in: *Militärwesen*, 1/1979, p. 6.

CHAPTER ELEVEN

Military Training

General principles

Communist military analysts take the view that no sharp distinction is possible between purely military and political training. As we have seen in the chapter on ideological indoctrination, training is seen in the NVA as a *unitary process of political and military instruction* carried out with the aim of "preparing servicemen and socialist combat collectives in all respects for armed combat"[1].

Since *political instruction* forms a large component of military instruction it is not surprising that it accounts for about 25 per cent of all training time. Even during the four weeks of *basic training* the young recruit, who would normally be fully occupied in adapting himself to his new environment, is subjected to Political Schooling as well. The book *Vom Sinn des Soldatseins* – The Meaning of Being a Soldier – is "ceremonially presented to him in the first hours of his service"[2] and he has to work his way through it during the month. Further political approaches are made to him through study discussions, films, lectures, excursions and conversations with "working-class veterans" and "brothers-in-arms" from the Soviet forces stationed in the country, the "regiment next door".

At the start of the 1979 training year Defence Minister Hoffmann, it is true, stressed the importance of discussing "specifically military aspects"[3] during Political Schooling lessons. The schooling is concerned with "the political content of our military task", he said, and its effectiveness is gauged by its impact on combat-readiness:

> The political morale of the troops, and hence the value of our ideological work, can largely be measured by standards of military order and discipline. One thing we know, and cannot emphasize too often: order and discipline are vital for the existence of our army, an integral part of the socialist way of life, the common factor in all the preconditions – ideological, technical, organizational, legal and moral – for a high level of combat-readiness.

As in every army, military training in the NVA has to adapt to *changing technical conditions and general social trends*. This too is reflected in Hoffmann's remarks:

> Modern warfare with all its demands and hardships enhances, for example, the role of command and obedience – even if some of our younger servicemen are inclined to believe the contrary. But growing importance

attaches at the same time to independent initiative on the part of the subordinate – and, of course, of the superior as well. More than ever, then, we need units to work together in an integrated fashion, while at the same time the individual soldier or NCO must display an unprecedented measure of independence and responsibility! This situation forces us to realize that the content and impact of a command – from the initial idea behind it, right through to its clear and concise formulation – have to be responsibly weighed and thought out, and that command and obedience, to a greater degree than in past years and earlier wars, must be linked in mutual trust.

Whichever aspect we concentrate on, one thing is always apparent. We can only cope with all the changes in military affairs that face our army, like every other army, to the extent that we can win the willingness of every serviceman, every subordinate, to put all their ability into the job. And these young men on whose brains and hands the effectiveness of our very costly, and very powerful, weapon systems depends are not going to respond to a commander quite in the fashion of left-turn and right-turn on the parade ground.

Though military and political training are regarded in the NVA as a single entity, distinctions emerge in practice which for clarity we can apply in the following description.

Training in the ranks

Military training begins as soon as a young man is called up for *enrolment* in his eighteenth year. Even those who receive no postal summons are in duty bound to report. "It is expected of every young man called up for service that he should prepare himself properly for the occasion, both in society's interest and in his own."[4] In addition to the sort of documents conscripts have to produce in other countries, in the GDR they must bring along evidence of their premilitary training in the GST, and Party and "mass organization" membership cards. In contrast to Western custom, the enrolment board includes not only army officers but representatives of enterprises and of government and social organizations. The medical examination is followed by an interview where the board adjudges suitability for particular arms and services. Young volunteers for service as privates, short-service NCOs or career soldiers are also given advice. All decisions are coordinated with military requirements, cadre needs in the NVA and other armed forces, and the board's individual findings.

The basis of the training programme is the 18 months of *basic military service,* plus the changeover of personnel that takes place every six months without overlapping.

Training is divided into *three half-year periods;* enlistments and discharges every spring and autumn mean that about one third of all personnel are

Basic training: learning to walk.

replaced each time – the so-called *Drittelfüllung*. The newly enlisted soldiers of the first half-year are for the most part quartered in advance with their *parent units,* but for training purposes are concentrated for four weeks in *recruit units,* where they receive basic training, while their colleagues of the second and third half-years undergo intensive individual training.

Once the basic training is over, recruits are finally incorporated in their parent units where they are given such simple jobs as rifle-loading and gun ammunition handling, while those in the second and third half-years take over positions vacated through discharge or promotion.

In the following training stages instruction is given in sections, platoons, companies and regiments, and includes practice with combined weapons. Additional divisional exercises and manoeuvres are held for the whole Military District towards the end of the training half-year.

Night training is given particular attention; between one-third and a half of all field training, combat training, firing practice, driving instruction and specialized training is done at night.

Part of the training programme is the period spent in *camps,* which every unit experiences both in the summer and winter half-years. The camps are usually set up in training areas where the recruits live in tents under war conditions for two to four weeks, eating battle rations.

Barrack duties are strict and occupy clearly prescribed periods of time.

Much time is devoted to *administration, servicing and care of weapons,* vehicles and other equipment and clothing. Maintenance days are set aside, especially after major exercises, which are also used for technical instruction and cadre schooling. Little time is left in the programme for learning service regulations or tactical, technical and political data and principles, so that these have to be absorbed partly in one's free time.

Basic military training

All servicemen in the NVA and Frontier Troops receive the same basic training in the first four weeks, whatever their later assignment. During this time, as in all armies, recruits are supposed to be *inured to soldierly discipline and order.* Considerable exertions are expected of them, physically, mentally and endurancewise. Training proper accounts for about eight hours each day, not including barrack duties such as cleaning quarters, cleaning equipment and mending clothes. Only on Saturdays is there any respite, apart from Sundays which are usually free. Exit permits and leave are seldom granted at all during basic training, since this would not be allowed by the time-span of the training, its purpose and the severe demands made of the soldiers.

Apart from Political Schooling, basic training comprises the following subjects:

— *drill practice;*

— *firing practice:* thorough familiarization with the automatic, followed by firing, prone, at fixed and snapshooting targets from up to 200 meters, testing both accuracy and speed of aim;

— *tactical training:* individual behaviour and movement over the battlefield;

— *protective training:* theoretical elements and basic skill in the use, care and servicing of personal defensive equipment against nuclear, chemical and biological weapons;

— *field engineering training;*

— *military topography:* terrain sketching, angle and distance estimation and its application on the march, taking bearings from nature;

— *physical training:* testing physical powers by the eight-part *Achtertest,* comprising 1. 20 push-ups, 2. running 100 m in 14.6 seconds; 3.

climbing a five-meter rope in 19 seconds; 4. hop, skip and jump; 5. 6 pull-ups on the horizontal bar; 6. running 3,000 m in 13 minutes 20 seconds; 7. grenade-throwing – 32 m; 8. running the 400 m obstacle course in 2 minutes 40 seconds. Additional tests in taking obstacles, close-quarter combat and grenade-throwing;

– *medical training:* hygiene; recognition of dangerous injuries; self-help and first-aid; use of the medical kit;

– *barrack duties:* service principles and regulations; disciplinary and complaints procedure, behaviour on and off duty, rights and duties, garrison and guard duty.

Individual training

A great number of hours are devoted during basic training to preparing recruits specifically for *functions they will exercise in the current half-year.* In the first half-year these will only be of the simplest kind, and training will only be given in the weapons and instruments with which the unit in question is equipped.

Recruits will naturally be most interested in new technology – fire guidance devices, radar or electronics. But this general military training provides the foundation for all the *complex specialized training* that is to come.

Weapon training and other types of combat training are done by numbers, in line with the great importance attached to *drill* generally. Parade drill, weapon drill and combat drill are successive stages in a routine which involves the rhythmic repetition of elementary military movements to a level of proficiency where such movements will be automatic even under the severest stress of nuclear missile warfare.

Individual training in the second or, as the case may be, third half-year differs from the earlier stages in that the old material is repeated in greater depth and extended to cover new ground, and a degree of *interchangeability of function* has to be achieved. Thus a trained gunner will have to become a trained gun-layer as well, a rifleman will be turned into a driver, a driver into a signaller and so forth, so that every soldier can undertake two or even three roles.

Training in sections or crews

The first half-year also features, during the individual training phase, exercises in large formations, over and above the instruction the soldier will in any case receive in the handling and effectiveness of the weapons used in his unit.

As soon as individual training proper is finished, *cooperation* begins in the smallest, basic units. Here for the first time older soldiers will undergo training together with the youngest contingent of their unit, and this will take up well over half the training time.

Apart from political instruction, the subjects dealt with in group training are similar to those in other armies. Night training takes up almost as much time as day training, and combat firing is practised by night as well. In all branches of the service combat in built-up areas, engagement with a suddenly emerging enemy and surmounting water obstacles are prominent items on the programme; technical servicing under battle conditions and combat drill occur frequently, too.

Training in the platoon

This belongs to the same phase as the group training just described, and the two overlap. Platoon training, too, is conducted from time to time in training areas, in camps or near the unit's base. Combat training alternates with revision of what was done in individual and group training periods.

It is at this point that the *combined effect of different types of weapons* is practised, and the field radio and other *means of communication* are brought into play.

Even during long periods of camp training, however, *Political Schooling* is not neglected. But the physical side of the training now concentrates on strenuous sports in a programme that includes contests for both individual and especially collective records in cross-country running, obstacle racing and swimming in uniform by entire platoons.

Company, battalion and regiment training

Training in companies, batteries, battalions and regiments – roughly *formation training* in the Western sense – is the longest and most important training phase, occupying two to three months in each training half-year. It includes the divisional exercises and manoeuvres at Military District level which round off each half-year and are conducted together with Soviet troops. Afterwards the soldiers return to their own company or battery training.

The core of the training programme is in any case the simulation of *fighting under war conditions*, with all the exertion and privations involved.

A glance at the following training schedules gives an idea of the aims of NVA instruction.

1. Combat training in the *motorized infantry companies* covers chiefly
– movement across country in extended order, with or without combat vehicles;
– the attack, from first approach to final charge; combat in depth; improvisation and conduct under nuclear attack; pursuit of the enemy;
– attack from prepared positions; charge; fighting for position; defence against counter-attack; flank and rear attack; bringing up combat vehicles and changing over to pursuit; attack in depth;
– attack over a water obstacle; preparation of weapons and vehicles for fording and swimming; thrust in depth;
– combat with parachutists and "counter-revolutionaries"; reconnaissance, encirclement, assault and destruction;
– defence, including occupation and fortification of defence positions; coordination of fire plans; planning the engagement and passing over to the offensive;

- company reconnaissance and cover;
- setting up camp and camp routine;
- conduct during rail, sea and air transport operations.

In addition, special stress is laid on field firing from different positions.

2. Training in an *armoured company* is analogous and emphasizes
- attack from the assembly area via the deployment sector to the points of assault; repulse of counter-attacks and pursuit of the evading enemy;
- firepower and counter-thrust in defence, including digging in and working out fire plans; coordination with motorized infantry and artillery;
- march, transport and camping;
- field firing.

3. Training in *artillery units* is similar. The battery practises
- movement in extended order;
- preparation of artillery for the attack, and fire support for armoured and infantry units;
- repulsing counter-attacks; anti-tank and anti-aircraft operations;
- deployment in defence;
- march, transport and camping;
- field firing.

In all units a great deal of time is devoted to *firing practice,* especially before and after exercises. A glance at the schedules shows to what extent the attack dominates all training. Indeed, the NVA regulations state that attack is the only road to success in a military operation.

In company training the *sports aspect* of physical exercise is completely superseded. The last trace of it is in the obstacle races varying from three to ten kilometers, the infantry having the longest ones. Otherwise, physical training is from this stage on purely for combat, e.g.

- combat courses involving climbing, water obstacles, wire entanglements, minefields, grenade throwing and close fighting;
- competitive construction of field positions, often in difficult postures;
- competitive ammunition carrying, mine-laying, mine removal, barrier removal, driving through water obstacles;
- competitive weapon drill for all specialists such as drivers, signallers, engineers, military police, chemical and technical personnel etc.

Drill training continues with emphasis on rigorous discipline at all times, including periods spent in camp or on field exercises. Rapid assembly practice, company drill and movement by numbers, with and without vehicles, are particularly stressed.

In this phase staff and support units seek maximum contact with armoured and infantry companies and artillery batteries under training. They not only turn up during the frequent battery, regimental and divisional exercises but also practise cooperation in larger formations with the companies and batteries.

Thus even in infantry company training we find signal troops, tanks, artillery, staff elements, rear services and even air force liaison personnel taking part. The process is facilitated by mixing weapons at regimental level and often bringing various elements together in the same barracks or training areas.

Tactical-operational training

Systematic transition to *formation training* occurs during March and April, and again in the summer, whenever company training is in progress. From that point on there is an increase in the frequency of large-area exercises, and in the number of formations involved.

The NVA does not in fact use the West German term *Verbandsausbildung* for "formation training", *Verband* being applied to brigades, divisions, corps, tactical and army-operational formations.

Tactical-operational training, like individual, section and platoon training, is supervised in detail "from above", i.e. by the *Ministry for Defence Training Administration.*

The competent desk in the Ministry prescribes "exercise themes" in advance, decides which units are to take part and lays down general guidelines. However, the timing and exact type of each exercise are only partly intimated to the commander affected, who can never display any initiative here. Many exercises start off with an alert which takes the commander by surprise as much as the men.

Simulation of war conditions is very prominent during exercises. In general all troops have to take part; very few are left behind on garrison duty and leave, exits and free time are virtually eliminated. Even during protracted exercises or series of continuous exercises troops are subjected to field conditions.

Camps are equally frequent in summer and winter, and highly spartan. In training areas, troops are sometimes quartered in barracks, but in general they live in tents or even under tarpaulins and other makeshifts. Camps are put up, given fire-cover and camouflaged as if in wartime.

On longer exercises units take all their military equipment with them as a *test of mobility and combat-readiness.*

Prime importance is attached to *manoeuvrability,* i.e. to the ability of men and officers to exercise movements and battle tactics at speed and in good order. Long marches, motorized or on foot, combat operations over large sectors without a break by day and night, in fair weather or foul, are characteristic for exercises at all levels up to the division and military district. Since 1961 the NVA has also taken part in the major Warsaw Pact joint exercises described in Chapter 3.

In a nutshell, the main scenarios of NVA exercises are these:

- stopping an attack launched across the state frontier;
- counter-attacking into "Agressor-land"; and
- destroying "diversionary" troops and parachutists.

Parachutists of the NVA. – In the foreground an airborne tank.

Where operational formations are exercising, however, the first scenario for the opening of hostilities appears designed for psychological purposes only: "*We are being attacked and have to defend ourselves*". The real tactical task is the "*counter*"-*attack*. "The conflict can only be resolved by offensive operations."

Air Force/Air Defence training

The NVA's Air Force/Air Defence comes under a separate *Command,* to which a number of Defence Ministry functions are delegated, including *training*. Since specialized service requires longer experience and most air force personnel join up for at least three years, a distinct training rotation system is laid down for them. *Basic training* is much the same as for other recruits, but is followed by markedly *specialized programmes for individual training in the different branches*. Of course, a large proportion of these men are regulars who will undergo training at NCO schools or the officers' college.

Relatively few in number, the air force soldiers are well equipped, and their training – which was often found inferior in the past – has also improved.

All planes, weapons and instruments are of Soviet origin, so that training is naturally based on the Soviet model. The East German air force has to rely greatly on Soviet assistance. Its main purpose – and hence its training – is oriented toward air defence; tactical support for the land forces is secondary.

People's Navy training

The People's Navy, similarly, has its own *Command* with certain Ministry for Defence functions, including again *training*. It, too, is small compared with the land forces. Its responsibilities in the Warsaw Pact context are

- to defend the East German coast;
- to engage enemy naval forces;
- to protect and maintain sea communications; and
- to support land forces in coastal operations.

Both nautical and weapon training, and political instruction, are the more intensive in the People's Navy because of the similarity of function in many ways with the Frontier Troops. The necessary experience and skills can for the most part be acquired only at sea. Both in training and service, the demands made on People's Navy personnel are severe, involving periods of exposure for several days at a time to continuous and increasing pressure, physical and psychological, with extreme variations in weather conditions. Crews are in addition frequently called upon to engage in contests and take on "self-commitment" tasks. The current standard of training is good.

NCO training

As in the Soviet forces, NCOs of the NVA were until 1965 regarded as *militarily unimportant*. In the Soviet case there was justification for this in the poor level of education and mental inflexibility of the lower ranks, who came mostly from a peasant background. Though they were from the start accorded disciplinary authority, their responsibilities were extraordinarily limited.

Their *increasing importance in modern warfare as unit leaders* led, however, to a complete revaluation of the NCO corps – first in the Soviet Union and then in the other Warsaw Pact countries. In 1965 the career description of the East German NCO was revised: he was no longer described as a "military skilled worker" but as a *"junior leader and aide to the unit commander"*. The increased demands made meant abandoning, in January 1966, the practice by which promotion to NCO was possible after a mere 12 months of basic service. To become an NCO one now has to sign up for at least three years, i.e. as a *short-service regular*.

The mainstay of the NCO corps, however, are *career soldiers* who sign on before the age of 26 for at least ten years' service and may stay in the NVA till they are 65. Every regular NCO can also apply to become an *ensign (Fähnrich)* or career officer.

Efforts are made to recruit young people as early as their 9th grade in school for NCO careers. Following acceptance by the local *Wehrkreiskommando* (enlistment office) the applicant is attached to an FDJ Candidates' Collective. The enlistment office then brings influence to bear on his vocational training with a view to his army intentions, and on his school leaving arrangements. A full year before the enlistment date – by which time the applicant must have finished his 10th grade satisfactorily and obtained qualification as a skilled worker – he undergoes a suitability test that takes in his political attitudes and character as well as general education, plus sports and medical checks.

The education of potential career NCOs continues at the special *NCO Schools,* starting with a five-to-ten months course that includes basic military training. The time devoted to each subject breaks down as follows in the case of the land forces:

– basic military training	15 per cent
– social sciences	20 per cent
– general military training	15–20 per cent
– weapon and technical training	40–45 per cent
– physical training	5 per cent

Once the course has been successfully concluded the applicant is confirmed as an NCO (or naval equivalent) and joins the forces for a term of two to three years with the possibility of promotion to platoon sergeant *(Unterfeldwebel)*. He then undergoes a career NCO's course of three to six months and passes to the higher rank on successful completion of the finishing test. In all branches this brings with it a state-recognized master's certificate equivalent to the corresponding civilian qualification.

Career NCOs, we read,

> enjoy extensive authority in every appointment, with full personal responsibility for leading military collectives and for safeguarding considerable material and financial resources. As soldiers in charge of others, they are political mentors, military instructors and experts in military technology combined[5].

An account dating from 1976 specifies the following possible careers for regular NCOs:

- Motorized infantry unit NCO;
- Tank commander;
- Gun or mortar commander in the artillery;
- Rocket launcher/mortar section leader;

- Plotter section leader in the rocket troops;
- Section leader in sound/radar unit;
- Commander of self-propelled AA gun in the army air defence;
- Section leader in meteorological artillery unit;
- NCO in the armour service, including section leader of a maintenance, repair or salvage crew, armour electrician, armoured gun or transport sergeant, tank equipment mechanic or motor transport sergeant;
- Rocket and weapon servicing NCO, maintenance specialist or maintenance crew leader;
- Military transport NCO (as section leader for railway/railbridge construction, road/roadbridge building or military transport);
- Rear services NCO for fuel and lubrication, catering, clothing and equipment;
- Engineer NCO for commander's requirements (leader of an engineer, blockade engineer or engineer reconnaissance section);
- Engineer NCO for technical requirements (leader of an engineer section, or section for construction of positions, road/bridge building, timber working, wellsinking and water treatment, amphibious vehicle repairs or engineering repairs; engineering machine driver);
- Chemical service NCO for commander's requirements (section leader for nuclear radiation and chemical reconnaissance and treatment, assayer, evaluator, laboratory head or assistant);
- Chemical services NCO for technical requirements (section leader for repair work, mechanic for nuclear radiation and chemical reconnaissance, or transport sergeant);
- Signals NCO for commander's requirements (section leader for medium-power short-wave equipment in a telegraph and telephone section, and other functions);
- Signals NCO for technical requirements (radio mechanic and senior engine mechanic, telephone mechanic, repair section leader, radio sergeant or signals equipment storekeeper);
- NCO for military topography;
- Medical NCO (section leader in a medical or maintenance section, medical orderly, disinfector, laboratory assistant or storeman in medical installation);
- NCO for reproduction technology (recording and reproduction);
- NCO for military polygraphy (printing technology);
- Military musician;
- NCO for aviation engineering (senior mechanic in a specialized field or repair facility);
- Air safety NCO (flight controller in flight monitoring or headquarter staffs);
- Aircraft supply NCO (mechanic or section leader in a technical aviation unit or oxygen supply facility);
- Air Force/Air Defence meteorological service NCO;
- AA rockets NCO (generator chargehand, senior circuit mechanic, testing-station section leader, sergeant or senior mechanic of a workshop, stock administrator);

– Radar NCO (radar station leader, senior radar mechanic in a workshop or operational crew leader);

– Petty officer for naval weapon requirements (commander of a combat station on a naval vessel in charge of navigation, gunnery, anti-mine and anti-submarine operations, torpedos, rockets or radar and missile guidance);

– Petty officer for engines (commander of combat station on a naval vessel in charge of ship's diesel engines, electric motors, boilers, turbines or pumps);

– Petty officer or NCO for radio signals (commander of a combat station on ship or land).

Those applying for NCO careers should preferably have a related vocational background and have obtained a "skilled worker" testimonial or other certificate of completion of training. Particularly in demand are candidates from the metallurgical or electrical fields. Keen activity in the Party's youth section, the FDJ, and in the premilitary GST, are expected. In the latter organization they will have been expected to earn the "Premilitary and technical proficiency" badge appropriate to the particular NCO career chosen. All would-be NCOs will be assumed to have earned their badges for swimming and sport.

Ensigns (Fähnriche)

The group of ensign ranks was introduced on the Soviet pattern by the standing orders on service careers of December 10, 1973[6]. An NCO can become an ensign through training or practical experience of the functions of NCO or ensign, and by undergoing an ensign course. During this process a serviceman remains treated as a short-service NCO or career NCO. On completing their specialist courses ensigns receive a civilian vocational title.

The option for ensign status should, where possible, be taken up in the 9th school grade. The following conditions then have to be met:

– completion of the 10th grade in a *Polytechnische Oberschule,*
– acquisition of a skilled trade,
– attendance at an NCO school and several years service thereafter as an NCO in the forces, and
– the one-year ensign course and completion of vocational schooling with the title of *Ingenieur.*

The first NVA and Frontier Troop staff sergeants to receive the rank of ensign – *Fähnrich* – were nominated by Deputy Defence Minister Kessler on January 3, 1974[7]. He described them as forming "a qualitatively new cadre category, the *Fähnrich Korps*". The NVA leaders expressed the hope that "the great treasure-house of political, military and vocational experience which you incorporate can be put to the service of our common cause for a long time ahead".

In general ensigns have the same uniforms and equipments as regular officers.

On September 1, 1979, further ensign ranks were introduced in the shape of senior ensign, staff ensign and senior staff ensign (*Oberfähnrich, Stabsfähnrich* and *Oberstabsfähnrich*), with promotion between grades after five years' service.

Officer cadre training

The SED realizes that the army's officer cadres are *one of the most important links in the all-embracing command-and-control chain* of a communist state. As the old Party leader Ulbricht himself had said in 1959[8], training NVA officers meant producing "reliable military functionaries with outstanding ideological and specialist qualifications".

The NVA officer has long been regarded as a man who,

> whatever his field of military competence, combines in himself the political educator and the military instructor, the pedagogue and the technician. Fighting power and combat-readiness are largely determined by him and by the example he sets[9].

As the scientific-technological revolution progresses, there is no upper bound to the expertise required of the officer. Looking forward to the coming decade General Professor Wiesner, Head of the Friedrich Engels Military Academy, laid down these requirements:

> The officer of the 1980s must distinguish himself by the thinking and behaviour of a steadfast communist, a military Party official;
>
> by strong conviction and unconditional loyalty to the Party and the people;
>
> by the knowledge and skill of an educated Marxist-Leninist and socialist soldier-specialist, who combines exact political, military and technical knowledge with practical mastery of his particular field;
>
> by discipline, initiative and persuasiveness;
>
> by strong willpower, exemplary conduct and organizational skills in teaching and training subordinates, so as to lead them in daily service as in battle and fill them with his own enthusiasm[10].

Any young man can apply *to become an officer* up to the age of 23[11]. A high degree of political reliability will be expected, and he must have proved his worth in social organizations, especially the FDJ. As soon as he reaches the 8th or 9th grade in school he will submit his application to the local enlistment office *(Wehrkreiskommando)* which, after a medical check and interview, will take him in charge from that point on. He will be expected during his premilitary training in the GST to have won proficiency badges appropriate to his chosen career.

There are three approaches to an officer's career:

1. Attendance at an Extended Secondary School *(Erweiterte Oberschule)* and school leaving examination *(Abitur);* qualification as a *skilled worker* in a one-year cadet training course; three or four years' study at an officers' college *(Offiziershochschule).*
2. Via the 10th grade of a *Polytechnische Oberschule* and vocational training with leaving examination, leading directly to the officers' college; or
3. via the 10th grade of a *Polytechnische Oberschule* and vocational training up to skilled worker level; matriculation from a one-year cadet course, and then entry to the officers' college.

The *officers' college course* lasts three years, or for aircraft captains, fighter pilots, naval officers and naval engineers four. It includes social sciences, military, technical, mathematical, scientific and specialist training, along with practical experience in the forces. Successful completion of this, and of the concluding officer's examination, leads to *appointment as a second lieutenant* and *"university-trained officer".* The young officer receives a certificate confirming his qualification in any of about twenty training categories or *Ausbildungsprofile,* giving him the title of *Hochschulingenieur, Hochschulingenieurökonom* or *Hochschulökonom.*

Once he is made second lieutenant the graduate steps into his *first officer function,* usually in the unit where he underwent his practical experience.

If he does well, he can expect to become a first lieutenant after two years and a captain after another three.

In all service careers it is possible to qualify as a political officer, staff officer or educational officer at an army teaching institute.

Several years' effective service with the troops entitles one to apply for attendance at a *military academy,* i.e. the Friedrich Engels Military Academy, the Wilhelm Pieck Army Political College, or some civilian institution. This paves the way to higher and more responsible posts.

The NVA officers' colleges

Up until 1963 army officer cadres were trained at one of thirteen *colleges for the various arms of service, special troops and services.* "By the early 60s, however, conditions were ripe for a necessary improvement in the system of developing officer cadres,"[12] and a single college was set up for each of the four main arms – Land Forces, Frontier Troops, Air Force/Air Defence and People's Navy. This made it possible to do more justice to the conditions of modern combat.

During 1968 and 1969 a third phase began in the evolution of officers' schools with the transition to higher education standards – *Hochschulausbildung.* The reasoning was explained thus:

The political and military leadership responsibility of officers had increased dramatically. They therefore required deeper scientific knowledge of the laws of development of a socialist society, as well as of military matters. Revolutionary military advances led to the re-equipment of the NVA with modern war technology, which continually develops and becomes more complex, putting more strain on the skill and knowledge of commanders. At the same time we had seen a rise in the general level of education and greater awareness among citizens of military age[13].

It was on February 25, 1971, that Minister Hoffmann conferred the status of *Hochschulen* – institutes of higher education – on the officers' schools, which had hitherto ranked as specialized technical colleges. The Ministry for Defence's *Offiziershochschulen* now comprise the following:

- the Ernst Thälmann Officers' College for the Land Forces, at Löbau;
- the Rosa Luxemburg Officers' College for the Frontier Troops, at Plauen;
- the Franz Mehring Officers' College for the Air Forces/Air Defence, at Kamenz; and
- the Karl Liebknecht Officers' College for the People's Navy, at Stralsund.

Other institutions of similar status at the disposal of the NVA and other defence agencies are

- the GDR Institute of Military History at Potsdam,
- the Military Signals and Transport Section of the Friedrich List Transport College in Dresden,
- the Department of Military Medicine in the Ernst Moritz Arndt University at Greifswald, and
- the Institute for Civil Defence at Beeskow.

The Ernst Thälmann Officers' College for the Land Forces

Founded on December 2, 1963, this college received its name and its military colours on March 1, 1964.

The military and political heritage of Ernst Thälmann is of particular significance for us ... His appreciation of the historic mission of his own class, his passionate internationalism and patriotism, made him an unflinching foe of imperialism ... As well as embodying Thälmann's spirit in turning young men into officers for our socialist army, the Officers' College became a centre for research and for preserving the military legacy of the German working class's revolutionary past[14].

The reorganization of the College in 1971 was to serve the following ends:

- Officers were to be trained for *employment in many roles*. Hence the new list of basic "career categories" – *Grundprofile* – and the large share of basic information given in the training.

– The *theoretical content* of the courses had to be extended to enable graduates to "adapt themselves creatively" to military innovations.

– Methods of thinking and working were to be imparted to graduates that would enable them to extend their knowledge and skill.

To meet these requirements the amount of basic training in the military, mathematical and natural sciences was increased. Special importance was attached to learning Russian. Classrooms, tutorial rooms and external training areas were extended and modernized.

According to the NVA press the following training categories are available for regular officers in the land forces[15]:

– Commander of a motorized infantry unit, starting as platoon commander in a motorized infantry, reconnaissance or anti-parachutist platoon;

– Commander of an armoured unit, starting as platoon commander of an armoured or reconnaissance platoon;

– Rocket unit commander, initially in charge of a command or firing platoon, or of a technical or meteorological platoon;

– Artillery unit commander, initially in charge of a command or firing platoon, in an artillery, tank-destroying, anti-tank rocket, mortar or grenade-projector battery, or platoon commander in a reconnaissance, survey or automatic artillery-reconnaissance unit;

– Commander of an engineers' unit, usually starting as commander of an engineering reconnaissance, technical engineering, road and position construction, or pontoon and land-bridging platoon;

– Chemical defence commander, usually starting in charge of a platoon for chemical reconnaissance, special treatment or chemical defence;

– AA artillery commander, for appointment mainly as commander of a command-and-rangefinding, firing, or AA guidance platoon;

– Commander or other officer of a signals unit, for appointment usually to a radio, telephone/telegraph, directional radio or mixed-technology signals platoon, or as a workshop officer;

– Radar service officer, for appointment as platoon commander in a repair unit, or as officer in charge of a radar station;

– Rocket service officer, for appointment as commander of a rocket service platoon;

– Weapon service officer, usually for appointment as platoon commander in a weapon repair unit, or as an ammunition officer;

– Tank and motor vehicle officer, usually for appointment as commander of a repair platoon, or as company second-in-command for technical equipment;

– Rear services officer, for appointment as supply officer to a battalion, as commander of a medical or motor transport platoon or, for outstanding graduates, as a regimental staff officer.

For some specialized functions regular officers can also be trained at civilian colleges, e.g. in the fields of physical training, finance, data processing and electronics, military construction, military transport, military topography and interpreting.

The Franz Mehring Air Force/Air Defence Officers' College

As in the preceding case, the elevation to *Hochschule* status of the Air Force/Air Defence officers' training centre affected the curriculum rather than the organization[16]. The further change formally signalized by the conferment of the Franz Mehring title on February 25, 1971, followed upon resolutions of the SED Central Committee and the GDR State Council on the Structuring of a *Uniform Socialist Education System;* it was also an application of the *Third Higher Education Reform* to the military sphere. Guidelines for the new curriculum were provided by the "training categories" laid down by the Chief of the Air Force/Air Defence, and the Requirements for Air Force/Air Defence Officers elaborated in the college itself.

Before the change, there had been doubts among the staff as to whether the new demands could be met without appreciably lengthening the courses. "Over-influenced by experience in civilian universities, these officers had conceived exaggerated views of the priority of certain training subjects."[17] However, it was only necessary to ask oneself the purpose of military training to realize

> that the main object was not to produce a university graduate but an NVA officer and political and military instructor, highly competent as a military specialist and with enough scientific and technical grounding to enable him to acquire fresh knowledge on his own.

To help accomplish the change, the "wisdom and experience of all the directorial and teaching staff" was supplemented by *Soviet advice.* As a result of close ties with the Soviet air force, there is a particularly active "interplay of experience" between training staff in the two countries.

As in all the NVA Officers' Colleges, officer cadets with school leaving certificates *(Abitur)* were trained to "skilled worker" standard for the first time in the 1974/1975 academic year. The training is subject to written agreements between the College and the employing enterprises. It proved difficult to assemble a uniform and efficient corps of instructors, drawn as these were from very disparate sources – leading cadres from the enterprises, teacher-training personnel, schoolteachers, senior officers in the College and officials of the Party and social organizations as well as "working-class brigades". The purpose was to give cadets, through this kind of vocational training, not only trade skills but heightened "class consciousness".

According to a description in the military press, the Air Force/Air Defence Officers' College offers among ten *training categories*[18]:

– Aircraft commander;

– Command staff officer, for appointment mostly as navigation officer, pilot or pilot/navigator;

– Flight engineer for airframe/driving gear, for appointment usually as section leader or head of technical services in a flight, or as platoon commander in an aero technical company.

– Flight engineer for special electric equipment, radio and radar, or weaponry;

– Officer for radar technology and automatic guidance systems;

– AA missile officer for electric and electronic equipment.

The Karl Liebknecht Officers' College for the People's Navy

"Karl Liebknecht's greatness as a man, his revolutionary conduct and passionate devotion to the Soviet Union have played a cardinal role", we read, in making cadet training the "anvil on which the People's Navy cadres are forged"[19]. Accordingly, *brotherhood-in-arms with the Soviet and other communist navies* is particularly stressed in the GDR sea forces. The Karl Liebknecht College cultivates close relationship with the M. V. Frunze Senior Naval Officers' School in Leningrad and the Polish equivalent, styled Heroes of the Westerplatte, in Gdynia.

It takes the Karl Liebknecht College in Stralsund four years – one year longer than in the Land Forces – to turn out naval officers and engineers as political and military commanders and instructors, with the university degree of Ingenieur.

In this case there are only two training categories[20].

– For naval officers, training inter alia in determination of position at sea; weather and marine science; magnetic and gyroscopic compasses; automatic pilot, sonar, course-measuring, radio bearings and collision avoidance; sea traffic law; use and effect of missiles, artillery, torpedos and mines; signalling equipment. After passing his final examination, and the traditional farewell on the Lenin Square in Stralsund, the graduate will have his first appointment as second officer on a warship or commander of a small vessel.

– For ship's engineers, there is training inter alia in basic mathematics, electronics, technical drawing, nature and testing of materials, mechanics and engine parts; accident prevention; electronics and mensuration; theory of heat; electric motors and installations; ship propulsion and its technical support. Appointment as engineer on large or small naval vessels.

Since the training course for marine officers is longer than elsewhere, great stress is laid on the *further education of officers* for the training battalions[21]. These last have to undergo in every training year some 300 hours of further instruction in

– general training subjects,

– physical training,

– military operational and specialized topics, and

– educational methods.

Further training projects are hampered by disparities of seniority and teaching experience among company officers, by the scope and variety of tasks assigned to them and by the need to ensure uninterrupted command of units. The centrally organized courses for company officers at the Officers' College cannot obviate the principle that every superior is directly responsible for the full training, and further training, of his subordinates.

The Friedrich Engels Military Academy

Set up by a Politburo decision on January 5, 1959, as the "first socialist military academy in the history of our people", the Dresden institution is responsible for training senior officers for all branches of the NVA, Frontier Troops and other armed forces.

The first step toward creating a *Hochschule* for NVA officers was taken as early as October 1956. Both before and after that date the NVA had sent its officers for academic qualification to the Soviet General Staff Academy, while junior officers of all services had attended other military schools in the U.S.S.R. Nowadays only those intended for general ranks, for the most part, go for two or three years to the General Staff or other Soviet military academies. Marine officers intended for promotion to admiral rank are trained at the First Baltic Marine School in Leningrad or the Second Baltic Marine School at Kaliningrad (former Königsberg).

In the early years of the NVA less than half the students at the Dresden Academy had been through an Officers' College. By 1965 the figure had reached 74 per cent and by 1968 89 per cent; since 1979 nearly all have attended an Officers' College and served satisfactorily with the troops[22]. As Defence Minister Hoffmann pointed out in February 1979 in a speech celebrating the Academy's 20th anniversary, the position among the instructors was initially even worse. "At that time only 20 per cent of the instructing officers had higher education. Today, every one has a degree. One comrade in four earned it at a Soviet academy. Meanwhile 40 per cent of those teaching here have taken a doctor's degree, 20 per cent have been appointed professors and over 50 per cent lecturers."[23]

The rising educational level of candidates made it possible on September 1, 1965, to do away with the "faculty of preliminary studies", though much of the subsequent training time still had to be spent on science and technical military studies. In the same year the military science teaching was modified in favour of an improved grounding in general. Principles and syllabuses could be worked out further in advance, making for more stability in the instruction generally. At the same time effect was given to the "Guidelines for the development of the Friedrich Engels Military Academy for the period 1965–1970" which had been settled by the National Defence Council on June 18, 1965.

In the third phase of its build-up, introduced in 1971 by the Resolutions of the 8th SED Party Congress and Directive No. 1/73 of the Defence Ministry, the Academy – like the NVA in general – was given the task of measuring its performance even more than before by the yardstick of the Soviet Army and of Soviet military science, which embodies the world's highest standards of military theory. For us this means, for example, adapting instruction even more closely to the conditions of modern combat, and making our attitudes more troop-oriented[24].

Since 1969 the Military Academy has been divided into five departments for

- the Land Forces, including territorial units,
- the Air Force/Air Defence,
- the Navy,
- the Frontier Troops, and
- Engineering.

These departments in turn cover twelve specialities, with an institute for each of them:

- operational arts and tactics,
- operational research,
- artillery and rockets,
- conduct of political work,
- troop commanding,
- mechanization and automation of troop commanding,
- armour and motor vehicle technology,
- project planning and control system, electronic data processing,
- cybernetics,
- military teaching theory and psychology,
- military sociology,
- military theory and doctrine.

The period of study – three years for *Direktstudium* and four in the *Diplomingenieur* course – is interrupted by troop command assignments. Most of the annual output of 230 to 240 graduates receive a degree Diplom as *Diplomgesellschaftswissenschaftler, Diplommilitärwissenschaftler* or *Diplomingenieur* and are simultaneously promoted to lieutenant-colonel or naval commander. They now rank as middle or senior command cadres.

After further experience with the troops for at least two years, graduates in some branches can apply for doctorates or professorships.

In addition to its teaching function the Military Academy has from the start engaged in research as well. One of its first, short-term tasks was to produce adequate teaching materials. Since the middle 'sixties members of the Academy have been presenting their own research papers on such subjects as the development of fraternal military relations, the theory of troop commanding and problems of political leadership in the forces. They have also come up with mathematical aides to commanders' decision-making and to the compilation of combat records.

With due regard to the "unity of teaching, research and degree studies" the new guidelines for social and military science research for the 'eighties, according to General Professor Wiesner, Head of the Military Academy, include these five points[25]:

- Firstly, intensification of scientific cooperation with the other fraternal socialist armies is needed ...
- Secondly, research tasks and aims must be derived, even more than before, from the practical needs of the troops and of teaching ...
- Thirdly, better research results can only be achieved by intensifying and developing interdisciplinary cooperation ...
- Fourthly, it will be necessary in social science research to pay more attention to the ideological class war. This means, for example, analysing the mental equipment of the NATO forces and drawing necessary conclusions for the fulfiment of our military class mission ...
- Fifthly, it must be made clear that the efficiency of scientific work depends on the professional standards of the researcher, on the material base and on its purposeful guidance, planning and organization.

These points apply, General Wiesner explained, not only to the Academy's research work but to its whole training function.

Today more than ever, further enhancement of fighting power and combat-readiness depends on qualitative factors. The consequence is that the demands made on the performance of command cadres and all servicemen will increase, producing fresh problems for the Military Academy in training officers[26].

One of these problems is clearly implied in the General's immediately following remarks to the Academy's scholar-graduates:

As the executor of the working class's will in the military sphere, the future graduate of the Military Academy must obey every command issued to him by Party, state and army leaders in the interest of protecting socialism.

Notes

[1] Militärlexikon, East Berlin 1973, p. 36.
[2] Militärische Grundausbildung, in: *Armeerundschau*, East Berlin 10/1975, p. 76.
[3] Army General Heinz *Hoffmann*, Zu einigen Führungs- und Erziehungsaufgaben im neuen Ausbildungsjahr, in: *Militärwesen*, East Berlin 1/1979, p. 8.
[4] Musterung, in: *Armeerundschau*, 3/1978, p. 42.
[5] Berufsunteroffiziere, in: *Armeerundschau* 3/1976, pp. 61–68.
[6] Beschluß des Staatsrates der DDR über den Dienst in den bewaffneten Organen und die militärischen Dienstgrade vom 10. Dezember 1973, *Gesetzblatt I*, No. 57, East Berlin, December 20, 1973, p. 559.
[7] *Volksarmee*, East Berlin 2/1974.
[8] Walter *Ulbricht*, Zur Eröffnung der ersten sozialistischen Militärakademie in der Geschichte Deutschlands, in: *Militärwesen*, special issue, February 1959.
[9] Offiziersberufe, in: *Armeerundschau*, 3/1975, p. 68.
[10] Lieutenant General Professor H. *Wiesner*, Head of the Friedrich Engels Military Academy, in: *Militärwesen*, 12/1978, p. 10 f.

[11] Cf. Offiziersberufe, loc. cit., note 9, pp. 68–75.

[12] Lieutenant General H.-G. *Ernst* of the Ernst Thälmann Officers' College, Die Heranbildung junger Kommandeure der Landstreitkräfte an der Offiziershochschule Ernst Thälmann, in: *Militärwesen*, 12/1975, A p. 98.

[13] Ibid., A p. 100.

[14] Ibid., A p. 98.

[15] Offiziersberufe, note 9.

[16] Cf. Major General M. *Lange* and others, Fünf Jahre Offiziershochschule der LSK/LV Franz Mehring, in: *Militärwesen*, 12/1975, B pp. 98–102.

[17] Ibid., B p. 99.

[18] Cf. Berufsoffiziere LSK/LV, in: *Armeerundschau*, 6/1974, pp. 36–38, and Offiziersberufe, loc. cit., note 9, pp. 73–75.

[19] Captain K. *Schulz* and others of the Karl Liebknecht Officers' College, Kaderschmiede der Volksmarine, in: *Militärwesen*, 12/1975, C pp. 98–102.

[20] Offiziersberufe, note 9, p. 75.

[21] Lieutenant General Professor H. *Wiesner*, Head of the Friedrich Engels Military Academy, 20 Jahre Militärakademie Friedrich Engels, in: *Militärwesen*, 12/1978, pp. 3–11.

[22] Cf. Major General W. *Otto* of the Friedrich Engels Military Academy, Zur Erziehung und Ausbildung von Offizierskadern an der Militärakademie Friedrich Engels, in: *Militärwesen*, 1/1974, pp. 50–55.

[23] *Neues Deutschland*, February 2, 1979.

[24] Lieutenant General Professor *Wiesner*, loc. cit., note 21, p. 6.

[25] Ibid., pp. 7–10.

[26] Ibid., p. 10.

CHAPTER TWELVE

Barrack Duties, Discipline and Internal Structure

The general rights and duties of servicemen in the NVA – and similarly of members of the GDR Frontier Troops and Civil Defence – are codified in the *regulations on interior or barrack duties*, known as the *Innendienstvorschrift*. This document also defines the mutual relations of members of the services and lays down the principles of internal discipline and the obligations of superiors and subordinates in all the principal functions within the regiment and unit. A revised *Innendienstvorschrift, DV 010/0/003*, came into force on December 1, 1978[1].

The supreme law governing the conduct of every serviceman is the NVA's *oath of allegiance* as formulated, after some changes, in 1962. It is extremely comprehensive; the socialist soldier evidently requires a detailed statement of his commitments.

I swear:

at all times loyally to serve my fatherland, the German Democratic Republic, and to protect it against any enemy when so ordered by the workers'-and-farmers' government;

I swear:

as a soldier of the National People's Army to be ready at all times, side by side with the Soviet Army and the armies of the socialist countries allied to us, to defend socialism against all enemies and to stake my life for the achievement of victory;

I swear:

to be an honourable, brave, disciplined and watchful soldier, to render unconditional obedience to my military superiors, to fulfil my orders with every determination and always strictly to observe military and state secrets;

I swear:

conscientiously to acquire military knowledge and observe military regulations, and always and everywhere to guard the honour of our Republic and of its National People's Army.

Should I ever violate this, my solemn military oath, may I suffer the stern penalties of the laws of our Republic and the contempt of the working people.

Servicemen enjoy the basic rights, and owe the basic duties, of all citizens according to the GDR Constitution, insofar as their exercise does not conflict with the requirements of socialist national defence.

The list of their duties differs in the main only terminologically from that of the West German *Bundeswehr*, or other Western armies. The same applies to the extensive rights accorded to members of the NVA. On the other hand the East German soldier enjoys rights specified in the *Innendienstvorschrift* which can only be granted in particular cases according to his superior's judgement.

Superiors and subordinates: seniors and juniors

Servicemen are classified by *rank-group* and *rank* in the Land Forces and Air Forces/Air Defence (and in the People's Navy) as follows:

Soldaten (Matrosen) – Equivalent in the British Forces: Privates.

> *Soldat (Matrose)* – Private, Aircraftman 2nd Class, (Ordinary Rating);
> *Gefreiter (Obermatrose)* – Private, Aircraftman 1st Class, (Ordinary Rating);
> *Stabsgefreiter (Stabsmatrose)* – Lance Corporal, Senior Aircraftman, (Able Rating);
> *Unteroffiziersschüler* – NCO Cadet;
> *Offiziersschüler* – Officer Cadet.

Unteroffiziere (Maate) – Corporals, Sergeants, (Petty Officers).

> *Unteroffizier (Maat)* – Corporal, (Leading Rating);
> *Unterfeldwebel (Obermaat)* – Lance Sergeant, (Petty Officer);
> *Feldwebel (Meister)* – Sergeant, (Petty Officer);
> *Oberfeldwebel (Obermeister)* – Staff Sergeant, Flight Sergeant, (Chief Petty Officer);
> *Stabsfeldwebel (Stabsobermeister)* – Warrant Officer.

Fähnriche – Ensigns, no equivalent in the British Forces.

> *Fähnrich;*
> *Oberfähnrich;*
> *Stabsfähnrich;*
> *Oberstabsfähnrich.*

Offiziere – Officers.

> a) *Leutnante* – Lieutenants;
> *Unterleutnant* – No equivalent in the British Forces;
> *Leutnant* – Second Lieutenant, Pilot Officer, (Acting Sub-Lieutenant);
> *Oberleutnant* – Lieutenant, Flying Officer, (Sub-Lieutenant).
> b) *Hauptleute (Kapitänleutnante)* – Captains;
> *Hauptmann (Kapitänleutnant)* – Captain, Flight Lieutenant, (Lieutenant).
> c) *Stabsoffiziere* – No equivalent in the British Forces.
> *Major (Korvettenkapitän)* – Major, Squadron Leader, (Lieutenant Commander);
> *Oberstleutnant (Fregattenkapitän)* – Lieutenant Colonel, Wing Commander, (Commander);
> *Oberst (Kapitän zur See)* – Colonel, Group Captain, (Captain).

Generale (Admirale) – Generals, (Admirals).

Generalmajor (Konteradmiral) – Brigadier, Air Commodore, (Commodore 1st and 2nd Class);

Generalleutnant (Vizeadmiral) – Major General, Air Vice Marshal, (Rear Admiral);

Generaloberst (Admiral) – Lieutenant General, Air Marshal, (Vice Admiral);

Armeegeneral (No rank in the People's Navy) – General, Air Chief Marshal, (Admiral).

Servicemen are divided by *function* into superiors and subordinates (*Vorgesetzte* and *Unterstellte*) and by terms of service into conscript privates, short-service privates, short-service NCOs, short-service officers, regular NCOs, ensigns and regular officers.

The first category by terms of service – *Soldaten im Grundwehrdienst* – comprises male citizens called up for military service under paragraph 21 of the Conscription Law[3].

Short-service NCOs and privates serve for at least three years, but can sign on for up to ten. The length of service for *short-service officers* is regulated by the Defence Ministry. Short-service privates or ratings can be promoted up to *Stabsgefreiter* (Lance Corporal, Leading Aircraftman) or *Stabsmatrose* (Able Rating). Short-service NCOs can advance to the rank of *Feldwebel* (Sergeant) or *Meister* (Petty Officer), short-service officers to that of *Hauptmann* (Captain, Flight Lieutenant) or *Kapitänleutnant* (Lieutenant or Lieutenant Commander).

Regular NCOs serve for at least ten years until they reach the retiring age for active service; this is usually 65, or 60 for women, but exceptions can be made.

The service period for *ensigns (Fähnriche)* and regular *officers (Berufsoffiziere)* is at least twenty-five years.

Subordination relationships are derived in principle from those of function. Those whose function puts them permanently or temporarily in charge of others are "direct superiors" *(direkte Vorgesetzte)* and those immediately in charge are "immediate superiors" (*unmittelbare Vorgesetzte*). Every direct superior has powers of command and discipline. *As sole Leader, Einzelleiter* (according to the principle of "sole command" or "one-man command"), he is responsible for the "unity of political, military, economic and administrative leadership". "This principle includes the creative utilization of the collective's wisdom by the direct superior at each level of command, just as much as the requirement of disciplined and unconditional fulfilment of orders."[4]

Right: Oath-taking ceremony.

Other kinds of superiors than the "direct" ones are

– all seconds-in-command with authority to issue orders in their own field of responsibility, and
– leaders and officers of the various special services, who can likewise issue orders to members of those services.
– Further, we read that "the regulations on the Rights and Duties of rank-seniors represent a complete innovation in the field of superior-subordinate relationships"[5].

This last means that *every rank-senior is superior to every rank-junior,* whenever the latter's direct superior is absent or if an abnormal situation arises, e.g. disturbance of public safety and order; circumstances prejudicial to military discipline and order or to the reputation of the NVA; or interruption of the prescribed command system during fulfilment of combat tasks or in the event of catastrophes, emergencies or impending danger. In such cases every rank-senior is entitled to issue orders, and obliged to take all necessary and possible measures. This new regulation eliminates the need which existed previously for the senior to declare himself "superior" in a particular situation, and to justify this vis-à-vis his rank-junior.

This right of command for the rank-senior arises, for example, when steps are necessary to cope with undisciplined behaviour by soldiers in public. Rank-juniors then have to comply with orders immediately, whichever part of the services the senior belongs to.

Issuing and carrying out orders

An order is the "supreme military directive". "In issuing an order the commander expresses not only his own will, but above all the will of the working class, the state and the people."[6] An order forms the basis for the strict command and leadership of servicemen and units. *Orders must be carried out unconditionally.*

Usually orders are issued by direct superiors. Within a company, for example, this means that the company commander passes them to the platoon commanders, these pass them to the section leaders and these to their men. Orders are to be concise and unambiguous so that all subordinates can understand them. Along with the right of command, a superior also carries responsibility for ensuring that an order does not infringe recognized international law or the penal code, for confirming that it has been carried out and for receiving the report of its completion. Responsibility for observance of national and international law lies solely with the superior, instead of being shared with the subordinate as in the West German forces.

An oral command has to be acknowledged with the words *"Zu Befehl!"* and then executed, after consideration of the best and fastest method of doing so.

Saluting

In accordance with the amended *Innendienstvorschrift* servicemen show their respect by saluting

– the Secretary General of the SED Party and the Chairman of the GDR State Council,
– the Prime Minister,
– the Speaker of the People's Chamber,
– when the National Anthem is played,
– memorials at national shrines for the Anti-fascist Resistance, and memorials to the fallen heroes of the Soviet Army,
– at parades for the dead and wreath-laying ceremonies,
– military banners,
– at the changing of the guards,
– state and military flags during flag parades,
– service flags when entering or leaving ships,
– members of other GDR armed forces or of other socialist armies of their own rank or higher,
– when entering or leaving rooms of superiors or of state organizations,
– when entering or leaving restaurants and the like.

Salutes of greeting from members of non-socialist armies are returned in kind.

Rules of conduct

Rules of conduct when on duty, or in public outside duty, are in general defined more exactly and clearly than before. They are considerably stricter than would be found acceptable in Western armies.

All NVA members are enjoined to *observe polite and correct manners in their mutual dealings*. The plural form of address – *Sie*, not *Du* – is in general use when on duty. Superiors and rank-seniors are addressed with the word *Genosse*, comrade, followed by the rank, e.g. *"Genosse Unteroffizier!"* Subordinates and rank-juniors are addressed as *"Genosse"* followed by their rank, or their surname.

With staff officers in the navy the full designation is now expected, e.g. *"Genosse Fregattenkapitän!"* The complete designation is now also applied to generals and admirals, e.g. *"Genosse Generalleutnant!"* And the Minister for National Defence is addressed as *"Genosse Minister"*.

Every serviceman is supposed to live according to the *"norms of socialist morality"*. The *Innendienstvorschrift* prescribes "modest and correct behaviour" at all times. When in uniform one is not supposed to play portable radios or tape recorders in public. Courtesy must be shown to civilians. Every member of the public is to be given help when he needs it, and backed up in the maintenance of public order.

In the interest of discipline and appearances hands should not be kept in uniform pockets. No soldier should sit down or smoke in the presence of his superior or rank-senior without permission. In public places, smoking in uniform is forbidden, with the exception of recreation areas, park benches or open-air restaurants.

When his superior approaches, a seated serviceman will rise and salute. Both for disciplinary and hygienic reasons all hair will be kept short; every soldier must be shaved for duty. Beards are in general forbidden.

Wearing of civilian clothes in off-duty hours and during leave is governed by the following rules. Officers, ensigns, regular NCOs, 4th year cadets and short-service NCOs from the 4th year of service require no special permission, nor do servicewomen of any length of service. All other NVA members have to request permission from a direct superior at company commander level or above.

Any instructions given to an NVA member in public by members of other GDR armed forces or customs officials in the exercise of their duty have to be complied with.

Except for officers and ensigns, NVA members are in principle only allowed to leave barracks if in possession of a duty pass or leave pass, or if permission has been entered in the duty logbook. All servicemen, officers and ensigns included, if they intend during leave to spend more than 24 hours elsewhere than at the place specified in the leave book, must write in that address as well. In theory, then, everyone can be contacted on leave within 24 hours.

Socialist relations between superior and subordinate

Even the amended version of the regulations shows that relations between superior and subordinate in the NVA are strictly *governed by military requirements,* and despite a few concessions to modernity the thinking behind them is *conservative and authoritarian.* The cooperative style of leadership that prevails increasingly in Western armies appears not to be possible in East Germany. In the NVA even personal relations between superior, equals and subordinates are considered *"socialist relations",* since the partners are "class comrades"[7]. What is particularly socialist about these relations may sometimes be hard for a Western observer to see. The communist terminology apart, the following catalogue of good and bad qualities in a superior corresponds in many details to notions held in Western armies. However, these *"essential socialist relations"*[8] in the NVA are enumerated thus:

– class pride, pride in membership of the working class and in the instrument of its power, the NVA;
– pride in solidarity, in the collective and its standard of performance, and in one's superior;
– respect for one's superior and strict compliance with his orders and instructions;
– relationship based on stringent demands and deep trust, on delegation of high responsibility, along with practical helpfulness and the creation of favourable conditions for creative initiative;

– helpfulness and solidarity, esprit de corps, mutual responsibility of the individual for the collective and vice versa;
– friendship, soldierly comradeship, trust, mutual respect, recognition and appreciation;
– candid, honourable and warm, yet critical, attitudes, sympathy and fellow-feeling, care and understanding for one another and direct concern for the life of one's comrade.

We are told further that socialist relations between superior and subordinate "are notable in that they are prescribed in service regulations, are confirmed by Party and government, and hence have the force of law". Which merely means that *all current NVA regulations are a priori "socialist"*.

Superiors in particular are enjoined to see that their socialist relations with their subordinates

– rest on the principle of strict subordination, which prescribes in detail the special powers of the commander (*Einzelleiter*) as well as the rights and duties of every serviceman;
– are marked by adherence to principle in political and military conduct;
– bear the stamp of high ideological and military standards, justice, sincerity and concern, mutual respect and trust, soldierly comradeship, tact, consideration, benevolence, approachability and warmth.

It is the duty of all superiors, especially those in command of companies and platoons, continually to acquire a *"socialist superior's personality"*.
A scientific investigation into behavioural and personality traits conducive to, or inhibitory of, *class-oriented relationships between superior and subordinate* produced the following findings[9]:

Conducive factors:
– constant open support for Party and government policies;
– setting a good example in dutiful and responsible service performance;
– exercise of international class-solidarity in word and deed (cf. unity of socialist patriotism and proletarian internationalism);
– a militant attitude to all hostile ideology;
– a clear concept of the enemy;
– good general education and possession of first-class specialist knowledge;
– persistence in acquiring political, military and specialist qualifications;
– a good-humoured way with young people;
– doggedness and perseverance;
– confidence in victory and deeprooted optimism in the performance of military duties;
– comradeliness and helpfulness in giving instruction and in daily intercourse with the troops;
– patience as a trainer;
– continual concern for outward appearances;

"Weapons from the workers' hands!" – A member of the Working Class Combat Groups hands over a submachine gun to a young soldier.

- imposing high standards on oneself;
- showing initiative.

Inhibitory factors:
– indecisiveness;
– frequent changes of mind;
– inefficiency in organizing work;
- favouritism;
-- lack of concern for others;
– giving ill-considered orders;
– vagueness in expressing oneself;
– failure to adapt to the language level of one's subordinates or fellow-members of a group;
– pretended omniscience;
– inadequate knowledge of detail in one's duties or in everyday life;

– mocking the deficiencies of one's subordinates or fellow-members of a group;
– failing to ask their opinions, or ignoring them when offered.

Service routines

Duties are organized according to a daily schedule *(Tagesdienstablaufplan)* with more precise deadlines than in the West German or other Western armies. The lengths of training periods each day are very meticulously laid down in the new *Innendienstvorschrift*, which gives the Duty Officer and *Duty NCO* the authority to ensure that they are adhered to.

The day begins with the Duty NCO sounding *reveille* on the bugle and giving the order "Company, rise!" In each room the room leader *(Stubenälteste)* is responsible for seeing that the others get up. *Morning exercise* follows, conducted by the section leader; this is compulsory for all except sick men, who report immediately after reveille to the Duty NCO; he enters them in the sickbook and sees that they are taken to the sickbay. All men *wash* stripped to the waist. *Cleaning of rooms* and barrack area has to be completed before *morning parade*, likewise bedmaking and tidying of rooms and lockers exactly as prescribed.

The morning, midday and evening *meals* are eaten communally. *Training* is compulsory for all servicemen, only the regimental commander being empowered to give exemption. From Monday to Friday the training day consists of seven 45 minute periods, a shorter period than in, for example, the West German army. Double periods are usual. After night-training at least six hours are allowed for sleeping, and the following day's training begins two hours after the men are woken. During manoeuvres, inspections and other complexities the training-day is unlimited and special schedules are laid down.

The day ends with the *tattoo (Zapfenstreich)*.

Servicemen quartered in barracks are allowed in their free time to *receive visits from citizens* of the GDR or other socialist states – but only if they are wives or relatives.

The daily schedule prescribes *periods of free time* for every soldier in the barrack. This is more clearly formulated in the new *Innendienstvorschrift*. Free time may not be curtailed unless required in the interest of combat-readiness. Social, cultural and sporting events are organized to occupy soldiers during their leisure, but attendance is voluntary.

Outside the company's quarters it is compulsory to *wear the correct uniform*. The commander issues the relevant rules for dress in the company club and other central premises. The regimental club, restaurants and visitors' room can normally only be entered in dress-uniform; only officers, ensigns and regular NCOs are allowed to wear service uniform in these places.

The numerous regulations in these matters are not only oppressive for the individual but give rise to much additional paperwork, just as the daily schedule's red tape does.

Accommodation

Except for regular officers and NCOs, and ensigns, all NVA servicemen are billetted in *barracks*. Short-service officers, NCOs and privates can apply for permission to live outside, but for the last two categories this is only given in special personal circumstances. NCO and officer cadets are in general exempt. Officers, ensigns and regular NCOs who have no nearby residence are housed in special hostels or in billets separate from their units.

The following *barrack-room rules* apply to NCOs and other ranks. Beds must not be close together. Uniforms must be hung up in lockers at night and underwear laid tidily on a stool, with boots cleaned and placed underneath.

NCOs and officer cadets are allowed to have their *own radios and gramophones* in their rooms. In privates' and NCO cadets' quarters one radio can be allowed per room by the company commander, provided there are no ring-main loudspeakers. Private TV sets in rooms occupied by officers, ensigns and regular NCOs require permission from the regimental commander.

Soldiers doing their conscript or reserve service are not allowed to have *private cars* in the barrack area. *Private cameras* belonging to servicemen living in barracks are registered, kept in store and only given out for exit and leave purposes.

Hygiene

The section on servicemen's hygiene in the amended *Innendienstvorschrift* is a new one. *Personal hygiene* includes regular washing – with cold water from the waist up in the morning, and at night the feet too. Teeth must be brushed twice a day, shaving and haircutting carried out in good time, the nails kept in order, showers taken regularly, underwear, socks, and bed linen changed, pyjamas worn at night, uniform, shoes and beds kept clean; men must report clean for medical treatment and no sports clothing may be worn under uniform. *Collective hygiene* involves cleanliness of rooms, lockers, toilets and other communal facilities, regular airing of rooms, cleaning of cutlery and eating utensils, removal of food waste, disposal of bottles and rubbish in the proper containers and avoidance of litter on streets and squares and around regimental premises.

NCOs and privates take a shower once a week. Canteen personnel and those engaged in dirty work do so daily, and extra showers must be facilitated for tank crews and repair and maintenance workers.

Clean laundry must be made available after each weekly shower. Underwear and towels are changed every week, bed linen every fortnight. Servicemen have to wash their own ties and socks.

Regular *inoculations* are given against smallpox, tetanus, typhoid and paratyphoid, and viral influenza.

All sick report to surgery for examination, where they are classified according to the nature and severity of their case as fit, partly fit, or unfit for duty. Those unfit are kept in the sickbay or sent elsewhere for treatment.

Requests and complaints

The 1978 version of the *Innendienstvorschrift* also changed the regulations on request and complaint procedure, with special reference to the Request Law *(Eingabegesetz)* of June 19, 1975.

In all service and personal matters every NVA serviceman is entitled to make oral or written requests or complaints to his superior. In matters not affecting his duties he is also entitled under law to direct them to popular representatives bodies and their members, and to any state or economic agency, socialist enterprise, industrial combine or state institution. In cases of jeopardy to security, fighting-power or combat-readiness servicemen can also apply to a superior at a higher level.

In general, however, requests and complaints are to be directed to one's immediate superior, who is usually able to make the necessary decision. If not, he is obliged to pass them on through proper channels.

A complaint against a superior should be directed to the superior's own immediate superior. It must be noted that a serviceman can only lodge a complaint on his own behalf; collective or proxy complaints are debarred. Nor is one allowed to present a complaint when on parade – except at question time – or on guard or day duty, during training periods or on combat tasks.

The intention to complain about an order does not justify non-compliance, unless carrying it out would obviously infringe international law or the penal code.

Servicemen are also entitled, provided they observe security requirements, to *write letters to the army press*. These periodicals treat such letters as requests and bring them to the attention of the writer's competent superior.

Requests and complaints have in principle to be dealt with in whatever quarter is best situated to make an informed decision. Superiors are wholly responsible for their processing.

The time-limits allowed for rulings are 28 days for the Defence Ministry, 20 days for high commands and equivalent staffs, 15 days for formation staffs and 10 for staffs of units. Within these deadlines a ruling has to be both made and notified to the originator.

The right of complaint in the NVA is largely similar to provisions in Western armies. What is remarkable is the simultaneous existence of a service procedure and of the right *to appeal directly to the SED Party's Central Committee*. Another unusual feature is the right to submit a letter to an NVA newspaper and have it treated as a request.

There also appears to be an inconsistency in the rule on complaining against an order that infringes *"recognized norms of international law or the penal code"*. The standing orders on complaint procedure appear to allow refusal of an order in such a case, whereas nothing of the kind is mentioned in the regulations on issuing and executing orders.

Garrison and guard duty

Another set of *"basic standing orders"*, concerning garrison and guard duty, was issued as DV 010/0/004 at the start of the 1978/79 training year. They were intended to strengthen the authority of servicemen performing these duties and spell out their tasks and obligations in such precise terms that no erroneous interpretation could arise. The Garrison Leader *(Standortälteste)*, Deputy Garrison Leader and Garrison Commandant are given wide rights and duties.

In garrison areas where there are units and ships of the People's Navy a Marine Garrison Commandant is appointed to back up the Garrison Leader and provide expertise in maritime matters. The garrison patrol system[10] has been tightened up in some respects as an important means of maintaining discipline and good order in public. All units in the area provide personnel for patrolling.

The rules laid down for guard duty begin with the admonition: *"Guard duty is a combat task"*[11]. Recently commanders of all companies contributing men for the purpose have been empowered to check guards without special instructions, as have their direct superiors, in addition to the officer in charge of the guard, who will be the Garrison Commander or Garrison Leader.

Rules of discipline

"The achievement of victory ... requires iron military discipline. Anyone who does not understand that knows nothing of the preconditions for the exercise of the workers' power", wrote Lenin[12]. In a socialist army, discipline is "not just a soldierly virtue ... but a requirement for the class struggle and its content is primarily a political one, determined by class interests"[13]. The concept of military discipline, then, has a "completely new content"[14] in so-

Right: Badges of Rank (Dienstgradabzeichen)

Left to right, 1st row: Cap badge (for Generals and the People's Navy gold-coloured, otherwise silver), Private without rank (motorized infantry), Private (artillery), Senior Aircraftman (air force), Corporal (engineers).

2nd row: Lance Sergeant (air force), Sergeant (signals), Staff Sergeant (rear services, Warrant Officer (armour), NCO Cadet (motorized infantry).

3rd row: Ensign (air force), Officer Cadet (rear services, 3rd year), Unterleutnant (frontier troops) (no equivalent in the British Forces), Pilot Officer (air force), Lieutenant (artillery).

4th row: Captain (armour), Major (engineers), Lieutenant Colonel (signals), Colonel (frontier troops), Lieutenant General (frontier troops) (equivalent to a Major General in the British Forces).

5th row: Colonel General (land forces) (equivalent to a Lieutenant General in the British Forces), General (land forces), Generals' (land forces) collar tab.

Dienstgradabzeichen

MÜTZENEMBLEM
(für Generale und
Volksmarine gold-
farben, sonst silbern)

SOLDAT
(Mot. Schützen)

GEFREITER
(Artillerie)

STABSGEFREITER
(Luftstreitkräfte)

UNTEROFFIZIER
(Pioniere und tech.
Truppen)

UNTERFELDWEBEL
(Luftverteidigung)

FELDWEBEL
(Nachrichten)

OBERFELDWEBEL
(Rückw. Dienste)

STABSFELDW.
(Panzer)

UFFZ.-SCHÜLER
(Mot.-Schützen)

FÄHNRICH (Luftstreitkräfte,
Ärmelabz. 3 Sterne ab 21., 2 ab
16., 1 Stern ab 11. Dienstjahr)

OFFZ. SCHÜLER
(Rückw. Dienste
3. Lehrjahr)

UNTERLEUTNANT
(Grenztruppen)

LEUTNANT
(Luft-Vertg.)

OBERLEUTNANT
(Artillerie)

HAUPTMANN
(Panzer)

MAJOR
(Pioniere u.
tech. Truppen)

OBERSTLEUT.
(Nachrichten)

OBERST
(Grenztruppen)

GENERALMAJOR
(Luftstreitkr.)

GENERALLEUTN.
(Grenztruppen)

GENERALOBERST (Landstreitkr.)

ARMEEGENERAL (Landstreitkr.)

GENERALE (Landstreitkräfte)
Kragenspiegel

MATROSE
(Seem. Laufbahn)

OBERMATROSE
(Tech. Laufbahn)

STABSMATROSE
(Küstendienstlaufb.)

UFFZ.-SCHÜLER

MAAT
(Seem. Laufbahn)

OBERMAAT
(Tech. Lfb.)

MEISTER
(Verw. Lfb.)

OBERMEISTER
(Tech. Lfb.)

STABSOBERMEISTER
(Seemänn. Laufbahn)

ÄRMELABZEICHEN
für Fähnriche der
Volksmarine
Untergrund Uni-
formblau
Sterne und Rand-
stickerei
goldfarben

FÄHNRICH
(Tech. Lfb.)

OFFZ.-SCHÜLER
(Seem. Laufb., 4. Lehrjahr)

UNTERLEUTNANT
(Med. Laufb.)

LEUTNANT
(Militärjustiz)

DIENSTFLAGGE DER VOLKSMARINE

OBERLEUTNANT(Musik)

KAPITÄNLEUTNANT (Küste)

ADMIRALSSTERN
(wird am Ärmel getragen)

Von rechts nach links:
ADMIRAL
VIZEADMIRAL
KONTERADMIRAL

Auch die Stabsoffiziere
tragen auf dem Ärmel
Laufbahnabzeichen

**KORVETTEN-
KAPITÄN**

**FREGATTEN-
KAPITÄN**

**KAPITÄN
ZUR SEE**

cialist forces, conditioned as it is by the technical revolution in military matters. The new and complex weapon systems require more finely tuned cooperation among the "collectives that operate them".

The new standing orders on disciplinary powers and responsibility which came into force on December 1, 1978, as *DV 010/0/006* put a stronger emphasis on political motivation, and prescribe a greater differentiation of authority. But in the field of disciplinary punishments, for example, they permit nothing that is not specifically provided for. The already elaborate *system of penalties and commendations* was further extended.

Every superior is charged to require a high level of discipline and to enforce it "by correct and sensible application of persuasion and force, praise and blame"[15].

Despite the further reinforcement of the "sole command" principle, *"social forces"* are also brought into the process of strengthening discipline, and it is possible for breaches of discipline to be dealt with by a *"collective"*. This corresponds to the "criticism and self-criticism" procedure commonly applied in the SED Party. In addition to commanders, Politorgans and Party and FDJ organizations are specified as having a role in the maintenance of discipline.

Contrary to previous regulations, the disciplinary powers now vested in superiors for meeting out praise and punishment are related to function, not rank. Particularly among the functions ranging from platoon commander to battalion commander powers of commendation are more elaborately specified than before, and full use of all variants is recommended, such as letters to places of employment, entries in the Book of Honour and photographs taken with the unit standard spread out in the background.

Additions to the range of disciplinary punishments are *Tadel* (censure) and *Verwarnung wegen Vernachlässigung der Dienstpflichten* (warning for neglect of duty). As the mildest of all measures, *Tadel* is not entered in the disciplinary records.

Moderate use of praise and punishment is urged, since their continual application means a loss of educative impact.

Left: Badges of Rank (Dienstgradabzeichen)
Left to right, 1st row: Sailor, Ordinary Rating, Able Rating.

2nd row: Leading Rating (executive career), Petty Officer (engineer's career), Petty Officer (administrative career), Chief Petty Officer (engineer's career), Warrant Officer (executive career), NCO Cadet.

3rd row: Ensign (engineer's career), Officer Cadet (executive career, 4th year), Unterleutnant (medical career) (no equivalent in the British Forces), Acting Sub-Lieutenant (military justice).

4th row: Sub-Lieutenant (music), Lieutenant (coast), Banner of the People's Navy.

5th row: Lieutenant Commander, Commander, Captain, Commodore, Rear Admiral, Vice Admiral, Admiral's pip.

Military jurisdiction

If "iron discipline" is to be maintained, the NVA obviously requires tough procedures to survive. Despite the extensive disciplinary measures, then, there is an equally *extensive system of military jurisdiction* which can make use of draconian penalties up to and including the death penalty.

In order to give backing to "commanders, Politorgans, military collectives and leaders of social organizations in the exercise of their responsibility for guaranteeing law and order and military discipline", *military courts*[16] are at hand to apply the criminal law to military personnel in the NVA, Frontier Troops, Ministry for Security, People's Police Alert Squads, Transport Police, conscientious objectors' Construction Units and Defence Ministry agencies. These courts can also deal with civilians where "military security" is involved. They form a constituent part of *"socialist law and administration of justice"* as laid down in Section IV of the Constitution, Articles 86–97[17]. Their *special status* is exemplified by their right both in peace time, and even more so in a "defence situation", to pass death sentences for a variety of offences on both civilian and military individuals.

Article 92 of the Constitution states that in military prosecutions "the Supreme Court, the Military High Courts and the Military Courts have jurisdiction". As soon as they were set up in 1963[18], a *Main Department for Military Courts (Hauptabteilung Militärgerichte)* was created in the Ministry of Justice. This is responsible for the personal, financial and material administration of Military High Courts and Military Courts and for the training and appointment of military judges. The Head of the Department reports to the Defence Minister and appropriate central agencies within the terms of his competence on all questions arising from the work of the courts.

Military judges are NVA officers with the degree of *Diplomjurist*. Like all judges in East Germany they are chosen for four years. Those in the military section of the Supreme Court are elected by parliament for the duration of its own life on the *recommendation of the National Defence Council;* those serving in the Military High Courts and Military Courts are appointed for the same term of office by the National Defence Council on the *recommendation of the Defence Minister.*

Senior military judges are appointed in the case of the Supreme Court by its president, in that of the Military High Courts by the Minister of Justice. In both cases they require the assent of the Defence Minister.

Military judges pass judgement *independently.* However, a judge can be *removed from office* by the same body that elected him, on the recommendation of the National Defence Council in the case of a Supreme Court military judge or on that of the Defence Ministry in the case of the two lower levels. Thus the judges are not truly independent, since they are answerable to the agencies that put them in office.

In criminal cases of first appeal the judges in Military Courts or High Courts are assisted by assessors *(Militärschöffen)* elected for four-year terms by members of units, offices and the military recruiting service. These assessors, of whom there were 1,715 in 1976, have an equal voice with the judges. They are answerable to those who elected them, but can be recalled by a regimental commander or his superior if the court so requests.

Even before the *Military Criminal Law* of January 24, 1962, provided the GDR with a separate system of military jurisdiction, a first step in that direction had been taken in November 1956 with the creation of *Military Prosecutors*. (In West Germany, by contrast, there is no military jurisdiction in peace time.) The Prosecutors act in close collaboration with commanders, Politorgans, SED and FDJ organizations and military "collectives".

As a component of the Public Prosecutors' service, East Germany's military prosecutors are controlled by the *Military Attorney-General (Militärober-staatsanwalt)*. He is a deputy of the *Attorney-General of the GDR (General-staatsanwalt der DDR)*, his professional superior, while at the same time, with the rank of major-general, he is responsible to the *Defence Minister* for military and disciplinary purposes. Under the *Militäroberstaatsanwalt* are *Militär-staatsanwälte (Military Attorneys)* for the various arms of service, military districts and formations of the NVA and for the recruiting service. All these prosecutors are NVA officers exercising their function "by virtue of their political ability and their jurisprudential and military training"[19]. They are appointed and recalled by the *Generalstaatsanwalt* under Article 98 (3) of the Constitution, are responsible to him in their work and follow his instructions.

The assistants *(Mitarbeiter)* of the Military Prosecutor's Office include servicemen who have been NCOs and then undergone training in criminal detection at a special school run by the Ministry of the Interior. They start work as investigators with the first lieutenant's rank *(Unterleutnant)* while studying law externally at the same time.

Military judges, assessors, prosecutors and assistants are all bound by the "class character of socialist law"[20]. "The basis and guidelines of socialist law are provided by the resolution and directives of the SED."

The *Penal Code*[21] of January 12, 1968, defines as *military crimes* all punishable acts committed by military personnel and prejudical to military discipline and combat-readiness. The *disciplinary responsibility* of military personnel guilty of *minor offences* is adjudged by their *commanders*. If there is evidence of criminal activity the commander will usually submit a report to the *military prosecutor*, who will initiate a fact-finding procedure. In certain cases every serviceman is in duty bound to report criminal activity known to him, and failure to do so can incur a prison sentence of up to ten years.

Proceedings are taken against the following types of *military crime:*

- desertion, punishable by sentence of up to 10 years, or by death in wartime;
- absence without permission – up to three years, or military detention;
- refusing or absconding from conscript service – up to five years, or death in wartime;
- refusal of an order or failure to execute an order – up to five years or military detention; death penalty in wartime;

- mutiny – up to eight years or military detention; death penalty in wartime;
- cowardice in the face of the enemy – at least one year, or death in wartime;
- infringement of regulations – up to five years, or military detention;
- assault, resistance or duresse against superiors, guards, patrols or other military personnel – up to ten years, or military detention, death penalty in wartime;
- betrayal of military secrets – up to ten years;
- impairment of serviceability of combat equipment – up to eight years, or military detention;
- criminal acts by a person in prison – up to ten years, or the death penalty in wartime;
- desecration of the dead or abuse of the wounded – imprisonment, or the death penalty in wartime.

Further punishable acts are

- the use of forbidden weapons,
- infringement of the rights of POWs,
- violation of the Red Cross emblem, and
- infringement of the rights of officers with a flag of truce.

Military courts can pronounce sentence on both servicemen and civilians for espionage, treason, "diversion" or sabotage, including the death penalty, even in time of peace.

Military detention, lasting from ten days to three months, can only be imposed on servicemen, and only on males. It is not entered in criminal records.

The *right to a defending officer,* though expressly laid down, is often not granted in practice. This is largely due to the concept of the function of legal counsels, who have to be guided by the "interests of society" rather than by the rights of the accused.

In the course of time the powers of the East German military courts have been gradually extended[22]. It can easily be shown that the practical interpretation of the definition of "highly dangerous crime against the state" is extraordinarily wide and elastic. In the view of a Swiss jurist "the rules of military jurisdiction in the GDR not only seem extreme in comparison with those in Western democratic countries, but in their scope and severity go beyond the corresponding regulations in other socialist states".

Leave, exits and exemption from duty

The regulations on these topics came into force on December 1, 1976, as *DV 010/0/007.* They are highly restrictive and on the whole no doubt vexatious.

The following categories of leave exist: recreational leave, extended short leave, short leave, special reward leave and recuperation leave. The last category, along with spa treatment, is covered by military health rules. Exits and exemptions from duty can also be granted. There is a legal entitlement to recreational leave, but not for the other forms, nor for exits or exemptions. No leave is generally granted before basic training is finished.

The length of *recreational leave* is governed by service status. During the eighteen months of conscript service 18 days leave are given, Sundays and public holidays not included.

Officer cadets and officer students of all study-years have a claim to 30 days recreational leave in the calendar year, including four Sundays or public holidays.

Soldiers, NCOs, short-service officers, regular NCOs, ensigns or regular officers who voluntarily sign on for longer terms receive correspondingly more leave.

Extended short leave means a weekend plus a day of recreational leave; it normally starts after duty on a Friday and ends with return to duty on Tuesday morning.

Short leave covers weekends or public holidays; it begins after duty on Saturday and ends on Monday morning, or begins when duty finishes on the day before the public holiday or holidays and ends on the day following.

Special leave is leave granted out of turn as a reward for outstanding achievement or for other special reasons, and lasts from two to five days. Special grounds include the need to prepare or finish off a work contract, acceptance as a member of a socialist organization prior to release from service, and preparation for entry to a university or vocational school.

All servicemen are entitled to a certain number of *free leave vouchers for travelling* by rail or coach from their place of residence or service to a recreational area, four per year (or six during the 18 months of conscript service) for those who live at a distance from their barracks, one per year for those who live near them.

Exits within barrack areas are conditional on proper performance of duties. The number given depends on the requirements of constant combat-readiness. In addition to those sick or on leave, not more than a further 15 per cent of the establishment can be given exits at any one time, subject to a maximum total of 30 per cent.

Exits apply, of course, from close of duty and are only valid within the barrack area. Conscript soldiers and reservists who have not done their service can go out till midnight once a week. Short-service soldiers, NCO cadets, officer cadets and reservists with completed service up to the rank of *Stabsfeldwebel* (Warrant officer) can receive exit passes as often as once a day, or for overnight absence.

No exits are needed for officers and ensigns within barrack area limits.

Short-service officers, regular NCOs, ensigns and regular officers can apply for permission to live outside barracks, but not NCO or officer cadets, and short-service privates and NCOs only in special personal circumstances.

Exemption from duty can be granted for a period determined by a superior, and is usually accompanied by permission to leave barracks for a prescribed time.

Uniform, equipment and badges of rank

For all branches of the NVA except the People's Navy the uniform is "stone grey", for the Navy dark blue. Other colours can be ordered for special troops by the Defence Ministry[23].

Uniforms have become steadily more handsome in the course of time. General Hoffmann and a few other highranking officers have for many years appeared occasionally in white uniforms.

Uniforms for privates and NCOs were generally improved for the 30th anniversary of the foundation of the Republic in October 1979. There is a new parade dress uniform consisting of a grey-collared parade or walking-out jacket, silver-grey shirt with shoulder-flaps, dark grey tie and trousers with belt-loops. Every soldier is issued with a green scarf in winter.

The collar and sleeve patches of the new jackets are as a rule covered with white purling in the land forces, so that the different branches can now only be told apart by the piping on their epaulettes. Jacket collars can as a rule be worn open. The new jacket material has a higher wool content, and the shirt is a cotton-polyester mixture.

For *going out,* soldiers wear the uniform jacket with belt outside, shirt and tie. *Parade uniform* consists of ankle boots, trousers worn straight, jacket, leather belt, shirt, tie and steel helmet.

Basic clothing and equipment for land and air forces, and frontier troops, comprises the following:

> 1 winter or peaked cap, 2 field caps, 1 greatcoat, 1 parade jacket, 1 service jacket, 2 shirts, 1 tie, 2 pairs of trousers, 2 field suits, 1 wool cap, 1 pullover, 1 pair of knitted gloves per winter-term, 3 or 4 pairs of socks, 5 small collars, 4 under-shirts, 4 pairs of pants, 2 pairs of boots, 1 pair of black shoes, 1 steel helmet, 1 helmet camouflage net, 1 webbing belt, 1 leather belt, 1 pair of patent braces, 1 pack frame, 1 two-part combat pack, 1 canteen, 1 set of eating utensils, 1 tent square, 1 blanket, 2 towels, 1 track suit, 1 sports shirt, 1 pair of shorts and 1 pair of gym shoes.

In addition all servicemen are issued with

> 2 two-part fatigue suits, 1 padded suit, 1 artificial fur-collar and 1 pair of mittens.

Most items of clothing are replaced after 18 months. Regular NCOs, ensigns and short-service officers have the same uniform and equipment as regular officers.

Since there are no metal branch-insignia in the NVA such as are worn in the Soviet and other Warsaw Pact armies, the "weapon colour" of the shoulder

On the 30th anniversary of the GDR a modified uniform was introduced into the NVA. The parade dress uniform now consists of grey-collared jacket, silver-grey shirt with shoulder-flaps, dark-grey tie and trousers with belt-loops.

strap or shoulder piece piping is important for distinguishing between branches of the services. The *colours* are these:

motorized infantry and reconnaissance	white
artillery	brick-red
armoured units	pink
engineers, chemical and other technical services	black
signals and radar units	yellow
anti-parachutists	orange
rear services, military jurisdiction and finance divisions	green
air force	light blue
air defence	grey
construction units	olive
frontier troops	light green
civil defence	raspberry.

Within any unit, men from other branches wear the colour of the unit's branch.

The peaked caps, parade-and-dress jackets and (among officers only) trousers also have piping – white for all land forces, light blue for the air force/air defence, and light green for the frontier troops.

In the People's Navy seamen and petty officers (*Maate*) wear cornflower-blue shoulder straps while higher ranks sport dark blue shoulder pieces.

In the general ranks the colours are for

land forces and air defence	crimson
air force	light blue
frontier troops	light green.

Privates also wear "career badges" (*Dienstlaufbahnzeichen*) to show their terms of service.

Officers wear a dagger with their dress uniform; officers in guards of honour carry sabres.

Officers have rank badges on their shoulder pieces, NCOs and other ranks on their straps. In the People's Navy rank-badges also appear on the sleeves.

Orders, badges of honour and efficiency

Over 4,000 different *marks of distinction are awarded by the East German state*, including orders, medals, prizes, honorary titles and badges. They can be conferred on collectives as well as on individuals.

The highest military order is the *Scharnhorst-Orden* initiated on February 17, 1966. It is associated with a money prize of five thousand marks.

Every grant of distinction requires the approval of the SED Party. Even in the cases of proficiency badges, the Party's cadre assessment is decisive.

Military catering

"Food not only keeps body and soul together; it helps the soldier above all to fulfil his combat and training tasks. And the quality and quantity of food provided no doubt have a considerable effect on the joys of service"[24].

There are *ten different food scales* in the NVA. Food Norm 110, which applies to most servicemen, is calculated to provide 4,200 calories a day; it is supposed to contain 130 g of protein, 150 g of fat, 550 g of carbohydrates and prescribed amounts of vitamins A, B and C. Many units contract directly for the supply of agricultural products in order to make sure of their fresh fruit and vegetables.

The average daily diet on Food Norm 110 comprises

120 g meat, 100 g sausages and meat products, 50 g butter, 200 g fresh milk, 100 g skimmed milk, 30 g fats, 20 g eggs, 45 g fish, 10 g high-fat cheese, 30 g low-fat cheese, 35 g jam, 40 g sugar and sweetstuffs, 1 kg potatoes, 300 g vegetables, 150 g fruit, 350 g rye bread, 150 g white bread or cake, 6 g coffee-substitute and tea, 70 g cereals, 25 g spices.

Pay and welfare

All NVA men on conscript service receive monthly pay[25] according to rank. The figures given below should be compared with the average employee's income in the GDR in 1977 of 839 East German Marks per month, including such "social income" items as family allowances and net of income tax and social security contributions. The skilled worker's salary then ranged between 800 and 900 Marks. (Basic consumer goods are, of course, cheap in the GDR, so far as they are available.)

Rank Land forces/Airforce/Navy	Monthly pay in Marks
Soldat/Matrose (Private/Aircraftman 2nd Class/Ordinary Rating)	120
Gefreiter/Obermatrose (Private/Aircraftman 1st Class/Ordinary Rating)	150
Stabsgefreiter/Stabsmatrose (Lance Corporal/Leading Aircraftman/Able Rating)	180
Unteroffizier/Maat (Corporal/Corporal/Leading Rating)	190
Unterfeldwebel/Obermaat (Sergeant/Sergeant/Petty Officer)	200
Feldwebel/Meister (Sergeant/Sergeant/Petty Officer)	210
Oberfeldwebel/Obermeister (Staff Sergeant/Flight Sergeant/Chief Petty Officer)	220
Stabsfeldwebel/Stabsobermeister (Warrant Officer 2nd Class)	230
Fähnrich (Ensign)	240
Unterleutnant (Sub-Lieutenant)	220
Leutnant (Second Lieutenant/Pilot Officer)	240
Oberleutnant (Lieutenant/Flying Officer)	260
Hauptmann/Kapitänleutnant (Captain/Flight Lieutenant/Lieutenant)	300
Major/Korvettenkapitän (Major/Squadron Leader/Lieutenant)	340
Oberstleutnant/Fregattenkapitän (Lieutenant Colonel/Wing Commander/Commander)	360
Oberst/Kapitän zur See (Colonel/Group Captain/Captain)	390

On the top of basic pay, performance bonuses can be granted when earned, also *Erschwerniszuschläge* in consideration of specially onerous physical or psychological work conditions. Both pay and bonuses are exempt from income tax or social security payments.

Short-service privates and NCOs and regular NCOs and officers on active service receive service emoluments *(Dienstbezüge)*, related to terms of service, rank, function and seniority; the same applies to servicewomen. Supplementary amounts, including hardship awards, can be added. Short-service NCOs performing the functions of regular NCOs or officers can have their emoluments made up to the same level. In contrast to army pay, these emoluments are liable to income tax and social security deductions.

Short-service soldiers in private and equivalent rank (e.g. seamen in mobile units, and anti-parachutist personnel) receive the same pay as conscripts during the first 18 months. Thereafter they receive rank-related emoluments, as well as a once-only "transition payment" of 1,500 Marks.

Examples of total monthly remuneration for given ranks:

Rank Land forces/Navy	Emolument in Marks
Unteroffizier/Maat	300
Fähnrich	450
Leutnant	600
Hauptmann/Kapitänleutnant	700
Major/Korvettenkapitän	750
Oberst/Kapitän zur See	900
Generalmajor/Konteradmiral	1,100
Armeegeneral	3,100

Examples of total monthly remuneration for *given functions:*

Section Leader *(Unteroffizier* to *Oberfeldwebel)*	125 to 450
Company Commander *(Oberleutnant* to *Major)*	525 to 625
Company Commander's Political Deputy	525 to 575
Battalion Commander	700 to 850
SED or FDJ Secretary, Battalion	650
Regimental Commander	1,100
Divisional Commander	2,000
Political Deputy to Head of Military District	2,000
Head of Military District	3,000

Seniority increases are based on rank and function, and progress from 5 per cent after 5 years' service to 20 per cent after 20 years.

Officer cadets receive a gross monthly remuneration of 300 Marks in their first year of training up to 500 in their fourth.

Bonuses for good performance and examplary behaviour in the fulfilment of duty can be awarded both to individuals and collectives.

Married short-service and regular NCOs, and married regular officers, receive a *housing allowance* in lieu of barrack maintenance. Single men or women can also claim this if they have children and run a household.

Servicemen who feed themselves outside barracks receive a *meal allowance*. This applies to married soldiers provided they satisfy the army that they can eat regularly outside without prejudice to their duties. Men on leave also receive meal allowances for the period in question.

Removal costs are payable to married regular NCOs and officers who move house under orders, or with approval, to their place of service or very near to it.

Female citizens of the GDR can volunteer for the NVA or Frontier Troops when they are 18. They enter either as short-service NCOs for at least three years, or as regular NCOs for at least ten.

Women and girls are not assigned directly to troop units; they work predominantly in the Ministry for Defence, the commands of the various services, the military regions, formation staffs or defence region and defence district headquarters.

In the administrative field they are employed mainly as clerks, secretaries or audiotypists, requiring vocational training as relevant as possible to the work. In the signals service they are used chiefly as telephonists or telegraphy and radio operators.

Trained nurses can be taken on into active service as medical NCOs in the NVA's medical facilities.

The NVA makes every effort to represent the work of women in its ranks as thoroughly feminine; it insists that there is no place for the kind of "gun-toting virago" that flourishes, in its view, in Western armies such as that of the USA. In the imperialist forces, we are told, women instead of receiving equal rights are imbued with the same "assassin morality" as the menfolk.

Men conscripted into the reserve service receive normal pay and retain their claim to their *civilian jobs*. They receive a compensatory sum throughout from their place of work.

The extent of *damage liability* borne by servicemen is determined by the Compensation Order *(Wiedergutmachungsverordnung)*[26]. Damage is defined as occurring when the NVA or Frontier Troops incur material or financial loss through culpable action. Any person acts culpably who deliberately, wantonly or negligently violates his service obligations and causes damage thereby. A soldier, for example, who leaves his unit without permission has to bear the whole cost incurred in bringing him back. Anyone causing damage under the influence of alcohol has to pay for it. The amount of compensation and manner of payment are decided by his commander.

Under the Promotion Order *(Förderungsverordnung)*[27] civil employment does not lapse when a man is called up for basic service; it is merely in abeyance. Enterprises are under obligation to keep in maximum contact with "their own soldiers" and their families. Soldiers released from active service have to be given *priority in re-employment* by their old enterprises, even if they are temporarily unfit for work. If they apply for new jobs minimum qualifications have to be accepted. The same applies to university and college entrance for short-service privates, NCOs and officers.

Regular ex-servicemen are entitled to a job with a salary equivalent to what they received in the army. There is a long list of parallels between NVA certificates and vocational titles and equivalent civilian qualifications.

In general it would be fair to say that the national economy has to bear a large share of the NVA's welfare obligations.

There is a Maintenance Order (*Unterhaltsverordnung*)[23] which prescribes the maintenance sums payable to conscripts' dependents. Maintenance is payable to a wife, if

- she is unfit for work and has no other income,
- there is at least one child under 16 in the household,
- she is released from work during pregnancy or after childbirth,
- she is attending school or a full-time study course,
- she is in vocational training and only in receipt of apprentice pay, or
- if she is an invalid, or has charge in her household of a member of the family in need of constant care.

If none of these circumstances apply she receives 100 Marks for herself and 60 Marks for each child.

Conscripts are also entitled to other forms of financial assistance, e.g. adjustment of instalment payments, and rent assistance. In the case of debts incurred before call-up to state and cooperative credit banks, state-owned enterprises and other agencies total or partial respite of payment may be granted.

Notes

[1] Cf. Innendienst, in: *Armeerundschau*, Militärverlag der DDR, East Berlin 1/1979, pp. 84–87; 2/1979, pp. 58–61; 3/1979, pp. 42–45.

[2] Anordnung des Nationalen Verteidigungsrates der DDR über den aktiven Wehrdienst in der NVA (Dienstlaufbahnordnung – NVA) of December 10, 1973, *Gesetzblatt*, pt. I, 1973, annex to par. 3, p. 561.

[3] Gesetz über die allgemeine Wehrpflicht (Wehrpflichtgesetz) of January 24, 1962, *Gesetzblatt*, pt. I, 1962, p. 2.

[4] Colonel H. *Wollmann*, Zu den neuen Grundsatzdienstvorschriften der NVA, in: *Militärwesen*, pub. Militärverlag der DDR (VEB), East Berlin 11/1978, p. 31.

[5] Ibid.

[6] Ibid.

[7] Lieutenant Colonel O. *Kroemke* of the Ernst Thälmann Officers' College, Gedanken zur Gestaltung sozialistischer Vorgesetzten-Unterstellten-Beziehungen, in: *Militärwesen*, 4/1976, p. 51.

[8] Ibid., p. 52.

[9] O. *Kroemke*, W. *Zschörnig*, Die klassenmäßige Erziehung der Offiziersschüler im Prozeß der Ausbildung unter den Bedingungen des Nutzens der Vorgesetzten-Unterstellten-Beziehungen, der Beziehungen innerhalb des Kollektivs und der zielstrebigen Arbeit mit einem 'Moralkodex für Offiziersschüler'. Dissertation presented at the Humboldt University, East Berlin 1972, p. 328 ff.

[10] Colonel H. *Wollmann*, Der Standortstreifendienst – Mittel zur Aufrechterhaltung militärischer Disziplin und Ordnung in der Öffentlichkeit, in: *Militärwesen*, 2/1979, pp. 30–33.

[11] Colonel H. *Wollmann*, Zu den neuen Grundsatzdienstvorschriften der NVA, loc. cit., p. 34.

[12] *Lenin*, Werke, vol. 30, East Berlin 1960, p. 424.

[13] Disziplin – Mutter des Sieges, in: *Militärwesen*, 3/1978, p. 86.

[14] Ibid.

[15] Note 11, ibid.

[16] Anordnung des Nationalen Verteidigungsrates der DDR über die Aufgaben, Zuständigkeit und Organisation der Militärgerichte (Militärgerichtsordnung) of September 27, 1974, *Gesetzblatt*, pt. I, 1974, p. 481.

[17] GDR Constitution of April 6, 1968, in the version of the Gesetz zur Ergänzung und Änderung der Verfassung der DDR vom 7. Oktober 1974, in: *Neues Deutschland*, September 28, 1974.

[18] Erlaß des Staatsrates über die Stellung und die Aufgaben der Gerichte für Militärstrafsachen (Militärgerichtsordnung) of April 4, 1963, *Gesetzblatt*, pt. I, 1963, p. 89.

[19] Militärlexikon, 1973, p. 251.

[20] Lieutenant Colonel H. *Härtel* of the Friedrich Engels Military Academy, Recht und Gesetzlichkeit in der NVA, in: *Militärwesen*, 12/1974, p. 54.

[21] The German Penal Code of 1871 applied in the GDR up to June 30, 1968. Not till January 12, 1968, did the Volkskammer pass a new Penal Code, which came into force on July 1, 1968. *Gesetzblatt*, pt. I, 1968, p. 1.

[22] Cf. Dr Miachel *Csizmas*, Die sozialistische Militärjustiz in der DDR, in: *Allgemeine Schweizerische Militärzeitschrift*, 10/1976, p. 374.

[23] Dritter Beschluß vom 18. September 1965 über die Einführung der Uniformen, der Dienstgradbezeichnungen und der Dienstgradabzeichen für die NVA, *Gesetzblatt*, pt. II, 1965, p. 700.

[24] Verpflegung in der NVA, in: *Armeerundschau*, 1/1974, p. 36.

[25] Verordnung über die Besoldung der Wehrpflichtigen für die Dauer des Dienstes in der NVA (Besoldungsverordnung) of January 24, 1962, *Gesetzblatt*, pt. II, 1962, p. 49. Various amendments have appeared subsequently (May 27, 1964, November 11, 1965, January 23, 1975) and directions for implementation issued. The figures given here applied in 1979.

[26] Verordnung über die materielle Verantwortlichkeit der Angehörigen der bewaffneten Organe – Wiedergutmachungsverordnung (WGVO) – of February 19, 1969, *Gesetzblatt*, pt. II, 1969, p. 159.

[27] Verordnung über die aus dem aktiven Wehrdienst entlassenen Angehörigen der NVA – Förderungsverordnung – of February 13, 1976, *Gesetzblatt*, pt. II, 1975, pp. 221–226; Erste Durchführungsbestimmung zur Förderungsverordnung, ibid., pp. 226–235.

[28] Verordnung über die Gewährung von Unterhaltsbeträgen und anderen finanziellen Leistungen an Angehörige der zum Grundwehrdienst einberufenen Wehrpflichtigen – Unterhaltsverordnung – of March 2, 1978, *Gesetzblatt*, pt. I, 1978, pp. 149–151; Erste Durchführungsbestimmung of April 2, 1978, ibid., pp. 152–154.

Index

Hoffmann, H. 11, 12, 13, 28, 29, 30, 35, 48, 62, 78, 79, 81, 86, 87, 94, 99, 100, 102, 107, 108, 109, 110, 111, 122, 136, 138, 145, 147, 156, 160, 162, 170, 171, 181, 186, 235, 239, 243, 246, 253, 272

Honecker, E. 19, 29, 37, 38, 44, 50, 67, 78, 95, 100, 102, 105, 106, 107, 108, 109, 160, 184, 186

Howitzers 208, 209

Hundertschaft (Hundred) 148, 151, 152, 155

Hungaria 33, 72, 73, 76, 79, 88, 89, 90, 91, 92, 96, 150, 183

Ideological war 37, 38

Ideology 28–30, 229–251

Indebtedness 186

India 99, 101

Individual command (Einzelleitung) 162, 170, 233, 278, 289

Industries 10, 175, 182, 183

Infantry weapons 194, 195 f.

Infra-red 197, 201, 209, 213

Infrastructure 173

Innovation movement 244, 246

Institute of Civil Defence 147

Intelligence 112, 113

Interkosmos programme 184

Internal structure 276–300

Iraq 101

Israel 99

Jet trainer 220

Joint Armed Forces 73, 74, 75, 79, 82, 83, 86, 94, 108

Joint Naval Forces 76, 85

Joint Secretariat 74

Joint (Supreme) Command 74, 76, 77, 82, 88, 94, 124

Kessler, H. 29, 80, 99, 100, 110, 160, 161, 163, 231, 265

Khrushchev, N. S. 35, 42, 43

Kondor-type patrol boats 129

Korea 24, 100, 181, 216

"Labour capital" 179

Land forces 112, 116–119, 195–216, 267, 268–270, 273, 296, 297, 298

Landing craft 120, 181, 195, 222, 226, 227

Leave 256, 292–294

Lenin, V. I. 12, 13, 26, 30, 55, 83, 98, 159, 288

Liberation movements 31, 33, 98, 100

Libya 100, 101

Local Councils 147, 174

Logistics 74, 113, 173

Machine guns 130, 145, 148, 182, 196, 197, 198, 201, 203, 209, 220

Main Political Administration (PHV) 86, 111, 113, 160, 162, 163, 164, 167, 233

Main Staff of the NVA 85, 110, 112, 160, 163

Maintenance 176

Manoeuvrability 191, 201, 260

Manoeuvres 85–88, 90, 93–98, 148, 240, 256, 258, 260

Marxism-Leninism 55, 229, 230

Mechanization and Automatization of Command 113, 273,

Medical services 264, 299

Microelectronic industry 185

Mielke, E. 11, 78, 108, 109, 145

MiG, see Fighter aircraft

Militarization of the economy 175

Military attorney 291

Military command 120 f.

Military council 74, 75

Military courts 113, 290

Military crimes 291 f.

Military districts 116, 166, 205, 208, 209, 212, 256

Military doctrine 10, 11, 30–35, 94, 273

Military-economic integration 182

Military economy 173–190

Military history 234–241, 248, 249, 268

Military jurisdiction 290–292, 295

Military leadership 107